Edited by
John Kirkby, Phil O'Keefe and Lloyd Timberlake

■
■
■

THE EARTHSCAN READER IN SUSTAINABLE DEVELOPMENT

■
■

EARTHSCAN
Earthscan Publications Ltd, London

First published in 1995 by
Earthscan Publications Limited
120 Pentonville Road, London N1 9JN

Copyright © ETC–UK, 1995

A catalogue record for this book is available from the British Library

ISBN: 1 85383 216 2 (Paperback)
      1 85383 223 5 (Hardback)

Copy-edited and typeset by Selro Publishing Services, Oxford
Printed in England by Clays Ltd, St Ives plc

Earthscan Publications Limited is an editorially independent subsidiary of Kogan Page
Limited and publishes in association with the International Institute for Environment
and Development and the WWF–UK.

THE EARTHSCAN READER IN SUSTAINABLE DEVELOPMENT

WITHDRAWN

■ Contents

■ Foreword

These readings have been selected from books published by Earthscan during the last few years. In two senses, then, it is *The Earthscan Reader in Sustainable Development*. The selection includes excerpts of varied length. In a few cases, entire chapters are included; in others a few pages only are used. The principle of selection was to represent a wide range of views on aspects of sustainability and development rather than provide a small number of key readings. Even though the number of excerpts is large, we are conscious that much excellent material could not be included. We do not apologize for concentrating on the Third World: this is our own major interest and we believe that this is the part of the world where problems of sustainable development are most pressing now, and will continue to be in the foreseeable future. Even so we have included a number of pieces on the global scale.

Many of the shorter excerpts are case studies of localities and involve consideration of the environmental predicament of households and individual people. We hope that in using the small scale we are able to convey a flavour of life as it is lived in the real world.

Suffering is experienced at the level of the individual person but we are unwilling to present one billion people simply as impotent victims. Several of the excerpts therefore examine the ways in which individual people, either acting individually or cooperating in small groups, can create better and sustainable livelihoods. The long history of successful locally-controlled resource management suggests that this is not an empty hope.

Many of the readings have overt and covert ethical standpoints. Ethical issues are far from simple at the global scale. Western ethics have evolved from Judaeo-Christian religious codes, with significant modifications during the last 400 years as part of the Enlightenment Project. Elites in non-Western societies, particularly if influenced by colonialism and its legacy of religious and educational structures may subscribe to Western ethics. For the majority of the world's people, however, Western ethics are alien. The position of women, children, other racial groups, other social groups, even other species may be very different throughout the Third World. Attempts to impose Western ethical judgements may be regarded as intellectual colonialism and may be vigorously rejected. Anodyne pronouncements about human rights conceal the real tensions between value systems. Whose value systems should prevail in the South?

The readings are arranged in ten sections; some of the excerpts could have been placed in other sections. This reflects the interconnectedness of the real world. Identification of suitable categories was on the basis of those used in Brundtland and at Rio. Environmental economics is included to give a flavour of the debate in environmental management within which it is one of the most important analytical methods.

■ Acknowledgements

The editors would like to thank Joan Hutchison, Donna Porter and Anne Welsh at ETC UK for the administrative support above and beyond the call of duty. Sincere thanks are also due to generations of undergraduates and graduate students of sustainable development at the University of Northumbria who have joined us, sometimes bemusedly, in debates around red-green issues. Most importantly, we acknowledge the inspiration provided by people, particularly in the Third World, to whom the daily struggle is one for sustainable development. Thanks also to ETC members, particularly Ray Baxter, Ian Cherrett, Ian Convery, Nick Emmel, Chris Howorth and Mike Sill for their helpful comments on the text. Finally, we thank Jonathan Sinclair Wilson and his colleagues at Earthscan for their patience and understanding in waiting for the production of the *Reader*.

■ Sustainable Development: An Introduction

History of the Concept

The World Commission on Environment and Development (WCED, 1987) Report, (commonly known as the Brundtland Report after its chairwoman), produced after 900 days of deliberation by an international group of politicians, civil servants and experts on environment and development, is the key statement of sustainable development. It marked the concept's political coming of age and established the content and structure of the present debate. The United Nations Conference on Environment and Development (UNCED) commonly known as the Rio conference of 1992 was the follow up to Brundtland and sought to move towards the achievement of Brundtland's aims.

The concept of sustainable development first appeared in the World Conservation Strategy (WCS) (IUCN, 1980), which had argued from a dominantly conservationist environmentalist standpoint (see Adams, 1990 for a history of the emergence of sustainable development). Issues raised by sustainability had been discussed for several years by WCS, and the clash between the interests of environmental conservation and development was very clear in the Stockholm Conference on the Human Environment in 1973.

Following the Brundtland Report, the ideal of sustainable development quickly became politically orthodox. Institutions giving grants or loans for development projects routinely demand an investigation of the sustainability and developmental components of the project. Many writers consider that the term is so widely and loosely used that it has now been devalued.

Definitions

According to Holmberg and Sandbrook (1992), 70 definitions are now current. Pearce et al (1989) include "A gallery of definitions" as an appendix to their book. The most widely quoted definition and effectively the official one is that of Brundtland (WCED, 1987) "[development that] meets the needs of the present without compromising the ability of future generations to meet their own needs". Many other definitions are variants of this, reflecting the disciplinary standpoint of the particular author — many of them say the same thing at much greater length. The apparently simple and clear Brundtland definition has caused heated discussion among theoreticians and practitioners of environment and development. To the authors' knowledge it has also launched a thousand student essays.

Clearly the Brundtland statement has a strong people-centred ethical stance, concentrating on the satisfaction of human needs (not human wants), rather than, for example, on protection of the environment in general, as WCS did, or on other species, as deep ecologists would. Redclift (1992) points out that the Brundtland Report does not specifically examine exactly what is meant by human needs. Basic needs to ensure survival are obviously included — nutrition, health and shelter, but it is not clear how much more than survival is involved in "needs". The concern with balancing the interests of present and future generations, the intergenerational criterion, is an ethical issue. Many people consider that it is presumptious to make assumptions about future human needs beyond the simple biological ones. In fact Brundtland is concerned also to secure intragenerational equity, in other words relative redistribution of resources towards the poor. Since the North is in general not interested in donating more than a token amount to the South, an improvement in their living conditions can be achieved only through economic growth in the South.

The rapid acceptance of the ideal of sustainable development is not surprising since it is interpretable in so many different ways. It fits nicely into political soundbites compared with its predecessor "ecodevelopment"; it is something with which everyone can agree, like "motherhood and apple pie" (Pearce et al, 1989, p1). But note the enigmatic quotation at the start of Pearce et al (1989) "Where are the lollipops in sustainable development? (Canadian politician 1988)". The European Union recognized a good slogan when it entitled its Fifth Environmental Action Plan, intended to run from 1994 to 2000, "Towards Sustainability". Both "sustainable" and "development" are rational and enlightened concepts. It is difficult to imagine that anyone, except out of perversity, could agree with the reverse. While no one would be likely to aim for the reverse — except as part of a war strategy (see below) — not everyone approves of the notion of sustainable development. Beckerman (1995, p1) regards it as a "catch phrase . . . repeated parrot fashion by environmental policy makers" and on page 8 says that "the value of the concept is vastly overrated". He prefers the obtaining of the highest feasible welfare as a more appropriate aim for society and believes that economic growth is the best way of achieving this. Forget environment and development and go for growth. Surprisingly, many environmentalists hate the term "sustainable development" precisely because "it appears to license economic growth" (Holmberg and Sandbrook, 1992, p21).

The acceptance of sustainable development as a basic aim for the world may also be explained by the perception, from the late 1960s, that the world is facing a meta crisis, including crises of development, environment and security.

The Crisis of Development
Though continuing attempts have been made through aid programmes since the Second World War to accomplish development in the South, it is clear that relatively little has been achieved. Dumont (1988) catalogues the failures of development initiatives in post-colonial Africa. The number of desperately poor people "the global underclass" (Eckholm, 1982) has remained steady at about one fifth of the human race. These are people who live on the edge of survival, at the mercy of the apocalyptic riders — death,

famine and disease (see Chapters 4 and 6 on health, urbanization and agriculture). Their living conditions, housing, health, nutrition are an insult to notions of equity. Since the 1960s, deterioration in the terms of trade for the South has intensified poverty. During the 1980s the growth of state debts and the impact of International Monetary Fund restructuring programmes (see Onimode, 1989) have caused governments to reduce their social programmes, with less expenditure on health, education and welfare, further depriving the poor. Increased emphasis on the production of agricultural commodities for export has reduced the scope for production of food for local consumption, again disproportionately affecting the poor.

Political economic changes within the countries of the South have increased the relative poverty of the poor (Patnaik, 1990; Harriss, 1990). Power and capital have been gained by merchants and the larger landowners. Urban elites have been able to acquire formerly common property land, as in eastern Sudan, to create large commercial farms, thus depriving pastoralists of their grazing lands. Commercial farms are usually mechanized so that few jobs are available. Utting (1993) shows how the rich and the multinational corporations have reduced people's access to forests in Central America. Commercial logging, large-scale cattle ranching, the "hamburger connection" and the expansion of export crops — coffee, bananas and cotton — have replaced forests, led to the breakdown of traditional resource management systems and to the marginalization and exclusion of the poor.

For the last 20 years it has been understood that underclasses can be recognized within the global underclass itself — people who find it even more difficult to survive. Three of these groups are indigenous people, children and women. Kemf (1993) draws attention to the predicament of the world's 300 million indigenous people, most of whom live in marginal areas far from economic core regions, who are politically impotent but in many cases seen by state governments as troublesome. Many of them live in marginal environments such as mountains, swamps or relict forests, which are ecologically valuable ecosystems. Outsiders, greedy for minerals or the products of the ecosystems, destroy their environments and in so doing, destroy their societies; indeed their diseases destroy the people. The indigenous people are excellent environmental guardians: if untouched their lives are infinitely sustainable. The loss is twofold: the loss of people (their distinctive livelihoods and unique languages, understanding and knowledge systems) and the loss of their environments.

"Every year 14 million children under the age of five die in the developing world, not in a drought or famine year, but in an ordinary year" (Timberlake and Thompson, 1990, p1). This is the stark end of the "children crisis", which Timberlake and Thompson attribute to underdevelopment itself — the effect of an international economic system favouring rich countries. Environmental degradation and the debt crisis contribute to the poverty, and consequent lack of access to resources, that creates the "children crisis". Seven million children, the street children, survive as they can with no support from adults. They are regarded as undesirable and are persecuted, even murdered by the police.

During the United Nations Decade for Women (1977–87), according to Sen and Grown (1988) women's living conditions deteriorated as commercialization devalued even further their contributions to human welfare. De Jesus (1990) in the three-year diary of a poor Brazilian woman living in a São Paulo *favela*, describes in detail her struggle to survive and support, unaided, her three children. This she did by gathering and selling scrap paper and scrap metal. Millions of women live in such conditions. As Boserup (1989) shows, one quarter of households in the South are female-headed; even if they are able to find paid employment, women are discriminated against and have to accept unskilled or semi-skilled low-paid jobs. Since men control most of the powerful institutions in the South (as in the world generally) (Seager, 1993), the only hope for women to improve their conditions is through self-empowerment and action at the grass roots, a conclusion reinforced by contributors to Shiva (1994). Lewenhak (1992) calls for a revaluation of women's work, most of which is unpaid and thus disregarded, for example in national economic accounting systems. Women are the main providers of childcare, education and health services (all unpaid). They are also the main producers of agricultural products and food and the main providers of fuel and water (also unpaid). This lack of payment for production, reproduction and social repro-duction, together with the many limitations on their freedom of action strikes the Western mind as immoral. However, as Boserup (1989) found, there are problems of empathizing (across cultures) from a Western ethical framework. For example, 85 per cent of Ivory Coast women prefer polygamy to monogamy and, though Westerners regard polygamy as exploitative, it is acceptable to local women. The notion, prevalent among Western liberal observers of the Third World during the 1960s, that there was an untapped pool of female labour, is clearly ridiculous.

The Environmental Crisis

Since the publication of *Limits to Growth* (Meadows, 1972) and the United Nations Conference on the Human Environment, many people have been persuaded that the earth's environment is rapidly deteriorating. Thus, while population rises by 100 million a year, earth's capacity to support humankind is reduced (see Chapter 3 on population). Two reasons are given for holding this pessimistic view: that resources are being consumed at an unsustainable rate and that resources are being degraded.

The world has an effectively finite stock of mineral resources. To some extent these are substitutable (for example oil for coal and vice versa) but the total stock is fixed. Similarly, there is a limit to the amount of land that might be cultivated or farmed in some way. An optimist might claim that intensification of inputs could raise produc-tivity, as has happened in the North — yields per hectare doubled in the last generation — but this demands extra resources (see Chapter 4 on agriculture). In the early 1970s total population numbers were regarded as the main cause for concern and since population growth was fastest in the South, it was possible to blame the people of the South for increasing stress on environment. Deeper analysis showed that if there was a population problem (see Chapter 3) it was caused by rates of resource consumption. The resource depletion cost of individual people in the North is much greater than that in the South: 80 per cent of the world's resource consumption is by 20 per cent of the people. This 20 per cent live mainly in the North. Since many resources are transferred (at prices favourable to the purchaser) from the South to the North, much of the cost in resource depletion is paid in the South.

For more than a century people have wanted to preserve species and ecosystems, but during the last few years the loss of biodiversity (see Chapter 1) has been viewed as a threat to sustainable development. This was a major concern at the UNCED conference in 1992. Over the last 20 years, increasing rates of forest loss, particularly species-rich moist tropical forest (Grainger, 1993), have also been identified as an alarming trend. Forests are probably important carbon sinks, reducing the effect of global warming; they are the homes of indigenous people; they are a protection against soil erosion and the siltation of reservoirs; and they moderate the severity of floods. Forests, and trees outside forests (Munslow et al, 1988), are valued as a source of fuelwood. Their disappearance leads to a crisis in energy production for the poor.

Resource degradation through misuse and pollution is the second component of the environmental crisis. In the North, pollution of air, land and water has long been identified as a problem: smoke control legislation was introduced in London in the thirteenth century. In the South the effects of pollution are also recognized as locally catastrophic (see Chapters 5 and 6). It is claimed, for example, that breathing the air of Mexico City for a day carries the same cancer risk as smoking 40 cigarettes a day. Atmospheric pollution through acid rain has been known since 1852 (McCormick, 1990), though it was 100 years before R A Smith's warning of the damage caused by acid rain was heeded. Acid precipitation, either as rain or dry fallout, is now a global phenomenon. It kills trees (more than two-thirds of Britain's forests are affected), acidifies soils, reduces crop yields, acidifies lakes, causes human health problems and corrodes stone buildings. Damage is most severe in industrial belts and during the last generation has intensified.

Emission of greenhouse gases (see Chapter 2 on climate change and energy) are possibly leading to changes in the earth's climate that will have major impacts on human welfare within the next generation. Decreases in the amount of ozone in the stratospheric ozone layer, first predicted in 1974, when it was calculated that chlorofluorocarbons (CFCs) would cause ozone depletion, were confirmed in 1985, first in southern and then in northern polar regions (Brown, 1994). The ozone layer shields against cancer-causing ultraviolet (UV radiation). CFC production increased greatly from 1960 to a peak in 1989, which was ten times the 1960 figure. There is now little doubt that human health is seriously threatened by increased UV radiation. At UN-sponsored conferences in Montreal (1987), London (1990) and Copenhagen (1992), governments agreed to phase out CFC production by 1996. Ozone loss will, however, continue because much CFC is already available in the atmosphere. The rapidity of the international response to ozone depletion is an encouraging sign that cooperation to maintain environmental quality is possible. But that a potentially catastrophic environmental problem could develop within less than 20 years is, to say the least, worrying.

Desertification is probably the most widely recognized form of resource degradation. It may affect as much as one-third of the world. Grainger (1990) discusses the causes, effects and possible remedial actions. Increased soil erosion, badly managed irrigation systems, fluctuations of climate, inappropriate land use, removal of trees, suppression of vegetation, over-use of ecologically sensitive environments, provision of water boreholes in semi-arid environments are a few of the vast number of factors that may cause desertification. The phenomenon is complex and it is not surprising that attempts to reverse desertification have had little success. Although desertification has occurred for thousands of years, it was recognized as a serious problem demanding immediate action only in 1977 at the United Nations Conference on Desertification. The United Nations Environmental Programme's Desertification Control Unit has recorded serious degradation of environments and people's lives, but experts are now questioning whether desertification is better regarded as a special case of environmental degradation. Certainly, areas of the world thousand of miles from deserts, and with high rainfall, show very similar patterns of degradation.

The Crisis of Global Insecurity

This is the third and probably most serious threat to sustainable development. Some of the broader aspects of global insecurity are considered in Chapter 8 (and Prins, 1993). When, 50 years ago, the United Nations Organization and the Bretton Woods institutions were created, it was hoped that an era of world peace and prosperity would follow. In fact, conflict, in the form of wars and trade wars have continued and possibly increased. Even the end of the Cold War has failed to lead to peace and cooperation. Constant competition between old and emerging super powers ensures the continuation of conflict. The creation of more powerful weaponry with greater killing power makes the devastation even greater. For tens, if not hundreds, of millions of people in the South, even survival is virtually impossible because these wars mainly take place there. Proxy wars, such as between Somalia and Ethiopia, colonial wars, post-colonial wars, resource wars such as the Kuwait conflict, and ethnic wars as in Rwanda devastate vast areas of the South. At a different level, wars within states, such as the secessionist wars in Ethiopia, Nigeria and Sudan have dominated people's lives for the last 50 years. All these wars include the deliberate killing of civilians, sabotage, the planting of mines, destruction of cities, towns, villages, irrigation systems and power installations, interference with planting and harvesting, and theft of food and livestock: in short, wars are destroying people, environments, livelihoods and any hope of sustainable development. Resources that might have been used to create development are used for destruction. Each year $1 trillion is spent on armies. Urdang (1989) describes the experience and effects of war in Mozambique and Wilson (1991) the effects of war in Eritrea. Refugeeism has become a way of life for millions. The number of refugees and displaced people is now about 70 million: at best they live in suspended animation. Aid for the South is now diverted from development to humanitarian assistance, from improvement of living conditions to achieving bare survival.

It is possible that new causes of conflict may arise in the future. The control of oil supplies has caused several conflicts in the past and it seems probable that in the Middle East further wars over oil may occur. But it is possible that conflict will also occur in the Middle East over the control of water supplies (Clarke, 1991). Clarke identifies the basins of the Tigris, Euphrates and Jordan as possible areas of conflict and considers that the water of the Ganges and Paraguay rivers may also be contested in the future.

As Brundtland (WCED, 1987) shows, these three crises interconnect and reinforce each other. The complexity and strength of the interconnections ensure that progress to sustainable development will not be easy and that, either incrementally through numerous small changes or radically through large structural changes, the functioning of the human system must change. Clearly, the prevailing economic, political and social systems are responsible for the misfit between the earth (nature) and the world (humanity). Changes to human systems can be achieved only on the basis of changes in ethical value systems; changes in what is regarded as acceptable behaviour in relation to people and to the environment. Some believe that it is only possible to achieve this through a centrally-driven, directive, command economy and society, dominated by a central government advised by experts. Alternatively, or possibly additionally, the emphasis might be on grass roots action, using the abilities of individuals, households and small communities. Whichever approach is used raises questions of equity, power and democracy.

The International Response to the Challenge of Sustainable Development

Two major attempts have been made by the international community to respond to the widely accepted need for a coordinated response to the triple crisis discussed above. These were the UN General Assembly's commissioning of WCED, chaired by Gro Harlem Brundtland to produce "a global agenda for change" (WCED, 1987, p ix), to propose long-term strategies, recommend ways of achieving international cooperation, consider ways by which international environmental concerns could be tackled and create a long-term agenda for action. The second, five years later and 20 years after the first global environmental conference in Stockholm in 1972, was the UNCED conference in Rio sometimes called the Earth Summit. This conference was also convened by the UN General Assembly. The following analysis of the two events draws on Grubb et al (1993); Middleton et al (1993), O'Keefe and Kirkby (1995) and O'Keefe et al (1993).

The Brundtland Analysis

Brundtland's analysis of the present state of the world starts from the identification of a mismatch between the capacities of the natural systems of the earth and humanity's ability to fit its activities into this framework. This has led to an interlocking series of crises of environment, development, security and energy. This interaction between global economy and global ecology entails environmental degradation, fuelled by a dramatic growth of population, particularly in Third World cities and by accelerating rates of economic activity. Poverty in the Third World, to a large extent the product of international and national economies, is the agent of environmental destruction.

The Brundtland Report suggests that the catastrophe of environment and development could be averted through sustainable development within a framework of equity. But inequity "is the planet's main environmental problem; it is also its main development problem" (WCED, 1987, p6). Power, the other side of the equity coin, is thus also the planet's main development problem: too much power in the North, with its grotesquely over-protected agriculture; too little power among the South's rural poor, whose artificially low farm produce prices subsidize politically dangerous urban areas, and too little power among the South's urban poor — yesterday's rural poor.

Two concepts underpin the Brundtland Commission's ideal of sustainability. First, and an overriding priority, is the achievement of basic needs for all humankind — in effect the uplift of the living conditions of the Fourth World — those living in absolute poverty in the Third World. Second, limits to development are seen as technical, cultural and social. Implicit in this is a rejection of the notion that limits to growth, as identified by the Club of Rome, are environmental (Meadows, 1972; Meadows et al, 1992). At the heart of the Brundtland Report is the belief (or is it a hope?) that equity, growth and environmental maintenance are simultaneously possible with each nation achieving its full economic potential and at the same time enhancing its resource base. The sunlit uplands indeed! A desirable end, but we must seriously question whether it is achievable. If equity is explicitly the overriding priority (in satisfying basic needs) then necessarily we downplay growth and environment (see Figure 1). Can technology and social change deliver the equity rabbit from the magician's hat and also encourage growth and the maintenance of environment as claimed by Brundtland? Figure 2 illustrates some aspects of Brundtland's components of sustainability. In general, mankind creates environments through management of both living and inanimate resources. Such environments may then be maintained or further improved. Failure of the maintenance programme leads to degradation. Growth occurs at different scales; it is possible, for example, to have growth at the global level, but not necessarily in each nation or within the rural and urban sectors of each nation. The issues of equity also entail global and intranational levels.

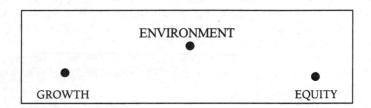

Figure 1 *The Main Components of Sustainability*

Possibly by "priority" Brundtland means the first aim to be achieved but not necessarily the most important. If this were so, UNCED as successor to Brundtland would surely address equity as its first aim too. UNCED did not start by asking questions about equity.

Figure 1 shows the main components of sustainability as interpreted by Brundtland. Different workers have conceived sustainability as relating to one only of these three variables, hence sustainable growth or sustainable environment. Brundtland believes that all three may be achieved as sustainable development.

Brundtland offered seven major proposals for a strategy to sustainable development which are listed in Table 2. It sought to revive growth but to change the quality of that growth; it sought to meet basic needs for employment, food, energy, water and sanitation but for a sustainable "population base". It sought to conserve and enhance natural resources but with an emphasis on refocusing technology to better manage risk. It sought to merge environment into economic decision making but realized this was impossible without transforming attitudes and practices.

Figure 2 breaks down the components of sustainability to indicate the complexity of sustainable development. It is possible, for example, to have growth at the global scale but not necessarily growth in each nation, or in both components of each nation.

It was unclear how growth would be revived or how a change in the quality of growth could be stimulated. The commitment to meet basic needs was a commitment to a subsistence level economy rather than a modern economy. Similarly the commitment to stabilize population, where there was little acknowledgement of the fact that population only seemed to stabilize with a high level of economic development, was rather vacuous. Discussion of the conservation and enhancement of natural resources

Table 1 Brundtland Takes Irreconcilable Positions

- Revive Growth
- Change Quality of Growth
- Meet Basic Needs
- Stabilize Population
- Conserve and Enhance Resources
- Reorient Technology and Manage Risk
- Put Environment into Economics

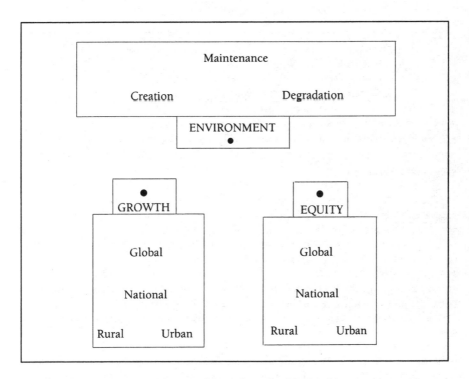

Figure 2 The Complexity of Sustainable Development

But Brundtland was an important political initiative not least because unlike other social democratic initiatives — the Pearson, Brandt and Palme Reports — it reported directly to the General Assembly of the United Nations. In turn, the United Nations General Assembly asked for a report back on progress in sustainability after five years. This report back was known as the United Nations Conference on Environment and Development (UNCED) which was held in Rio de Janeiro, Brazil in 1992. What is striking about UNCED in how far the agenda had been turned "green" and anti-developmental in the five years from the Brundtland Report. Details of this change are shown in Table 3 where the agendas of Brundtland and UNCED are compared. This change in agenda was not simply because the lawyers had taken over but because the sustainable debate had been driven by Northern governments, using Northern environmental NGOs such as Friends of the Earth and Greenpeace to pursue a status quo development framework that was essentially against the South. The North turned "green" and the South was turned away.

Table 2 Brundtland — Major Proposals

- Reviving Growth
- Changing the Quality of Growth
- Meeting Essential Needs for Jobs, Food, Energy, Water and Sanitation
- Ensuring a Sustainable Level of Population
- Conserving and Enhancing the Resource Base
- Reorienting Technology and Managing Risks
- Merging Environment and Economics in Decision-making

Source: WCED (1987).

The Rio conference was the largest environmental conference ever and some 30,000 people attended. It was also the largest ever meeting of heads of state (more than 100). The intention was to build on Brundtland's hopes and achievement, to respond to pressing global environmental problems, to agree major treaties on biodiversity, climate change and forest management; and to achieve agreement on principles and actions for sustainable development. Over two years at a series of four preparatory committees (prepcoms) an agenda was agreed and agreements substantially achieved so that only the more controversial sections were discussed at Rio (Grubb et al, 1993).

During the Rio conference there was continuous dispute over finance, control and the relative importance of consumption rates and population. Within the North there was also a conflict between the desirability of voluntarism as opposed to control. The final outcome from the conference was better than was feared during the conference itself, though the fundamentally different priorities of the Northern states demanding environmental sustainability and the Southern states demanding development ensure that agreements will be reached only with difficulty.

The unholy alliance between Northern money, Northern self-interest and soft green concerns with the conservation of "pure" ecosystems has ensured that Rio 1992 is predominantly about the unimpaired growth of the North, implying accelerated extraction of resources from the South (driven by IMF adjustment programmes) and it is about maintenance of the global commons, at present being degraded largely by the North. Current interest in "debt for nature" exchanges has concentrated on narrowly conceived biosphere conservation, with implicit exclusion of the interests of Third World people. (What use are biosphere reserves to them?) Why not some "debt for equity" agreements to help the urban poor of the Third World — or for that matter to help any Third World people? Cosmetic identification of reserves for aboriginal people reveals a limited view of equity. Perhaps the indigenous knowledge held in these museums will hold a cancer or AIDS cure for MNCs? The real Northern concerns of trade, economy and foreign policy wormed their way into the environmental and development agenda constructed by Brundtland. In fact, as a comparison between the report and the conference shows (Table 3), the lack of relationship between them is bewildering, when one is explicitly a follow-up to the other.

Table 3 The Mismatch of Agenda

BRUNDTLAND	UNCED
A Threatened Future	Conventions on Climate Change
Sustainable Development	Forests
International Economy	Biodiversity, Biotechnology, Land Resources
Population and Human Resources	Hazardous Wastes
Food Security	Toxic Chemicals
Energy	Freshwater
Industry	
Urbanization	Action for Sustainable Development into the Twenty-First Century
The Commons	Environmental Awareness
Conflict — environment and development	Poverty and Environment
Proposals for Institutional and Legal Change	Finance
	Agenda 21 — Cross Sectoral Issues
	The Earth Charter

Source: Middleton et al (1993).

The outcomes from Rio (Grubb et al, 1993) were:

1. Convention on Biological Diversity
2. Framework Convention on Climatic Change
3. Principles of Forest Management
4. Agenda 21
5. The Rio Declaration on Environment and Development

The Convention on Biological Diversity was negotiated independently of UNCED under the UNDP, but was signed at Rio. It is a legally binding treaty. It seeks to conserve biodiversity, species and ecosystems and sets rules for their use. The North feared the restriction on the development of biotechnology and the USA refused to sign largely for this reason. Other Northern countries, while signing, were uneasy that they could be committed to large expenses in paying for programmes to protect biodiversity. There were 155 signatories at Rio.

Response to climatic change was also negotiated outside the UNCED structure. The Framework Convention agrees an outline legal response to what are resolved to be serious issues and accepts the need for a precautionary approach pending further scientific knowledge. Northern countries agreed to pay the full incremental cost of measures taken by the South. Northern countries agreed also to stabilize their output of greenhouse gases at 1990 levels by 2000, 153 states signed the Framework Convention on Climate Change at Rio.

Principles of Forest Management are strong on well meaning statements but weak on commitment. They stress the right of states to manage their own resources and fail to set up a legal framework for forest management for sustainability.

Agenda 21 is a vast document of 40 chapters. It may be regarded as a broad action plan for sustainable development and/or a manual of good practice for sustainable development. Four groups of topics are considered:

1. *Social and economic development*, including: international cooperation, poverty, sustainable consumption, population, health, settlements, and integration of environment with development.
2. *Resource management*, including: atmosphere, land resource planning, deforestation, fragile ecosystems, mountains, rural development, biodiversity, biotechnologies, oceans, freshwater, toxic waste, hazardous waste, solid wastes and sewage and radioactive wastes.
3. *Strengthening the participation of major groups*. This includes virtually everyone: women, children, indigenous people and NGOs are among the groups specified.
4. *Means of implementation* includes finance, institutions, technology transfer, sciences, education, capacity building, international institutions, law and information for decision making.

Agenda 21 also recommended creating an international Commission for Sustainable Development.

The *Rio Declaration on Environmental Development* comprises 27 principles for the achievement of sustainable development. On the surface they appear bland and uncontroversial: they were in fact bitterly contested. Many stress development issues. The first and presumably most important is "human beings are at the centre of concerns for sustainable development. They are entitled to a healthy and productive life in harmony with nature". On the surface at least, it appears that Brundtland's equity cornerstone has been incorporated in Rio.

Conclusion

The world has made a start in developing a programme for sustainable development, though the dilution of Brundtland's high ideals at Rio has been a setback. *Realpolitik* rules and justice is the advantage of the stronger. There are, however, some hopeful signs. At least the world is now aware of the political economic nature of the debate and of the need for coordinated action at the international level. The success of negotiations for a reduction of CFCs shows that states can act in the common interest. Environment is on the media agenda, development, unfortunately less so. Even here, the increased awareness of the plight of children, women in the South, indigenous people and refugees may broaden into a concern for all disadvantaged people who see development rather than humanitarian aid as the long-term aim. For the editors, though, the greatest successes are those achieved at the grass roots by ordinary people showing their ability to create, rebuild and maintain their own bits of environment, cooperating to build sustainable lives. Empowerment is the key and the challenge.

References

Adams, W M (1990) *Green Development*, Routledge, London
Beckerman, W (1995) *Small is Stupid: Blowing the Whistle on the Greens*, Duckworth, London
Boserup, E (1989) *Women's Role in Economic Development*, Earthscan, London
Brown, L (1994) "CFC Production Falling", in L Brown, H Kane and E Ayres, *Vital Signs 1993–1994: The Trends that are Shaping our Future*, Earthscan, London, pp66–7
Clarke, R (1991) *Water: The International Crisis*, Earthscan, London
De Jesus, C M (1990) *Beyond All Pity: The Diary of Carolina Maria de Jesus*, Earthscan, London
Dumount, R (1988) *False Start in Africa*, Earthscan, London
Eckholm, E P (1982) *Down to Earth: Environment and Human Needs*, Norton, New York and London
Grainger, A (1990) *The Threatening Desert: Controlling Desertification*, Earthscan, London
—— (1993) *Controlling Tropical Deforestation*, Earthscan, London
Grubb, M, M Koch, A Munson, F Sullivan and K Thompson (1993) *The Earth Summit Agreements: A Guide and Assessment*, Earthscan, London
Harris, B (1990) "Another Awkward Class: Merchants and Agrarian Change in India", in H Berstein, B Craw, M Mackintosh and C Mackintosh, *The Food Question: Profits versus People?*, Earthscan, London, pp91–103
Holmberg, J and R Sandbrook (1992) "Sustainable Development: What is to be Done?", in J Holmberg (ed) *Policies for a Small Planet*, Earthscan, London, pp19–38
IUCN (1980) "World Conservation Strategy: Living Resource Conservation for Sustainable Development", IUCN, UNEP and WWF, Gland, Switzerland
Kemf, E (ed) (1993) *Indigenous Peoples and Protected Areas*, Earthscan, London
Lewenhak, S (1992) *The Revolution of Women's Work*, Earthscan, London
McCormick, J (1990) *Acid Earth: The Global Threat of Acid Pollution*, Earthscan, London
Meadows, D H (1972) *The Limits to Growth*, Unwise Books, New York
Meadows, D H, D L Meadows and J Randers (1992) *Beyond the Limits: Global Collapse of a Sustainable Future*, Earthscan, London
Middleton, N, P O'Keefe and S Moyo (1993) *Tears of the Crocodile: From Rio to Reality in the Developing World*, Pluto Press, London and Boulder, CO
Munslow, B, Y Katerere, A Ferf and P O'Keefe (1988) *The Fuelwood Trap: A Study of the SADCC Region*, Earthscan, London
O'Keefe, P and S J Kirkby (1995) *Adding Value to Nature*. Division of Geography and Environmental Management, Departmental Occasional Papers, new Series No 12
O'Keefe, P, S J Kirkby and C Howarth (1993) "Whatever Happened in Brazil 1992: An Earth Charter for Whom?", in J Dahl, D Drakakis-Smith and A Narmen, *Land, Food and Basic Needs in Developing Countries*, the Department of Geography, University of Goteborg
Onimode, B (1989) *The IMF, The World Bank and the African Debt*: Vol 2 *The Social and Political Impact*, Zed Books, London and New Jersey
Patnaik, U. (1990) "Some Economic and Political Consequences of the Green Revolution in India", in H Berstein, B Craw, M Mackintosh and C Martin, *The Food Question: Profits versus People?*, Earthscan, London, pp80–90

Pearce, D, A Markandaya and E B Barbier (1989) *Blueprint for a Green Economy*, Earthscan, London

Prins, G (ed) (1993) *Threats Without Enemies: Facing Environmental Insecurity*, Earthscan, London

Redclift, M (1992) "The Meaning of Sustainable Development", *Geoforum*, vol 23, no 3, pp395–403

Seager, J (1993) *Earth Follies: Feminism, Politics and The Environment*, Earthscan, London

Sen, G and C Grown (1988) *Development Crises and Alternative Visions: Third World Women's Perspectives*, Earthscan, London

Shiva, V (ed) (1994) *Close to Home: Women Reconnect Ecology, Health and Development*, Earthscan, London

Timberlake, L and L Thompson (1990) *When the Bough Breaks: Our Children, Our Environment*, Earthscan, London

Utting, P (1993) *Trees, People and Power*, Earthscan, London

Urdang, S (1989) "And Still They Dance", *Women, War and the Struggle for Change in Mozambique*, Earthscan, London

WCED (1987) *Our Common Future*, Oxford University Press, Oxford

Wilson, A (1991) *The Challenge Road: Women and the Eitrean Revolution*, Earthscan, London

Chapter 1 | BIODIVERSITY

Maintenance of biodiversity is a long-term priority for sustainable development. Biodiversity covers a wide range of aspects of living things: genetic diversity within individual species, the diversity of species themselves and the diversity of ecosystems within which individual organisms live. Since the Neolithic age, human beings have manipulated the genepool of useful species, through breeding for desired qualities. A wild genepool allows continued improvements and reduces the risk of catastrophic losses through disease of domesticated species.

Unfortunately, due to human activities, this rate of extinction of species has increased, possibly to 1000 times the "normal" rate. The anthropogenic rate of extinctions is on the scale of the catastrophic mass extinctions which punctuate geological time. Unquestionably, biological resources are the most significant component of natural capital. Martyn Murray reviews the significance of this loss, indicates the profoundness of our ignorance of this cornucopia of riches and explains how we are squandering our heritage. He outlines the conflict of interests between North and South shown in the discussion of the biodiversity treaty at Rio and concludes by reviewing some of the actions needed to protect biodiversity.

Ed Ayres shows the rapid depletion of one set of resources, marine mammals, which in principle could have been used indefinitely, if a suitable management system had been implemented. Practical methods of maintaining collections of wild genetic resources, either in nature reserves or in zoos and gene banks are reviewed by Robert and Christine Prescott-Allen. Most success so far has been in zoos and gene banks though the need is for effective wild gene pool management. Peter Utting discusses the success of conservation in a variety of protected areas in Costa Rica covering almost 30 per cent of the country. Debt-for-nature scoops have been used to buy land for conservation, though the environmental benefits and social impact of such schemes are questionable. The case study of the Carara Biological Reserve points out the conflicts that may occur when conservation areas are created. Abby Munson provides a concise review of the UNCED Convention on Biological Diversity.

The Value of Biodiversity
Martyn Murray

> *It is permissible to lament the altered aspect of the Earth's surface, together with the disappearance of numberless noble and beautiful forms.*
>
> (W H Hudson, 1895)

Earth's biosphere, a thin interlocking layer of land surfaces, oceans and atmosphere, embraces a variety of living organisms so great that most have not yet been named. To the naturalist, the diversity of life to be found in the biosphere and the intricacy of the interactions among the different life forms are the greatest wonder of the world: they have immeasurable intrinsic value. Being so hard to measure in the monetary terms which dominate the modern world, or to exchange in a utilitarian marketplace the validity of this value of biodiversity is challenged daily by our crowded societies. Other peoples and other cultures have had less difficulty in respecting such values. In 1855 Chief Seattle of the Suguamish Indians was compelled to "sell" his lands along the Puget Sound of Washington State to the advancing whites. Famously he replied: "How can you buy or sell the sky? We do not own the freshness of the air or the sparkle of the water. How then can you buy them from us? Every part of the Earth is sacred to my people, holy in their memory and experience." But American Indians could not halt the immense intellectual commitment and technological capacity to subdue nature possessed by the white man and with which today he has imbued a global culture. Chief Seattle continued his address in burning words which set the agenda for an evaluation of biodiversity in the closing years of this millennium:

> We know that the white man does not understand our ways. He is a stranger who comes in the night and takes from the land whatever he needs. The earth is not his friend but his enemy, and when he has conquered it he moves on. He kidnaps the earth from his children. His appetite will devour the earth and leave behind a desert. If all the beasts were gone, we would die from a great loneliness of the spirit, for whatever happens to the beasts, happens also to us. All things are connected. Whatever befalls the earth, befalls the children of the earth.

Chief Seattle's commentary has great poignancy for us in the closing years of the twentieth century. An expanding human population, growing per capita energy consumption and increasing waste production are eroding and altering natural habitats in every country; and the loss of wild places is accelerating, causing widespread extinctions of plant and animal species. There is a growing realization that the present variety of living organisms will not be maintained, unless the value of biodiversity is revealed and appraised in terms corresponding directly with those used in managing the global economy. So paradoxically, immeasurable intrinsic value may only be protected in the short term by finding ways to do what Chief Seattle thought impossible: placing extrinsic value on biodiversity.

While ways to cost biodiversity have only just begun to be investigated, finding an equitable distribution of benefits arising from biodiversity has already proved to be a thorny problem. Failure to reach agreement in this area in 1992 led to the refusal of the US government to sign the Convention on the Conservation of Biological Diversity at the Earth Summit. One contributory factor underlying this disagreement was a difference in interpretation of the meaning of biodiversity. A definition of biodiversity, acceptable to lawyers and economists, as well as to biologists, is obviously needed, and is the first topic to be addressed in this chapter.

What is Biodiversity?

Biodiversity is often used as a synonym for species diversity which has been broadly defined as the number of species of plant, animal and "lower organism" within a given area. Of course, there is much more to life's diversity than can be contained in one summary statistic. Each species is composed of many individual plants or animals which may differ from one another in subtle and sometimes not so subtle ways. Some of these differences are the result of the particular environment in which the individual develops and others are due to genetic inheritance. Inheritance is controlled by genes, which are the basic units conferring biological distinctiveness at every level of comparison, from molecules to man. So it is important to understand their basic properties.

Every individual carries in every cell of its body a library of genetic information whose physical form is long chains of DNA (deoxyribonucleic acid) molecules. DNA has the property of being able to undergo biochemical reactions which result in identical copies being formed, or replicated. Certain sections of DNA retain their selfsame identity over evolutionary time, replicated copies being passed on functionally unchanged from one generation to the next. These sections of DNA operate by directing the synthesis of protein molecules, which are fundamental to the life and work of the cell and thus to the make-up and behaviour of the individual who carries them. These DNA sections are known as genes.

Physical maps, which give the location of different genes along the DNA molecule, are currently being assembled for several species of plant and animal, but producing each map is an enormous undertaking. Not surprisingly, more progress has been made with simpler organisms. The estimated numbers of different genes expressed by the bacterium *Escherichia coli*, bakers' yeast, and a small nematode (roundworm) are: 3500–4000, 7000–8000 and 25 000, respectively. Thale cress and the horse chestnut also have about 25 000 different genes and this number may be typical of higher plants. In fruit fly the number is put at about 15 000 different genes and in mammals, including man, estimates vary between 10 000 and 100 000 genes.

Genes directing synthesis of proteins that are fundamental to life processes have been conserved with little functional change since early in the story of life. For example, cytochrome c is a small protein with an important role in capturing energy from food that first appeared between between one-and-a-half to two billion years ago. Similar variants of cytochrome c are found today in such diverse species as yeast, pumpkin, wheat, screw-worm fly, grey whale and man. Many other genes, such as those conferring differences in body size, form, structure, disease resistance, chemistry of toxins and behaviour are far more recently derived and may be confined to a single species. When a species becomes extinct, unique genetic information in these genes is lost forever.

As a general rule, the more similar the DNA of two species, the more recently they shared a common ancestor. Man and chimpanzee have been shown to be close cousins, sharing over 98 per cent of their DNA structure. By comparison, the DNA of certain "relic species" or "living fossils", such as the coelacanth fish and the Chinese maidenhair tree, have many differences from those of their nearest relatives, for each is the sole surviving representative of a long-independent lineage. Two distinctive species represent a more important part of biodiversity than two similar ones as the former carry many more unique genes. Conservation biologists have devised new methods for putting conservation efforts in order of priority which take into account the genetical distinctiveness of species, in addition to considerations of numerical rarity and of geographic distribution, which had previously been used.

Biological diversity incorporates the idea of distinctiveness at every level of life from molecules, to cells, to individuals, to species, to assemblages of species and to eco-systems. This distinctiveness derives from the influences (or expressions) of very many different genes. Thus biodiversity is the product of many different genes. For our pragmatic purpose, we may define global biodiversity as the total number of genes on Earth.

A Task with a Time Limit

Hawaii once had a wealth of land snails paralleled nowhere else on Earth with well over 1000 endemic species, including the beautifully coloured and patterned little agate shells or Oahu tree snails. However, within the last 100 years, about 600 of these irreplaceable species have become extinct. The river systems of Malaysia's tropical forests were once rich in freshwater fish, with 266 species described and named. In a recent four-year survey, less than half this number could be found. Island species and aquatic species in isolated inland waters are particularly susceptible to extinction due to their restricted geographic ranges and their vulnerability to introduced predators, so that these examples are not broadly representative of mainland species. Nevertheless, they have sounded a clear warning of what is likely to happen on a wider scale if present practices continue.

Quantitative information on extinction rates is not yet available for the vast majority of species and geographic regions, but estimates can be inferred from observed rates of loss of natural habitats, and from empirical rules relating numbers of species to area of habitat. A recent analysis predicts the loss of 2 to 8 per cent of all currently existing species over the next 25 years. Current estimates of global extinction rates are not yet precise, but what is not disputed is that extinction rates are accelerating. In geological time there have been spectacular mass extinctions of highly successful groups — the trilobites and the dinosaurs, for example — and these have been attributed to a variety of natural processes, yet over the next 50 years the cataclysmic extinction of thousands or millions of species will be of a similar order, and it will have been due primarily to man's mass mismanagement of the planet.

The desire to understand life and the nature of living organisms has captured the human imagination since prehistory, but this quest has been given special impetus by the present-day global threat to biodiversity. Biologists are seeking to find the principles underlying the diversity of all living organisms, and they recognize that this task now has a time limit.

The first undertaking in any scientific endeavour is to take stock, and this is where the difficulties in studying biodiversity begin. The system of nomenclature used today was worked out by Carolus Linnaeus of Sweden whose *Systema Naturae*, with the names of 9000 species of plant and animal, was published in 1758. Although all human cultures have classified nature, this was the beginning of the formal classification of life on Earth. Since then a total of between 1.4 and 1.8 million species have been collected, described and named. Biologists are confident that the majority of vertebrates and higher plants that exist (estimates of 50 000 and 300 000 respectively) have been formally described, but accept that there are probably many more insect species than the 950 000 that have been catalogued.

Just a few years ago the total number of species on Earth, including those not yet discovered, was thought to be in the order of three million. Then about ten years ago Terry L Erwin of the Smithsonian Institution reported his findings on the range of beetles collected from the canopy of tropical trees, and used this information to estimate that 30 million kinds of insect may occur in the tropics alone. This phenomenal new total was reckoned in an interesting way. First, the canopies of 19 individual trees belonging to one Panamanian species were sampled for beetles by fogging with insecticide, producing about 1200 species in all. Many of these species were vagrants appearing on other tree species, but some were specialists. So Erwin adjusted this figure downward to estimate the average number of beetle species that were specialized exclusively on a single species of tropical tree. Upward adjustments were then made to convert beetle numbers to insect numbers, and again to convert the number of canopy insects to the number of insects at any height above ground. The resulting figure of 600 insect species was multiplied by 50 000 — the number of species of tropical trees — yielding 30 million species of tropical insect. Much more research is required to test the accuracy of each step in Erwin's calculation. Meanwhile, parallel studies by Peter Hammond of the Natural History Museum, in moist tropical forest on Sulawesi, suggests a substantially lower but still massive figure of 8 million insect species worldwide. Adding this figure to conservative estimates for other groups, he suggests 12.5 million species as the global total for all kinds of organism.

A completely different approach to calculating numbers of species is to employ one or more empirical rules relating species number to ecological parameters such as structure of food chains, area of habitats, range sizes and body sizes. For example, Robert May compiled numbers of named species to reveal that for organisms ranging in size from one centimetre to a few metres, a tenfold reduction in length corresponded approximately to a hundredfold increase in the number of species. Extrapolating down to smaller-sized organisms that are less well catalogued, he arrived at a global total of around 10 million species.

The need for much more basic information, especially from such species-rich groups as insects, nematodes, mites, fungi and bacteria and from poorly known areas, is self-evident. Meanwhile there remains the possibility that even our most careful estimate of species richness, taken from the current base of scientific knowledge, will be wildly upset by future discoveries. A recent survey of animal life on the deep-ocean floor gave rise to a preliminary estimate of 10 million bottom-dwelling species.

Beyond this exercise of taking stock is the need to understand the pattern of biological diversity over space and time. The basic tool for understanding, conserving and describing biodiversity is the species distribution map. So far, only a few well-studied groups have been charted. Biologists truly have an enormous task ahead of them.

The Basis for Insecurity

The greatest immediate threat to terrestrial biodiversity is the loss and fragmentation of natural habitats, especially in the tropics. Major alteration of tropical forests began in about AD 1600 and has accelerated during the past 50 years. In 1980, 113 000 km^2 of tropical forest was cleared, but by 1990 annual clearance was 169 000 km^2. If this rate continues to accelerate the last area of tropical forest will disappear in about AD 2040.

According to a report from the Food and Agricultural Organization of the United Nations, shifting cultivation, otherwise known as slash-and-burn farming, is the principal cause of forest loss in Africa, Asia and the Americas, accounting for 70 per cent, 50 per cent and 35 per cent of forest loss respectively. In the past, traditional societies included a fallow period of ten years or more in their shifting rotation which allowed for regrowth of the forest, but today this practice is rare as numbers of cultivators have greatly increased, and often they are immigrant farmers without knowledge of appropriate farming methods. Exploitation for timber and clearance of forest for plantation crops, such as rubber, oil palm, tea, coffee, sugar cane and cacao, also contribute to deforestation. Often there is a progression in the pattern of land use in which roads that were constructed to transport timber from logging operations, set in hitherto remote forested areas, facilitate access by hunters, encourage settlement and farming, and lead to further loss of forest.

Two other major habitat classes of particular importance for biodiversity are wetlands and coral reefs. Wetlands include areas of marsh, swamp and open shallow water, which are important breeding grounds for many species. Loss of wetlands has not yet been quantified in most countries but it may be severe: for example, over 90 per cent of the wetlands of New Zealand have been lost since the arrival of European settlers. The causes of wetland loss include drainage for land development, construction of dams and dykes, hydrological alterations brought about by depletion of underground aquifers, and pollution. Coral reefs have been likened to rainforests of the seas because of their enormous variety of marine life, including reef fishes, molluscs, crustaceans and the corals themselves. Major threats from humans include pollution, sedimentation and over-exploitation.

Potentially just as damaging to biodiversity as the steady erosion of natural habitats is the sudden impact of global climate change. One cause of particular concern is the possibility of rapid stepwise changes to the environment caused by climatic systems with positive feedbacks. One such example would be an increase in warm surface currents caused by melting of sea ice, which in turn accelerates the melting process. Rapid changes in patterns of precipitation and temperature are likely to cause extinctions of many species in areas of high biodiversity. A different type of threat, also associated with climatic change, is the potential for increased invasion of native communities by alien and exotic species. Judging from the effect of recent introductions to Australia, New Zealand and southern Africa, an increase in alien invasions alone could precipitate mass extinctions.

The various threats to biodiversity discussed above are concerned with the proximal causes of loss of species. The more fundamental causes are embedded in the contemporary condition of humanity, compounded by geometric growth in many human populations, and exacerbated by poverty and the aspirations of all people for a better quality of life. In a recent article in *Science* ("Biodiversity Studies: Science and Policy", 1991), Paul Ehrlich and Edward Wilson point out that the expected increase in global economic activity that is predicted as necessary to meet the demands and aspirations of the human population, which is itself projected as doubling over the next half century, make the destruction of most of the world's biodiversity virtually inevitable, if business continues as usual.

The Value of Biodiversity

Current practices of land use reflect the legitimate economic interests of powerful interested parties, including governments, development banks and companies, landholders, farmers and others. But it is now widely understood that the costs of depleting biodiversity are not being factored into the accounts when decisions are made on land development. This may be partly because the value of biodiversity is not yet sufficiently explicit, partly because the benefits arising from the utilization of biodiversity have been acquired in the past without recompense, and partly because what recompense has been received has seldom been transferred to the local level.

Two principal uses of wild plants and animals are cited as providing a strong economic justification for conservation of global biodiversity. One is concerned with sustaining our food production and the other with protecting our health.

Although the number of major crops is small (there are about 200 domesticated species of food plant each comprising many cultivated varieties, or cultivars), their continuing productivity is underpinned by a reservoir of genes present in a much larger number of related wild species. These wild genes can be incorporated through plant breeding programmes. For example, genes from wild grasses provide today's crop of wheat (*Triticum aestivum*) with resistance to rust diseases, tolerance of drought, winter hardiness and higher kernel protein content. The development of high-yielding cultivars for intensive agriculture has led to a great reliance on genetically uniform crops and the loss of genetic diversity. This genetic erosion is now recognized as a major threat to the long-term maintenance of global food supplies. Natural predators such as viruses, bacteria, nematodes, aphids and others are very efficient at finding weaknesses in crops and, unlike their genetically uniform prey, they are constantly evolving. In several dramatic cases, major crop failures have been averted by the discovery of resistant genes in wild relatives of food plants.

The value of conserving wild relatives of the major food crop species is well recognized, but while this may be a forceful argument for conserving centres of diversity of wild crop plants, it is not a sufficient economic reason for blanket preservation of wild plants and animals in other parts of the world. A much greater range of plants is used for medicinal purposes. The World Health Organization lists over 21 000 plants that are used in traditional medicine, of which some 5000 species have been investigated as sources of new drugs for orthodox medicine at present, some 119 pure chemical compounds extracted from 90 species of higher plant have found uses in drugs and preparations, and almost a quarter of all medical prescriptions are for drugs extracted or derived from plants and micro-organisms. The total market for plant-derived medicines is estimated at US\$ 43 billion per annum.

Chemical substances in plants with medicinal applications are usually the compounds that have evolved as chemical defences against insects, pathogens and other natural enemies. The rosy periwinkle (*Catharanthus roseus*) of Madagascar has given rise to anti-cancer drugs vincristine and vinblastine. These drugs are difficult to synthesize in the laboratory, and so it remains cheaper to extract their precursors from leaves collected from living plants. Natural products are seldom used directly in orthodox medicine, but the compounds extracted from them often form the starting point in a search for synthetic compounds that retain useful activity while minimizing unwanted side effects. The great value of natural products is as a source of novelty and as a source of leads in developing new drugs and useful chemicals. Since 1950, 3000 antibiotics have been developed from *Actinomycetes* (a group of bacteria) alone. Despite these successes, and the financial benefits arising from the use of wild plants and animals, the present market system does not provide economic incentives for conserving biodiversity.

One problem is the lack of clear pricing. Economists have estimated the direct retail value of genes and gene products taken from specific medicinal plants and wild relatives of crop plants, but the cost of developing them for commercial use is less easy to establish. One reason for expecting the cost to be high arises from the difficulty in predicting which of many wild species will eventually have an economic value. The discovery of new drugs has been likened to a lottery in which hundreds of plant extracts must be screened before one is found that can be developed to a successful product.

In recent times, the process of screening natural product has been greatly speeded up by combining modern molecular techniques with a system of pre-election, using either the medicinal knowledge of traditional peoples or the observations of field ecologists. Presumably, these improved procedures have reduced the cost of developing commercially successful products from natural sources, but more explicit information is required. A plant that has already been screened for useful chemical activities is just as likely to provide useful chemicals in the future as one that has not. As techniques improve, more and more biological activity is being discovered in natural products. The number of compounds isolated from each of the well-studied plants, such as the rosy periwinkle, can approach 100, and even well-studied organisms can be regarded as untested with respect to a new assay. This implies that mining wild species for their current batch of useful products, and then discarding them, would be counterproductive in the long term.

Even though the diversity of known animal species is much higher, far more use is made of genes and gene products extracted from plants and micro-organisms. As with food plants, there are only a small number of economically important domestic species of animal. Domesticated vertebrates account for just 28 species, but the seven main mammalian livestock species are subdivided into some 3237 breeds. The differentiation into many breeds is what maintains the genetic heterogeneity of domesticated animals. While a strong case can therefore be made for conserving rare breeds, thus retaining the broad genetic base of domestic animals, the same argument is much less forceful when applied to conservation of related wild species.

Many animal products are used locally in traditional medicines and there is a substantial international trade in substances such as deer antlers, tendons and musk, bears' gall bladders and rhino horn. Some animal products are also used in the development of orthodox medicines. Snake venoms contain powerful anticoagulants, neurotoxins and cytotoxin that have potential and actual application in bleeding disorders, cancer treatment and as anaesthetics. Spider venoms are being investigated as potential sources for the development of new insecticides. However, insects, while representing an estimated 64 per cent of all species on Earth, have never been systematically studied for useful biochemical products. This is a serious handicap to any attempt to place an economic value on biodiversity. One reason why insects are neglected is that many of their toxins may have similar chemical bases to those in plants, but it also has to be admitted that the necessary scientific and technical expertise is, quite simply, lacking.

The potential utility of new scientific research is well illustrated by current work investigating the sensory capacity of the antennae of various insect species. In the moist tropics, many insects specialize on single plant species. The plant components that act as toxicants or repellents to most potential predators, can also be an attractant to specialist insects. Volatile chemicals are released by plants and employed by insects as cues to the identification and location of food plants. The insects perceive these "semiochemicals" through sensilla, specialized receptor organs located on the antennae. Using extremely fine microelectrodes implanted into the base of sensilla, scientists have found that some receptors are precisely tuned to the perception of one particular compound, or a narrow range of structural types, and this new technique has enabled them to isolate and identify novel components from complex chemical extracts of plants. In fact, these discoveries promise to throw open a new door for re-exploration of the tropical flora by way of the chemical receptors of insect species. Another promising area for new research concerns the adaptations of insects to their food plants, which frequently contain toxic secondary compounds. Bruchid beetles, for example, are able to detoxify amino acids in the seeds of their food plants. The study of the detoxification process in insects is still in its infancy. How soon these promising lines of new research will deliver improved methods of crop protection, or more effective medical treatments, remains to be seen, but the potential is clearly enormous. A major increase in funding of research into the chemical ecology of tropical insects and plants is now an urgent priority.

A survey of the opinions of opinion-leaders in matters concerning tropical rainforests, revealed that many believe the most forceful arguments for convincing others to conserve forests were those based on sound commercial management for timber and non-timber products. But, in the personal beliefs of the same respondents, the most important reasons for conserving rainforests were to do with their biological uniqueness. Conversion of rainforest for other uses has been likened to burning libraries full of volumes that have not even been read. And in reading through a genetic library, it is not just the painstaking mapping of genes that is revealing but the elucidation of many varied and surprising interactions between species: mimicries and deceits, elaborate harvesting strategies, ways to avoid predation, obtain pollination, or sow seed. These and other such interchanges bring the forest to life and provide us with the stories and visions that, as Daniel Janzen has said, make up the real value of the natural world for humanity.

The knowledge that such natural phenomena are irreplaceable gives special impetus to the Prince of Wales's moral imperative which casts humankind in the role of temporary steward, with the responsibility to use natural resources in a sustainable way, and to pass them on to future generations in good order. Few would argue with such a principle, or with the urgency with which it needs to be adopted, but finding a path forward that is equitable to all nations and peoples, and round which many complex conflicts and differences can be resolved, is a challenge that is as formidable to our political leaders as it is fundamental to our future. The UN Conference on Environment and Development (the Earth Summit), held in June 1992 at Rio de Janeiro was organized as a major new initiative to help find just such an equitable pathway; and biodiversity was one of its prime concerns.

Conflicts of the Earth Summit

Curiously enough, the value of biodiversity was not the object of disagreement among the heads of state meeting in Rio. What stalled the biodiversity treaty, causing international furore, was a conflict over the marketing of biodiversity. In a nutshell: who gets paid for natural products that have been improved with biotechnology, and how much? In opposing camps were the US government, which had incorporated in its patent legislation the possibility of protection for "anything under the sun that is made by man" and the southern nations, stewards of the greatest abundance of biodiversity on the planet.

In the past, developed countries have taken advantage of tropical genetic resources to improve their agricultural and pharmaceutical industries, at little or no cost. They have argued that it is not the products found in plants that are offered for sale, but derivatives which have been isolated and synthesize at considerable expense, and they have pointed out that legal protection of these derivatives is needed to safeguard the large investments required for future work. At Rio, the response of Malaysia's prime minister, Dr Mahathir Mohammad, was hard-hitting and to the point: "Rainforest is not a common inheritance unless you are willing to pay for it. You don't pay, you expect us to pay for it. No go!"

During negotiations, the proposed rules for governing intellectual property rights on genetic resources and biotechnology were amended so as to exclude from consideration the international crop germplasm collections, and to admit the possibility of patenting genetic materials. Even so, the United States Bush Administration refused to sign the final version of the Convention on Biological Diversity. Despite this failure to find common ground, the meetings at Rio did set in motion a large, if slow-moving, wheel of change. The convention was signed by 153 governments who thus committed themselves in principle to supporting the treaty, with all its implications for minimizing future losses of biodiversity.

An equally important outcome of the Rio meetings was a recognition that the conservation of biodiversity could not be approached in the same way as the regulation of the atmosphere and climate. Developing countries have now refused to consider biodiversity as something belonging to the world community, insisting instead that it is the property of individual nations, in the same sense as any other marketable resource. While this viewpoint will have to be accommodated in future negotiations over biodiversity, so may demands for some form of restrictive covenant. The latter could take the form of an obligation incorporated into an international treaty or convention.

With many of the substantive provisions of the Convention on Biological Diversity still undecided, the caretakers of the treaty have a major task in front of them. What sort of devices can they set up to ensure that the framework of the convention is forged into an effective international instrument that secures biodiversity for generations to come?

Reducing Insecurities

The list of actions needed to protect biodiversity is indeed long, ranging from new species inventories to improved *ex situ* propagation and breeding facilities, to measures aimed at limiting the damage of human encroachment into the natural world. Finding workable ways to implement these activities is even more important than naming them. We can briefly summarize four central provisions that will have great importance in securing biodiversity in the long term, these being: putting a proper economic value on biodiversity; adopting a new environmental economics that manages renewable natural resources; completing a global inventory of plant and animal species; and establishing management systems to monitor and deal with environmental problems.

Economic Values

First, as we have seen earlier, there is the need to reach agreement on the issue of compensating developing countries for conserving and making available genetic diversity, while maintaining incentives for developed countries to market genetic resources. The collection and storage of genetic material without compensation is clearly inequitable and will lead to conflict. The National Biodiversity Institute (INBio) of Costa Rica has shown that local action can lead the way forward. The institute recently negotiated and signed a contract with the drugs company, Merck in which it agreed to supply plant extracts that will be screened for pharmaceuticals in return for US $1 million over a two-year period. INBio also has formal agreements over payment of royalties in other collaborative research ventures in which patentable products could be developed from natural sources. As Costa Rica continues with its ambitious ten-year plan to complete the first detailed biological inventory of a tropical country, it is also acquiring the technology to screen natural compounds in its own laboratories. If these plans are seen to succeed, other countries can be expected to set up similar institutions, and one can even envisage the emergence of cartels of gene and gene product producers with participating member-countries mapping onto floristic provinces or regions with high species diversity.

Environmental Economics

Second, there is the fundamental need to combine principles of conservation with economic development, so as to change a "throughput economy" still largely grounded on the theory and practice of trade in depletable resources, such as oil or coal, to one that can deal with renewable natural resources, such as tropical forests and marine fisheries, and can recognize the "invisible" transactions taking place outside the usual marketplace. Though this question has been examined in the one context by Dr Leggett and in the other by Professor Dürr, I need to refer to it here too. Invisible benefits might include storm protection and water purification by coastal wetlands, protection of watersheds by upland forest, and protection of primary food plants and medicinal plants by natural habitats. Since we cannot see such values in Chief Seattle's way, we must stick realistic costings upon such benefits. Only then will it be possible for managers correctly to frame the different options available for land use and sustainable development, because a mangrove swamp will turn out to be more valuable as a mangrove swamp than as a beach hotel.

The vision of a future in which biodiversity is confined to a global network of "fortress parks" is giving way to one in which much larger areas of publicly and privately owned lands are subject to sustainable resource extraction, while still providing for the maintenance of biodiversity. The new environmental economics will be an essential underpinning for conservation of biodiversity within these "protected landscapes". Experience has shown that local control of natural resources is more effective than centralized planning, though central agencies can help with education programmes and technical assistance. Thus, it will be important that benefits accruing from the use of biodiversity are returned to local communities. Furthermore, environmental economics will need to be underpinned by certain basic rights of the citizens of every country, such as the right of access to information about the environment, including levels of pollution; the rights of consultation and involvement before development; and the right of redress or compensation if the environment is damaged.

A Global Inventory

The third provision for safeguarding biodiversity is an inventory of the biological wealth of this planet, with a source catalogue of plant and animal species. This inventory is as vital for the rational utilization of biodiversity as it is for the development of a rational strategy for conserving biodiversity. Producing a global catalogue of species is quite feasible with modern information technology, provided that sufficient human resources are made available. The "parataxonomist programme" recently initiated by INBio in Costa Rica has demonstrated how a modest course of skilled training, combined with ongoing support and supervision of graduates, is sufficient to equip rural adults with the skills necessary to conduct a serious national inventory of animals and plants. Similar national programmes could be integrated with an international database containing information on identification traits, taxonomic affinities, distribution, ecology and genetics of each species, which could itself be made effectively available to developing countries on CD-ROM. Further technological assistance may soon appear in the form of multi-media databases, in which images, sound and video can be stored and displayed on microcomputers to assist with identification of specimens in remote locations.

The United Nations Environment Programme has already initiated a programme of country studies that would provide a natural framework for assembling a global inventory. Recognizing that local participation is the key to success, this programme aims to establish a national biodiversity unit in each country to serve as a coordinating centre for the gathering of data on the status, utilization and economic values of bio-diversity. This important initiative, in which developing countries will be assisted in setting up their own management capability, provides a framework for building a relationship of goodwill and trust between developing and developed nations in an area of mutual concern and interest.

Environmental Management

The fourth provision for securing biodiversity is the establishment of management systems to give warning of impending environmental problems and to implement effective conservation actions. As Kenton Miller has pointed out, at present there is no quick-response monitoring system that can provide reliable and targeted information, stimulate rapid and effective action, and track compliance with international agree-ments. Even with good scientific monitoring, experience shows that the environmental crunch often comes because of a failure in basic management. Environmental problems usually appear rapidly, as for example with the recent drought in southern Africa. The response to this type of problem involves many people working together for the first time, and for this reason it requires new management structures.

To cope with a serious drought, for example, park officials, botanists, wildlife biologists, veterinarians, agronomists, meteorologists, hydrologists, local community leaders, private landowners and central government representatives would all be needed to review available options and plan a response that minimized losses in biodiversity. Inevitably, disagreements and conflicts would arise from the different backgrounds, different responsibilities and different points of view. By the time these were worked out, the window in time within which effective management could have been imple-mented might have passed, leaving room only for ineffective actions. In other words, environmental crises have all too often been accompanied by management crises. The lesson that has to be learnt is one of pre-establishing a management system in which predictable scenarios (and many are easily predictable) have been discussed beforehand, and the rational management alternatives expounded.

Conclusion

In looking ahead at the prospects for minimizing losses in biodiversity, sooner or later one has to face up to all of the major insecurities jeopardizing our future on Earth. But what would it mean to lose a substantial portion of biodiversity? If we are looking for a fundamental concept for the practical value of biodiversity to humankind, it is this. Every species of plant and animal survives in the face of constant challenges from novel forms of micro-organism, parasite, pest and predator. It is now thought by leading evolutionary biologists that the whole process of sex itself has evolved and is maintained by the need to recombine genes to find new genetic variety to counter these antagonists, which are themselves eventually able to counter adapt. In wealthy nations the misery caused by disease, plague and pestilence is largely controlled by modern medicines and medical research, which rely heavily on drugs derived from a wide variety of natural products. Similarly, the essential production of high-yielding food plants relies on a variety of disease-resistant genes originating in wild plant relatives. As the human population goes through its final projected doubling of size to an estimated 10 billion, or tripling, humankind will need to call on the full diversity of genetic defences and resources on the planet in order to sustain this extraordinary new equilibrium and to realize a measure of freedom from hunger, illness and pain. It is to be hoped that the practical need to place an economic value on biodiversity will coincide with a broader reassessment of our relationship with the living world and our responsibility towards it, so that eventually we can understand and value fully what Chief Seattle was saying to us a century and a half ago.

■ Many Marine Mammal Populations Declining
Ed Ayres

Population collapses and extinctions of the Earth's plant and animal species are now taking place at several thousand times the natural "background" rate of biodiversity loss that has prevailed throughout the planet's biological history (Ryan, 1992). Losses of marine mammals — whales, dolphins, seals, manatees, and the like — constitute only a tiny portion of the overall devastation, but have caused particular concern because they serve as highly visible indicators of the difficulties other species, including humans, face. They are also of interest because they share much in common with us: they are at the top of their food chain, compete with humans for many of the same food sources, and may be affected by many of the same kinds of pollutants or environmental disruptions.

Public alarm has been particularly aroused by the growing frequency of such mysterious occurrences as the dying-off of bottlenose dolphins off the US Atlantic coast in 1987–88, which may have cut the region's population in half; the sudden deaths of more than 14 000 seals in northern Europe the following year; and the highly publicized self-strandings of whales — sometimes whole schools at a time (NOAA, 1991; Harwood and Reijnders, 1988). Of the 1200 whale-beachings known to have taken place in the past two centuries, two-thirds have occurred since the 1950s (Anon, 1993). Yet for all the concern these events cause, they represent only a small portion of the overall losses taking place in the marine mammal world.

Like human cultures, sea mammal populations have had widely varying fortunes over the past century of unprecedented change in the geophysical and biological environment. But it is noteworthy that in recent years many species have declined drastically in population, and some appear headed for extinction. (See Table 1.1)

Globally, most whales and porpoises are declining (International Whaling Commission, 1992; Nowack, 1993). The blue whale, for example — the largest animal on Earth — once numbered about 200 000 but is now estimated at fewer than 2000. The humpback whale, once at 125 000 is now at about 10 000. The sei whale has dropped from 200 000 in pre-industrial times to 25 000 today; the fin whale from 470 000 to 110 000; and the right whale, from 200 000 to 3000 (NOAA, 1992; Nowack, 1991).

Table 1.1 Changes in Marine Mammal Populations Since Mid-Century

Species	Population at mid-century	Current population*
Declines		
Sei Whale	200 000	25 000
Fin Whale	470 000	110 000
Blue Whale	200 000	2 000
Humpback Whale	125 000	10 000
Right Whale	200 000	30 900
Bowhead Whale	120 000	6 000
Northern Sea Lion	154 000	66 000
Juan Fernandez Fur Seal	4 000 000	600
Hawaiian monk seal	1500	1000
Recoveries		
Grey Whale	10 000	21 000
Galapagos fur seal	near extinction	30 000
Antarctic fur seal	near extinction	1 530 000
Walrus	50 000	280 000
Dugong	30 000	55 000

* Late 1980s to present.
Source: National Oceanic and Atmospheric Administration (NOAA), Office of Protected Resources, *Marine Mammal Protection Act of 1972. Annual Report 1988–89* (Washington, DC: US Department of Commerce, 1992); NOAA, *Our Living Oceans; The First Annual Report on the Status of US Living Marine Resources* (Washington, DC: 1991); Ron Nowack, Office of Scientific authority, US Fish and Wildlife Service, Arlington, VA, private communication, January 1993.

For some species, global populations are unknown — but regional trends follow a similar pattern. Dolphins off the Pacific coast of Mexico and Central America have declined by about half since purse-seine nets (huge sieve-like traps) were introduced in 1959 for yellow-fin tuna fishing (Norris, 1992). Although the problem was partially alleviated by the invention of a modified net allowing some dolphins to escape, some 20 000–50 000 dolphins are still drowned in the nets each year (NOAA, 1991).

Ironically, protections instituted to protect some marine mammals have increased pressure on others. In Japan, the national appetite for whale meat has heightened the demand for Dall's porpoise. Although the world's population of this animal is estimated at 2.2 million, Japanese hunters were killing 40 000 per year by 1988 — considered by some marine biologists to be an unsustainable pressure on the species (Norris, 1992).

Among the pinnipeds (sea mammals with four flippers), many species appear to be stable — but others are in sharp decline. The northern sea lion dropped from about 154 000 in 1960 to 66 000 in 1990 (Nowack, 1993). The Juan Fernandez fur seal, once numbering 4 million worldwide, has declined to about 600 (NOAA, 1991). And the decline can be extremely rapid: off the coast of Namibia, the seal population collapsed in just four years when overfishing depleted the animals' food supply, whereas 54 000 seal pups survived in 1985, only 3000 lived past ten months of age in 1989 (Anon,

1990). In the Bering Sea, the Steller's sea cow was killed off within 27 years of its discovery by nonindigenous hunters (Animal Welfare Institute, 1993).

The causes of decline are many — most of them resulting from human activity. Some mammals are still targets for hunters. Many more are killed in "incidental take" when caught in fishers' nets (NOAA, 1991). Others, such as the bottlenose dolphins whose population collapsed along the northern Atlantic coast in 1987–88, may have been killed by pollutants (Harwood and Reijnders, 1988). In Europe, thousands of seals have died of viral diseases in recent years — possibly because their immune systems had been weakened by pollutants or other environmental disruptions (NOAA, 1991). And there are other human intrusions as well. In Florida, the leading cause of death of manatees is collisions with boats (Van Meter, 1989).

During the heyday of unrestricted commercial fishing in the latter half of the nineteenth century, many sea mammals were hunted nearly to extinction. Others thrived well into the twentieth century but came under increasing pressure after the first modern factory ship began processing whales at sea in 1925. Commercial whaling boomed in the 1930s, with 46 000 whales — mostly blue whales — killed in the Antarctic region alone in the 1937–38 season. By the 1950s, the blue whale was extinct commercially. Given protection in 1965, its population began to rebound (MacDonald, 1984).

Similarly, at least four species of fur seals were decimated in the eighteenth and nineteenth centuries but have since recovered. The Antarctic variety — nearly extinct by 1900 — now numbers about 1.5 million. In the north Pacific, the North American grey whale declined to about 10 000 in mid-century, but has since rebounded to about 21 000. Two other species of grey whale, however — in the Atlantic and west Pacific — have been lost (Nowack, 1993).

Protections have brought some stability to the world's overall population of marine mammals: the US Marine Mammal Protection Act was passed in 1972, the 38-nation International Whaling Commission began a moratorium on commercial whaling in 1986, the European Council of Ministers banned purse-seining of marine mammals in 1992, and members of the United Nations resolved to ban driftnets by 1993 (IUCN, 1980; Thorne-Miller and Catena, 1991; Norris, 1992).

These protections appear precarious, however, in view of the growing appearance of conflict between short-term human economic demands and longer-term sustainability of marine activities. Both Norway and Iceland have said their economies depend on a resumption of commercial whaling, and the global whaling ban is under siege (MacLeod, 1992).

More generally, the growing global demand for fish not only threatens continued attrition of mammals through injuries by boats or fishing gear, it also depletes the mammals' own food supplies. And even if fishing demands can be brought into line with the oceans' carrying capacity, the effects of other human-caused disruptions — notably pollution and atmospheric ozone depletion, which appears to be killing some of the phytoplankton that are a primary link in the marine food chain — have become growing problems (Stetson, 1992). Future trends among marine mammals may be a telling measure of stability in human society itself.

References
Animal Welfare Institute (1983) *The Endangered Species Handbook*, Washington, DC

Anon (1990) "Namibian Seals Face Extinction", *African,* March

—— (1993) "Lost Angels: The Great Australian Whale Rescue," Storyteller Productions, Arts and Entertainment Network, 28 January

Harwood, J and P Reijnders (1988) "Seals, Sense and Sensibility", *New Scientist*, 15 October

IUCN, World Wildlife Fund and UN Environment Programme (1980) *World Conservation Strategy*. Gland, Switzerland

International Whaling Commission (1992) Cambridge UK, private communication, September

MacDonald, D (ed) (1984) *The Encyclopedia of Mammals*, Facts on File, New York

MacLeod, A (1992) "World Whaling Body Shaken by Attempts to Resume the Hunt", *Christian Science Monitor*, 6 July

NOAA (1991) *Our Living Oceans: The First Annual Report on the Status of US Living Marine Resources*, Washington, DC

—— (1992) *Marine Mammal Protection Act of 1972*, Annual Report 1988–89, Department of Commerce, Washington, DC

Norris (1992) "Dolphins in Crisis", *National Geographic*, September

Nowack, R (1991) *Walker's Mammals of the World*, Johns Hopkins University Press, Baltimore

—— (1993) Personal communication

Ryan, J C (1992) *Life Support: Conserving Biological Diversity*, Worldwatch Paper 108, Washington, DC

Stetson, M (1992) "Saving Nature's Sunscreen", *World Watch*, March/April

Thorne-Miller, B and J Catena (1991) *The Living Ocean: Understanding and Protecting Marine Biodiversity*, Friends of the Earth, Washington, DC

Van Meter, V B (1989) "Analysis of Propeller Wounds on Manatees in Florida", *The West Indian Manatee in Florida*, Florida Light & Power Company

The Evolution of International Whaling Law
Greg Rose and Saundra Crane

Whales ... belong to no single nation nor to any group of nations but rather they are the wards of the entire world.

(Acheson, 1946)

Whales have evolved over millions of years while commercial exploitation of them has taken place for only a few hundred. In those latter years whale populations have been subjected to intensive hunting and some species have been pushed near the point of extinction. International laws for their protection have developed slowly and haltingly, failing to arrest the species' decline. Even today, political and commercial interests continue to impede the progress of legal measures for the whales' protection.

The central international legal arrangement for the protection of whales is provided by the 1946 International Convention for the Regulation of Whaling (ICRW) and the International Whaling Commission (IWC) established thereunder (ICRW, 1946). However, since its signature 47 years ago, the ICRW has become too far removed from the realities of current political needs to meet adequately the needs of whale conservation. The reason that it has survived in its current anachronistic form is simply that its members are divided into two deadlocked camps: pro-whaling and anti-whaling countries. Any change in the balance between them may cause the machinery to collapse and so it remains static and antiquated.

This chapter aims to provide an understanding of the challenges facing the IWC in its attempts to "manage whale stocks" today. These include deciding what whales are under its jurisdiction; whether to maintain the commercial moratorium; how to formulate "revised management procedures"; whether to extend greatly the Indian Ocean whale sanctuary; how properly to manage "scientific", "pirate" and "aboriginal" whaling; and how to collaborate with fishing organizations to prevent whales from being drowned in fishing nets. A grasp of these issues requires familiarization with the ICRW, some aspects of the international law of the sea and with those political pressures which have shaped the role of the IWC since it was established.

Economic History of Whaling

For thousands of years aboriginal hunting of whales has been a subsistence and cultural activity. Commercial whaling began with the Basques in the Bay of Biscay in the eleventh century. Hunted intensively for their meat, oil and whalebone (for use in furniture and clothing), right whale populations deteriorated rapidly. The Basques extended their hunting grounds to the north Atlantic, where they were joined by British and Dutch hunters. The Basque industry ended in the sixteenth century as a result of stiff competition from the British and Dutch and as a result of the increasing rarity of right whales. The latter also caused a decline in the Dutch industry by the seventeenth century, but German and French hunters and European settlers in America readily filled the gap with other whale stocks (Smith, 1984).

Illustrative of whaling practices at the time is the story of the grey whales, which breed off the coast of southern California in US waters. Their nursery was discovered in 1851 and commercial whalers proceeded to slaughter the local population to the point of extinction. With the nursery depleted, the whalers destroyed their own industry in addition to decimating the California grey whale. When the American Civil War limited US participation in whaling and the petroleum oil industry emerged, much North American commercial whaling came to an end in the late 1800s (Smith, 1984).

As target species were depleted, the types of species hunted and the areas in which they were hunted needed to be continually expanded. To remain economically efficient, the industry required larger ships that sailed on longer journeys to the South Pacific and Indian Oceans in search of unexploited stocks. By the 1890s new technologies had greatly improved efficiency. The Norwegians had invented the harpoon gun, which enabled whalers to hunt the faster swimming whales by firing an explosive shell into the animal, killing it upon detonation (Birnie, 1989). Around this time, steam engines allowed ships to engage in pelagic or high-seas whaling as far away as the Antarctic seas. Approximately 10 000 whales were harvested there in 1901 (D'Amato and Chopra, 1991). The First World War inhibited the industry's operation, but by 1925 the invention of the slip-stern ship enabled whalers to pull the captured animal on board for processing. By the end of the 1930s, 85 per cent of the worlds' catch came from the Antarctic, with nearly 55 000 whales killed there in 1938 (Andersen, 1989).

Gradual recognition dawned in the 1930s that the industry's future was threatened by a rapid global decline in whale stocks. An annual catch of 43 219 whales also created a surplus in the whale-oil market, which led to lower prices (D'Amato and Chopra, 1991). The industry decided to take measures to protect its commercial interests in the same manner as cartels would, and steps were taken to limit catches through private agreements (Birnie, 1989). In 1931 a coordinated international effort to establish catch limits was made by the adoption of the Convention for the Regulation of Whaling (Convention for the Regulation of Whaling, 1931). These international legal developments need to be seen in the context of the international law of the sea, as it existed then and today.

International Law of the Sea

States have territorial sovereignty over all the resources within their "territorial seas". Territorial seas once extended three nautical miles out from the shoreline, but this limit was increased during the 1970s and 1980s to a maximum of 12 nautical miles from the shoreline. Beyond the territorial sea is the "exclusive economic zone" (EEZ) coastal states may claim, and it extends to 200 nautical miles from the shoreline. It is different from the territorial sea in that the coastal state has fewer rights over activities unrelated to economic resource utilization in that area (for example, it has less control over the movements of foreign vessels). In the EEZ, the coastal state has exclusive jurisdiction over economic resources, the most important of which is fisheries. An area known as the "high seas" extends from the outer edge of a state's EEZ (or territorial sea if it has not claimed an EEZ) to the outer edge of another state's EEZ or territorial waters. In its territorial waters and EEZ ("coastal waters"), the coastal state has sovereign rights to exploit the economic resources there. These resources include whales, which are in general considered a part of the national fishery resource. Any whale conservation measures taken in the territorial seas are voluntary only.

Somewhat more controversial in international law are the international duties to conserve fishery resources in the EEZ. The 1982 UN Convention on the Law of the Sea (UNCLOS) sets out these duties and, although almost all states have signed the convention, it has not yet come into force. Therefore, one can only say that these conservation duties are still evolving as rules of law outside of UNCLOS and are not yet binding as treaty law. Unless it has signed a voluntary agreement not to do so, the coastal state may legally choose to exploit and deplete the fisheries resources in its EEZ. Even within the terms of UNCLOS, the obligation to conserve fisheries is vague. However, in the cases of marine mammals and highly migratory species — both of which include cateceans — UNCLOS requires at least that states cooperate to conserve, manage and study them. Yet, when the convention comes into force, this obligation will not be compulsory in the sense of being subject to binding decision by an international tribunal; rather, it will offer political leverage to conservation interests.

On the high seas, all states have equal access to the waters and rights to use the economic resources contained therein. Whales, like other resources in the high seas, belong to no one and are not subject to exclusive control by any state, they are "free for all". However, the International Court of Justice has recognized that there is a general obligation for states to cooperate in fisheries conservation on the high seas (ICJ, 1973). Again, however, the duty is vague. When it comes into force, UNCLOS will require that states cooperate to ensure the conservation of cetaceans and, in relation to the high seas, this obligation is compulsory.

Threats to the IWC
The IWC is at another crossroads: having achieved little in its attempts to conserve whale stocks in its first years, it has since imposed a full moratorium on commercial whaling. Now, as the pressure to resume commercial whaling continues and the RMP takes shape, the IWC must decide whether its obligations to the whaling industry require the resumption of commercial whaling. The risk of deciding not to permit active commercial whaling in the near future is that pro-whaling states, such as Norway, Russia and Japan, may withdraw from the IWC.

In 1988 Iceland held a meeting in Reykjavik attended by Canada, Japan, Norway, the former USSR, the Faroe Islands and Greenland, to "discuss their common situation in light of the development in the IWC" (Andersen, 1989). Canada is no longer a member of the IWC and Iceland withdrew in 1992. In its opening statement at the IWC's forty-fourth meeting, Norway delivered a threat that its continued participation in the IWC depended on a liberal interpretation of proposed RMP for minke whales (IWC, 1992). At the forty-fifth meeting in 1993, Japan expressed doubts about its future participation but has indicated that it will remain, for the present, in order to lobby against the Southern Ocean Sanctuary proposal.

On 9 April 1992, an agreement was signed by Greenland, the Faroe Islands, Iceland and Norway forming a new organization called the North Atlantic Marine Mammals Conservation Organization (NAMMCO). Its members can produce more whale products than they consume. The largest consumer market remains closed to them since IWC members have agreed by resolution not to import whale products from non-member countries. However, if Japan should leave the IWC and join NAMMCO, both producer and consumer markets would be brought together in an organization outside the auspices of the IWC.

One of the earliest international influences on the IWC was the establishment of the South Pacific Commission (SPC) by Chile, Peru and Ecuador (Birnie, 1989), which had as its objective the management of marine fauna of the waters in their recently declared 200-mile fisheries zones. This undermined the IWC, since the SPC announced it would follow IWC regulations except when they conflicted with "just needs for national consumption and industrial supplies". NAMMCO is likely to pose an even more seriously undermining threat, as its participants are likely to be the core of today's pro-whaling states supporting commercial trade in whale products.

Is it legal to form an organization in competition with, and that undermines, the IWC? As noted above, Article 65 of the 1982 UNCLOS mandates that states cooperate in the protection of cetaceans by working with "appropriate international organizations". The argument has been put forward by countries such as Iceland that UNCLOS allows states to decide independently whether an international organization is appropriate to the task of managing and conserving marine mammals. Yet this would also encourage states to operate without real coordination through their own puppet organizations. A much more sensible interpretation of the law is that there must be objective reasons for deciding that an organization is appropriate.

Clearly and objectively, the IWC qualifies as an "appropriate organization" for the conservation of cateceans. This fact was recognized by consensus of the international community in Chapter 17 and Agenda 21 of the 1992 UNCED (UNCED, 1992). It reiterates the language of Article 65 and goes further to emphasize that "states recognize the responsibility of the International Whaling Commission for the conservation and management of whale stocks and regulation of whaling pursuant to the 1946 Convention" (Para 17.66 (a)). It is unlikely that NAMMCO is an appropriate organization. It is a fledgling that lacks the resources and expertise of the IWC.

Conclusion

The role of international law in the conservation of whales has been fundamental. Remarkably, the rules set by IWC have usually been observed rather than breached. Many legal controversies and crises have arisen from the ambiguity of its 1946 convention and, consequently, the proper scope of the mandate of the IWC. Revision of the convention is required to deal effectively with these issues. Discussions concerning revision have taken place but amendments require adoption of protocols and, to be effective, unanimous agreement among the commission's member countries. Polarization between pro- and anti-whaling states has therefore prevented successful amendment so far. It seems that any substantial conservationist revision to the convention would result in the withdrawal of pro-whaling countries.

Consequently, we find that the central international legal document for the conservation of whales, the ICRW, has not really been greened in the almost 50 years of its existence. It remains a fishing, rather than a wildlife, conservation convention. However, many of the members of the IWC have succeeded in having it adopt more conservative regulations, resolutions and practices than the ICRW ever originally contemplated. Further, other international laws, such as wildlife treaties, are rapidly filling the legal lacunae and becoming more effective regional tools for conservation. This is especially true in the northern hemisphere where EC and North Sea regional achievements have been adopted concerning cetacean habitats, trade and protection.

A more politically practical approach to revision of the ICRW than wholesale reformulation is, in the short term, to tinker with it so that it continues to work more efficiently. For example, a protocol to the ICRW may allow the commission to deal with the management of small cetaceans in a more rational manner. Although the moratorium is conceived as a temporary measure, there are other options legally available to the IWC within the current convention to avoid reinstituting commercial whaling. These include the placement of species within the NMP protected stock classification (which prohibits hunting), or the adoption of a revised management scheme with very strict or negligible catch limits and strong monitoring and enforcement procedures. As long as the categorization of whale stocks has a scientific basis, the commission can maintain an "indefinite" ban on species exhibiting depleted levels. Sanctuaries may also become a primary mechanism for ensuring that sufficient time is given for the recovery of many populations. Yet, a disadvantage in each proposal for any measure other than a full ban on commercial whaling is that some trade in high value whale products would be legitimized and would give cover to increased smuggling by pirate operations.

In the longer term, therefore, states concerned about their image within the international community, may begin to perceive a pro-whaling stance as a political liability. With public support for commercial whaling diminishing while whale-watching in Japan gains popularity (Schoenberger, 1991), the Japanese government may soon find itself in the untenable position of supporting an industry unwanted by most of its citizens or the international community. Whaling still provides an economic return in the smaller coastal communities of the pro-whaling countries, but its national economic importance has been marginal.

In contrast, the global economic importance of whale-watching is growing. In 1991, the whale-watching industry worldwide had direct revenues of US$ 75 592 000 and total revenues of US$ 317 881 000. It may be that the convention can be interpreted or amended to include commercial whale-watching operations as a new branch of the whaling industry to be protected by the IWC. Moves in this direction were renewed in 1993 when a resolution proposed by Great Britain was passed (IWC, 1992). It requested member states to assess the scientific and economic value of whale-watching, the IWC secretariat to consolidate a report and a working group to be established on the subject to make recommendations to the next meeting of the IWC.

In its 47 years of existence, the IWC has evolved to embrace various cetacean species and management philosophies. As the scope of its work increases it must work in new ways with other regional organizations, particularly to protect incidental catches of small cetaceans. However, the commission still remains the most appropriate international organization to regulate whaling. To do its work better it needs more modern and efficient legal machinery than the 1946 convention. Eventually, it will get it, for one thing is becoming clear: the IWC is surviving its many trials but large-scale commercial whale catching is not.

References

Acheson, D (1946) Acting US Secretary of State, opening address, IWC/11, 1

Andersen, S (1989) "Science and Politics in the International Management of Whales", *Marine Policy*, vol 13, pp99–101

Birnie, P (1989) "International Legal Issues in the Management and Protection of Whales: A Review of Four Decades of Experience", *Natural Resources Journal*, vol 29, pp901–4

Convention for the Regulation of Whaling (1931), 24 September, 49 Stat 3079, TS No 880, 155 LNTS 349

D'Amato, A and S K Chopra (1991) "Whales: Their Emerging Right to Life", *American Journal of International Law*, vol 85, pp21–9

ICJ (1973) Fisheries Jurisdiction, Report 3

ICRW (1946) *International Convention for the Regulation of Whaling with Schedule Whaling Regulations*, 2 December, 161 UNTS 72

IWC (1992) IWC/44/OS Norway, 44th meeting

Schoenberger, K (1991) "Friends for Whales in Japan", *Los Angeles Times*, 4 January

Smith, G (1984) "The International Whaling commission: Analysis of the Past and Reflections on the Future", *Natural Resources Journal*, vol 16, pp901–4

UNCED (1992) Agenda 21, Chapter 17

■ Conservation of
Wild Genetic Resources
Robert Prescott-Allen

There are two ways of conserving wild genetic resources: *in situ* (in nature reserves) and *ex situ* (in zoos and gene banks). Both are needed. Neither is being done as effectively as it should.

In situ conservation is the maintenance of a wild gene pool in its native habitat, in a national park or nature reserve, for example. *Ex situ* conservation is the maintenance of the resource outside its native habitat: either the whole organism (plant or animal) in a botanical garden, plantation, zoo or breed farm; or just the germplasm (seed, pollen, sperm, ova, budwood or cells) in a seed bank, sperm bank, and so on.

The International Board for Plant Genetic Resources (IBPGR) distinguishes three types of *ex situ* crop germplasm collection, which can usefully be applied to all genetic resources and to *in situ* as well as *ex situ* systems:

* *Base collections* for long-term maintenance of genetic material;
* *Active collections* for medium-term maintenance of genetic material, multiplication and distribution, evaluation and documentation;
* *Working collections* serving the short term needs of individual breeders and breeding programmes.

The primary aim of a base collection (type 1) is the security of the germplasm it conserves. The primary aim of a working collection (type 3) is the convenience of the breeders and breeding programmes it serves. So as one moves from 1 to 3 convenience increases but security decreases.

By far the greatest amount of progress has been made in the *ex situ* conservation of crop genetic resources. Since the IBPGR was set up in 1974, it has promoted the development of an impressive network of national and international base collections covering more than 20 of the world's most important crops. These include wheat, rice, maize, barley, oats, sorghum, millet, potato, *Phaseolus* beans, pigeon pea, peanut, chickpea, peas, cowpea, winged bean, onion and garlic, bell and chili pepper, tomato, eggplant, cabbages, and sugar beet (IBPGR, 1982). The scale of this achievement can be realized by comparing the situation in 1975, when only eight institutions in the world had facilities for long-term seed storage, with the situation seven years later, when the number had quadrupled to 33 (Plunkett et al, 1983).

Although most of these collections include wild species, the bulk of the germplasm they maintain is of the crops themselves. There are two good reasons for this. First, the domesticated material is generally more useful than the wild material. Second, it has generally been more threatened. Much of the impetus to the collection and main-tenance of genetic resources during the last two decades has been due to the growing recognition that many valuable landraces of crops and livestock have been irretrievably lost and the remainder are rapidly disappearing.

Landraces (primitive or traditional cultivars and breeds) can be made extinct with a suddenness that befalls only a few of the most endangered species. With most wild species, extinction is a fairly gradual process; only species with an extremely small distribution can be eliminated completely in, say, one episode of habitat destruction. Landraces have been totally lost as a result of simple abandonment by the farmers who grew them. The landraces may be displaced in one or two seasons by more productive modern cultivars, including emergency seed sent in by famine-relief operations. Between 1930 and the mid-1960s the proportion of the Greek wheat crop grown to traditional landraces fell from 80 per cent to 10 per cent (Bennett, 1973a).

A 1973 report illustrates dramatically the problems of conserving landraces: "When this survey was made, Afghanistan's native wheats seemed safer from genetic erosion than almost any others. Since then, two years of drought, harvest failures and catas-trophic famine have drastically changed the picture. Thousands of tonnes of seeds have been imported. Introduced varieties now predominate in many parts of the country. In mountain areas where previously only indigenous varieties have ever grown, introduced varieties have now widely replaced them. Afghanistan is a warning that genetic erosion does not follow a predictable course, and that genetic conservation programmes must never be relaxed, even in regions considered safe from genetic erosion (Bennett, 1973b). This last statement applies equally forcibly to wild genetic resources. The threats to landraces have not and are unlikely to diminish. The need to collect and conserve them remains a priority. But the importance and vulnerability of the wild gene pools are growing rapidly. These now need to be given the level of attention first accorded to landraces a decade ago.

An IBPGR survey of the 20 major collections of wheat in the world (Australia, Canada (2), Czechoslovakia, France, Germany, Hungary, India, Israel, Italy, Japan (3), the Netherlands, Turkey, UK, USA (2) and the USSR) (Corbet and Hill, 1980) illus-trates the gap. Excluding duplicates, the 20 collections together hold some 4000 samples of *Aegilops* species and more than 40 000 samples of *Triticum* species. The two most commonly cultivated wheats naturally dominate the collections: there are 9000 samples of macaroni wheat (the *durum* form of *T. turgidum turgidum*), and 24 500 samples of bread wheat (*T. aestivum vulgare*). The survey classifies as underrepresented in the world collection any taxon (species, subspecies or variety) that is represented by fewer than 100 samples. Of the 17 taxa that are considered underrepresented, nine are domesticated (various primitive *Triticum taxa*), and eight are wild (species of *Aegilops*).

Superficially, therefore, it would appear that the wild genetic resources of wheat are no worse off than the primitive domesticated genetic resources. The wild taxa, however, are much more patchily represented and hence less of their genetic variation is likely to be protected than is that of the cultivated forms. Of the 17 domesticated taxa (one species + 11 subspecies + five varieties), 12 (or 7 per cent) are represented by samples from each country in which the taxa occur. But of the 24 wild taxa (20 *Aegilops* species + one species and three subspecies of *Triticum*), only five (or 21 per cent) are represented by samples from all the countries of their natural distribution. There is not necessarily any relationship between the number of countries in which a species occurs and its genetic variation. But the variability of a species cannot be known until it has been adequately sampled; and it is clear from the survey that most of the wild relatives of wheat have not been.

The situation for wheat is good compared with rice and maize. There are 38 active and base collections of rice listed in the *IBPGR director of germplasm collections* (Toll et al, 1980): six in developed countries, the rest in developing countries. Only 12 report holdings of wild species, and only five of these (in Japan, Nigeria, the Philippines, the USSR and the USA) have long-term storage facilities. Of 53 active and base collections of maize (22 in developed countries, 31 in developing countries) (7), only six include wild species and only one of these (in the USA) can maintain them long term.

Many more of the germplasm collections of food legumes include wild species: 29 out of 66 (31 in developed countries; 35 in developing countries). Ten of these are base collections: six among developed countries — Belgium, German Democratic Republic, Italy, Sweden, the USA and the USSR; and four among developing countries: Argentina, Colombia, Costa Rica and Nigeria (Hymowitz and Newell, 1977). However, these collections usually include a greater number of crops (*Phaseolus* beans, *Vigna* beans, soybeans, peanuts, chickpeas, lentils) than the cereal collections, and there are far fewer individual accessions (samples). For example, the US collection of soybean and its wild relatives, the most comprehensive in the world, contains some 7200 accessions. This is quite small compared with the collections of cereal crops (such as wheat, rice and sorghum) which are from two to five times larger (84). Even so, soybean cultivars make up 90 per cent of the collection; the wild GP1 species *Glycine Soja* accounts for only 7 per cent and samples of the six GP3 species for only 3 per cent, a mere 197 samples (Hymowitz and Newell, 1980).

Seed-propagated crops with seeds that can be dried and cold-stored for up to a century, like cereals and legumes, are relatively easy to maintain. Crops that are maintained vegetatively (like bananas), or crops like cacao whose seeds cannot be dried and then stored without killing them, are harder to keep safe. Many crops, including timber trees, fall into this category: mango, rubber, chestnuts, oaks, walnuts, cinnamon, avocado, majoganies, coffee, citrus and cacao are among them (King and Roberts, 1979). With such crops there are severe physical constraints on the amount, and therefore the diversity, of the germplasm that can be stored.

The *ex situ* collections of crop genetic resource centres and provenance collections of tree breeders are probably doing quite well compared to other *ex situ* systems such as zoos and botanical gardens. Within-species variation is after all the stock-in-trade of agricultural and silvicultural gene banks. Zoos and botanical gardens tend to operate at the species level, since their logistical problems are even greater than those of cacao or banana or sugarcane conservationists. William G Conway, director of the New York Zoological Society, has remarked that all the zoo animal enclosures in the world could comfortably fit within the borough of Brooklyn (Conway, nd). It is therefore sensible for them to concentrate their captive breeding efforts towards providing a safety net for species close to extinction, rather than attempting to maintain a wide range of the gene pools of less endangered species. This would include saving the wild relatives of live-stock species from extinction; captive breeding programmes have been successfully carried out in the case of the European bison (*Bison bonasus*) and Przewalski's horse (*Equus ferus*). The former became extinct in the wild, but was increased from surviving zoo animals and has been reintroduced in Poland. The latter is believed to be extinct in the wild and exists only as a zoo animal. The present population of about 265 horses is descended from nine animals obtained from Mongolia at the beginning of this century. According to Conway, the population today could have been as high as 1000 but for the application of arbitrary restrictions in the breeding programmes, limiting the male line to a few stallions. A substantial portion of the population, he writes, "is beginning to show the effects of inbreeding depression in lowered vitality and various anomalies" (Conway, 1980).

Botanical gardens face lesser but similar problems. Like zoos they can and do combine whole organism and germplasm maintenance. But since crop relatives are generally smaller than livestock relatives and many plants are inbreeders, whereas all the animals are outbreeders, botanical gardens are less limited than zoos in the role they can play. Similarly, the maintenance of plant germplasm (pollen, seeds), while not without its problems (some of which have yet to be overcome), is generally easier than the maintenance of animal germplasm (semen, ova). So one can envisage botanical gardens making a greater contribution to *ex situ* conservation of wild genetic resources. For example, they could maintain samples of a wide range of gene pools of locally occurring crop relatives; and could act as bridging institutions between agricultural and silvicultural *ex situ* gene banks on one side, and *in situ* gene banks on the other.

In Situ Gene Banks

At present *in situ* gene banks are more a hope than a reality. There are many national parks, nature reserves, biosphere reserves and countless other protected areas, but as far as we are aware the number of genuine *in situ* gene banks can be counted on the fingers of one hand. The USSR has apparently established a reserve in the Kopet-Dag moun-tains (Turkmen SSR) to protect wild forage grasses, wild apricot, pistachio and almond, and one in the Caucasus to protect wild wheat and wild fruit trees (Brezhnev, 1975). Sri Lanka has set up a reserve for wild medicinal plants, and India is planning sanctuaries to protect wild relatives of banana, citrus, rice, sugarcane and mango (IBPGR, 1978).

Otherwise, the world's protected areas continue to be designed and operated with little if any consideration for the maintenance of wild genetic resources. In 1980, on behalf of IBPGR and the IUCN, we surveyed the government agencies responsible for protected areas in a sample of 50 countries. The survey was concerned only with the wild relatives of crops and not with other wild genetic resources. Nevertheless, from the 30 per cent response it was clear that by and large protected areas are currently ill-equipped to service the potential users of the genetic resources they may maintain.

A minimum requirement is documentation. Yet fewer than half the countries that replied had compiled lists of the species occurring in their protected areas — and then only for a small minority of the reserves. For the time being, therefore, it is impossible to tell how many wild relatives of crops occur in protected areas, and thus impossible to decide whether new areas are needed and, if so, where. Lack of information also means that it is seldom possible to determine whether a particular wild gene pool requires special management. It may be that a reserve is ostensibly protecting populations of wild cereals or wild grapes, but that in practice those populations are being overgrazed by herbivores that the reserve is also attempting to maintain.

In addition, the absence of documentation reduces the value of nature reserves to the users of genetic resources; even if a reserve is protecting valuable gene pools, there is no way the users can know about it. Users are likely to face other obstacles as well. Fewer than 15 per cent of the countries surveyed permit the collection of germplasm (seeds, budwood), and almost 25 per cent do not allow collection for any purpose.

Another unmet need is adequate liaison between the agencies responsible for protected areas, and those responsible for research and the protection of crop genetic resources. Even if important wild genetic resources *are* being maintained in a protected area, the potential users may not know about it, may not be allowed access to the resources, or may be hampered by the lack of facilities for research or standby storage of any material collected.

In the late 1960s and early 1970s, before the establishment of IBPGR and the major international *ex situ* gene banks, and before the establishment of the first biosphere reserves, the scientific leaders of the genetic resources community were emphatic about the need for both *ex situ* and *in situ* conservation. Recommendation 39 of the United Nations Conference on the Human Environment (Stockholm, 1972) for example, recommended both static (*ex situ*) and dynamic (*in situ*) ways of preserving wild plant and animal gene pools.

Implicit (and sometimes explicit) in the concept of biosphere reserves, as it was developed in the early 1970s, was the idea of conserving genetic diversity at several levels: the ecosystem, the species and the gene pool. But in practice, biosphere reserves, like national parks and other protected areas, have been selected and managed with the first two levels of diversity in mind, not the third.

Why is it that the *in situ* conservation of wild genetic resources has made so little progress? In my analysis, the reason is a combination of sectoralism and prejudice. The various kinds of protected areas have been set up with numerous, sometimes conflicting, aims:

- to protect wildernesses and sacred groves and other areas symbolic of the relationship between a particular society and the natural world;
- to provide amenity and recreation;
- to serve as sites for eduction and scientific research;
- to safeguard ecosystems that play key positions in ecological processes, such as the role of watershed forests in regulating local and regional hydrology;
- to act as a reserve in the regeneration of a resource such as timber, game, or sport fish;
- to protect habitats critical for the survival of an endangered species;
- to conserve entire ecosystems that may be threatened, such as a coral reef.

Agencies administering protected areas have tended to emphasize some types of goal at the expense of others, depending on their mandates — water management, fisheries, forestry, national parks, wildlife, tourism and recreation, and science.

There have been only two overarching, integrating approaches to the jungle of conflicting mandates: the philosophy of national parks, promoting a combination of preservation of natural areas and biological diversity with facilities for public recreation; and the concept of a world network of areas conserving representative and unique examples of the biological diversity of the planet, of which *biosphere reserves* coordinated by UNESCO (United Nations Education, Scientific and Cultural Organization) are the most coherent expression.

There is a place for *in situ* gene banks in both schemes — which, of course, overlap. However, the criteria for selecting protected areas under these schemes have concentrated on features of outstanding beauty and interest, and examples of the diversity of ecosystems and of species rather than on variation *within* species. Thus Dr Michael Batisse (deputy assistant director-general for science at UNESCO) explains (Batisse, 1982) that "each biosphere reserve should include one or more of the following:

- representative examples of natural biomes;
- unique communities or areas with unusual features of exceptional interest;
- examples of harmonious landscape resulting from traditional patterns of land-use; and/or
- examples of modified or degraded ecosystems that are capable of being restored to more-or-less natural conditions."

There is nothing in this that would prevent a biosphere reserve being an *in situ* gene bank (or vice versa), and in fact the biosphere reserve system has great potential for the development of *in situ* gene banks. But nor is there anything that makes clear that within-species variation is one of the objects of conservation.

Indeed, Dr Batisse wrote earlier that one of the primary objectives of biosphere reserves is to safeguard "the genetic diversity on which their continuing evolution depends" (Batisse, 1982). The phrase "on which their continuing evolution depends" reveals an unconscious and traditional bias. There are two reasons for conserving within-species variation. First, because genetic variation is essential for species to adapt and survive. Second, because genetic variation is the raw material of domestication and of the continued survival and improvement of domesticates. Both reasons are equally valid, but each requires distinctly different approaches to conservation. Conservationists have generally thought only of the first rather than of the second.

The Difficulties
While wildlife conservationists and the protected areas community have been slow to put genetic resources on their agenda, the genetic resources community has been just as slow to turn its attention to *in situ* conservation. For reasons already given, *ex situ* conservation took priority, but in addition many people in the genetic resources community have been frankly sceptical that *in situ* conservation is either necessary or possible. They see three main obstacles that rule out protected areas as a means of conserving wild genetic resources: problems of use, problems of security, and problems of coverage.

First, there are problems of use. *Ex situ* gene banks can be sited wherever is most convenient to the users of the resources they house. *In situ* gene banks by definition have to be where the resources are. Wild species protected in nature reserves will often be far from the breeders that need them — in some cases continents apart. Examples are bananas (wild in Southeast Asia, cultivated in the Caribbean and Central America), rubber (wild in South America, cultivated in Southeast Asia), and eucalyptus (wild in Australia but grown all over the world). This is a valid objection only if *in situ* gene banks are intended as active or working collections, which clearly cannot be except in special circumstances. One such circumstance would be reserves protecting the genetic resources of a country's timber trees, which will often be close to (and may include) areas being logged and grown to plantations. Generally, however, the main contribution of *in situ* gene banks will be as base collections, safeguarding wild genetic resources over the long term. The location of a base collection does not matter as long as it is safe.

Second, there are problems of security. Genetic resource users fear that *in situ* gene banks would be vulnerable to periodic disturbance by poachers, firewood collectors and livestock, or to outright destruction by development, or by the pressures of population growth. They could be invaded by farmers, or be dismembered by the flick of a legislative pen or a bribe. *Ex situ* gene banks, it is argued, can keep everything safely under one roof and are much easier to protect. This is true. Protected areas are intrinsically more vulnerable than *ex situ* collections to changes in land use for whatever cause. However, it is easy to exaggerate both the insecurity of *in situ* gene banks and the security of *ex situ* gene banks. The greater the perceived value of a protected area the longer it is likely to last, and conserving wild genetic resources will increase a protected area's value to society.

For their part, *ex situ* collections are vulnerable to human error. Many have been lost in the past and it is unlikely that future losses, while they can be reduced, can be avoided altogether.

• From 1929 to 1931, two US Department of Agriculture seed explorers collected 4000 samples of soybean seed from China, Japan and Korea; today less than a third of their collection still survives, the rest having been thrown out or lost.
• Maintenance problems have led to considerable losses of sugarcane clones (IBPGR, 1982). Of some 1000 clones collected from Papua New Guinea from 1875 to 1955, only 281 were remaining in 1958, and 204 by 1975. A major sugarcane collection, which included important wild material, was reduced by half in the 18 years since the collection was made (Berding and Koike, 1980).
• Several valuable collections of wild grape species have been almost entirely lost due to lack of continuity in the breeding programmes that initiated the collections; remaining collections are experiencing problems of maintenance (Prescott-Allen and Prescott-Allen, 1986).
• More sensitive species like wild cocoa suffer maintenance problems from the point of collection, well before they even arrive at the *ex situ* gene bank: collections in Brazil have been lost due to airline delays (Prescott-Allen and Prescott-Allen, 1986).
• The difficulties of maintaining wild species *ex situ* arise either because they are poorly adapted to the location, such as the wild African rices *Oryza barthii* and *O. longistaminata* at the International Rice Research Institute in the Philippines

(Harlan, 1981); or because they are difficult to germinate and grow out, such as some of the wild sunflowers (Prescott-Allen and Prescott-Allen, 1981) and chickpeas (van der Maesen, 1979).

The third problem with *in situ* gene banks is that of coverage. Attempts to safeguard adequate samples of the genetic variation of wild species may, it is argued, take up so much land that they are quite impractical. This may or may not be so. In practice, the conservation of wild genetic resources has been so badly neglected that little is known of the distribution of potentially valuable wild gene pools. It is very doubtful that all the important wild germplasm can be protected in any way — either *ex situ* or *in situ*. It is already disappearing. But it seems highly likely that a worthwhile proportion of surviving genetic variation could be saved and that the establishment of effective *in situ* gene banks would increase that proportion.

One advantage of *in situ* gene banks is that they can serve several sectors at once. Gene pools of value to agriculture, forestry and aquaculture may very well overlap and hence be conserved in the same protected area. Another advantage is that evolution can continue within a protected area. This is especially important for pest and disease resistance. In the wild, resistant species can co-evolve with parasites and pathogens, providing the breeder with a dynamic reservoir of resistance that is lost when the material is transferred to the deep freeze of an *ex situ* gene bank. Areas that have a rich diversity of pest and disease races, and a corresponding richness in the diversity of resistant plants, would be excellent candidates as *in situ* gene banks: parasite and pathogen parks. Central Mexico (late blight and wild potatoes), central USA (*Phylloxera* and wild grapes), Israel (rusts and wild oats), southwestern USSR (rusts and wild wheats) might be good places to start.

Yet another advantage of *in situ* gene banks is that they can double as living laboratories. Maintenance of a species in its natural habitat allows the breeder to study its ecology and so obtain information that might otherwise be overlooked. Several valuable characteristics of wild tomatoes have been discovered in this way: high soluble solids, tolerance of intense tropical moisture and temperatures, tolerance of saline soils, insect resistance and drought resistance (Rick, 1974; Rick, 1981).

The problem with discussing the pros and cons of *ex situ* and *in situ* gene banks is that it appears that they are in competition. They are not. As we stated at the beginning of this chapter, both are needed. They complement each other, the strengths of one compensating for the other's weaknesses. Fortunately, a convergence of opinion appears to be emerging among genetic resource users and the wildlife conservationists and protected areas community. IBPGR took the initiative in commissioning a position report on the *in situ* conservation of the wild relatives of crops. And the United Nations Environment Programme (UNEP) and FAO have been active in getting experts together to decide on the best ways of getting *in situ* conservation off the ground. These meetings have included one on the *in situ* conservation of forest genetic resources (FAO and UNEP, 1981) and one conserving the genetic resources of fish (FAO, 1981).

IUCN, the leading scientific non-governmental conservation body, is actively pursuing ways of integrating the new concept of *in situ* gene banks into the well-established procedures of conserving threatened species and managing national parks and nature reserves. UNESCO, too, has recognized that biosphere reserves and *in situ* gene banks are perfect partners. Some wild gene pools can be maintained passively: leave them along, protect them from harm, and they will persist. Other wild gene pools will have to be maintained actively: many wild species in primary gene pools flourish only in fairly disturbed environments, and the *in situ* gene banker will need to maintain that level of disturbance to maintain the populations concerned. The concept of core and buffer zones in the biosphere reserves provides very well for the combination of preservation and active management that much *in situ* gene banking is likely to call for. New ways of maintaining, and new ways of using the newest resource are being developed, as they must be, side by side.

References

Batisse, M (1982) "The Biosphere Reserve: A Tool for Environmental Conservation and Management", *Environment Conservation*, pp101–12

Bennett, E (1973a) "Mediterranean: Wheats of the Mediterranean Basin", in O H Frankel (ed) *Survey of Crop Genetic Resources in their Centres of Diversity: First Report*, pp1–8

—— (1973b) "Near East: Cereals: Afghanistan", in O H Frankel (ed) *Survey of Crop Genetic Resources in their Centres of Diversity: First Report*, pp22–4

Berding, N and N and H Koike (1980) "Germplasm Conservation of the *Saccharum* Complex: A Collection from the Indonesian Archipelago", *Hawaiian Planters' Record*, vol 59, pp87–176

Brezhnev, D D (1975) "Plant Exploration in the USSR", in O H Frankel. and J G Hawkes (eds) *Crop Genetic Resources for Today and Tomorrow*, pp147–150

Conway, W G (nd) *Gene Banks for Higher Animal*

—— (1980) "An Overview of Captive Propagation", in M E Soule and B A Wilcox (eds) *Conservation Biology: An Evolutionary — Ecological Perspective*, pp199–208

Corbett, G B and J E Hill (1980) *A World List of Mammalian Species*, British Museum, London

FAO (1981) *Conservation of the Genetic Resource of fish?: Problems and Recommendations*, FAO, Rome

FAO and UNEP (1981) *Report on the FAO/UNEP Expert Consultation on situ Conservation of Forest Genetic Resources*, FAO, Rome

Harlan, J R (1973) "Genetic Resources of some Major Field Crops in Africa", in O H Frankel (ed) *Survey of Crop Genetic Resources in their Centres of Diversity: First Report*, pp45–64

Hymowitz, T and C A Newell (1977) "Current Thoughts in Origins, Present Status and Future Soyabeans", in D S Seigler (ed) *Crop Resources*, pp197–209

—— (1980) "Taxonomy, Speciation, Domestication, Dissemination, Germplasm Resources and Variation in the Genus *Glycine*", in R J Summerfield and A H Bunting (eds) *Advances in Legume Science*, pp251–264

IBPGR (1978) *Report of IBPGR Working Group on the Genetic Resources of Bananas and Plantains*, IBPGR, Rome

—— (1982) *Consultative Group on International Agricultural Research: Annual Report*, IBPGR, Rome

King, M W and E H Roberts (1979) *The Storage of Recalcitrant Seeds — Achievements and Possible Approaches*, IBPGR, Rome

Maesen, L van der (1979) "Genetic Resource of Grain Legume in the Middle East", in G C Hawtin and G J Chancellor (eds) *Food Legumes Improvement and Development*, pp140–6

Plunkett, D L, N J L Smith, J T Williams and N M Anishetty (1983) "Crop Germplasm Conservation and Developing Countries, *Science*, vol 220

Prescott-Allen, R and C (1982) *What's Wildlife Worth? Economic Contributions of Wild Plants and Animals to Developing Countries*, Earthscan, London

—— (1986) *The First Resource: Wild Species in the North America Economy*, Yale University Press, New Haven, CT

Rick, C M (1974) "High Soluble-Solids Content in Large Fruited Tomato Lines Derived from a Wild Green Fruited Species", *Hilgardia*, vol 42, pp493–510

—— (1981) "The Potential of Exotic Germplasm for Tomato Improvement", unpublished ms

Toll, J, N M Anishetty and G Ayad (1980) *Directory of Germplasm Collection, 3, Cereals, III, Rice*, IBPGR, Rome

■ Costa Rica
Peter Utting

Since the creation of the country's first reserve in 1963 and the enactment of the 1969 Forest Law, more has been done in Costa Rica to protect forest resources than in any other Central American country. By 1990, 80 national parks and reserves of different categories, covering 1.5 million hectares, or 29.3 per cent of the national territory, had been legally constituted as protected areas (MIRENEM, 1990, pp19–20). Some 65 per cent of these protected areas are covered with forest.

In addition to protecting forest resources, these areas have been created with the objective of preserving biodiversity and natural habitats (national parks, biological reserves and wildlife refuges); protecting the environment through the sustainable use of natural resources (forest reserves and protectorate zones); and protecting cultural forms, life systems and methods of resource use in areas where Indian populations are concentrated (indigenous reserves).

NGOs have played a major role in the establishment and administration of protected areas and in supporting numerous projects in these areas. The role of foreign NGOs has been reinforced by the fact that several international agencies have their Central American headquarters in Costa Rica. Political stability and democracy have given Costa Rica a comparative advantage in obtaining external aid and support from many international agencies. The country's forest protection programmes also enjoy considerable public support, due partly to a relatively effective programme of environmental education over the past two decades.

An important development that has strengthened the capacity of the state to undertake forest protection and environmental protection initiatives during the 1980s has been the process of institutional consolidation. It was noted earlier that the existence of weak institutions has been a major constraint, which has undermined the conservation approach in the different Central American countries. The situation in Costa Rica is somewhat different. The main agencies with responsibility for protected areas (other than the indigenous reserves) — namely the National Parks Service (SPN), the General Forestry Directorate (DGF), and the Wildlife Division — moved from the Ministry of Agriculture and Livestock (MAG) to strengthen the Ministry of Natural Resources, Energy and Mines (MIRENEM), which was set up in 1988.

During the late 1980s, the existence of the SPN facilitated the reception of funds via the debt-for-nature swap mechanism. The latter involves the conversion of foreign debt titles, available at a discount on the secondary market, into local currency for investment in conservation programmes (Bruggemann, 1990, personal communication).

This mechanism was instituted in 1987 with the purpose of reducing the national debt, generating funds for environmental protection, and, through ecotourism, involving the business sector in conservation. The debt-for-nature swap mechanism enables conservation (for example WWF, Nature Conservancy) or bilateral (for example Sweden, the Netherlands) agencies to purchase foreign loans at a discount on the understanding that the national government will provide funds in local currency at a dollar equivalent that exceeds considerably the cost to the purchaser. Such funds are used to purchase national park and reserve land, provide financial incentives for reforestation schemes, as well as institutional support for environmental organizations. By mid-1991, Costa Rica accounted for 44 per cent of the total value of the world's debt-for-nature swaps. Between 1987 and mid-1991, some $80 million of national debt was purchased for $12.5 million and converted into $42 million of local currency commitments (see Table 1.2).

Table 1.2 Costa Rica Debt-For-Nature Swaps, 1988 to Mid-1991

Date	Purchaser	Cost to purchaser	Face value of debt ($)	Funds generated $ equivalent[*]
1988	Netherlands	5 000 000	33 000 000	9 000 000
1988	FPN/WWF	918 000	5 400 000	4 050 000
1989	Sweden	3 500 000	24 500 000	17 100 000
1989	NC	784 000	5 600 000	1 680 000
1990	Sweden/WWF/NC	1 953 473	10 753 631	9 602 904
1991	RA/MCL/NC[**]	360 000	600 000	540 000
Sub-total		12 515 473	79,853,631	41 972 904
World total		16 705 000	98 445 000	61 064 000

*   Dollar equivalent of local currency. Conservation funds generated do not include interest on bonds when government pays in bonds rather than cash.
** Debt donated by Bank of America.

Source: Based on Mahony (1992, Table 1, p98).

By the early 1990s, the initial enthusiasm for debt-for-nature swaps had waned to some extent. What, in World Bank parlance, had seemed like a definite "win-win" situation — in which all those involved (international banks, the national government, NGOs, environmentalists, local landowners) stood to benefit — turned out, in practice, to involve a number of trade-offs, unexpected costs and a somewhat skewed distribution of benefits.

Clear winners in this exercise have been the northern financial institutions. As Mahony points out, not only have they been able to recover some of the debt, but they have done so by employing mechanisms (including not only debt swaps but also debt restructuring) which ensure that the discount rate on outstanding debt rises as the debt is paid off. As the price of the debt on the resale market increases the government is likely to find itself in a situation of having to repay the same amount as before the debt-for-nature swap took place (Mahony, 1992 p99). Hence the benefits to the Costa Rican government are not as straightforward as one might assume.

In the case of Costa Rica, the value at which one dollar's-worth of debt was purchased on the secondary market increased sharply from 13 cents in January 1989 to 51 cents in November 1991 (CEPAL, 1991, Table 20). Under such conditions it is to be expected that the debt-for-nature swap phenomenon will be relatively short-lived. This is because the increase in the discount rate will scare off potential purchasers, and the government will be reluctant to comply with the so-called multiplier effect whereby it commits considerably more than the sum paid by the purchaser.

In actual fact, the amount of debt which has been cancelled through the debt-for-nature swap mechanism is only a tiny fraction of the country's total debt. In 1990, Costa Rica's total external debt amounted to $3772 million (World Bank, 1992). As indicated in Table 1.2, debt-for-nature swaps accounted for just $79 million or 2 per cent of the total debt. By making available large amounts of local currency, debt-for-nature swaps also run the risk of fuelling inflationary pressures. Clear tensions have arisen in the context of economic stabilization programmes which attempt to control the money supply and reduce government deficits. In 1990, a debt-for-nature swap programme was approved which would have converted 100 million dollars of debt over a five-year period. Later that year, however, the programme was temporarily suspended and scaled down by the Central Bank given the fear that large-scale purchases of land would have inflationary effects (Bradley et al, 1990a, vol 2, p102).

Doubts have also arisen concerning the ability of the government to honour its commitments and the implications of debt swaps for other forms of government spending on environment. Donations are often in the form of bonds which are redeemable in several years' time. As Mahony (1992, pp100) points out: "There is no guarantee that Costa Rica will honour these bonds ... any more than it will pay back the rest of its debt.... But even if the government did honour this new debt, it could cut its other environmental spending to make up the cost."

Perhaps the major question mark surrounding the debt-for-nature swap mechanism concerns the capacity of government agencies and NGOs effectively to implement protected area status and to do so in a way that benefits local populations.

While Costa Rica is often held up as a sort of model for other countries in the region, forest protection initiatives have experienced serious limitations. While the conservation drive began in earnest during the late 1960s it proved extremely difficult to contain deforestation over the following two decades. Most of Costa Rica's forests are now located in protected areas, but the expropriation of private holdings in such areas still has a long way to go. According to the Costa Rican Tropical Forestry Action Plan, "real protection in many of these areas is relatively weak" since current regulations still permit landowners to exploit forest resources (MIRENEM, 1990, p5).

Since the 1960s, numerous laws have been introduced in Costa Rica to protect forests. A study conducted by the Costa Rican environmental group CEDARENA has shown, however, the limited effectiveness of much of this legislation. While legislation passed in 1961 (ley de Tierras y Colonización), for example, attempted to bring a halt to spontaneous settlement of public lands, "this provision in the law has been largely ignored by settlers and weakly enforced by the government. . . . The history of toleration of mass invasions of public lands in the three decades since the public domain was placed legally off limits to settlers . . . suggests that the state is not serious about excluding settlers from state land" (CEDARENA, 1990).

The legislation and procedures governing the establishment and administration of protected areas is flawed in numerous respects. While the process of creating such areas requires a preliminary study of the demographic and land tenure situation in the area, it does not automatically involve a socio-economic study of the affected population. Once a protected area is established, private land within the boundary of the area must be purchased. This procedure demands enormous resources. The state must compensate not only those with legal title to the land, but also those with possession rights or who have made improvements on the land (such as fences, or the planting of perennial crops). About 10 per cent of the area administered by the SPN is still privately owned (DEA, 1990) while the percentage is even higher in most other categories of protected areas.

The legislation ignores the fate of those who must leave the protected areas. Once paid, residents must fend for themselves elsewhere. Only in a few instances has the state facilitated access to land elsewhere or alternative employment.

The enforcement of regulations governing land use in protected areas has been generally weak. Penalties for infringing the laws vary from fines to prison sentences, which in the case of forest fires range from six months to three years. However, both the lack of control and the nature of the legal system often mean that penalties do not act as a deterrent. The legal system is both extremely slow and, at the local level, culprits are often treated lightly. The lack of control is a function not only of limited human and material resources such as vehicles, but also the policy of forest protection authorities to deflate social tensions. Controlling deforestation in the indigenous reserves has proved difficult. The forestry department has no inspectors in these areas. According to the Indigenous Law, land in the reserves is common property, to be administered by local community organizations known as integral development associations (ADIs). The ADIs must authorize the felling of trees. In practice, however, many people fail to obtain the required authorization.

Not only have state institutions and NGOs been severely stretched in their efforts to enforce protected area status but, for many years, their activities remained uncoordinated. It was not until the late 1980s that the state attempted to devise a more coordinated and systematic approach by creating regional conservation units. These are bodies which oversee the work of the different institutions and agencies working in a group of protected areas in close proximity to one another. By 1991, 11 such units were in existence.

The Carara Biological Reserve

To examine in more detail the nature of social conflicts which arise when conservation areas are created or expanded, a case study was undertaken of the Carara Biological Reserve in the central-Pacific region of Costa Rica.

The Carara Reserve

While the Carara Reserve cannot be considered one of the hot spots of social conflict in

Costa Rica, several problems have arisen that reflect some of the fundamental weaknesses in the conservationist approach that has characterized Costa Rica's environmental protection policy over the past two decades.

The reserve was created in 1978 in an area of 7700 hectares. Its aim was to protect the last remnants of forest and the considerable biodiversity which exists in what constitutes a transition zone between the drier northern region of the country and the more humid region to the south.

Local residents had always used the area for hunting and, to a lesser degree, for forest products. Tensions soon arose when the authorities attempted to enforce regulations. During the early years forest guards adopted an aggressive attitude, which aggravated frictions between the communities and the reserve administration. Local residents recalled how hunting dogs were occasionally shot by guards and how the refrigerators of local restaurants or *cantinas* were searched for illicit supplies of meat.

There was no attempt to encourage the participation of the community in conservation activities. It was not until the mid-1980s, when a Peace Corps volunteer began an environmental education campaign, that someone thought to explain the *raison d'être* of the reserve to the local population.

Enforcing regulations, however, proved difficult. Whereas the reserve management plan estimated that approximately 30 guards would be required, only seven existed. While the hunting activities of local residents declined over time, professional poachers from the Central Valley increased their activities as demand for live exotic animals grew.

The reserve contained both dense forest and two degraded areas in the mountainous southern and eastern areas of the reserve. Peasant farmers produced basic grains in the southern part while land-seeking peasants subsequently invaded the eastern part. When the reserve was created, little account was taken of the situation of those who used the land. Peasants in the southern area struggled for six years to force the Institute for Agrarian Development (IDA) and the SPN to establish settlements. Peasants in the eastern zone were able to enlist the support of a politician to back their cause. In 1983, nearly 3000 hectares of the reserve were handed over to the IDA for settlements.

The creation of these settlements clearly reduced pressure on the forest area but did little to improve the living conditions of the peasants involved. The settlements received some technical, material and financial support from government agencies such as the IDA and Ministry of Agriculture (MAG) as well as the EEC which implemented a rural development project. Much of this support, however, was highly inappropriate for the types of producers and biophysical conditions of the area. Subsistence peasant producers with poor education and using rudimentary technology were suddenly expected to engage in efficient cash-crop production of fruit and vegetables, employing sophisticated modern inputs. Goats and bees were introduced: the goats ate the crops and, according to some accounts, the bees left the area in search of better conditions. Moreover, no account was taken of the buffer zone character of the area; the need, for example, to grow crops that would not be eaten by natural predators from the forest was overlooked, as was the appropriateness of reforestation and agroforestry schemes.

Conflicts of interest also developed between the SPN, which administers the reserve, and the EEC project supporting a cooperative settlement located to the north of the reserve. To improve access to the settlement, the agencies supporting the settlement pushed for a road to be built through part of the reserve to avoid the more costly alternative of constructing a bridge over a nearby river. While an environmental impact study was conducted to determine what impact the road might have, no one foresaw the growth in the number of tourists visiting the area. Visits to the reserve rose from 5000 in 1987 to 15 000 in 1990, creating a situation the reserve authorities could not control. Not only has wildlife in the area been affected by the influx of tourists, but local communities have not benefited from the tourist boom. There has been no attempt to involve local residents in tourist projects. By law, it is illegal for local residents to engage in commercial activities in national parks or reserves.

References
Bradley, T et al (1990a) *Costa Rica Natural Resource Policy Inventory*, USAID/ROCAP, vol 11, San José
Bruggemann, (1990) Personal communication
CEDARENA (1990) *Tortuguero Region Case Studies*, CEDARENA, San José
CEPAL (1991) *Balance Preliminar de la Economía de America Latina y el Caribe 1991*, United Nations, Santiago
DEA (1990) *Parques Nacionales y Areas Afines de Costa Rica 1990*, DEA/SPN/MIRENEM, San José
Mohony, R (1992) "Debt for Nature Swaps: Who Really Benefits?", *The Ecologist*, vol 22, no 3, pp97–103
MIRENEM (1990) *Plan de Acción Forestal para Costa Rica: Documentos Base*, Ministerio de Recursos Naturales, Energia y Minas de Costa Rica, San José
World Bank (1992) *World Development Report 1992: Development and the Environment*, Oxford University Press, New York

■ The United Nations Convention on Biological Diversity
Abby Munson

Historical Beginnings

Biodiversity is the global composite of genes, species and ecosystems. The rapid acceleration of loss of species and ecosystem degradation has caused rising concern among scientists, policymakers, and the public. UNEP estimates there are about 30 million species on Earth, of which only about one and a half million have ever been described, and that about one-quarter of the Earth's species risk extinction within the next 30 years.

In 1987, amid overwhelming scientific evidence of growing biological erosion, UNEP called on governments to examine the possibility of establishing an international legal instrument on the conservation and sustainable use of biodiversity. The USA was the first to call for the creation of a comprehensive convention. A year later an ad hoc working group of experts on biological diversity was initiated by UNEP to discuss the matter. It met three times between November 1988 and July 1990. As a result of the report by the group, UNEP set up a working group of legal and technical experts.

Two meetings later this group was transformed into the Intergovernmental Negotiating Committee for a Convention on Biological Diversity. This body met five times between June 1991 and May 1992. Negotiations soon focused on an argument between countries over exchange of biological resources in return for access to technologies, particularly biotechnology. Countries with the greatest diversity of species — primarily the developing countries — insisted on sovereign rights over genetic resources within their territories, as well as access to benefits resulting from the use of such resources in the shape of biotechnology. These demands were unacceptable to certain countries, who viewed biodiversity as a common heritage of humankind, and biotechnology as the concern of industry and best advanced with minimal or no government interference.

The final draft of the Biodiversity Convention was completed on 22 May 1992 in Nairobi, under the auspices of UNEP. The final product reflects compromise by both sides (UNEP, 1992).

The Convention

The preamble sets the tone for the whole convention, recognizing the wide ranging implications of biodiversity conservation and use, its "ecological, genetic, social, economic, scientific, educational, cultural, recreational and aesthetic" values. It introduces principles and criteria that underpin the understanding and implementation of the convention, affirming that "states have sovereign rights over their own biological resources" while also being responsible for "conserving their biological diversity and for using their biological resources in a sustainable manner"; including a precautionary note by declaring that a "lack of full scientific certainty should not be a reason for postponing measures to avoid or minimize such a threat" of significant reduction or loss of biological diversity; and acknowledging the need for "new and additional financial resources" and "appropriate access to relevant technologies" for developing countries.

Unlike other conventions, such as the Convention on International Trade in Endangered Species (CITES), this convention establishes a wider context for all biological diversity protection, as well as sustainable use of the components of biodiversity. The interdependence of developed and developing nations in maintaining biological diversity is recognized, as is the need for new and additional financial contributions from the developed world. Acknowledging these things makes this convention an important and successful start towards maintaining and sustainably using biological diversity.

The objectives of the convention, set out in Article 1, are the "conservation of biological diversity, the sustainable use of its components and the fair and equitable sharing of the benefits arising out of the utilization of genetic resources, including by appropriate access to genetic resources and by appropriate transfer of relevant technologies".

Throughout the negotiations, certain governments stressed that the convention primarily needed to tackle biological erosion on a global scale and that to include matters of technology transfer and finance among its objectives would inevitably lead to the neglect of more detailed action on methods for conservation and sustainable use of biodiversity itself.

Article 2, on the use of terms, lists definitions of terms used in the convention such as biological diversity and biological resources. Articles 3, 4 and 5, on principle, jurisdictional scope and cooperation respectively, establish parameters of the legal scope of the biodiversity convention. They remind contracting parties that the convention relies very much on the voluntary compliance of national states. Article 3, the convention's only guiding principle, is a direct transposition of the 1972 Stockholm principle, which acknowledges contracting parties' "sovereign right to exploit their own resources", while ensuring such activities "do not cause damage to the environment of other states or areas beyond the limits of national jurisdiction".[*]

Article 4 limits each party's obligations under the convention to "areas within the limits of its national jurisdiction" and activities "carried out under its jurisdiction or control, within the area of its national jurisdiction or beyond the limits or its jurisdiction". Article 5 reaffirms the importance of contracting parties to cooperate

---

[*] This principle formed Principle 21 of the Stockholm Declaration some 20 years ago, and has surfaced on a number of occasions in conventions and declarations since, without appearing to have achieved much impact on national policy making.

through "competent international organizations, in respect of areas beyond national jurisdiction".

Article 6, on general measures for conservation and sustainable use, states that each contracting party; "shall, in accordance with its particular conditions and capabilities, develop national strategies, plans or programmes of the conservation and sustainable use of biological diversity or adapt for this purpose existing strategies, plans or programmes which shall reflect, *inter alia*, the measures set out in this convention relevant to the contracting party concerned". Such national plans will be crucial in the process of building up an accurate picture of existing biodiversity, conservation requirements, future sustainable uses, as well as effective coordination between nations. However, there is no requirement for governments to establish "new" plans, and the scope and detail of national strategies, plans or programmes receives no comment. These limitations led to strong criticism from conservationists.

Article 7, on the identification and monitoring of biological diversity and its components, requires each contracting party "as far as possible and as appropriate" to "identify components of biological diversity important for its conservation and sustainable use", and to monitor the identified components of biological diversity, "paying particular attention to those requiring urgent conservation measures and those which offer the greatest potential for sustainable use". This may encourage governments to neglect the conservation of those species with aesthetic or cultural value only. Also, contracting parties are only required to "monitor" activities "which have or are likely to have significant adverse impacts on the conservation and sustainable use of biological diversity".

Article 8 is devoted to *in situ* conservation, meaning conservation where genetic resources exist within ecosystems and natural habitats (or, in the case of cultivated species, in the surroundings in which they have developed their "distinctive properties"). The article consists of a list of initiatives, which can be split into three main tasks.

- straightforward conservation: establish "protected areas" or "areas where special measures need to be taken to conserve biological diversity"; "regulate or manage biological resources important for the conservation of biodiversity" and "rehabilitate and restore" degraded ecosystems;
- protection of indigenous people and their knowledge: "subject to its national legislation, respect, preserve and maintain knowledge, innovations and practices of indigenous and local communities embodying traditional lifestyles relevant for the conservation and sustainable use of biological diversity and promote their wider application" and "encourage the equitable sharing of the benefits"; and
- protection against potentially hazardous biotechnology products and exotic species: develop legislation and/or regulatory provisions to protect "threatened species", and "establish or maintain means to regulate, manage or control the risks associated with the use and release of living modified organisms resulting from biotechnology".

Article 9 is devoted to *ex situ* conservation, which is the conservation of components of biological diversity "outside their natural habitats". It stresses the need to carry out conservation in the "country of origin", and the need for contracting parties to rehabilitate "threatened species".

Article 10, on the sustainable use of components of biological diversity, was the subject of much heated debate between countries with a direct interest in the use of biological resources and those more interested in conservation. As a compromise, the article calls for the adoption of measures to "avoid or minimize adverse impacts on biological diversity", to protect "traditional cultural practices" — but only if "compatible with conservation or sustainable use requirements".

Article 11, on incentive measures, obliges each contracting party to establish policies that act as "incentives for conservation and sustainable use of components of biological diversity". This is important as it contrasts with economic incentives that have historically ignored sustainable use and conservation — such as agricultural subsidies.

Articles 12 and 13, on research and training, and on public education and awareness, are general and will almost certainly receive more detailed attention at a later date, after the convention has been ratified.

Article 14, on impact assessment and minimizing adverse impacts, establishes that each contracting party "as far as possible and as appropriate shall introduce appropriate procedures requiring environmental impact assessment of its proposed projects" that are "likely to have significant adverse effects" on biodiversity, with the motive of reducing such effect. The article defers the subject of liability for damage to biological diversity for elaboration in a protocol.

Article 15, on access to genetic resources, is very important. It acknowledges the "sovereign rights" of states over their natural resource and the authority of states to determine access to their own genetic resources. The negotiations therefore established that genetic resources can no longer be viewed as a common resource. But the article also established a *quid pro quo* obligation to protect domestic genetic resources, to use them sustainably, to facilitate their use by others, "and not to impose restrictions that run counter to the objectives of this convention".

Article 15 adds that contracting parties "as appropriate shall take legislative, administrative or policy measures . . . with the aim of sharing in a fair and equitable way the results of research and development and the benefits arising from commercial and other utilization of genetic resources with the contracting party providing such resources". Acknowledging that contracting parties must share the benefits of any profits arising from work on genetic resources is commendable, especially in the light of disagreement on this issue. However, the article is still vague as to what "fair and equitable" means, due to the qualification added to the text that such policies should be agreed "as appropriate", and that any sharing shall be on "mutually agreed terms". Also the obligations do not apply to parties with *ex situ* genetic material in their possession collected before the convention enters into force.

Article 16, on access to and the transfer of technology, recognizes "that technology includes biotechnology, and that both access to and transfer of technology among contracting parties are essential elements of the attainment of the objectives of this convention". Article 16 elaborates that access to and transfer of technology "shall be provided and/or facilitated under fair and most favourable terms, including on concessional and preferential terms". Some business interests fear that this will be used by some countries to justify compulsory licensing of patents. However, none of the above terms such as "fair and most favourable" have been defined, so the meaning is somewhat vague and, furthermore, any technology transfer agreement between contracting paries must "recognize" and be "consistent with the adequate and effective protection of intellectual property rights". Consequently, most governments and observers judge that the convention does not in fact pose a significant "threat to business interest", a concern expressed primarily by the USA.

Article 17, on the exchange of information states that contracting parties shall facilitate exchange of information "from all public available sources". Article 18, on technical and scientific cooperation, stresses the importance of promoting joint research programmes and joint ventures for relevant technologies.

Article 19, on handling biotechnology and distributing its benefits, requires each contracting party to provide participation in biotechnological research activities and, especially developing countries, to promote "priority access on a fair and equitable basis . . . to the results and benefits arising from biotechnologies based upon genetic resources provided by those contracting parties". Such access is qualified by being "on mutually agreed terms".

Article 19 adds that contracting parties shall "consider the need for and modalities of a protocol setting out appropriate procedures, including, in particular, advanced informed agreement, in the field of the safe transfer, handling and use of any living modified organism resulting from biotechnology that may have adverse effect on the conservation and sustainable use of biological diversity". The biodiversity convention goes further than Agenda 21 (Chapter 16) on biosafety. It obliges contracting parties to consider the need for a protocol on biosafety, whereas Agenda 21 merely requires governments to consider the need for guidelines.

Article 20 on financial resources declares that it is every contracting party's duty to provide "in accordance with its capabilities" financial support for national activities laid out in the convention. It goes on to say that the "developed country parties shall provide new and additional financial resources to enable developing country parties to meet the agreed full incremental costs to them of implementing measures which fulfil the obligations of this convention and to benefit from its provisions".

Article 21, on financial mechanisms, caused controversy over the working of paragraph 1, which states that:

> There shall be a mechanism for the provision of financial resources to developing country parties for the purposes of this convention on a grant or concessional basis. . . . The mechanism shall function under the authority and guidance of, and be accountable to, the conference of the parties. . . . The conference of the parties shall determine the policy, strategy, programme priorities and eligibility criteria relating to the access to and utilization of such resource. The contribution shall be such as to take into account the need for predictability, adequacy and timely flow of funds . . . in accordance with the amount of resources needed to be decided periodically by the conference of the parties and the importance of burden-sharing among the contributing parties.

Placing the funding mechanism under the "authority and guidance of" the conference of parties differs from the wording in the Climate Convention, which refers just to "guidance". The governments of 19 developed countries signed a declaration after the final negotiation in Nairobi stating that Article 21 should not be construed in such a way as to make the poor decide the amount of individual contributions to be provided by donor countries. Some governments repeated this reservation when signing the Biodiversity Convention in Rio, with additional statements to that effect. Donors are further protected from being forced into contributions they do not want to make by Article 23, which ensures that the rules of procedure for the conference of the parties are decided by consensus. Article 39 makes the GEF the interim financial mechanism, and the GEF is likely to remain in this role given the donor countries' firm support for it.

Article 22, on relationships with other international conventions, affirms that the convention will not interfere with any contracting party's commitment to other international laws "except where the exercise of these rights and obligations would cause a serious damage or threat to biological diversity".

The conference of the parties will transmit information such as national reports, carry out scientific reviews, and have the mandate "to set up protocols" and make "amendments to the convention" itself, as well as to protocols.

A secretariat is established by the convention to perform administrative tasks for the conference of the parties as well as to "coordinate with other relevant international bodies". A subsidiary body on scientific, technical and technological advice is also set up to provide the conference of the parties with such advice as required.

The last ten or more articles deal primarily with institutional arrangements. These include most importantly the following: each contracting party must report to the conference of the parties on the action it has taken related to the convention; the settlement of disputes should be by negotiation if possible and, if not, Annex II sets out a procedure for compulsory arbitration; no reservations are permitted; and states should cooperate in the formulation and adoption of protocols. In Annex I provision is made for listing important ecosystems, habitats, species, communities, genomes and genes. This is important in the absence of a separate article on global lists.

By the close of the Rio conference, 155 governments had signed on to this convention, which will enter into force 90 days after 30 signatories have ratified it. The convention requires ratifying nations to meet within one year of its entry into force to establish a permanent funding mechanism. Realistically this means the conference of the parties is not expected to meet for a few years, given the time constraint governments face in putting the convention before their own national legislatures.

Limitations, Controversies and Prospects

Many of those involved were cautious about the prospects for successful negotiation of a biodiversity convention given the limited time frame, and the size and complexity of the task. Given that, it was a remarkable achievement for governments to arrive at a consensus on the need for a more global and comprehensive approach to conserving and using biological resources; on the need for new and additional finances, with developed countries making the predominant contribution; and on an agreement in principle to exchange fairly genetic resources for access to and transfer of technology.

However, the convention is not free from criticism. Jacques Delors declared that the European Commission "regards the convention on biodiversity as being too timid"

(Delors, 1992). UNEPs executive director, Mostafa Tolba (1992), stated that the negotiations had resulted in "the minimum on which the international community can agree". The convention clearly has not achieved the paradigm shift in government policy needed to ensure immediate biological conservation and sustainable use. The convention generalizes the activities each national government should undertake but fails to set out a framework for truly international action for the conservation of species. Added to this, the language in the convention is weak, with obligations commonly being qualified by "as appropriate" or "as far as possible".

In the end game, however, the USA was the only government not prepared to commit itself to signing the convention. President Bush protested that it posed a threat to the US biotechnology industry and put American jobs at risk. This was, he argued, due to a restrictive regulatory agenda for genetically manipulated products and a failure to protect intellectual property rights. Concern that Articles 20 and 21 gave unsatisfactory mechanisms for controlling finances, with too much power to the conference of parties, was also an important factor in the US decision. For a while there were rumours that the UK and Japanese governments would not sign the convention, due both to their concerns about the financial arrangements and a desire to avoid isolating the US government.* However, when it became clear that they would sign, and that no other government would support the US position, behind the scenes some members of the US delegation attempted to reach a compromise in the text of the convention so that the USA could change its position, but to no avail.** There is a risk, in fact, of such isolationism backfiring in that if business transactions proceed under the terms of the convention elsewhere in the world, the US biotechnology industry may experience isolation.

As a result of the prolonged arguments over access to genetic diversity and technology transfer, the convention concentrated too heavily on these issues and on financing at the expense of focusing on methods to conserve biodiversity.

The omission of an article on the preparation of global lists of globally important areas and species on which to focus international attention, due to developing countries seeing these as a potential threat to their sovereignty, may be a case in point. The convention also arguably places too much emphasis on biotechnology and technological fixes to reverse the loss of biodiversity. Globe International (1992) points out the dangers of this creating "a reliance on the 'diversity' created through technology which would replace the respect for the diversity found in nature".

Conclusion: Biotechnology and the Future of Third World Development

Biotechnology represents a challenge and an opportunity for countries of the South. On the one hand the "biorevolution" threatens to exacerbate North–South technical disparities, reinforce patterns of Third World dependency and inequality, and create even

---

* The UK and Japanese governments did after some hesitation sign the convention at Rio, but ratification will depend on the issues of financial control being sorted out.

** Divisions between some US negotiators and the White House were apparent. A leaked memo destroyed any attempt at finding a compromise for the convention. It has been suggested that those who leaked the memo hoped it would cause other countries not to sign the Biodiversity Convention, thus causing developing countries to realize what had happened and refuse to sign the Climate Convention.

more pronounced socioeconomic differentiation among low-income countries, as many critics have warned. On the other hand, biotechnologies in agriculture, non-farm industry, health care and so on could make major contributions to improving living standards and enhancing accumulation in the Third World. But they will be able to do so neither automatically nor painlessly.

Perhaps the most crucial aspect of biotechnology for development compared with previous industrial technologies is that it is relatively inexpensive and thus potentially accessible to most developing nations. By contrast, a "turnkey" steel, oil refining, auto assembly or chemical facility and a pilot bioprocessing production facility could be established with a capital investment of $50 million. Relatively inexpensive biotechnology facilities can also provide R & D for many sectors — agriculture, food manufacturing, pharmaceuticals, energy, forestry, mining, chemicals — while a conventional industrial plant is limited to one sector. Especially for the poorest Third World countries, $50 million is a major government commitment, but even more would be needed for the scale-up and commercialization of biotechnology products. But given the "multivalency" of R & D facilities, these investment requirements are modest. Unfortunately, the political economy of international biotechnology will tend to limit the development gains possible. Third World countries will have to do more on their own — either individually or as members of a Third World consortium — than they have in the past to establish biotechnology R & D programmes that can contribute to achieving equitable development.

References
Delors, J (1992) Speech to the Plenary, UNCED, Rio, 13 June
Globe International (1992) *Agenda 21: Conserving Biodiversity: The Human Element. The Role of Biotechnology and Agriculture*, Convention on Biological Diversity and UNCED, Background Report and Action Agenda, discussion document, 5 February
Tolba, M (1992) Speech to the Plenary, UNCED, Rio de Janeiro, 4 June
UNEP (1992) "The State of the Global Environment", *Our Planet*, vol 4, no 2

Chapter 2 | CLIMATE CHANGE and ENERGY

In the early 1970s the shock to the global economic system caused by OPEC's rising oil prices drew attention to the implications of fuel shortages. Subsequently, the problems of energy production in the biomass economies of the Third World became apparent. The world recognized a global energy crisis. But also during the last 20 years the threat of climate change, caused largely by energy production, has forcefully demonstrated the linkage between economic activity and the global ecosystem. Unlike many aspects of the global environmental crisis, the countries of the North are directly and seriously threatened by climate change and energy shortages. For countries of the South these were simply additional environmental problems, though some low-lying states like Bangladesh and the Maldives might be drowned out of existence. Florentin Krause, Wilfrid Bach and John Kooney discuss the suggested causes and probable effects on environment and society of anticipated climate change. Robert Hill, Phil O'Keefe and Colin Snape examine the scope for energy policy to respond to the challenge to realize sustainable development for present and future generations.

A Target-Based, Least Cost Approach to Climate Stabilization

Florentin Krause, Wilfrid Bach and John Kooney

Wait-and-See Versus Risk Minimization

Despite recent progress in putting the threat of global warming onto the international agenda, the debate over the greenhouse effect continues to be shaped by two diametrically opposed viewpoints. These views can be characterized as follows:

Don't act until you are certain or wait-and-see. Analysts holding to this view believe that current scientific uncertainties are still too large to warrant costly preventive action. Instead, more research should be pursued to reduce scientific uncertainties.

Act now to minimize risk. Those holding to this view believe that current uncertainty cuts both ways: if major warming should come true, inaction could have catastrophic consequences. Society should therefore pursue investments and policies now to minimize such risks.

The competition between these two viewpoints revolves around the following fundamental issues:

- Which aspects, if any, of the global warming threat are scientifically established facts and which are not?
- How costly would prevention be compared with adaption?
- Would there be winners and losers, or would the consequences of global warming be catastrophic for the world as a whole?
- Is there reason to believe that remaining uncertainties could be satisfactorily resolved in a time frame that would still allow preventive global action later?
- Would improved scientific modelling tools reliably be able to distinguish between winners and losers?
- What is established scientific fact and what is uncertain?

The scientific community is in complete agreement that the atmospheric greenhouse effect governs global temperature (Schneider, 1989). In fact, heat entrapment due to radiative forcing of gases is one of the oldest and most well-established experimental findings of modern science, going back some 150 years. Moreover, the greenhouse effect is the only basis on which the enormous differences in atmospheric temperatures and climate between planets like Mars, Venus and Earth can be explained.

What is also certain is that the atmospheric concentrations of a number of greenhouse gases have been rising and are continuing to rise, as shown by ongoing measurements in a global network of monitoring stations (Wuebbles and Edmonds, 1988). There is compelling evidence that these increases must be attributed to human activities (Dickinson and Cicerone, 1986).

Furthermore, data from trapped air samples in ice cores have shown that for the last 150 000 years, atmospheric carbon dioxide and methane concentrations have closely tracked the surface temperature changes brought on by glacial and interglacial periods. (Budyoko et al, 1987; Sundquist and Broecker, 1985; Schneider and Linder, 1984).

There is also virtually no debate in the scientific community that continuing rises in the atmospheric concentrations of carbon dioxide and other greenhouse gases will lead to global warming (CDAC, 1983; Schneider, 1989).

Finally, scientific research to date has firmly established the risk of catastrophic consequences from future climate warming. There is ample physical evidence that past changes in the earth's surface temperature were related to major changes in sea levels, ice cover, forest cover and regional climates. If these changes were to occur again in the world of today, their consequences would likely be catastrophic: imagine, for example, a global sea level rise of several metres. Though they might not occur, similar outcomes cannot be excluded as a consequence of future global warming.

What is uncertain is how much warming the earth will experience for a given increase in greenhouse gas concentrations (the climate sensitivity). It is also uncertain what the precise global and regional magnitudes and kinds of impacts will be — whether impacts will arrive gradually or suddenly; whether they will be catastrophic everywhere or only in some regions, and if so, where; and what monetary costs and benefits would be associated with these impacts.

The wait-and-see policy ignores that incurring risks has its own cost. Costs are only seen as existing on the prevention side of the ledger, while the risk-reducing benefits of preventive action are discounted. The principal rationale, namely that scientific uncertainty could be sufficiently resolved through research eventually to allow the application of conventional cost-benefit analysis, is faulty. The continued attractiveness of a wait-and-see policy among some constituencies is mainly explained by a lack of information about the nature of the problem, as well as by unbridled technological optimism, and in some cases, vested economic interests in the status quo.

The risk minimization approach to global warming, on the other hand, relies on a properly scientific outlook — not just in terms of the facts and risks that science has already established beyond question, but also in recognizing the inherent limits to striving for scientific certainty or, for that matter, for comprehensive and reliable monetary assessments of potential impacts. In this paradigm, risks contribute to real costs. These risk-based costs can be expressed in the following simple equation:

$$(\text{low or uncertain probability}) \times (\text{catastrophic consequences})$$
$$= (\text{major risk to society})$$

This perspective on risks is by no means unique to global warming. Huge military outlays are routinely made on the basis of this formula. Given the magnitude of climate risks, global warming — as well as other environmental threats — could be treated as a new type of threat to global security (Brundtland, 1988). Just as military expenditures are justified as precautionary measures that buy insurance against perceived risks and threats, precautionary measures to reduce greenhouse gas emission could be seen as a form of insurance against the risk and threat of climate change.

The realization that the emission of trace gases might change the climate of the planet goes back more than 150 years. Fourier was probably the first to discuss the CO_2 greenhouse effect in 1827 by comparing it with the warming of air isolated under a glass plate (Bach, 1982 and 1984). In 1903, Arrhenius made the first climate change calculation — a CO_2 increase by a factor of 2.5–3 would increase the global mean surface temperature by 8–9°C. In 1941, Flohn noted that man-made CO_2 production perturbs the carbon cycle leading to a continual CO_2 increase in the atmosphere. In 1957, Revelle and Suess concluded that human activities were initiating a global geophysical experiment that would lead to detectable climate changes in a few decades. In the same year, Keeling and co-workers started the first CO_2 measurement programme on Mauna Loa (Hawaii) and at the South Pole as part of the international geophysical year.

In 1969 and 1970, a group of scientists undertook the first major studies on the climatic effects of human activities. The results were a "Study of Critical Environmental Problems" (SCEP, 1970) and a "Study on Man's Impact on Climate" (SMIC, 1971). Both served as input to the 1972 UN Conference on the Human Environment. As a reaction to the growing concern that human activities might alter climate, in 1979 the World Meteorological Organization convened a World Climate Conference in Geneva (WMO, 1979). An important outcome of this meeting was an urgent appeal to the world's nations:

- to take full advantage of man's present knowledge of climate;
- to take steps to improve significantly that knowledge; and
- to foresee and to prevent potential man-made changes in climate that might be adverse to the wellbeing of humanity.

Since then, a number of national programmes and initiatives have emerged. For example, in preparation for the German Climate Programme, a series of international conferences were held, sponsored by the Federal Environmental Agency of the FRG. These were "Man's Impact on Climate" (Bach et al, 1980) and "Food/Climate Interactions" (Bach et al, 1981). These meetings led to the formulation of a low-climate-risk energy strategy, which would

- promote the more efficient end use of energy;
- secure the expeditious development of energy sources that add little or no CO_2 to the atmosphere; and
- keep global fossil fuel, and hence CO_2 emissions, at the present level.

These conferences initiated a shift in emphasis from calls for more studies to calls for immediate policy action.

In the wake of these calls for action, many countries started their own climate programmes. In the USA, the Carbon Dioxide Assessment Committee of the National Academy of Sciences issued a major report (CDAC, 1983), followed by a study on greenhouse gases by the US EPA (Seidel and Keyes, 1983) and a major five-volume report on the effects of changes in ozone and climate by EPA and UNEP (Titus, 1986). More recently, the US EPA published an analysis of climate stabilization options (Lashof and Tirpak, 1989). Canada has established a CO_2 and climate programme (Hengeveld, 1987). In the Netherlands, an assessment of the CO_2 problems was undertaken by a Committee of the Health Council of the Netherlands (CHCN, 1983). Various activities on trace gases and climate were initiated within the EEC and the World Meteorological Organization (WMO, 1985).

In 1986, upon the recommendation of the 1985 Villach meeting, an Advisory Group on Greenhouse Gases (AGGG) was set up jointly by ICSU, WMO and UNEP. Its tasks are to review global and regional studies on greenhouse gases and to evaluate the rates of greenhouse gas increases and their effects. The annually recurring ozone hole over Antarctica has led to an initiative among 17 European research centres to set up EUROPICA (European Programme in Chemistry of the Atmosphere). While ozone will be the focal point of this scientific mission, many of the climate-related trace gases will also be studied. In 1986, ICSU also launched a decades-long International Geosphere-Biosphere Programme (IGBP). Its objectives are: "to describe and understand the interactive physical, chemical and biological processes that regulate the total Earth system, the unique environment it provides for life, the changes that are occurring in that system, and the manner by which these changes are influenced by human actions".

A second World Climate Conference was held in 1990. In preparation for this meeting the following conferences were held:

- UNEP/WMO/ICSU "Assessment Conference on the Role of Carbon Dioxide and Radiatively-Active Constituents in Climate Variation and Associated Impacts", Villach, October 1985.
- UNEP/WMO/ICSU "The Effects of Future Climatic Changes on the World's Bioclimatic Regions and their Management Implications: A New Technical Agenda", Villach, September/October 1987.
- Government of the Netherlands/EC/WMO "Interrelated Bioclimatic Land Use Changes", Noordwijkerhout, October 1987.
- UNEP/RBF/GMF "Priorities for Future Management: A New Policy Agenda", Bellagio, November, 1987.
- EEC/Government of the Netherlands, EEB/IPSEP "Energy Policy and Climate Change: What Can Western Europe Do?", Brussels, June 1988.
- Ministry of the Environment of Canada/UNEP/WMO "World Conference on the Changing Atmosphere: Implications for Global Security", Toronto, June 1988.
- INCSTD/UNEP/WMO "Climate Change and Variability, and Social, Economic and Technological Development", Hamburg, November 1988.
- First meeting of the Intergovernmental Panel on Climate Change (IPCC) under the sponsorship of UNEP and WMO, Geneva, November 1988.

This panel consisted of three working groups on modelling, impact studies and response strategies. The purpose of the IPCC was to prepare the Second World Climate Conference in 1990 and to work toward a global climate convention.

The establishment of the IPCC is symbolic of a major broadening of the international climate warming agenda from basic research to preventive policy action. Several other milestones in this process should be mentioned:

- In 1987, the US Congress passed a Global Climate Protection Act that ordered the EPA, the Office of Technology Assessment and the Department of Energy to prepare reports on specific policy actions that could limit global warming.
- In the same year, West Germany established a special standing parliamentary commission, the Enquête Commission on "Precautionary Measures for the Protection of the Earth's Atmosphere". Its express mandate was to identify and evaluate specific measures that can reduce the emission of trace gases that endanger the world's climate and ozone layer. A final report was planned for 1990.
- In June 1988, the Toronto World Conference on the Changing Atmosphere called for a 20 per cent reduction of fossil carbon dioxide releases by 2005. Two heads of state appealed for a global convention to deal with the greenhouse effect.
- In the wake of the Toronto meeting several far-reaching legislative proposals were introduced in the US Congress that called for reductions in carbon dioxide emissions in addition to reduction in chloroflurocarbon emissions.
- In the US–Soviet summit held at the end of 1988, greenhouse warming was recognized for the first time as an issue at that level.
- In February 1989, the government of Canada sponsored an "International Meeting of Legal and Policy Experts: Protection of the Atmosphere", in Ottawa, with the purpose of examining formulations and principles for a global climate convention.
- In April 1989, the OECD's International Energy Agency held the first major international expert seminar on energy technologies for reducing emissions of greenhouse gases, attended by more than 200 participants from 24 nations.
- At the IPCC meeting in Geneva in May 1989, more than 20 participants supported a global climate convention.
- The Helsinki Declaration of May 1989 brought a major increase in the numbers of governments supporting action on the ozone and greenhouse problems.
- Around the same time, the Dutch government adopted a target to return fossil carbon emission to the 1990 level by 2000, and the Swedish parliament voted to limit fossil carbon releases to present levels.
- During the Group of Seven Summit in July 1989 in Paris, global warming became an agenda item.

Events are proceeding so rapidly that the above chronology will soon be hopelessly out of date. Underlying this rising tide of international activity is the growing recognition of the enormous risks entailed in climate warming.

In summary, the greenhouse effect has been known as a scientific possibility for more than a century. But only in the last two decades has this threat begun to be taken seriously, and only during the last few years have preventive measures entered the international political arena. Most scientific analysts now agree that the only way to address the greenhouse threat is to reduce the emissions that drive global warming.

■ *Florentin Krause, Wilfrid Bach and John Kooney*

Driving Forces of Climate Change

The causes of climatic change are complex and there are many theories and possible mechanisms. We limit our discussion to the driving forces created by trace gases related to human activity, since those are the only ones we can influence through policy action.

The Greenhouse Effect

Like a window pane in a greenhouse, a number of gases in the earth's atmosphere let solar radiation (visible light) pass to the surface of the earth while trapping infrared (IR) radiation, also known as heat radiation, that is re-emitted by the surface of the earth. This heat radiation would have otherwise escaped to space. It is this trapping of infrared radiation that is referred to as the greenhouse effect (Ramanathan et al, 1987).

Gases that influence the surface — atmosphere radiation balance — are also called radiatively active or greenhouse gases (GHG). Even in the absence of human interference, the greenhouse effect is constantly in operation in maintaining the Earth's climate. A number of natural constituents of the atmosphere are radiatively active. The most important are water vapour, carbon dioxide (CO_2), and clouds. These contribute roughly 90 per cent to the natural greenhouse effect, whereas naturally occurring ozone (O_3) methane (CH_4) and other gases account for the remainder.

Human activities cause the emission of a number of greenhouse gases. These emissions create a change in the radiative balance of the surface atmosphere system (radiative forcing). Because the concentrations of natural and anthropogenic greenhouse gases are small compared with the principal atmospheric constituents of oxygen and nitrogen, these gases are also called trace gases.

Important Trace Gases

Trace gases fall into three categories: (1) radiatively active trace gases such as water vapour (H_2), carbon dioxide (CO_2), ozone (O_3), methane (CH_4), nitrous oxide (N_2) and the chlorofluorocarbons (CFCs) which exert direct climatic effects; (2) chemically/photochemically active trace gases such as carbon monoxide (CO), nitrogen oxides (NO_x) and sulphur dioxide (SO_2) which exert indirect climate effects through the chemistry that determined the atmospheric concentrations of hydroxyl radicals (OH), CH_4 and O_3; and (3) aerosol emissions. Table 2.1 lists most greenhouse gases.

Feedback Mechanisms

Greenhouse warming has the potential to produce many complex feedbacks that are the major source of current climate modelling uncertainties. These feedbacks could substantially increase the sensitivity of the climate system to human perturbation. They can be categorized as follows (Lashof, 1989): Geophysical climate feedbacks (due to physical as opposed to chemical or biochemical processes); they include:

• increased water vapour due to warmer and wetter climate;
• decreased reflectiveness (albedo) of the earth's surface due to shrinking snow and ice cover; and
• increases in clouds due to greater evaporation.

70

Table 2.1 Overview of Greenhouse Gases in the Atmosphere

Trace Gas	Chemical Symbol	Trace Gas	Chemical Symbol
Carbon Group		Halogen Group	
Carbon monoxide	CO	Trichlorofluoromethane	CFCl3
Carbon dioxide	CO2	(Freon 11)	
Methane	CH4	Dichlorodifluoromethane	CF2Cl2
		(Freon 12)	
Oxygen Group		Chlorotrifluoromethane	CF3Cl
Ozone	O3	(Freon 13)	
		Dichlorofluoromethane	CFHCl2
Nitrogen Group		(Freon 21)	
Nitrous oxide	N2O	Chlorodifluoromethane	CF2HCl
Nitrous dioxide	NO2	(Freon 22)	
Dinitrogen pentoxide	N2O5	Trichlorofluoromethane	CF3CCl3
Nitric acid	HNO3	(Freon 113)	
Ammonia	NH3	Dichlorotetrafluoroethane	C2F4Cl2
		(Freon 114)	
Sulphur group		Chloropentafluoroethane	C2F5Cl
Sulphur dioxide	SO2	(Freon 115)	
Sulphur hexafluoride	SF6	Hexafluoroethane	C2F6
Carbonyl sulphide	COS	(Freon 116)	
Carbon disulphide	CS2	Methyl bromide	CH3Br
Hydrogen sulphide	H2S	Ethylene bromide	BrCH2CH2Br
		Bromotrifluoromethane	CF3Br
Non-methane hydrocarbons		Methyl chloride	CH3Cl
Acetylene	C2H2	Methylene chloride	CH2Cl2
Acetalehyde	CH3CHO	Dichloroethane	CH2ClCH2Cl
Formaldehyde	HCHO	Trichloroethylene	C2HCl3
Ethylene	C2H4	Tetrachloroetylene	C2Cl4
Ethane	C2H6	methyl chloroform	CH3CCl3
Propane	C3H8	Carbon tetrafluoride	CF4
Butane	C4H10	Carbontetrachloride	CCl4
Methyl pentane	C4H14		
Others			
peroxyacetyle nitrate	PAN		

Sources: WMO (1982); Chamberlain et al (1982); Ramanathan et al (1985).

Biogeochemical feedbacks, including

- physical effects of warming (release of methane from hydrates in sediments changes in ocean circulation and mixing affecting CO2 uptake);
- climate-chemical feedbacks (changes in hydroxyl concentrations and tropospheric ozone due to more water vapour, shifts in the CO2/carbonate equilibrium in the ocean);
- short-term biological responses to warming (increased microbial activity and there-

fore methane releases from soil organic matter, carbon dioxide fertilization of plant growth, increased plant respiration, increased non-methane hydrocarbons from vegetation).
• Effects due to the reorganization of ecosystems (changes in surface albedo, changes in terrestrial carbon storage, and changes in the biological pumping of carbon from the ocean surface to deep waters).

At this time, the biochemical feedbacks have not been incorporated in current climate methods.

Implications for Climate Stabilization
Inertia and feedback mechanisms mean that full warming impacts from greenhouse gas emissions manifest only with delay. The full warming impact from a change in greenhouse gas concentrations is also referred to as the equilibrium warming, while temperature effects on the way to reaching this equilibrium are called transient warming. If emissions continue at a sufficient rate to maintain raised levels of atmospheric concentrations, the transient warming will eventually converge on the equilibrium warming.

The full warming impact could be avoided if concentrations of trace gases in the atmosphere could be made to decline again before the impact of previous emissions has fully materialized. This possibility is important to recognize, though the degree to which such a reversal is possible is limited by both practical and physical factors. For the gases with long atmospheric residence times, just holding emission rates constant will lead to inexorable rises in atmospheric concentrations, and a complete cessation will only lead to slow declines in concentrations. However, the short-lived greenhouse gases respond quickly to cuts in emissions, among them methane and ozone. Since both are related to air pollution sources, controlling the air pollution emissions that govern their tropospheric chemistry is one area where short-term reductions in radiative forcing could be obtained.

Anticipated Global Climate Changes

Anticipated Warming
The degree of climate change the world is likely to experience depends on future atmospheric greenhouse gas concentrations. Warming predictions also depend on the climate sensitivity assumed in the mathematical models used for calculating warming. According to established scientific consensus, a doubling of carbon dioxide levels or equivalent changes in atmospheric composition would raise the mean surface temperature of the globe anywhere from 1.5 to 4.5°C (CDAC, 1983). The currently most widely used models predict a narrower range of 3 to 5.5°C (Dickinson and Cicerone, 1986). When a broader range of possible feedback effects of Section C is added, average warming from doubled CO_2 could be as high as 6.3 to 8°C or more (Lashof, 1989). However, the same study suggests that the different feedbacks might well produce stabilizing interactive dynamics rather than just being linearly additive. They also would probably lose much of their potency if a substantial warming is realized and the absorption bands of greenhouse gases saturate.

This global average surface warming would be unevenly distributed. For example, if low latitudes were to experience a warming of about 2°C, high latitudes would likely see as much as 4 to 10°C during the winter months.

Unprecedentedness and Climatic Throwback

The enormity of these changes can only be grasped if we compare them to the climate history of the earth:

- A 1 to 1.5° global average warming would represent a climate not experienced since the Holocene period at the beginning of agricultural civilization (some 6000 years ago).
- A 2 to 2.5° warming would represent a climate not experienced since the Eem-Sangamon interglacial period some 125 000 years ago. At that time, human communities existed as hunter-gatherer societies, and the west Antarctic ice shield seemed to have partially disintegrated, raising sea levels up by 5 to 7 metres.
- A 3 to 4° warming would represent a climate not experienced since human beings appeared on earth some two million years ago. The last time the Earth was this warm was between three and five million years ago, in the Pliocene period.
- A global average warming of 5° or more would mean a climate not experienced for tens of millions of years, when there were no glaciers in the Antarctic, Iceland and Greenland or on mountain ranges like the Sierra Nevada.

Two qualifications are in order: first, the availability of data and therefore our knowledge about the environmental conditions during previous warm periods, drops off steeply as we go further back in geological time. Second, some of the evidence in the earth's historic climate record suggests that the climate system, once sufficiently disturbed, may find a new equilibrium quickly and abruptly, without the gradual response in proportion to rising concentrations that current models predict (Broecker, 1987).

Secondary Climate Changes

One major effect global warming will have is to create warmer oceans. The warmer oceans will evaporate more moisture. The excess moisture in the atmosphere will make the climate more humid and wetter overall. And global circulation patterns in the oceans and atmosphere will be affected.

While the uncertainties surrounding more specific predictions of impacts are often very great, the following geophysical and biospheric changes are expected to materialize:

- Rising sea levels by at least 0.5 to 1.5 metres over the next few decades, and by as much as several metres over the longer term.
- Lower snowpacks and receding glaciers.
- Shifts in ocean currents and changed precipitation patterns in all regions.
- More frequent occurrences of weather conditions now considered extreme.
- Increased storms, floods and avalanches, and significant seasonal changes in the availability of water run-off.
- Loss of soil moisture due to increased evaporation, and an increase in the duration and frequency of heat waves and drought conditions.

- Reduction in precipitation in the mid-latitude continental regions of North America and Eurasia.
- More stagnant air masses and displacement of high pressure systems.
- Changes and reorganizations of natural and agricultural ecosystems.

Impacts on Society

A growing amount of research is being done on how climate changes might affect human society, but the prediction of many impacts remains highly speculative at this time. Below we summarize some of the most likely practical consequences of climate warming, along with the risk of well-established impacts. A more detailed review can be found, for example, in Kates et al (1985); Parry et al (1988) and in Smith and Tirpak (1988), who specifically discuss the USA.

The likelihood and extent of many impacts, particularly those having to do with the feedback effects of climate warming on geophysical and ecological processes, are highly uncertain at this time. Often, there are countervailing feedback forces at work. These can make it difficult to determine the net direction of impact (Lashof, 1989). However, prudent policy making should be particularly concerned with the downside risks and should not rely on the most optimistic interpretations of available evidence.

Food Security

Human history, if replete with famines caused by deterioration in regional climates and even highly mechanized and chemical-intensive agriculture, is critically dependent on climate.[*] Under favourable conditions, increased CO_2 levels and higher temperature could increase agricultural yields. But many crop yields are delicately dependent on a particular mix of temperatures, soil conditions and rainfall patterns. High latitude regions that could in principle become available for agriculture may not provide such favourable conditions. Furthermore, a number of weed plants seem to be more efficient than crops in utilizing atmospheric carbon dioxide. Warmer weather could also encourage the spread of certain plant pests (Bach et al, 1981).[**]

A recent study by the US Environmental Protection Agency predicts that warming of several degrees would force major redistributions of cropping zones and changes in farming practices (Smith and Tirpak, 1988). The study found that while some areas might gain a few tens of per cent in yields, other areas could suffer reductions of 50 per cent. Drier conditions are expected for the grain belts in the US Midwest. Semi-arid regions would be particularly strongly affected. The same goes for the wheat growing Kazakstan region of the former Soviet Union.

Impacts on agricultural productivity could be particularly severe in developing countries. Notably in the semi-arid regions, small irregularities in climate are sufficient to create major disruption. Heat stress could also severely reduce rice plant reproduction in the world's rice growing regions. Such impacts could have disastrous effects

---

* The 1988 drought in the USA was a reminder of this dependence. For the first time in decades, the largest grain exporter in the world failed to produce more wheat than that needed to meet domestic demand.

** Again, the 1988 US drought is a case in point. The unusually hot conditions resulted in the infection of significant portions of the US corn harvest with aflatoxin-producing moulds. Aflatoxins are potent carcinogens.

on poor rural subsistence farmers in the developing world. Unlike farmers in industrial countries, most Third World peasants do not have recourse to modern fuels and machinery to buffer against fundamental changes in their environment. These farmers' major productive asset is their intuitive knowledge of the local climate, and the cultural "software" that has been built around this knowledge. Global warming could make both worthless.

Reduced yields and less-than-needed yield improvements in the developing countries, combined with higher food prices worldwide and possibly the loss of surplus production and reserves in industrial countries, could lead to more suffering in the Third World. In the international markets, scarce supplies would go to those who can pay the highest price. Such shifts in fortunes could bring geopolitical instability and international polarization similar to the events surrounding the oil crises of the 1970s.

Impacts of Forests and Species Diversity

While most attention has been given to impacts on agricultural systems, important disruptions are expected for relatively unmanaged ecosystems. Where soil conditions and rainfall permit, global warming would allow forests to extend upward in altitude and poleward in latitudes. Unfortunately, the rate of warming the world might experience over the next number of decades could far outstrip the capacity of forests to migrate. A warming of several degrees over a 100-year period would greatly exceed natural rates of change, pushing forests poleward by 2.5 kilometres a year, compared with less than one kilometre a year in fast migration tree specifies (CEC, 1986).

If forests cannot keep up with this rate, the result would be rapid dieback of existing forests while new species would take root much more slowly. The rapid appearance of acid rain damage in the forests of central Europe illustrates the vulnerability of these ecosystems, and continued air pollution stresses from fossil fuel consumption could further aggravate these impacts. The result could be a period of many decades in which forest cover and/or forest productivity in the mid-latitudes would be greatly diminished.

Climate change might not just disrupt mid-latitude forests, but could also lead to serious damage to tropical forests, due to greater evaporation and changes in the regional distribution of rainfall. This, in turn, could exacerbate current losses in species diversity. Most of the world's biological species are found in these forests, and human-induced deforestation is already producing species losses at an alarming rate.

Landuse and Human Settlements

Warming of several degrees could, within the next 50 to 100 years, result in a sea level rise of 0.5 to 1.5 metres. Global warming could also eventually break up the west Antarctic ice shield and lead to a sea level rise of several metres, though this process would probably take several hundred years.

Even a modest sea level rise would threaten the coastal settlements in which half of humanity lives. In the USA also, an estimated 12 million people — close to 5 per cent of the population — could become homeless. High tides and storm surges would penetrate further inland. Salinity would move upstream, penetrating into groundwater and bays, and forming inland salt lakes in many areas. Rich farmland in coastal river deltas would be lost unless expensive dykes were built. Developing countries, particularly in Asia, may find the cost of such measures prohibitive.

Economic impacts would be aggravated by the fact that many major infrastructural and industrial investments are located near the shore. Airports, waste dumps, harbour facilities, bridges, drainage systems, irrigation systems, water treatment plants, chemical factors and power plants all would require protective investments or rebuilding to protect them from flooding. Smith and Tirpak (1988) estimate for the USA that protection against a one metre rise in sea levels would cost a cumulative $123–175 billion (1985 dollars) by the year 2100. Again, Third World countries would be particularly hard hit.

Freshwater Supplies

Warming could reduce stream flows and increase pressure on groundwater supplies in many regions, while worsening the pollution from waste discharge into smaller flows. For example, it is estimated that viable farm acreage in the arid regions of the USA could be reduced by one third (Waggoner, 1989). Regions and nations sharing watersheds could experience conflicts in the form of water wars.

Other Impacts

Other impacts could involve human health risks due to extreme heat stress and the more vigorous transmission of tropical and other diseases over larger areas; increases in energy consumption for air conditioning (Linder and Inglis, 1988); losses in hydro power availability; and losses in revenue from tourism and fisheries.

Planning Uncertainty

A major impact, and one that is frequently overlooked, is the great increase in planning uncertainty. Climate change could be producing impacts rapidly in some regions but slowly in others, and at different speeds during different phases of the warming process. Such uncertainty would have an impact on all levels of human activity, including the very investments aimed at adapting to climate change — whether planning for flood control systems, adjusting hydro dams and irrigation systems to irregular run-off, or selecting food crops for changing growing seasons. Society might find itself engaged in a constant treadmill, trying to catch up with perpetual change in an environment that no longer works.

References

Bach, W (1982) *Gefahr fur unser Klima: Wege aus der CO2-Bedrohung durch sinnvollen Energieeisatz*, K Muller, Karlsruhe
—— (1984) *Our Threatened Climate: Ways of Averting the CO2 Problem through Rational Energy Use*, Reidel Publishing Company, Dordrecht (English translation of Bach 1982)
Bach, W, J Pankrath and J Williams (eds) (1980) *Interactions of Energy and Climate*, Reidel Publishing Company, Dordrecht
Bach, W, J Pankrath and S H Schneider (eds) (1981) *Food–Climate Interactions*, Reidel Publishing Company, Dordrecht
Broecker, W S (1987) "Testimony before the US Senate Subcommittee on Environmental Protection", 28 January, Washington, DC; see also *Nature*, vol 328, p123
Brundtland Commission (1988) *Our Common Future*. Report to the United Nations Commission on Environment and Development, United Nations, New York
Budyko, M I, A B Ronov and A L Yanhin (1987) *History of the Earth's Atmosphere*, Springer-Verlag Publishing, Berlin

CDAC (1983) *Changing Climate*, Natural Resources Council, National Academy Press, Washington, DC

CEC (1986) "Climate Change and Associated Impacts", Proceedings of Symposium on COs and other Greenhouse Gases: Climate and Associated Impacts, Brussels, 3–5 November

Chamberlain, J W, H M Foley, G J MacDonald and M A Ruderman (1982) "Climate Effects on Minor Atmospheric Constituents", in W Clark (ed) *Carbon Dioxide Review*, Oxford, pp253–77

CHCN (1983) *Report on CO2 Problem*, The Hague, The Netherlands

Dickinson, R E and R J Cicerone (1986) "Future Global Warming Forms Trace Gases", *Nature*, vol 319, pp109–14

Henegeveld, H G (1987) *Understanding CO2 and Climate*, Annual Report 1986, Canadian Climate Centre, Ottawa (and other years)

Kates, R W, J H Ausubel and M Barberian (eds) (1985) *Climate Impact Assessment: Studies of the Interactions of Climate and Society*, John Wiley & Sons, New York

Lashof, D A (1989) "The Dynamic Greenhouse: Feedback Processes that may Influence Future Concentrations of Atmospheric Trace Gases and Climate Change", *Climate Change* (forthcoming)

Lashof, D A and D Tirpak (1989) "Policy Options for Stabilizing Global Climate", draft report to the US Congress, February

Linder, K and M Inglis (1988) "The Potential Impacts of Climate Change on Electric Utilities: Regional and National Estimates", Report of ICF to the US Environmental Protection Agency

Parry, M L et al (1988) *The Impact of Climate Variations on Agriculture*, vol 1: "Assessments in Semi-Arid Regions", vol 2: "Assessments in Cool Temperature and Cold Regions", Reidel, Kluiver Academie, Holland

Ramanathan, V et al (1985) "Trace Gas Trends and their Potential Role in Climate Change", *JGR Journal of Geo-Physical Research*, vol 90, pp5547–66

——— (1987) "Climate–Chemical Interactions and Effects of Changing Atmospheric Trace Gases", *Reviews of Geophysics*, vol 25, no 7, pp1441–82

SCEP (1970) "Report of the Study of Critical Environment Problems", *Man's Impact on the Global Environment*, MIT Press, Cambridge, MA

Schneider, S H (1989) "The Greenhouse Effect: Science and Policy", *Science*, vol 243, no 4892, pp771–81, 10 February

Schneider, S H and R Linder (1984) *The Coevolution of Climate and Life*, Sierra Club Books, San Francisco

Seidel and Keyes (1983) *Can We Delay a Greenhouse Warning?*, US Environmental Protection Agency, Washington, DC

SMIC (1971) "Report on the Study of Man's Impact on Climate", *Inadvertent Climate Modification*, MIT Press, Cambridge, MA

Smith, J B and D Tirpak (eds) (1988) *The Potential Effect of a Global Climate Change on the United States*, Draft report to Congress, October

Sundquist, E T and W S Brocker (eds) (1985) *The Carbon Cycle and Atmospheric COs: Natural Variations Archean to Present*, American Geophysical Union, Washington, DC

Titus, J G (ed) (1986) *Effects of Changes in Stratospheric Ozone and Global Climate*, vols 1–4, US Environmental Protection Agency/UNEP, Washington, DC

Waggoner, P E (ed) (1989) *Climate Change and US Water Resources*, Wiley, New York

WMO (1979) *World Climate Conference*, WMO–No 537, Geneva

——— (1982) "The Stratosphere 1981: Theory and Measurements", Global Ozone Research and Monitoring Project, Report No 11, Geneva

——— (1985) "Atmospheric ozone 1985", vols. I–III, Global Ozone Research and Monitoring Project, Report, No.16, Geneva. WMO, 1985

Wuebbles, D J and J Edmonds (1988) *A Primer on Greenhouse Gases*, US DOE, Washington, DC

Energy Planning
Robert Hill, Phil O'Keefe and Colin Snape

Energy in the Global Village

The world is rapidly becoming a single global village. In it, developed families cannot deny the existence of the poor. The major initiative for changing matters must, however, lie with the poor themselves. Development aid is no more than a small contribution to the alleviation of poverty.

Developing countries face three serious problems. These are:

- Increasing ecological destruction;
- Low levels of economic development; and
- Problems with maintaining political pluralism.

Problems, addressed correctly, can produce solutions that generate new opportunities and these must provide opportunities for sustainability.

Over the past decade, as aid has increasingly been focused on poverty alleviation, discussion on designing sustainable responses to development challenges has emerged. But there is little point in addressing vital issues if they simply re-emerge in a more acute manner in another generation. The basic policy aim of development can be summarized by the wish: "May today's children die of old age, having confidence in the future".

Several development problems, particularly those concerned with the environment such as population growth, the greenhouse effect, ecological degradation and natural resource exhaustion, only appear as problems after a long delay. If such problems are not addressed immediately they accumulate, creating conditions in the system that can not be repaired. Prevention is usually cheaper than cure and, even if a firm diagnosis is not yet available, paying now for prevention is a wise precaution. It is precisely because these time delayed problems are difficult to handle in the future that they need to be addressed as policy issues now. A starting point is the definition of a clear energy policy with a long-term perspective.

We have in mind a perspective which runs to the mid twenty-first century when, though many readers of this chapter will be dead, power plant built now will still be operating. Medium-term policies, up to 2010, will have to make significant progress towards long-term objectives. This means the full implementation of energy efficiency measures and the use of renewable energy sources. Short-term action, which includes formulating an energy policy, must be focused on institutional developments that can secure a sustainable energy future and on the immediate introduction of efficiency measures. Efficiency is the key which, among other things, makes energy resources available for alternative purposes. Short-term initiatives must not undermine the longer term.

It is not immediately evident that an energy policy for development is needed. For most economic activity, energy is just an input and it is neither difficult nor expensive to obtain. However, precisely because of this, energy markets are a poor guide to developing a sustainable energy future. Energy is never an item of final consumption, but only a means of providing services and satisfying basic needs. Energy, however, differs from other economic inputs in that it is associated with a number of macro-economic problems with a wide spatial and a long temporal impact.

Energy is used in all sectors of society. In energy policy, however, it is important to distinguish different levels of energy issues. The first and most important is energy as an environmental issue where it co-determines the level of sustainable development. Crudely, this is a situation where energy issues put the existence of a nation state at risk. At a global level, climate change resulting from enhanced global warming is another such issue.

Energy is also a strategic issue influencing national development and energy scarcity. Policies here address issues of natural resource exploitation, fuel switching, energy for industrialization, transport and rural electrification. Separate from these two levels are matters relating to secondary energy, including discussion of energy forms, pricing, availability and quality as well as of management techniques, institutions and technologies for the delivery of energy. These secondary questions must be dealt with in a broader policy framework that demonstrates a commitment to long-term institutional development.

The Parameters for the Global Village Energy Future

Present energy consumption in developed countries is 7 kW per capita, but only 1.1 kW per capita in the developing countries. Technology already exists for a reduction from 7 to 3 kW per capita in the developed world and it is theoretically possible to achieve a 3 kW per capita world by 2060 but only if, both for economic and environmental reasons, energy efficiency and the use of renewables are adopted more or less everywhere.

Fossil fuel prices, when left to the market, have not provided an incentive for improving energy efficiency or for employing renewable energy on a large scale. The prices of hydrocarbons must be monitored because, although these resources are underpriced, neither the costs for resource depletion nor for the externalities associated with production and use are included, they are the bench mark for costing any intervention in the energy sector. Governments also need to monitor energy markets proactively so as to determine how they should intervene to create a sustainable energy future. This problem is particularly acute when addressing policy issues to minimize environmental damage.

Current world energy use is 10 TW (10 watts) and rising rapidly and most of it is obtained from non-renewable resources. Gross world annual photosynthesis, the essential but only conditionally renewable resource, is some 100 TW. In the longer term, photosynthetic production will neither be a major energy source nor a carbon sink. This points up the need to address long-term problems of sustainability by concentrating on efficiency and on the use of renewables that directly convert incoming solar radiation to productive energy.

Global warming is the problem that most clearly establishes the direction of a long-term sustainable energy future. To avoid the enhanced greenhouse effect and, by implication, climatic disaster, the human population must emit no more carbon dioxide than it does today. In crude terms, this probably means an upper limit of carbon emissions of five billion tonnes a year. Assuming that demographic change produces a steady state population of 15 billion, per capita consumption would have to be reduced to 0.5 kW per year. This is roughly ten to twenty times less than developed countries use now.

The trend towards greater urbanization in developing countries is unlikely to change, so an accelerating transition to hydrocarbon fuels is inevitable. However, experience has shown that the potential for change is much greater in urban than in rural environments. The urban opportunity is the "Coca Cola" opportunity because energy, like soft drinks, is a universal service already commoditized and advertised. Assistance for urban development should be designed to ensure that best practice prevails. Energy efficiency programmes, coupled with health, sanitation and waste programmes, can be integrated into urban development as a priority. There should also be a renewed emphasis on efficient public transport.

The section below highlights two possible and contrasting trends in development, which will produce different commercial energy futures. They suggest that for some countries there will be an increase in energy use at a rate above the growth of gross national product.

Energy Policy and Markets

It is necessary to recognize that to design a sustainable energy policy for the future, it is not enough to rely on market signals that are derived from the appraisal of volume and price for energy commodities. Market information does not include the costs of resource depletion and of pollution. It also excludes those substantial energy resources collected as "free goods" for use in households in developing countries. At best, the market indicates what energy future is profitable, not what is sustainable. By focusing on profitability, the market emphasizes short-term solutions: by focusing on least-cost investment, the market reinforces the short-term outlook.

The limitations of the market cannot be addressed by a simple technology push involving the rapid transfer of existing technology from developed to developing countries. Such a transfer is focused on energy supply, not on energy consumption. In most cases, developed countries themselves do not supply technologies designed for a sustainable energy future and the beneficiaries of investment in developing countries tend to be the rich, not the poor.

The design of energy policy calls for a focus on energy consumers by sector of economic activity. This will require the strengthening of institutional arrangements so that consumer need can be secured. An emphasis on security, on economic maximization, successfully pervades the energy policy of developed countries — the best demonstration of this was the minimal impact of the Gulf War on energy supplies. Security for energy consumers must be matched by an emphasis on energy efficiency. Again reliance on market signals gives the wrong message — while it is cheaper to save a unit of energy than to produce a new one, it is more profitable, for any individual electricity company, to produce a new unit of energy than to save one.

Beyond the market, in the household energy sector dominated by woody biomass fuels, it is difficult to price energy goods. A tree, for example, is usually a free good available to an entire community or, often, to all. Even a nominal price for the tree as wood energy is difficult to calculate because it is simultaneously a resource for fodder, fencing and fruit. Designing woody biomass projects, if a nominal price for woodfuel can be accepted, is hazardous at best. Signals from the energy market are important but they cannot drive an energy policy committed to a long-term sustainable energy future focused on securing stable supplies for consumers. Such security is provided by emphasizing efficiency and by supporting the local management of renewable energy resources.

Towards a Sustainable Energy Future
The present concept of "development" is based on the Western model of society. Europe uses about 5kW and the USA 10kW per person and are dominated by production from fossil fuels. But these levels are only possible so long as they are limited to no more than a small fraction of the global population.

If non-carbon energy sources are to become dominant, then the world energy price must be significantly higher than it is today. The present Northern societal structure (large turnover of goods, high mobility) is poorly adapted for the sorts of price level needed and its technologies are far from optimal. The Western model is therefore not one for best future practice in developing countries. Developing countries must aim to achieve wellbeing at historically high international energy prices and the developed world will have to transform itself within the same framework.

Figure 2.1 demonstrates the route that developing countries must take to achieve the goal of sustainable energy and they should be helped to find the shortest route to it. This will need both societal and technological change, the beginnings of which exist neither in the developed nor in the developing world. Introducing them is the challenge to societal and technological research and innovation, and a task to be shared by all countries.

National Energy and Environment Policy
In the Netherlands, the national energy policy, focused on conservation, got enormous encouragement in the wake of the oil crisis. Overall, energy consumption was reduced by almost 2 per cent a year, while the economy continued to grow. At the beginning of the 1980s, however, the economic growth rate was not high. This, combined with a small shift towards less energy-intensive sectors of industry, made total energy consumption in 1985 just about the same as it had been in 1973. The annual energy efficiency improvement rate has, at the present time, fallen to less than half of what it was in the period between 1973 and 1985.

The CO_2 and climate issue is taking a prominent position in the concerns of the industrialized nations particularly through the International Energy Agency, the IPCC and the European Union. It is becoming so serious that it has prompted international action. However, developing countries with large fossil fuel reserves (China, with its coal, and the OPEC countries) might have less interest in participating in CO_2 reductions, as international sales and inland use of these fuels are a major source of income and a motor for development: in the short term, economic constraint can override environmental concerns.

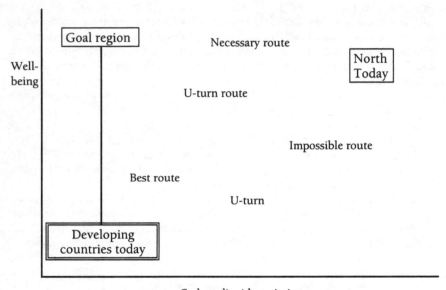

Source: after Ferguson

Figure 2.1 *Future Environmental Paths*

Designing Sustainable Energy Policy

Developing countries have been excluded from much of the discussion on global environmental change. Furthermore, their short-term economic and energy security problems imply that, if a new mode of energy and development is not found, they will increasingly contribute a substantial proportion of carbon emissions.

Sustainable energy policies start from the point of consumption, not of supply. This is an emphasis on end-use which, in turn, allows for a focus on energy efficiency. Looking at end-use also allows certain sectors of the energy economies of developing countries to be highlighted, particularly those of household energy and of energy transition in urban areas, notably in transport. In fact the main objective of an end-use orientation is to enable a sustainable energy economy, which gives particular emphasis to household energy needs, to be built in developing countries.

End-use

End-use is a worm's eye view of the energy problem. It starts with the people or organizations using energy rather than with supply.

End-use and supply are the opposite ends of a chain which runs from the energy source, through transformation and distribution to the services the end-user wants. End-use analysis begins by defining major energy consumption sectors. In general, these are households, industry, transport, agriculture and commerce. Major sub-sectors within the household sector are used to differentiate between driving power and heating requirements; within transport, the major sub-sectors are passenger and freight requirements.

In rural households, the dominant end-use is cooking, though there are numerous others such as space and water heating, ironing and light. These end-uses vary from region to region depending on socio-economic, cultural and ecological considerations. A disaggregated end-use approach can capture the complexity of this situation allowing a range of solutions to be offered.

For each end-use, such as cooking, there is a further level of disaggregation associated with:

- fuel type,
- technology,
- energy intensity,
- social class of users

Examining each end-use from this level of disaggregation allows for a clear analysis of policy options. These run from fuel switching, through technology transfer and energy intensity, to government intervention on behalf of certain end-users.

Global Warming

The major environmental challenge facing humanity over the next 100 years is climate change. Scientific advisers and policy makers now accept that the rate of climatic change might be more substantial than at any point in the last 10 000 years. This is because the greenhouse effect, which produces temperatures that allow people to live on earth, is being enhanced.

The Earth's climate is driven by many factors. The primary force is radiant energy from the sun, and the reflection or absorption and reradiation of this energy by atmospheric gas molecules, clouds, and the surface of the Earth itself. A portion of this reradiated energy leaves the atmosphere and over the long term, a balance is maintained between the solar energy entering the atmosphere and the energy leaving it. The net result of these natural processes is the "greenhouse effect" — a warming of the Earth's atmosphere and surface. Water vapour (in the form of clouds) and carbon dioxide (CO_2) are major contributors to this effect, with smaller but still significant contributions coming from methane (CH_4), nitrous oxide (N_2O) and ozone (O_3).

Human activities during the last century have resulted in significant increases in concentrations of CO_2, CH_4 and N_2O as well as the introduction of chlorofluoro-carbons (CFCs). As concentrations increase more radiation should be trapped to further warm the Earth's surface and atmosphere. This should lead to an "enhanced" greenhouse effect and a warmer climate which, in turn, will probably produce a parallel rise in sea level of between 0.4 and 0.6 metres (OTA, 1992). The consequent threat of flooding is not limited only to the Netherlands. Some ten million of the world's population live less than three metres above sea level. Substantial areas, from inhabited Pacific atolls to the coastal areas of Egypt and Bangladesh, will become increasingly prone to flooding. If flooding is accompanied by major shifts in global atmospheric pressure, substantial alterations in global food production systems could occur. The impact of such change is difficult to predict but has to be considered as potentially enormous.

The cause of this enhancement of the greenhouse gases is readily identifiable. Over half comes from burning fossil fuel which releases carbon dioxide. A second substantial contribution comes from change in land use, particularly deforestation which accompanies the clearance of land for agriculture. A third is of chlorofluorocarbons (CFCs) used for coolants, propellants and solvents (CFCs also damage the ozone layer). In addition to these three dominant gases, there are others such as methane and nitrous oxide which are related to agriculture, but which also contribute to the enhanced greenhouse effect. Natural gas is predominantly methane and so when it is released it too adds to greenhouse enhancement. The problem, however, is that the developed and the developing world produce these gases in different quantities.

The developing world is largely responsible for changes in land use as it seeks to bring more land into productive agricultural activity: the developed world is, however, responsible for most of the production of carbon dioxide and CFCs. In the not too distant future, the newly emerging industrial countries (NEICs), including India and China, are likely to develop energy intensive industries, which will substantially increase their releases of both carbon dioxides and CFCs. Their demand for access to functions of the ecoscope is likely to increase the problems of the enhanced greenhouse effect.

Urban Air Pollution

Developing countries are urbanizing rapidly and by 2050, half the world's population will live in cities. This change of habitat is itself producing environmental problems. The combustion of hydrocarbons has led to levels of air pollution in the cities of developing countries which rank among the highest in the world. Transport is the largest contributor but the combustion of hydrocarbons, in electricity generating units and households, also add to them. Emissions of nitrogen oxides, particulates, sulphur dioxide, carbon dioxide and carbon monoxide are high. Coal is the most polluting of all the fossil fuels in terms of emissions per unit of energy consumed, particularly when fired in inefficient plants as in many developing countries.

These urban environmental problems are paralleled by more regional problems of which the greatest is acid rain. Sulphur oxides (SO_2) and nitrogen oxides, emitted by the combustion of carbon fuels, have increased acid precipitation. On a global scale, over 60 per cent of this problem is currently due to the emission of sulphur oxides, largely from coal-fired power stations. Smoke stacks work against the local dry deposition of sulphur oxides which, because of the altitude of emission, tend to be transported from the site of pollution. Prevailing meteorological conditions, notably wind direction and rainfall, tend to deposit sulphur and nitrogen oxides in mountainous areas from which they flow into fresh water systems, including reservoirs and lakes. The acidification of lakes and rivers is linked to acid precipitation and has impacts on a variety of aquatic organisms in the food chain. The growing use of coal in the Third World, particularly of high sulphur coal, will increase acid deposition unless suitable scrubbing technology is attached to coal-fired power plants. Urbanization can consequently produce not just urban but also rural pollution. More emphasis will be placed in our policy on reducing the effects of air pollution by supporting energy efficiency in the transport sector, by energy and environmental audits in industry and by increasing accessibility to environmentally benign technology in the power production sector.

Deforestation

It is a mistake to attribute large-scale deforestation to wood cutting for energy; more important processes are land clearance, grazing and bushfires. However, in local instances, fuelwood consumption can be a major contributing process particularly near settlements and in sensitive ecosystems. For example, in the arid zones of developing countries, like the Sahel, stands of trees are being destroyed or threatened by fuelwood cutting. Either there is no replanting or it is insufficient to maintain existing stocks and yields: natural recovery is also hampered by livestock grazing. The most serious problems arise not from the rural population but from the urban population, which demands a steady supply of fuelwood and charcoal. Loggers have a wide variety of resources from which to cut and will simply look elsewhere if any village or rural region tries to collect a selling price (in stumpage fees). In short, local people have no bargaining power with which to enhance their management of local resources.

Experience shows, however, that the only people who can protect and replant trees are local villagers. Planting by authorities is difficult to manage on the required scale and expensive. But as long as prices to producers remain low and levels of responsibility remain unclear, local people often have little interest in planting or protecting trees and, consequently, sustainable wood production is virtually impossible.

Charcoal

In rural areas cutting fuelwood for conversion to charcoal (essentially an urban fuel) is a major source of income and non-agricultural employment. End-users prefer charcoal to woodfuels for a number of reasons. It is cleaner, produces less smoke, is easier to handle, easier to light, involves shorter cooking times, and is free from insect attack and wetting. It is usually made by stacking wood, covering it with a layer of earth and letting it burn with a limited supply of air. The efficiency of these simple earthen kilns is low, typically ranging from 40 to 60 per cent (ETC, 1995). One bag of charcoal is equivalent in volume to ten bags of wood.

Charcoal is a "priced" fuel and because it is popular and its method of production is poor, a number of ways to promote efficiency in both production and use now exist. The introduction of more efficient kilns is one obvious move. If capital investment is made, ranging from a few hundred dollars for simple modifications to traditional kilns (ETC, 1995) to $100 000 or more for a modern continuous retort, higher energy efficiencies can be achieved (OTA, 1992).

The source of wood is also a matter for concern. Indiscriminate felling for charcoal has had detrimental effects, especially when it happens close to urban areas, where, among other things, woodland as an amenity is destroyed. One option is to identify charcoal production areas which can then be institutionalized and improved. It is a mistake to ban charcoal production altogether, as in The Gambia, because, where there is sufficient demand, banning simply leads to cross frontier transfers. This, in turn, can impoverish other areas (in the case of The Gambia it is the Cassamance region of Senegal) that have no forms of redress.

As even the best traditional rural technologies lose 60 per cent of the energy content of wood in converting it into charcoal, and as the more customary loss is around 75 per cent, urban household demand exacerbates deforestation. Even though charcoal stoves use slightly less energy than the corresponding wood stoves, in the end changing over from wood to charcoal doubles, if not triples, wood consumption.

A global problem that parallels both energy use and changes in land use is the conservation of tropical rainforests and their biological diversity. They account, very roughly, for 50 per cent of all species of flora and fauna. Since 1950, over 10 000 species have been lost largely through the destruction of tropical rainforests. However, although it does not have such an immediate impact on biodiversity, deforestation is larger in scale in semi arid and arid regions than in tropical rainforests where logging and land clearance are for agriculture, not for fuelwood.

More emphasis has to be given, in energy policies, to the sustainable management of local land-use systems in which woody biomass for energy is just one component. Energy efficiency technologies that reduce the cost and secure the supplies of energy for rural and low-income urban households must also be emphasized.

Energy and Equity

Meeting the challenge of maintaining and enhancing the ecoscope is not simply a matter of polluting less and moving from non-renewable to renewable resources, but also of equity. Solving one environmental problem can frequently lead to others and, in the end, no solution will work without greater equity in access to the ecoscope.

The operation of an expanding, open economic system in a finite closed ecoscope poses several policy issues. It is important to screen technologies to minimize ecoscope disruption, to use environmental impact (EIA) and cost-benefit (CBA) analyses and environmental profiles to outline the impact of investment on the ecoscope. But the major problem remains. It is that current energy production technologies are largely hydrocarbon based and cause significant environmental damage. Yet it is precisely these technologies that developing countries need most for their national economic development.

We have already remarked that there is a significant difference in the consumption of primary energy between developed and developing countries. The latter consume less than 28 per cent of world energy — taken together, all developing countries consume only the equivalent of 25 per cent of the US fossil energy consumption. In developing countries, changes in energy prices do not have an immediate impact on fuel consumption, because household use is fixed at a virtually irreducible level by the need to cook food.

Rural women and children pay an increasing price in time in gathering biomass fuels to secure their energy subsistence. It is commonly two to three hours per day and in some cases can be up to five hours. Poorer urban households pay an increasing cash price because, for most of them, collecting fuel is not possible as supplies around towns become more and more depleted.

A proportion of income in urban areas is spent on switching to more advanced fuels. In Addis Ababa, for example, by 1986, 70 per cent of households had switched to kerosene because wood and charcoal prices had risen. Paradoxically, as the price of energy rises, the demand does not fall. Therefore in developing countries, over the last 20 years, oil consumption continued to grow steadily, reflecting the original low consumption base, while in developed countries it varied following the movement in oil prices. This indicated both a higher volume of consumption and an ability to lower consumption through investment in energy efficiency.

Developing countries must have a right to the economic opportunities enjoyed by developed countries. For that purpose, more investment in state-of-the-art technologies that maximize efficiency, minimize environmental damage and are budget neutral, especially for poor people, is needed. Furthermore, the concentration of energy investment in urban economic centres does not encourage significant rural development without which rural resource depletion and migration to urban centres will grow.

Economics and Politics of Energy Resource Depletion
The very size of energy production and consumption technologies, and the environmental problems associated with them have made their impact global rather than local. The scale of this impact poses special problems for the costing of global environmental damage. Conventional economic analysis cannot handle the costs of pollution and of the depletion of common property resources because common property, like climate or air quality, cannot be privatized and thus are outside the market place. Different mechanisms have to be found to ensure equity in access to ecoscope both within and between nations and, in the developing world, equity is closely tied to the alleviation of poverty, which will lead to an increase in energy consumption.

Several factors in developing countries will cause the use of commercial energy to rise more rapidly than gross national product. First, the growth of urban households will result in an increase in the commercial provision of goods and services and thus in energy demand. Second, there will be a move from traditional biomass fuels to modern fuels and technologies at the very moment when they are available and affordable, especially in urban areas. Third, the building of commercial industrial and transport infrastructures will require the use of large quantities of energy-intensive material. Fourth, modern manufacturing technologies have increased the access of the poor to a range of consumer goods which demand energy (for example, radios and torches).

These factors are counter-balanced by others, which will moderate a rapid increase in energy demand. First, the high cost of developing national energy infrastructure will limit its rapid expansion except in developing countries, notably China and India, which have sufficient hydrocarbon resources to pursue such investment. Second, energy efficiency improvements worldwide will become accessible to developing countries. Third, when poverty is alleviated by economic development, structural changes will shift investment from energy-intensive infrastructure to higher value-added goods.

Energy use in developing countries will depend on how these opposing economic factors operate. At low levels of development, the first set of factors predominate while, at higher levels of development the converse is true. For rapidly industrializing countries, growth rates in energy use will be substantially slower than those in the gross national product. The challenge for energy policy-makers is to establish strategies now without being able to predict the future for which they are designed.

Increased energy efficiency will enable developing countries to destroy the direct links between increases in standards of living and increases in energy use. To date, however, the energy transition model for developing countries that seems most probable is that followed by the Soviet Union and eastern Europe where a level of industrial development, and thus a level of improved income, was built on a high per capita consumption of primary energy. This is the route that will result in environmental problems. Within developing countries, economic development is an important determinant of energy consumption, and thus of equity, but it is not the only one. Energy intensity varies enormously between and within countries. In the years immediately before 1973, global energy intensity rose, but after 1973, there was a sharp drop in developed countries which reflected the growing importance of energy efficiency and conservation not matched in developing countries. Differences in energy intensity reflect differences in urbanization, the quality of industrial structure and levels of technology.

Some projections suggest that by 2010 commercial energy consumption for developing countries could be 2.5 times higher than in 1985, suggesting a growth rate of 3.8 per cent (OTA, 1991). More conservative figures suggest that with an annual increase of 3.3 per cent, commercial consumption in developing countries will be three times higher than in 1985 while consumption of traditional fuels will grow by 25 per cent over the same period. Policies addressing the probable environmental impact of such a growth of commercial energy, which will largely be a growth in hydrocarbon consumption, will require an emphasis on models of best practice for urban energy consumption. This emphasis must include energy intensity in industry by concentrating on value-adding processes and by improving accessibility to best practice technology from developed to developing countries. Most importantly, it requires an end-use analysis of energy, where energy consumption requirements are accurately matched to energy supplies. Such an approach will limit reliance on over-engineered single supply solutions and will create space for energy efficiency improvements and an expanded use of new and renewable sources of energy. The Dutch government's policy emphasizes an end-use approach because it maximizes equity in, and access to, energy services while simultaneously minimizing environmental damage.

There is little doubt that a key issue in equity is the access of poorer households to fuel supplies. Their need for energy is irreducible but the cost in collection time or in cash has been rising over the last 20 years. Institutional support for poorer households must concentrate on minimizing the risk of fuel shortage. In rural areas, especially in the case of refugees (the most vulnerable of the vulnerable), where fuel scarcity is compounded by large local increases in population, policy must provide greater access to and control of productive resources by local people. In the case of refugee settlements in Sudan, government policy puts a ceiling on their access to resources by insisting that it should be no better than that of other local people. At the same time, the activities of commercial farmers and commercial charcoal producers have led to a great reduction in the amount of fuelwood available. Initiatives aimed at improving local fuel supplies through farm woodlands, social forestry and community forestry have, however, in some cases, been successful.

Another way of supporting the more disadvantaged in both rural and urban areas is through income support schemes that allow for the purchase of energy. In rural areas such income may be achieved by smallholder cash cropping, service industry and domestic-based manufacturing industries. Experience of Dutch supported refugee schemes in Tanzania and Sudan shows that even in the case of refugees, it is possible to achieve sustainable development within a project.

Energy and National Development

The use of different fuels in developing countries varies enormously — they use 80 per cent of biomass fuel but only 23 per cent of commercial energy. Several developing countries — China, India, Mexico, Brazil and South Africa — are among the largest energy consumers. Just three — China, India and Brazil — account for 45 per cent while, at the other end of the scale, the 50 countries of Africa use less than 3 per cent of total energy consumption in the developing world. The developing countries are expected to increase their share of global energy consumption to 40 per cent by 2020, which will account for almost 60 per cent of the global increase.

Most public investment is in electricity production and transmission, a commitment to capital expenditure that seems increasingly unsustainable. Africa alone will require US $110 billion of capital investment in energy technology by 2010, largely in the electricity sector. Such investment is unlikely to occur without substantial private capital resources.

It is not just capital investment, but also recurrent expenditure which dominates discussion of the impact of energy costs on the national economy. Energy imports are, for the non-oil producing countries, a significant factor of recurrent expenditure.

In the energy sector, the level and stability of prices are of great influence on national economies. Stable prices encourage short-term financial stability and make possible opportunities for long-term sustainable development. Commercial energy markets are dominated by oil so that, quintessentially, sustainable energy development needs a stable oil market. In the medium to long term, the long-run marginal supply price of oil is expected to be relatively constant. National, European and global policy aimed at limiting price instability in the oil market caused by political upheaval must be accompanied by questions about the real cost of energy, including the externalities of pollution, so that the global issue of carbon taxes can be addressed. The best investment in the energy sector for minimizing the impact of political and price disruption is efficiency rather than an expansion in supply lines.

The scale of future investment in the energy sector is projected as being very large. The World Bank estimates that US $125 billion (which is double current investment) is needed to supply developing countries with electricity. It also estimates that electricity currently accounts for 50 per cent of all investment; oil, including refineries, 40 per cent; and natural gas and coal 5 per cent each. Over half the cost of energy investment is in foreign exchange and only coal has low foreign-exchange costs. Financing this level of foreign capital resources will prove increasingly difficult for national economies over the next investment cycle, leading them, where resources are nationally available, to coal-fired commercial energy futures. Developing countries need support to build a policy framework that enables them to seek less energy-intensive development paths.

Energy as a Productive Factor

The productive sector of developing countries consumes between 40 and 60 per cent of commercial energy. The primary energy services are process heat and, to a lesser degree, mechanical drive. The form of energy provision is basically determined by whether industries are cottage, small factories or large-scale processing units. In developing countries, although the modern sector is the largest energy consumer, as much as 70 per cent of industrial production can be in cottage industry, which causes severe problems for energy delivery.

Process heat, ranging from low temperature heat for food processing through to high temperature processing of steel and cement, are energy demands with lower efficiencies than those obtainable in the developed world. Modern large-scale industries operate at significantly lower efficiencies in developing countries and a few energy intensive materials — steel, cement, fertilizer and paper — account for most industrial energy use. Mechanical drive is largely met by electric motors. Again, efficiencies are low because of poor maintenance, repair and rewind, as well as power variation. Energy use is dominated by the provision of basic metals and this could be the emerging energy pattern for all developing countries if a positive emphasis on energy efficiency is not pursued.

Other major sectors of energy demand are transport, residential and services. They consume slightly less energy but are nonetheless extremely important in consumption patterns. In many developing countries transport consumes more than a quarter of total commercial energy and most of it is oil derived. Although developing countries have only a small fraction of automobiles per person compared with developed countries, that fraction is growing. These automobiles are in many cases very inefficient and are a major cause of pollution. This is partly due to the "transfer of relics" from the North to the South (vehicles that would not get a sale in the North are sold or donated to developing countries), and partly due to low scrappage rates.

The increase in the private ownership of cars and the rapid rates of urbanization combine to create urban congestion, which lowers vehicle efficiency and, in turn, adds to urban air pollution. Improvements both in engine efficiency and to infrastructure could lead to greater energy efficiency. The major challenge, however, is mass public transport.

Public services include health, education, utilities and government institutions. These tend to be arranged so that the highest level and most energy consuming activities are concentrated in large urban and elite areas, particularly in capital cities, which often have public service facilities comparable to those of developed countries. These include high energy consumption for lighting, office facilities and other equipment. Electrification has been extended to the level of small towns in many places, but intensity of use in secondary institutions, (for example, small hospitals and clinics) is much less than in large administrative centres.

Most opportunities for efficient energy use in developed countries are relevant to developing countries. In particular, where energy-efficient investment reduces overall capital requirements, such investments should be made, since capital is scarce. It is difficult to achieve this because many policy instruments available to developed countries, such as rebate programmes, cannot work in developing countries where there are few fiscal mechanisms for delivering rebates to the poor. What is needed is a review of the product cycle of the entire energy system, from end use to supply, which examines the effect of improved efficiency on saving foreign exchange and in minimizing environmental damage.

It should be noted that energy efficiency, and the use of a localized resource base, together with an emphasis on the production and use of renewable resources, can lead to the development of less energy-intensive industries, which will maintain prosperity while minimizing damage to the ecoscope.

Energy and Basic Needs

Enhancing economic development and improving opportunities has not led to the eradication of poverty. Consequently, more tailor-made programmes have been developed that concentrate on basic human needs. This, it is hoped, will reduce the rate of migration from country to towns and, therefore, the cost of rapid uncontrolled urbanization.

Basic needs programmes aim to provide minimum standards of nutrition, shelter, clothing, sanitation, health, education and employment in rural areas. Energy is not specifically part of these programmes but is indirectly required for the satisfaction of these needs and it usually comes from biomass fuels. Two thirds of the world's developing population, some 2.6 billion people, live in rural areas with little access to commercial energy supplies and technologies. Biomass fuels provide the heating and cooking needs of these populations and we have already commented on some of the problems associated with them.

Traditional energy products are part of a complex, interdependent biological system not of a simple, geological resource like fossil fuels. Despite frequently being outside the commercial energy market, there are benefits and costs associated with traditional energy use. The benefits associated with the integration of biomass fuel production integrated into local land-use management systems include the maintenance of ecological stability and the provision of a range of products for food, fodder and shelter. The costs associated with deforestation are related to the environment (soil erosion, land degradation and loss of carbon sink) as well as to the time women and children spend travelling to seek energy supplies. Cooking is the single largest end-use of biomass in rural areas and responsibility for producing, collecting and purchasing fuel falls largely to women. Biomass fuels are frequently sold in urban markets and are thus sources of family income.

Investing in fuel switching in urban areas is a positive way of reducing demand for biomass fuels, particularly when the urban energy economy relies on charcoal, which is more demanding on biomass resources than burning wood. The introduction of improved cooking stoves that conserve energy is helpful, particularly when such programmes are focused on urban areas where both the fuel and the technologies are already commercialized. An emphasis on enhancing biomass fuel supplies is useful but only when such programmes have an integrated approach to total land use and to household production. It is also crucial to strengthen local organization in sharing energy conservation practices, like fire and food management techniques.

Access to biomass fuels is restricted by rules and regulations that govern the local management of common property resources. This remains a relatively unexplored area since, while customary controls have been eroded by the imposition of statutory government, government has been unable to replicate traditional resource management. Building local environmental management capacity is a central challenge if basic needs, and the parallel provision of biomass energy resources, are to be met. More attention should be given to the structure of management of natural resources at local levels, of which sustainable land-use management should form an integral part.

Women and Energy

Women not only provide the backbone of rural Third World agriculture, undertaking some 70 per cent of all farming activities, but they also dominate household energy collection, and utilization. Added to the time spent collecting wood (bundles may weigh up to 50 kilos) is an hour and a half pounding or grinding foods, and anything from one to six hours fetching water.

As land degradation spreads, especially in sensitive environments, women have to spend more hours walking greater distances to collect fuelwood. In this situation there may also be a corresponding shortage of water. This dual increase in the burden on women creates serious problems for other tasks such as planting, weeding and harvesting and this accelerates the impoverishment of women. So far it has proved difficult to design specific energy projects for women that can successfully break this vicious circle. Attaching an energy component to an ongoing women's project offers better development opportunities.

The burden on women is caused by the gender division of labour; men are largely the income generators and women largely do the unpaid, unrecognized work. Women frequently have no access to opportunities to generate income and, as a consequence, have few opportunities for purchasing energy or labour saving devices. They are not only constrained by societal traps but also by finance. In a systematic end-use approach, the views of women will be central to the design of programmes and projects in which energy is included.

Training and extension programmes in agroforestry specifically designed for women must be strengthened to include income generation and security of energy supply. To this end more support should be given to "training of trainers" programmes in local biomass production linked to the continuing training programmes for low investment agriculture.

Energy Efficiency

A central feature of an end-use energy strategy is the pursuit of cost-effective opportunities for more efficient energy use in the modern sector. Just as many of the energy efficient technologies used in industrialized countries are relevant to the modern sectors of developing countries, so also are many measures being considered for promoting the adoption of energy efficient technologies.

Improving energy efficiency is influenced by market forces and they are clearly important. A properly functioning market has a more important role in implementing end-use energy strategies than in implementing those for conventional energy. The complexities of energy end-use decision making can generally be dealt with more effectively by buyers and sellers; they know what is needed, what is affordable and what energy using devices cost to produce. The public sector is relatively bad at monitoring users' needs and preferences; besides, replacing the myriad interactions of buyers and sellers with procedures and rules invariably produces black markets. There is a clear advocative and stimulating role for NGOs here.

Nevertheless, public sector interactions in the market are needed because of market biases, market frictions and inherent market failings. Existing "market biases" in the form of price controls and various energy producer and consumer subsidies promote economic inefficiency and are slowing adjustments to a new sustainable energy economy based on real prices. Market interventions are needed to remove such biases, to create a more even-handed treatment of investments in energy supply and energy efficiency improvements.

Compared with developed countries energy efficiency investment in developing countries is low, but there are several possible interventionary policy instruments for promoting it:

- Eliminating energy supply subsidies.
- Rationalizing energy prices.
- Improving the flow of information.
- Targeting energy performance.
- Promoting comprehensive energy service delivery.
- Making finance available for energy efficiency investments

Power Output and Costs of Generation Technology

Generation technologies, of which there is a large range, must be judged by their power output and cost and both must match end-use.

Fossil fuel and hydro generation dominate all power requirements. By 1995 they will account for some 55 and 37 per cent respectively of all electricity supply in developing countries and both can be scaled down to power demands of less than 1 kW. Renewables other than hydro generation can deal with low power demands; solar and wind power are particularly suited to the purpose. Table 2.2 outlines the minimum and maximum figures for each fuel source. Actual economic performance depends on the type of technology and, especially with renewables, on local conditions. Economic capacity must also be considered against the nature of demand for base and peak electricity. Given the low demand for electricity in rural areas, generation flexibility is important, which suggests a system based on peak power, not on base-load requirements.

Table 2.2 gives a range of costs associated with different combinations of fuel-technology for electricity generation. Comparative capital costs favour fossil generation rather than renewables, but fuel, operation and maintenance costs, which together are recurrent, are higher for conventional fuels than for renewables. Of particular note is the recurrent cost of small-scale diesel generation. The comparative delivered cost per unit of electricity indicates the relative cheapness of conventional generation, with the exception of small-scale diesel generation, and the high maximum costs of all renewables except hydro generation. Comparative costs do not totally explain the dominance of grid extension and stand alone in diesel generation for rural electrification programmes. To understand the complexity of this issue, analysis of end-use demand is necessary.

Table 2.2 Costs Associated with Different Fuel-Technology Combinations for Electricity Generation

	Comparative Capital Costs* US$/kW (000's)	Comparative Fuel & O&M Costs** US cents/kWh Externalities not included	Comparative Costs of Delivered Power** US cents/kWh
Coal	1.0–2.0	2.0–4.0	5–10
Fuel Oil	0.5–1.0	3.0–6.0	9–14
Natural Gas	0.4–0.9	2.5–5.5	6–12
Nuclear	1.0–1.5	1.5–3.0	6–15
Small Diesel	0.4–1.0	8.0–30	10–80
Solar	4.0–10	0.0–1.0	9–90

Notes: * $/kW; ** cents/kW
Source: World Bank, adapted from FINESSE.

Fuel Switch and Renewable Energies

Fuel substitution and renewables (including biomass) are the joint priorities in any consideration of energy supply. Fuel substitution must be determined by end-use demands. Households, particularly those in urban areas of developing countries, must be persuaded to a switch from biomass to kerosene. In the world at large, a move from non-renewable to renewable resources and, within the hydrocarbon sub-sector, from coal to natural gas should be encouraged. Rural households will continue to depend heavily on woody biomass for their sources of energy, but our policy will promote the establishment of local small-scale generation plant for development opportunities.

The quality, reliability and durability of a small-scale electricity generation plant has often been assessed in the field, and what is apparent is that performance is largely determined by the characteristics of the site. Thus biomass-fired plant depends on the availability of biomass feedstock, micro-hydro plant needs a river, even wind generation depends on a suitable site, though to a lesser extent than the other two. Because the technologies are place dependent, they tend to rely on local construction. Biomass generation in particular and, to a lesser extent, wind generation have encouraged local manufacturing with the consequence that quality, reliability and durability have been questionable. Even with photovoltaic generation, where the modules are internationally manufactured to a high standard but parts of the system are locally made, there has been difficulty in maintaining electricity supply.

For a variety of reasons all renewable technologies are unable, from time to time, to provide continuous supply. Biomass and hydro resources are seasonal, although biomass generation can meet peak load more successfully. Wind generation is variable and is best paired with diesel generation backup, although the size and costs of the backup equipment have carefully to be considered. Solar generation varies by day, by season and with weather conditions. The product of all these technologies requires storage, essentially batteries, which increases both cost and maintenance problems.

Because renewable generation technologies are site specific, comparison between them is difficult, but photovoltaic generation is the simplest answer to the problem of rural electrification. Because the system will have been well manufactured and because it requires the least skilled servicing, it is the most reliable and durable technology. Furthermore, as its use becomes more widespread module costs are declining. However, all renewable technologies must be compared with stand-alone diesel generation and any comparison between renewable energy technologies must recognize that they are site-specific. Thus photovoltaic generation might not be the only answer for particular communities in particular places.

Policy Support

It is only during the last 20 years that most government and donor agencies have paid any attention to energy as a policy issue and the main approach during this time has been to see the energy "crisis" as a problem of supply. Diagnoses of problems and designs for their solution have both been premised on simple models of supply "gaps". Solutions have been sought by applying single technologies (whether forestry, stove technologies, individual renewables or large-scale hydrocarbons) and, with a few notable exceptions, they have failed to have a lasting impact on the problems.

Some policies (for example, kerosene subsidies) can distort the operation of energy markets and prevent the setting of real energy prices. Strategies for each energy sub-sector should be developed and, at the same time, energy planning institutions should be strengthened and reformed so creating a capacity for effective strategic implementation. There are four interrelated levels of policy support:

- The improvement of the information base on which policies are developed.
- The correction of market failures and the improved functioning of markets.
- The development of energy sector strategies.
- The strengthening of energy planning institutions.

Providing better information and removing policy distortions will create the pre-conditions for effective energy policies which need coordinating through strategies for energy sub-sectors which, in turn, are able to capture the local specificity of energy problems and opportunities. This will determine the mixes of technical packages appropriate to the enhancement of supply, of conservation and of fuel switching. It will also provide a structure for forming priorities and for institutional relationships between planning agencies and local communities.

Agroforestry and the Fuelwood Problem in Africa

Fuelwood is the issue at the centre of energy planning. That wood energy cannot be provided by planting fuelwood trees is at last being recognized. Agroforestry, in which trees are a multi-purpose resource in a land-use system, seems to provide an opportunity for addressing the problem. However, women, who are usually the wood gatherers and farmers of Africa, need to be key participants in any solution. More importantly, energy systems in urban areas need to be addressed. Many of them still rely heavily on charcoal. By encouraging a change from charcoal to fuels, which are both preferable and more easily obtained, the pressure on rural wood resources could be reduced. As we have already remarked, this transition will ease the problem of wood depletion and rural environmental degradation.

Given Africa's heavy dependence on wood for energy, the call is now for a form of forestry which will contribute to the process of sustainable development (sustainable development was characterized by the Brundtland Commission as that which is equitable and which meets the needs of the present without compromising the ability of future generations to meet their own needs). Implicit in this is a need for new forestry initiatives that contribute to a participatory, equitable, decentralized and self-sustaining process of rural development throughout Africa. Fuelwood stress is also conditioned by social and demographic trends within African countries; both overall population growth and rates of urbanization are exacerbating the problems. In particular, fuelwood policies do not fully consider the significance of urbanization processes. Urban growth rates of 10 per cent are the norm in Africa and what were rural societies are becoming increasingly urban. Population growth in rural areas affects fuelwood use in much the same way as it does other forms of resource exploitation.

However, the varying circumstances of different people and places make generalization about fuelwood stress problematic and the problems can rarely be summarized. Fuelwood use and scarcity reflect complex and variable interactions between local production systems and the environmental resource on which they are based. The significance and origins of fuelwood problems vary as much as do local environments and societies.

Given this, a number of criteria must be satisfied before a sustainable energy policy can reflect the heterogenous nature of fuelwood supply and end-use:

- Biomass resources in different areas must be measured and this will give an indication of the maximum available as potential fuel. The areas taken will equate to agro-climatic zones, which are a broad indication of land productivity.
- The characteristic rural economy, including population densities, forms of settlement and dominant types of agriculture must be identified. This will indicate the level of demand for energy and the characteristic patterns of land management.
- The socio-economic condition of the area must be described because it determines access to the resource base for fuel by different sections of the local community.
- Factors which produce significant exports of woodfuel resources, such as commercial logging and the influence of urban woodfuel and charcoal markets must be incorporated.
- Major forms of structural change that seriously affect the fuelwood situation in a locality must be analysed. They will include land colonization, demographic change and urbanization, major developments such as roads and hydroelectric power schemes and catastrophic drought or conflict.

This is a complex list of criteria, but their consideration is essential if fuelwood problems and solutions are to relate to the condition of the people experiencing fuelwood stress.

The African Fuelwood Experience
Most forestry plans in the past 15 to 20 years have treated the biomass problem simply

as one of supply and demand. It was argued that people were extracting more biomass than the environment could sustainably produce and the solution was self evident — if projected demand exceeded supply, either plant more trees or devise policies to reduce demand. As a result, foresters tried to increase tree supplies by various large-scale means like monocultural plantations, peri-urban wood lots, community wood lots and increased policing of forests and woodlands. Their object was to plant as many trees as quickly as possible. Unfortunately, and all too often, decisions to spend large sums of money planting trees have been taken without considering other options or the consequences of existing market and policy failures. Foresters have only themselves to blame for excluding options and courting failure (Van Gelder and O'Keefe, 1995).

The Kenyan Experience
In 1980, there was an attempt in Kenya to address the broad energy and development problem, particularly of fuelwood, in a systematic manner. Fuel switching was considered but, because of the comparative expense of oil, it seemed insufficiently attractive. Energy conservation was mooted but, especially for fuelwood, there were substantial limits to investment in it. Finally, the analysts looked at the possibility of expanding wood energy supplies and this led to the formulation of the Kenyan Woodfuel Development Programme (KWDP). This programme was run from the Ministry of Energy but had a level of contact with the district forestry administration.

The KWDP was focused on the Kakemega and Kisii districts of western Kenya. Being densely populated and undergoing rapid land consolidation, they were thought to be the best areas in which to explore potential models of agroforestry. Early surveys came to the striking conclusion that deforestation does not necessarily occur in densely populated areas. Quite the reverse — there is much evidence to suggest that farmers, given the necessary inputs, will increase the amount of woody biomass on their farms.

Towards Solutions
Although there has been much work in recent years on local demand for trees and tree products, it has largely been led from social science and has not addressed the issues of local production. What is urgently needed is a new form of social forestry that provides wood near where people live. This requires integrating wood into existing land-use patterns in the farming system; it requires production design for a new agroforestry.

It is important, even at the risk of repetition, to correct the three most popular misconceptions about the problem of declining wood resources. First, it is frequently assumed that deforestation is caused by commercial logging and cutting for fuelwood; this is simply not true — agricultural colonization is the major cause. Second, it is frequently assumed that forests are a primary source of woodfuel for rural people; this is wrong — in Africa over 90 per cent of biomass fuel comes from agroforestry. Third, it is assumed that rural people fell trees for domestic energy use — this happens very infrequently because woodfuel is a residue from other uses of wood in the rural economy. Quite simply, woodfuel is what is left over.

Any new agroforestry project must recognize that:

• trees can be combined with crops and/or animals in many different systems of land use;

◼ "Carrying Capacity", "Over Population" and Environmental Degradation
The Ecologist

The term "carrying capacity" originally derived from the biological sciences, where it was used to denote the optimum number of given species a specific ecosystem is able to sustain without interfering with its basic structure and stability. For global managers, it is a concept that has a particular significance because it provides a seemingly "objective" measure of how many people can survive or flourish on a particular area of land at particular levels of consumption and technology. If "carrying capacity" is exceeded, the reasoning goes, then population can be said to be "objectively" excessive relative to land, consumption and technology.

It is not as easy as all that, however, to remove the concept of "overpopulation" from the realm of moral criticism and debate. Outsiders' claims that a given area of land has a certain "carrying capacity" are open to criticism in three different ways. First, the number of people who can live on a piece of land depends largely on their culture, which determines both their needs and their ways of life. The nature and success of their farming systems, for example, cannot easily be predicted in advance on the model of outsiders' cultures. Second, the fact that the question of consumption and technology levels must be raised in any discussion of "carrying capacity" means that the normative issues of what sort of society or economy people desire cannot be evaded when talking of "overpopulation". Third, a given land area's "carrying capacity" will depend largely on what happens outside its borders: upstream deforestation, global commodity price fluctuations, greenhouse gas emissions, acid rain and so forth. Local inhabitants will always be justified in pointing out that their land could support a great many more people if damaging external influences were curbed and, on this ground, in calling into question the presumption of those partly responsible for such influences in suggesting "proper" local population levels.

This latter problem might be evaded, of course, by an attempt to determine global carrying capacity. However, this is usually acknowledged to be technically far-fetched even if the world's peoples could be induced to accept uniform global consumption levels and technology. And it would of course leave wide open the question of which local "populations" would have to be "adjusted" to meet the purported "global" requirements.

Lack of Explanatory Power

One response to such arguments is that while "overpopulation" cannot be precisely or "objectively" defined, there are at least unambiguous statistical correlations between "population" and environmental degradation on a national scale. On close examination, however, even this assertion turns out to be problematic. Malaysia, for example, although having only a tenth as many people as neighbouring Indonesia, has cleared fully 40 per cent as much forest as Indonesia has done. Central America, with a "population" density of only 57 persons per square kilometre, has cleared 410 000 square kilometres of forests, or 82 per cent of its original forest cover, while France, covering the same land area with double the number of people, has cleared less. And those who would explain the destruction of half a million square kilometres of Brazilian Amazonian forests between 1975 and 1988 in Malthusian terms "overlook the inconvenient fact that although the Amazon forms over 60 per cent of Brazilian national territory, less than 10 per cent of Brazil's population lives there".

If "population" and "population" density are poorly correlated with specific examples of environmental degradation, "population" increase is equally poorly correlated with rates of environmental degradation. Costa Rica and Cameroon, for example, are clearing their forests faster than Guatemala and Zaire respectively, despite having lower "population" growth rates. Thailand's rate of forest encroachment, similarly, has varied less closely with the rate of population increase than with changes in political climate, villagers' security, road and dam building, and logging concessions.

To confuse the issue still further, there are many instances of environmental degradation resulting from the outflow of people from a given area of land. In Africa, for example, there are many areas where fallow periods have been reduced, not because there is a shortage of land due to "population pressure" but because there is a shortage of farm labour due to urban migration. The longer a plot of cleared bush is left fallow, the more labour is required to clear it again for agriculture: hence, it makes economic (if not ecological) sense to reduce the fallow period. In such cases, the problems associated with reduced fallow periods result not from overpopulation but from local depopulation.

Exploitative Relations

Indeed, the closer one looks at the relationship between human numbers and environmental degradation, the clearer it becomes that, at root, the key issue is not simply how many? But *how is society organized*? In the case of deforestation, for example, the periods of most rapid destruction "have not necessarily been at the times when population was most rapidly expanding. They have occurred when the exploitation of subordinate groups (as well as of resources) has intensified". The halving of Central America's forest area between 1950 and 1990, for example, is due not to a "population explosion" but to the concentration of land in the hands of a limited number of rich ranchers and landowners raising bananas, cotton, coffee and cattle. Peasants have been used as land-clearers only to be pushed into the hills, where they displace others and are forced to cut yet more forest. Elsewhere, transnational corporations such as Finland's Jaakko Poyry Oy, the USA's Scott Paper, and Japan's Marubeni often supervise forest plunder, with additional destruction resulting from expropriative cattle-raising, road, hydro-electric and industrial projects.

In the Amazon, most land cleared of forest produces little in the way of food and often was not cleared for that purpose. Migration into the forests has much more to do with structural changes in the regions of emigration than with "population" growth. Thus, decline in access to land, as it occurred in northeastern Brazil, stimulated emigration. In the case of migrants from the south of Brazil, the expansion of mechanized agriculture and the flooding of enormous areas of agricultural land forced small farmers out of their holdings. Finally, the threat of violence and lack of employment have also expelled farmers from their holdings. Since more than half of all agriculturalists in Brazil rely on wage labour as well as cropping for their income, activities like mechanization, which reduce rural employment, are often as disastrous to peasants as brute expulsion from their lands.

For those who would avoid such issues, the concept of "carrying capacity" offers a welcome life belt. Seemingly objective, it depoliticizes what is a highly political issue by reducing the debate to one of mathematics. In its recommendations to UNCED on sustainable agriculture, for example, the UN Food and Agriculture Organization (FAO) argues that governments should "evaluate the carrying and population supporting capacity of major agricultural areas" and, where such areas are deemed to be "over-populated", take steps to change "the man/land ratio" (*sic*) by "facilitating the accommodation of migrating populations into better-endowed areas". Elsewhere, FAO is more candid, specifically recommending "transmigration" programmes. Peasants who have been forced onto marginal lands as a result of the best quality land being taken over for intensive export-oriented agriculture may thus be liable to resettlement because officials calculate that they are a threat to local "carrying capacity": yet does FAO consider the alternative option that ecological stress in marginal areas might be better relieved by reclaiming the best farm land for peasant agriculture. In effect, far from being a neutral and objective measure of ecological stress, carrying capacity is already being used as a means of preventing radical social change.

■ The Population Debate
Frances Moore Lappé and Rachel Shurman

What Set Off the Population Explosion?

The widely accepted explanation of what tripped the population wire in the Third World is that a rapid drop in death rates occurred without a parallel drop in birth rates. With more people living longer, but as many babies still being born, populations began to grow fast.

While a similar shift was typical of the first stage of a transition to slow population growth in the now industrial countries, what has happened in the Third World is different. The mortality decline there has been sharper than that which occurred in western Europe and the United States, and it happened against a backdrop of higher initial birth races (Teitelbaum, 1975).

What accounts for this sharp drop in deaths? Here, demographers hardly agree. Some point to the introduction of vaccines, antibiotics and pesticides from the industrial countries; others stress improvement in education, sanitation and nutrition. And why haven't birth rates declined, too? They have, but not nearly enough to prevent rapid population growth in most Third World countries. But don't be too alarmed, many population experts tell us. It is only a matter of time before a decline in birth rates will mimic the decline in death rates. The world's population will thus level off or plateau, they predict, about a century from now at about 10 billion, double the world's current population (UNFPA, 1986).

We're not so sanguine. While death rates may be brought down, at least somewhat, by imported technologies or public health initiatives, birth rates are not so easily affected. They reflect intensely personal choices in response to a host of economic, social and cultural forces. Until the forces underpinning high birth rates start to change, we doubt that it is possible to predict the timing of a human population plateau. Some demographers share our concern. "Forget plateaux" says population specialist Phillip Cutright. Such projections are likely to be "wishful thinking," he warns (personal communication, 1988). And recent data confirm Cutright's scepticism. Global population is growing faster than expected because many of the most populous nations — China, India, Pakistan, Egypt and Iran to name a few — are not following the expected pattern of a smooth and continuous fertility decline (Population Reference Bureau, 1988).

Population: What's the Problem?

To make our own analysis most clear, let us begin with a brief outline of the main schools of thought concerning the nature of the population problem. We present three alternative perspectives and then our own.

More people–no problem perspective. To some, population growth is no threat at all. To the contrary, it may actually contribute to economic development and higher living standards.

Julian Simon, author of *The Ultimate Resource*, is perhaps the best-known advocate of this position. Writing in *Science*, Simon argues that in industrial countries, additional people stimulate higher productivity (Simon, 1980). Growing populations in Third World countries also "have a positive net effect on the general standard of living" apparent only in the long term (Simon, 1980). According to Simon, productivity will be raised not only through economies of scale and larger markets, but also through the addition of more people's contributions to knowledge and technical progress (see also Simon, 1981). Simon and his supporters marshal largely historical evidence. If improvements in technology and productivity have surpassed growth in population so far, they ask, why not indefinitely?

While Simon's view is not widely accepted, his influence can be easily detected in recent mainstream pronouncements on population. In 1986, a report by the National Academy of Sciences downplayed population as a problem, stating that "concern about the impact of rapid population growth on resource exhaustion has often been exaggerated" (National Academy of Sciences, 1986).

In our view, Simon's perspective must first be rejected on ethical grounds. It implies that the impact of population growth can be judged solely by how it affects human wellbeing, ignoring any responsibility towards the integrity of the larger ecosphere. Second, its presumption that population growth is not a problem because of infinite human ingenuity to discover replacements for any depleted resource is blind to the fact that the natural world is a delicate, interacting system, not merely an emporium of separate, replaceable parts. Simon fails to consider the possibility that our efforts to support ever larger numbers is destroying that delicate environmental balance. Because we reject this perspective's first premises, we do not examine it in depth.

People-versus-resources perspective. The much more widely held view, that which has shaped popular understanding since the 1960s, stands Simon's position on its head: people are pitted against finite resources and we are fast overrunning the earth's capacity to support us. In fact, current environmental degradation and hunger suggest that in some places we have already pushed beyond the earth's limits.

This conceptualization of the problem came vividly into popular consciousness with Paul Ehrlich's *The Population Bomb*, first published in 1968. Ehrlich convinced many people that fast-growing populations meant that we had reached the earth's limits to feed people. Ehrlich (1968) wrote: "The battle to feed all of humanity is over. In the 1970s the world will undergo famines — hundreds of millions of people are going to starve to death in spite of the crash programmes embarked upon now."

In *Famine 1975!*, published the year before Ehrlich's book, William and Paul Paddock warned that catastrophe was imminent (Paddock and Paddock, 1975).

By the 1980s, emphasis within the people-versus-resources perspective was less on the danger of humanity simply running out of land to feed itself than on the destruction of the environment by expanding populations. Ehrlich's underlying assumptions have continued to hold sway in the popular consciousness. Perhaps the most widely read expression of this view today comes from the Worldwatch Institute in Washington DC. In a 1986 Worldwatch publication, Lester Brown and Jodi Jacobson describe the threat of continuing high rates of growth: "Our contemporary world is being divided in two by demographic forces.... In the... half where birth rates remain high, rapid population growth is beginning to overwhelm local life-support systems ... leading to ecological deterioration and declining living standards" (Brown and Jacobson, 1986). And, according to them, this process is already well under way in many Third World countries.

An extreme version of this perspective is found in the work of biologist Garrett Hardin. He takes the answer to the question "What is the population problem?" a step further towards strict biological determinism. As the influential economist Thomas Malthus argued in the early nineteenth century, Hardin claims that our biology drives us to reproduce at a rate faster than our resources can sustain. Without government policies to prevent it, we are destined to overrun our resource base, with hunger the tragic outcome (Hardin, 1974).

For Hardin, of immediate concern is not the threat of global food shortage, but population-caused food shortages at the national and local levels. In his view, the populations of some countries have already overrun their biological "carrying capacities". To Hardin, Ethiopia's repeated famines clinch his case (Moore Lappé, 1987). His views are now echoed by some hard-line environmentalists, like Earth First! founder Dave Foreman.

This extreme neo-Malthusian view is generally discredited. But a soft-pedalled version — still posing people against resources as the essential problem — captures considerable media attention and dominates the popular understanding of the problem today.

Much of our prior work, especially *Food First and World Hunger: Twelve Myths*, is a refutation of this still-influential resources-versus-people perspective. We demonstrate the illogicality of seeing population as a root cause of hunger when in so many cases population density and hunger are not demonstrably related. China, for instance, has only half as much cropped land per person as India, yet Indians suffer widespread and severe hunger while the Chinese do not. Sri Lanka has only half the farmland per person of Bangladesh, yet when effective government policies kept food affordable, Sri Lankans were considerably better fed than Bangladeshis. Costa Rica, with less than half of Honduras' cropped acres per person, boasts a life expectancy — one indicator of nutrition — 14 years longer than that of Honduras and close to that of the industrial countries (Urban and Vollrath, 1984; World Bank, 1985; Kissinger, 1984). And Cuba, which leads the Third World in life expectancy, low infant mortality rates and good nutrition, has a population density similar to Mexico's, where hunger is rampant.

This lack of a clear link between population density and hunger (highlighted in Table 3.1) is a strong rebuttal to the people-versus-resources conception of the problem. Many other factors beyond sheer numbers obviously determine whether people eat adequately; among them are whether or not people have access to land to grow food, or have jobs providing them with money to buy it.

The same simplistic formulation must be rejected when it comes to environmental destruction. An obvious example is the ecological havoc now being wrought in the Brazilian Amazon. The slash-and-burn agriculture of Brazilian peasants often gets the blame. But if land in Brazil were not the monopoly of the few — with 2 per cent of the landowners controlling 60 per cent of the arable land — poor Brazilians would not be forced to settle in the Amazon, destroying the irreplaceable rain forest. And surely the logging and cattle ranching, also destroying rain forests, reflect not population pressure but market demand for meat and wood by better-off consumers, largely in the industrial countries.

Table 3.1 *Hunger and Population Density*
(acres of cropland* per person in 1980, selected countries)

Population Density	Significant Hunger		Less Hunger	
High	Burundi	.070	Singapore	.007
	Bangladesh	.25	Japan	.10
	El Salvador	.37	South Korea	.14
	Haiti	.38	China	.25
	Rwanda	.47	Israel	.26
			Mauritius	.28
			North Korea	.31
			Sri Lanka	.36
Moderate	Philippines	.50	Venezuela	.54
	India	.60	Costa Rica	.54
	Guinea	.72	Malaysia	.76
	Mexico	.85	Cuba	.80
	Burkino Faso	.93		
	Thailand	.93		
	Nigeria	.93		
Low	Honduras	1.15	Hungary	1.23
	South Africa	1.17	Chile	1.24
	Brazil	1.24	Uruguay	1.61
	Afghanistan	1.28	United States	2.07
	Angola	1.29	Argentina	3.11
	Chad	1.68		

* Cropland consists of arable land and land in permanent crops.
Source: Adapted from Urban and Vollrath (1984).

The social perspective. Fortunately, over the past two decades, an outline has emerged of a strikingly different answer to the question, "What is the problem?" It draws on the research of scores of anthropologists, sociologists and economists. This newer perspective has taken hold in such varied institutions as the World Resources Institute, the Population Reference Bureau, the UN Fund for Population Activities and the World Bank. In the 1980s, some from the food-versus-resources perspective, including the Worldwatch Institute, acknowledged the findings of the social scientists.

The social perspective takes a look beneath the threat of populations overrunning resources to ask why Third World populations are growing so fast, pointing to a complex interaction of economic, social and cultural forces that keeps Third World fertility high. They include the low status of women, the high death rates of children and the lack of old-age security.

This perspective presents a powerful challenge to the people-versus-resources view in which growing populations deplete per capita resources, leading to hunger and environmental degradation. In the social perspective it is the realities of poverty that lead to both rapid population growth and hunger. High fertility becomes an effect more than a cause of poverty and hunger.

The power-structures perspective. Building on the previous work of the Institute for Food and Development Policy, in this report we seek to synthesize crucial insights emerging from this social perspective, while pushing its analysis still further.

Peeling away another layer, we ask what lies behind the poverty and insecurity keeping birth rates high. In answering, we add a critical dimension without which we believe it is impossible to understand population patterns: power. By this we mean, very concretely, the relative ability of people to have a say in decisions that shape their lives, from those decisions made at the family level to those that are international in scope.

How society distributes power determines which human rights are acknowledged and protected. We find it most fruitful to view the varied forces keeping birth rates high as aspects of a systematic denial of essential human rights — understood to include not only political liberties, but access to life-sustaining resources and to educational and economic opportunity.

In our common search for solutions, we challenge all who are beginning to grasp the true social — rather than biological — roots of rapid population growth to follow through on the logical consequences of this deeper analysis. Unfortunately, it is in defining solutions that the promising social perspective falls flat. It describes the link between poverty and high fertility, but it fails to confront the forces that generate and perpetuate poverty.

The consequences are momentous. Ignoring the social roots of hunger while still trying to reduce birth rates leads almost inexorably to more coercive birth control technologies and programmes that jeopardize people's health and self-determination.

Finally, we call for a shift in the entire debate about the population problem to incorporate insights emerging from environmentalists and from the land stewardship movement. Drawing on ancient insights from diverse cultures, they point to our much larger responsibility. We must halt human population growth not just to ensure the wellbeing of humanity but to restore the interdependent biotic community in which we human beings must learn to see ourselves as members not masters.

References
Brown, L and J L Jacobson (1986) "Our Demographically Divided World", *WorldWatch*, Paper no 74, Washington, DC
Cutright, Phillip (1988) Personal communication. Cutright is with the Department of Sociology, Indiana University, Bloomington
Ehrlich, P (1968) *The Population Bomb*, Ballantine Books, New York
Hardin, G (1974) "Living on a Lifeboat", *BioScience*, 24, pp561–68

Kissinger Commission Report (1984) *Report of the National Bipartisan Commission on Central America*, Washington, DC

Moore Lappé, F (1987) Views expressed in televised debate, July

National Academy of Sciences (1986) Working Group on Population Growth and Economic Development, *Population Growth and Economic Development: Policy Questions*, 17, Washington, DC

Paddock, W and P Paddock (1975) *Famine 1975!*, Little, Brown & Company, Boston

Population Reference Bureau (1988) News Release, 28 April

Simon, J (1980) "Resources, Population, Environment: An Oversupply of False Bad News", *Science*, 208, 27 June, 1434

—— (1981) *The Ultimate Resource*, Princeton University Press, NJ

Teitelbaum, M S (1975) "Relevance of Demographic Transition Theory for Developing Countries", *Science*, 188, 2 May, pp420–25

UN Fund for Population Activities (1986) *Annual Report*, UNFPA, New York

Urban, F and T Vollrath (1984) *Patterns and Trends in World Agricultural Landuse*, Table 2, US Department of Agriculture, Economic Research Service, Foreign Agricultural Economic Report no 198, Washington, DC

World Bank (1985) *World Development Report*, Table 1, 174, Oxford University Press, New York

The Politics of Population Policies
Mira Shiva

There are growing numbers of people who view population policies as dangerously close to being racist, sexist and imperialist, as well as anti-poor. These individuals and groups are equally concerned about the health of the nation and the health of its people and are asking some extremely uncomfortable questions for which there are no easy answers. They want to know why so many corporate giants sit on the board of the International Planned Parenthood Federation — representatives of Dupont Chemicals, US Sugar Corporation, General Motors, Chase Manhattan Bank, International Nickel, Marconi, RCA, Xerox and Gulf Oil. They want to know why population policies and research in fertility control are supported by the defence wings of certain countries and why population is seen as a "security threat" by them, requiring "stringent action, bordering on subtle coercion of national governments and, through them, of their people — which in almost every case happen to be the women". They say, if stringent population policy was an anti-poverty measure, then those countries in Latin America which have had 80 per cent of their women sterilized should have begun to lead a qualitatively better life, rather than become poorer and more deprived. There should have been fewer poor and fewer street children in Brazil, which brought down its birth rate by 50 per cent within 20 years — something its northern neighbours took several centuries to accomplish.

Hunger, poverty and national indebtedness have worsened dramatically for most Third World countries. Denied social security, the poor in these countries continue to look to their children to provide labour and social security, especially in agrarian societies. Consequently, they look upon solutions that are "good for them", coming from outside, with doubt and suspicion. For those involved in health work, population control policies have been a double tragedy, first because they failed to meet women's contraceptive needs and second because they eclipsed other necessary health care work.

India was the first country in the developing world to formulate its national population policy in 1951 with the First Five Year Plan. It was centrally planned, financed and monitored, and implemented at the state and local levels in a typically top-down manner. It did not require the statistical evidence provided by the Planning

Commission's mid-term evaluation report to demonstrate that the policy was a failure; recipients of the service had been saying all along that it was not meeting their needs. The predictable bureaucratic response was to change the nomenclature from "family planning" to "family welfare" and "maternal and child health". But the strategies, attitudes and methodology with regard to family planning and therefore the treatment of women, remained unchanged. Unfortunately, no one was really listening to the people. After all, foreign experts' solutions are always right, especially when they are handed out with funds. In their view, women were prone to breeding like rabbits. and therefore their fertility had to be curbed.

How different the scenario would have been had the obvious been recognized at the outset: that female literacy, the guarantee of a minimum wage, and social and political awareness, especially in relation to women's status, have a great deal more to do with opting for a small family norm than do technology-centred, coercive population control programmes. Where the former are not ensured and where women are subordinate in everything, from access to food, education and skill development to freedom in decision-making, equal wages and access to productive resources, birth rates are always higher. They are high when the survival of children is not ensured, when there is a repressive compulsion to produce male children, when female children do not count. "Demographic fundamentalism" is what Ashish Bose calls the craze for male children. When women have no easy access to safe and effective contraception and absolutely no control over their fertility or sexuality, the freedom not to conceive is not in their hands: they do not have the right to say "No". It is ironic and tragic that brain-washed, insensitive or desensitized health workers should mouth slogans that hold women "guilty" of producing too many children when the women themselves have had little or no say in matters related to conception.

No one cared to listen to what the women had to say — listening with sympathy to their problems and constraints was not part of the population policy. Had those whose hearts bleed for the soaring population of India cared to listen, they would have recognized the need to strengthen the hands of women (educationally, economically and socially) early enough so that they could be helped to make choices about conception and contraception.

The insensitivity and dehumanization of the programme can be seen in its almost total neglect of all other aspects of women's health problems. The incidence of gynaecological problems — trichomoniasis, moniliasis, acute chronic pelvic inflammatory disease, sexually transmitted diseases of the cervix and urinary tract infection — is significant. A community-based study by Drs Rani and Abhay Bang (1989) carried out in Ghadhcharoli, a tribal district in Maharashtra, found that 92 per cent of women were suffering from gynaecological diseases, 52 per cent with symptoms including pain, discomfort, leucorrhea and dyspareunia (pain during sexual intercourse); other health problems related to child-bearing, nutritional deficiencies, communicable diseases and infections also seemed to merit no concern. Only fertility receives sustained attention.

It is well known that maternal mortality in India is shockingly, embarrassingly high, worse than in many poorer nations. It is also well known that 20 per cent of it is related to iron deficiency anaemia and its complications. Most causes of maternal mortality are preventable. Why is it then that women continue to be poorly nourished and to die during childbirth? Is childbirth the cause of death, or is the failure to diagnose, prevent and treat the reasons for maternal mortality (all connected with women's status and their access to food, education and health care) responsible? High maternal mortality is just another symptom of a deep-rooted, widely prevalent and socially accepted gender bias which begins at birth and continues until death. Now, with amniocentesis and pre-natal sex determination, it can be seen even prior to birth. If all the money spent on family planning, where "target setting" resulted in manipulated "target meeting" attempts and where the magic of incentives linked with sterilization made even conscientious health workers neglect spacing methods and other aspects of health care, had been used more judiciously to meet women's needs, the results would have been more encouraging. The focus on meeting targets led to large-scale corruption; statistics were concocted. Family planning camps carried out as many tube ectomies as possible, without after-care or accountability, leaving women with complications and a great deal of dissatisfaction. This in itself turned women against sterilization and was far more influential than all the propaganda, including the money incentive.

As a consequence of this misguided policy, not only were women deprived of much needed health care, they were also denied the knowledge and provision of other non-incentive-related and non-terminal spacing methods that were sorely needed by them and by the nation. It is not surprising that when they began to recognize the lack of genuine concern or interest in solving their health problems and experienced only aggressive and sometimes subtly coercive manipulation, they became alienated from the health care system. No one really cared about how the family planning programmes were run, how satisfied the recipients were and what problems they faced. In such a situation, the failure to achieve any significant drop in the birth rate was only to be expected.

According to Ashish Bose the major reasons for the failure of the family planning programme have been (i) undesirable foreign orientation; (ii) monopoly on the part of bureaucrats; (iii) monopoly on the part of the central government; (iv) sole concern for quantitative targets and their achievement, irrespective of their impact on birth rate; and (v) neglect of women's health. Who should be held responsible for the billions of rupees wasted on this futile exercise, undertaken with the guidance of foreign experts and tied foreign aid? If it were just a question of waste, it might have been explained away: what is regrettable is that a sensitively conceived programme, which could have met the genuine contraceptive needs of many women, was never allowed to take shape. The involvement of women is necessary for the success of any programme like this, especially if the very people on whom its successful implementation depends have been alienated by target chasers (who should have been healthcare providers). The loss has to be calculated in more than just monetary terms. The social costs of this misadventure have been tremendous. If our health services had addressed women's health problems and their genuine contraceptive needs, women today would have been the greatest supporters of a humane and sensitively implemented family planning programme. It is the failure of our programmes, policies and governments to respond to their concerns that has made women refuse to participate in a 40-year-old attempt to regulate their fertility.

The Myth of Choice
In a society in which a woman has no choice about when and to whom she gets

married, when and how many times she conceives, or even how much she should eat while she is pregnant or lactating, and in which she is in no position to avail herself of minimal rest from strenuous work in the terminal stages of her pregnancy, does she really have any choice regarding contraceptive methods? Can she be expected to make an informed decision when she has no access to information, when often the only alternative open to her is sterilization?

A powerful deterrent to using commonly prescribed, non-terminal methods of contraception has been the serious lack of accessible healthcare. None of the many thousands of women in whom Dalkon shields had been inserted could seek advice or compensation for serious complications, simply because they had no access to their own medical records. Again, when roughly 50 per cent of our people live below or on the poverty line and are nutritionally deficient and prone to infection, the insertion of IUCDs into women with gynaecological infections often causes chronic pelvic inflammatory diseases. These in turn can cause adhesions in the Fallopian tubes, which may result in infertility, ectopic pregnancies and so on. When the number of women involved runs into several millions the potential magnitude of the problem is self-evident.

Although policy advisors, policy makers and health officials responsible for implementation utter the usual reassuring rhetoric on the importance and safety of the various technologies, actual experiences belie their promises. The apparently "successful" vasectomy camps of Kerala, when repeated in Uttar Pradesh, led to tetanus deaths and had to be abandoned: the laparoscopic method of female sterilization, considered a "revolutionary step" by our national family planning programme, led to callous over-use of this technology. Air, pumped through bicycle pumps, was used to inflate the abdomen, rather than carbon dioxide. The question then arises: will the use of newer contraceptive technologies be caring, sensitive and objective or will the same callousness prevail because it is intrinsic in a programme that has failed, from the outset, to consider the social reality of our people and their basic need for treatment with care and dignity?

This leads us to a related question. Why is most contraceptive research aimed at women? Why is it that when recognition of the hazards of hormonal contraceptives has led to lower and lower doses of hormones in contraceptive pills in the North, long-acting injectable contraceptives are considered safe and effective for anaemic, malnourished, infection-ridden underweight women in the South? If a woman in the North voluntarily chooses such a contraceptive, hers may be considered an informed choice. She is usually in good health and if she happens to develop complications, she has access to follow-up diagnosis and proper treatment. At the best of times, this cannot be assumed for the majority of women in the South. Significant menstrual problems are a recognized side-effect of long-acting hormonal contraceptives; such blood loss in an already severely anaemic woman can compound the problem considerably.

Similarly, what effect would the contraceptive pill have on a foetus if it were given to a pregnant woman? The teratogenic effects of hormones have been recognized and it is unlikely that they are insignificant in the case of long-acting hormonal contraceptives. Fears have been raised by women's organizations and health and consumer groups about an excessive preoccupation with meeting targets without due warning about side effects.

Objections have been raised to the conducting of trials in violation of the Helsinki Declaration of 1964, which demands informed consent and guides physicians in biomedical research involving human subjects. Public interest litigation has been filed in the Supreme Court of India by several women's organizations, which felt that the bias underlying studies undertaken without full ethical clearance would definitely lead to one-sided results, which would then in turn form the basis of family planning policy-making.

If growing population is a major health problem, then the hugeness of the market for new reproductive technologies is staggering. It is little wonder that many pharmaceutical companies have been heavily involved in researching contraceptive technology.

Public memory is short, but we would do well to remember the case of Dr Michael Briggs, consultant to the World Health Organization and actively involved in the preparation of a technical report series on female sex hormones. Dr Briggs testified to the safety of hormonal contraceptives, thus obliging the pharmaceutical companies in whose pay he was. Dr Isobel Gal, on the other hand, who in 1967 had showed the link between teratogenesis and hormonal pregnancy tests and warned about the effect of hormonal preparations in pregnancy on the unborn foetus, had her research work abruptly stopped because it was a threat to vested interests and the rapidly increasing hormonal preparations market. She was hounded, criticized and belittled, her work was discredited, but her long and lonely battle warned others involved with women's issues, consumer rights, health and human rights of the danger of using hormones in pregnancy.

Thalidomide was supposed to be safe for women and unborn babies, as was dimethyl stilboestrol. No one expected children to be born without arms and legs as a result of the use of the former, daughters to develop adenocarcinoma of the vagina in young adulthood, sons with abnormalities in the testes, or the women themselves to develop breast and cervical cancer years later.

The question is not merely one of side effects: it has to do with denial of information; about who benefits and who loses when decisions are made regarding certain technologies; about who controls them and who is controlled by them; who pays in terms of money and who in terms of health; who carries out and who sponsors the research. If the safety of certain technological options is being challenged and increasingly subjected to external control, it is for good reasons. Experience has shown that if provided with unbiased information and safe and effective alternatives, women avoid technologies that are hazardous to their health. It has often been said that potentially hazardous contraceptives are less hazardous than childbirth; such a sentiment can only succeed in perpetuating the failures of yesteryear.

If we are serious about an effective decrease in population growth then the approach to the problem has to be more comprehensive and rational. Technological fixes alone will not solve the problem. After all, why have anti-TB drugs not controlled tuberculosis or anti-malarials not eradicated malaria? And why have the great Green Revolution and the presence of food reserves not succeeded in removing malnutrition and hunger?

Reference
Bang, Abhay and Rani (1989) *The Lancet*, 14 June

Stabilizing Population: The Biggest Challenge
John Rowley and Johan Holmberg

Population Growth and the Environment
One of the most confusing and contentious aspects of the population issue is the relative importance of population growth as a factor in sustainable development.

It is unfortunate, but understandable, that the debate about population has become polarized on ideological grounds. On the one side there are those motivated by lingering Malthusian fears of human populations swamping the Earth and swarming over national borders. On the other there are those who see such concerns as diverting attention from radical political, economic and social reforms. Yet others have religious or other fears over the issues of family planning and women's rights.

Because population is usually seen as a problem for developing countries — where 95 per cent of the projected 3.2 billion growth in numbers by 2025 is expected to take place — the contribution of developed countries' populations to environmental problems such as waste and pollution is sometimes overlooked. It has been calculated, for example, that the average Swiss pours 2000 times more toxic waste into the environment than the average Sahelian farmer (Pradervand, 1991). If levels of waste and consumption do not change, the 57 million extra Northerners expected during the 1990s will pollute the Earth more than the extra 911 million southerners (Harrison, 1992).

Fortunately, there is a growing consensus that it is unhelpful to take up polar positions on population. As long ago as 1984, at the International Population Conference in Mexico City, governments agreed that population and development problems should be tackled as closely interrelated ones (Rowley, 1984). In terms of environmental impact, *population* is now more clearly seen as a multiplier of the interaction between *consumption per person* and the *technologies* to supply that consumption and dispose of the waste (Ehrlich and Ehrlich, 1991). This relationship can be described by the model $I = P \times A \times T$, where I is environmental impact, P is population, A affluence (or per capita consumption) and T technology.

According to Barry Commoner, technology will often be the major actor in this equation. He has calculated, for example, that in measuring the causes of pollution from nitrates, cars and electricity in 65 developing countries, between 1970 and 1980, population was a less important factor than technology, though it was, nevertheless, responsible for between 24 and 31 per cent of the increase in pollution (Commoner, 1989). Others maintain that population is frequently a crucial factor. It has, for instance, been argued that population growth at 1.9 per cent a year from 1950 to 1985 was a major factor in the increase of global carbon dioxide emissions from 2349 million tonnes to 6793 million tonnes, an annual increase of 3.1 per cent (Harrison, 1992).

In the case of agriculture, increased population will frequently lead to new technologies that allow for greater productivity without necessarily damaging the land. But in some situations new technology may not be affordable or easy to apply. One situation is where slash-and-burn farming is common. This is a form of rotational cultivation that can be highly sustainable if population density is low and if there is no pressure to produce crops for export. It is particularly suitable for tropical upland areas with low soil fertility. Unfortunately, in many regions of the world, increased population densities and competition for scarce forest resources have undermined the system. A huge influx of migrants into hills and mountains in Vietnam, Indonesia and the Philippines has shorted the rotational cycle and prevented forest regeneration (Rambo, 1990). Elsewhere, pioneering slash-and-burn, which clears plots of primary forest and uses them intensively until the fertility is destroyed, is also unsustainable. In large areas of Africa, increased use of land once allowed to lie fallow for several years has led directly to deforestation, loss of species, loss of soil fertility and increased erosion.

There is no doubt that population has had a major impact on deforestation in developing countries. In the 15 years to 1986, forest and woodland shrank by 125 million hectares, while the farmed areas increased by 58.7 million hectares. A similar amount of land was used up by houses, factories and roads, while pasture increased by 7.9 million hectares (FAO, 1987). In the same period, population in developing countries grew by 2.2 per cent a year, perhaps accounting for some four-fifths of the loss of forest cover (Harrison, 1992). Along with the loss of trees has gone some of the protection against erosion, since not everywhere will adequate manure or compost have been applied to make up for the loss of organic content in the soil, nor action taken to compensate for loss of the holding action of roots on sloping land. And with the loss of trees goes loss of species.

But if population is an important factor in environmental degradation and the perpetuation of poverty, it is only one factor among many. Those who argue that unequal landholdings are a major factor in forcing poor people on to a marginal land are quite right — especially in Latin America.

In countries such as Brazil and Guatemala, the unequal distribution of land is a more important cause of severe pressure on marginal land than an overall land shortage (Thiesenhusen, 1989). Poverty itself is a cause of much resource damage — forcing the poor and landless to move into forest lands, to use marginal land or to deplete inshore fisheries. Moreover, many of the pressures on developing countries' resources come from the developed world, which extracts massive amounts of hardwoods, cash crops, meat and minerals to feed its often wasteful appetites.

Poverty, low agricultural prices and appalling communications often prevent poor farmers from making the investments or applying the technologies that would enable them to increase yields to feed increased numbers. Some causes of poverty stretch back to bankers in Washington, London or Geneva, who hold the purse-strings on national debts, or to corrupt governments nearer home. Population, nevertheless, remains a fundamental factor in the environmental impact equation, whatever the level of consumption or technology.

Slowing population growth could, for example, play a major role in slowing carbon dioxide emissions from the developing countries, which on present trends will grow from 0.8 tons to 1.67 tons per person by 2025. Nafis Sadik, the executive director of the United Nations Population Fund, has pointed out that if the UN's low rather than medium population projection could be achieved, this would reduce emissions in the year 2025 by 1.3 billion tonnes — enough to offset 84 per cent of present deforestation rates (Sadik, 1990). A summary of global population trends is provided in Box 3.1 below.

Box 3.1 POPULATION: THE FACTS

World population has more than doubled from 2.5 billion in 1950 to 5.4 billion today. The fundamental reason for this increase is the continuing fall in death rates, which has not been accompanied by an equivalent fall in birth rates.

According to the United Nations medium variant, world population will reach 10 billion by 2050 and level out at about 11.6 billion towards the end of the twenty-second century. This assumes that developing world fertility will be at replacement level of just over two children per women by 2050. But even if that were achieved today world population would still grow to 8.4 billion before stabilizing. The medium-high projection puts population at 12.5 billion, the medium-low at 7.8 billion by the middle of the next century.

The rate of population growth peaked in the late 1960s and is now about 1.7 per cent. But the annual additions will peak some time towards the end of the decade at around 100 million and then slowly decline. Nearly all these additional people will live in the developing world and it is projected that over 80 per cent of the increase in these countries up to the year 2025 will be in urban areas.

Around 37 per cent of people in developing countries are under 15 years of age and as they reach sexual maturity their fertility will have a major impact on future population growth.

Fertility in the developed world is below replacement level of 2.0 to 2.1 births per woman. Only the momentum of unbalanced age distribution and immigration keeps population growing.

Slowing population growth is conceivably the biggest challenge facing development planners in the Third World. The necessary policies are complex and slow acting, as those who have been attempting to include them in national conservation strategies have found. In Pakistan, where population has grown from 30 million to 114 million since 1950 and threatens to reach 200 million by 2010, it is now realized that the best hope is merely to delay the achievement of that total by six to ten years (Box 3.2). But if that can be done, the time can be used to ease the pressures on the cities and phase in other development and distribution strategies. And there is a chance that another fateful doubling to 400 million might be averted. Where population growth rates have been brought down sharply, as in Thailand or Korea, the benefits in per capita social investment and reduced pressure on the environment are already being felt.

Box 3.2 *PAKISTAN: A CONSERVATION STRATEGY*

Many countries have begun work on a National Conservation Strategy (NCS) based upon the model of the World Conservation Strategy *published in 1980 and its successor* Caring for the Earth: A Strategy for Sustainability *(IUCN, UNEP and WWF, 1991). But few strategy documents have incorporated population factors as well as the Pakistani NCS, coordinated by the IUCN office in Karachi.*

This recently completed report states that it may be possible for the country, with a present population of 114 million, to accommodate 200 million people — the number expected to live there around the year 2010 — by adopting the suggested sustainable development programmes. But, the report says:

there is no possibility of accommodating the 400 million people projected to be living in this country by 2035–40 if existing trends in population growth continue. If this is allowed to occur, Pakistan will become an international charity case, like Haiti, Ethiopia, Sudan and Bangladesh — dependent on the goodwill of others, with no realistic opportunity to improve the lot of its people and no expectations other than a continuing decline in living standards for the vast bulk of them.

(IUCN, UNEP and WWF, 1991)

The report then charts out three broad options available to policy-makers "faced with this inexorable momentum of population growth". The first of these is to continue on the current path with no overt political commitment to population planning and low levels of funding for a "population welfare programme". The result: not much slowing in the march to 200 million people by the year 2010.

The second option would involve firm political support for fertility reduction and for upgrading the status of women, aided by a multisectoral programme which significantly shifts funds to social sectors, such as education and health.

The third option would follow the second path but add on a policy to sustain the natural resource base. Key items in this policy would support out-migration from the fragile ecological areas such as uplands, rangelands and deserts, and retention of populations in the more robust canal-irrigated areas. This in turn would allow a sustainable rate of urbanization.

Such a policy, says the report, could give Pakistan an extra six to ten years before a population of 200 million is reached and would have "enormous distributional and environmental consequences". It would also increase the likelihood that food needs could be met in most regions of the country.

The NCS of Pakistan suggests setting specific targets for fertility reduction, which would bring average family size down from 6.5 children to half that over 20

---

years — "an enormous but not impossible task". It would like to see a return to the 1981 levels of population in the fragile ecological zones through out-migration — though it admits this will not be possible in rapidly growing regions such as Baluchistan where there is no tradition of emigration.

The report also suggests a target for population retention in the fertile irrigated areas of at least 40 per cent. One way to do this would be to make the villages more inviting to stay in — with better health facilities, better water supplies, a paved market road and a reliable source of electricity. In addition, it supports the idea of developing agriculture-based rural industries.

Whether Pakistan can develop the political will and administrative capacity to implement such a plan is open to question. However, integrated planning of this kind would be an essential first step towards a pattern of sustainable development in the country.

The same might be said of China, though in that case there is widespread agreement that population has already grossly overshot the environmental carrying capacity of the country. According to Dr Qu Geping, vice-chairman of the Environmental Protection Commission and administrator of the National Environmental Protection Agency, studies show that, based upon China's natural resources and the level of its science and technology, the country's 9.6 million square kilometres can appropriately support about 700 million people. However, this limit is now exceeded by 400 million people and may be exceeded by 600 million by the end of the century. According to Dr Qu, "a large number of our environmental problems result directly or indirectly from the pounding of population increase". These include deforestation, grassland degradation, desert encroachment, water resource shortage and waste of mineral resources (Qu Geping, 1989). In fact, China's total cultivated area has fallen by 17 million hectares since 1957 and in nine provinces there is less than 0.067 of a hectare per person, below what is necessary for self-sustaining agriculture. But the situation would have been much worse if China had not managed to bring its total fertility rate down from an average of 5.8 children in the 1970s to 2.4 children in the late 1980s (Ni Shaoxiang, 1989). The official policy of levelling out the population at 1.4 to 1.5 billion some time in the next century looks over-ambitious, but the nightmare of 2 billion people crowded on to a shrinking resource base has been averted.

Population Planning: Lessons from Experience

One of the lessons from such examples is that action in countries with too rapid population growth needs to be taken urgently. Because policies take time to achieve results and because population growth feeds on itself, it is imperative not to delay. But what policies should be pursued and how should they relate to other actions to conserve the environment, to tackle poverty and to sustain development? It is here that the lessons of successful population planning have much to offer. There need be no conflict, and there are potentially strong synergies between what we now know must be done to slow population growth and what will also alleviate poverty, improve the lives of women and children and empower communities to act in their own interest.

The particular nexus of activities necessary to slow population growth rates was well described in the *State of the World's Children 1991* report by UNICEF (1991). This argued that four broad factors work together to bring about the transition to lower birth rates: economic and social progress improvements for women, family planning programmes and reduced infant and child deaths. These four factors act together "in a cat's cradle of synergisms". For example, "women's advancement (and especially secondary education) makes family planning more likely; family planning reduces both child deaths and child births; slower population growth can assist economic progress; economic progress can lead to lower birth rates". All these factors acting together will exert a far greater downward pressure on birth rates than any one of them acting alone. The link between the level of child deaths and the take-up of family planning is especially strong. Few countries have a rate of acceptance of family planning beyond 35 per cent of couples in the child-bearing age as long as under-five mortality rates remain much above 100 per 1000 births. It is equally uncommon to find under-five mortality rates below 100 if family planning acceptance remains much below the 35 per cent mark.

"In the context of overall development", the report says,

> all of these basic factors in fertility decline — improvements in the lives of women, reduced child deaths and the availability of family planning — are important in themselves. All of them make a direct contribution to improving the lives of millions of people; the fact that they also make a strong synergistic contribution to solving the population problem and that they can all be accomplished at a relatively modest cost, adds up to what should be an irresistible case for simultaneous action on all these fronts in the decade ahead.
>
> (UNICEF, 1991)

In its 1992 report UNICEF stresses, particularly, the special benefits of "the responsible planning of births" which it calls "one of the most effective and least expensive ways of improving the quality of life on earth". Indeed, it argues that family planning could bring more benefits to more people at less cost than any other single technology now available to mankind. It could save the lives of perhaps one-quarter to one-third of the 500 000 women who now die every year from causes related to pregnancy and giving birth. It could prevent many if not most of the more than 50 000 illegal abortions which are now performed on women *every single day* and which result in the deaths of 150 000 young women every year. In addition, it could not only save the lives of several million children each year — the majority of whom die from preventable "high risk", badly spaced and timed births — but also significantly improve the nutritional health and quality of live of children throughout the developing world (UNICEF, 1992).

Equally pertinent is the importance of environmental improvements in the nexus of factors which, interacting together, can achieve a sustainable future. Safe, sufficient and affordable water supplies, sanitation, sustainable farming technologies, healthy low-cost housing, affordable sources of fuel whose use does not imply unhealthy levels of indoor air pollution: these are all part of a package of basic needs which will help child survival, improve living standards and create the conditions under which population policies and transition to the small family norm can be brought about.

That still leaves open the question of how, in the real world, these changes can be encouraged. In much of Africa and Latin America investments in social sectors such as health and education have been falling. In India some 250 million people live in extreme poverty (World Bank, 1990). In Mexico, per capita income fell by 9 per cent in the 1980s while the working population grew by 3 per cent every year. Overall income disparities between rich and poor countries are widening. In 1976, the countries classified by the World Bank as low income, the poorest countries, on average had a per capita income of only 2.4 per cent of the per capita income of countries defined as high income; in 1982 the figure was 2.2; and in 1988 it had fallen to 1.9.

This situation calls for fundamental changes in policies to bring about a fairer relationship between rich and poor — at a national as well as the international level. It calls for agreements and incentives to deal with the global environmental threats such as climate change and the loss of biodiversity. The political will must be found by governments to increase the priority given to social investments in people and in conservation. Issues of education, health and housing, of land reform, soil conservation, clean water and sanitation must come higher up the agenda. As will be argued below, a new morality of consumption has to be found. But the one essential investment will be in people themselves.

There is now plenty of evidence in this book and elsewhere that the empowerment of people to take as much charge as possible of their own environment and their own common needs is the only way forward to truly sustainable development. Empowerment, the active involvement of the beneficiaries of development in the design and implementation of activities intended to improve their welfare, has in preceding chapters been cited as an essential ingredient of primary environmental care. As shown below, there is plenty of evidence to suggest that empowerment, particularly of women, is equally important in bringing about successful family planning services in that country and has halved average family size in 20 years.

While in the North environmentally polluting consumption and technologies have led to what Pierre Pradervand has dubbed "wealth-generated ecocide", the destruction of impoverished environments in the South constitutes "ecocide by poverty". In the North, the problem can be solved if government and people find the will to apply the available solutions. In the South, it will require a strategy of popular action among individuals and groups, supported by government, to develop the knowledge and faith to apply the synergistic solutions discussed above.

This does not mean that people's organizations have to be involved in activities which tackle simultaneously all the interventions needed to meet basic needs, achieve slow population growth and care for the environment. Sometimes planting trees and improving water supplies might form part of an approach aimed at increasing incomes and productivity. Family planning activities might be linked with other family concerns such as child weighing, maternal care, immunization and income-generating schemes.

References

Commoner, B (1989) "Rapid Population Growth and Environmental Stress" in *Consequences of Rapid Population Growth in Developing countries*, proceedings of UN expert group meeting, August 1988, ESA/P/WP 110, United Nations, New York

Ehrlich, P R and A H Ehrlich (1991) *The Population Explosion*, Hutchinson, London

FAO (1987) *Production Year Book*, FAO, Rome

Harrison, P (1992) *The Third Revolution*, I B Tauris and St Martin's Press, London

IUCN, UNEP and WWF (1991) *National Conservation Strategy of Pakistan*, National Planning Commission in collaboration with the IUCN, Islamabad

■ *John Rowley and Johan Holmberg*

Ni Shaoxiang (1989) "Population Pressures on Resources and the Environment", *Earthwatch*, 34, IPPF, UNPFA and IUCN, London

Pradervand, P (1991) "The Interaction of Population and Natural Resources", background document for Social Services Division, IUCN, Gland, Switzerland

Qu Geping (1989) "Over the Limit", *Earthwatch*, 34, IPPF, UNPFA and IUCN, London

Rambo, T (1990) "Slash-and-Burn Farmers: Victims or Villains?", *Earthwatch*, 39, IPPF, UNPFA and IUCN, London

Rowley, J (1984) "A Watershed of Ideas", *People*, vol 11, no 4, IPPF, London

Sadik, N (1990) *The State of World Population 1990*, UNPFA, New York

Thiesenhusen, W C (ed) (1989) *Searching for Agricultural Reform in Latin America*, Unwin Hyman, Boston, MA

UNICEF (1991) *The State of the World's Children*, UNICEF, New York

—— (1992) *The State of the World's Children*, UNICEF, New York

World Bank (1990) *World Development Report 1990*, Oxford University Press, Oxford

Chapter 4 **█ AGRICULTURE**

Some 10 per cent of humankind are continuously hungry. They and a further 10 per cent are at risk of starvation through the effects of natural hazards. Most of these people live in the Third World. Provision of food for this global under-class is one of the world's immediate environmental challenges. The simple explanation of "too many people" does not work: hunger and famine have existed for thousands of years. They are not the effect of rising populations. Nor are hunger and famine created by an inability to produce food at the global scale, but by the inability of people to produce or purchase sufficient food within their own countries. Increasing food production in Third World countries may be achievable through increasing yield per unit of farmed land. Jules Pretty et al critically examine the idea that a technical fix, the Green Revolution, is removing the threat of hunger and starvation. They explore the reasons why the high yields achievable on research stations are difficult to achieve and maintain on many Third World farms. As an alternative strategy, they argue for building on traditional low external impact farming systems, particularly for smallholder farmers. Their account stresses the value of indigenous knowledge and technologies and considers ways in which these may be supported. In the original chapter, they review the changes in institutional, economic and legal frameworks needed to support low external input agriculture.

Utsa Patnaik examines some of the negative consequences of the Green Revolution in India, one of the countries where the high external input model is widely believed to have been successful. She shows that there have been marked regional and class differences in the benefits. The effect has been to increase total food supply but at the cost of intra-generational equity: the poor have lost. In the original chapter she concludes by examining the tensions created in the Punjab and Assam, resulting in a strengthening of secessionist tendencies.

Gordon Conway and Edward Barbier discuss the effects of some of the government of Indonesia's agricultural policies on environmental sustainability and environmental degradation. Many of these effects are negative both in marginal and better quality environments. They conclude by indicating ways in which these policies might be modified.

Regenerating Agriculture: The Agroecology of Low-External Input and Community-Based Development
Jules Pretty, Irene Guijt,
Ian Scoones and John Thompson

Despite an agricultural revolution in the South over the course of a single generation that has produced enormous benefits for farmers, consumers and economies, many of the poorest rural people are yet to benefit. They live in regions with poor-quality soils and unpredictable rainfall. Either they are remote from agricultural services that promote the package of inputs necessary to add value, or they cannot afford to take a risk by adopting the whole package. More importantly, many simply find the package unsuitable for their needs and tastes. In addition, inappropriate use of inputs imposes costs in terms of both economic efficiency and the external costs imposed on others from agricultural pollution and environmental degradation.

If the projected world population of 8 to 13 billion people is to be fed, new efforts based on maximizing the use of renewable resources internal to the farm, rather than on a high external input approach, will be required. These will be centred on agro-ecological technologies capable of achieving permanent improvements to agricultural production that do not damage the environment.

This chapter argues that low-external input technologies improve pest management, conserve oil, water and nutrients, recycle wastes and utilize local sources of water efficiently. The selection of elements appropriate to local livelihoods will best be made by rural people, who know most about local conditions. This participation in planning, implementation and maintenance has been shown to produce highly effective, efficient and sustainable solutions, but generally only on a small scale. The final element of the challenge for fostering this new revolution lies in the support by national governments in the form of appropriate institutional and legal frameworks and economic incentives to make these islands of success more widespread.

An Agricultural Revolution

Over the last 25 years, farmers in the Third World have risen to an enormous global challenge. Although the global population has grown from 3.3 to 5.3 billion, food production per person has risen even more steeply. Farmers have both intensified their use of resources to produce more from the same amount of land and expanded into uncultivated lands. As a result, each one of us has now on average some 7 per cent more food than the prior generation at the same age. This has been agriculture's Green Revolution.

The success of the Green Revolution lay in simplicity. Agricultural scientists bred new varieties of staple cereals that (1) matured quickly, so permitting two or three crops to be grown each year, (2) were day-length insensitive, so could be extended to farmers at a wide range of latitudes, and (3) were producers of more grain at the expense of straw. These modern varieties (MVs) were distributed to farmers together with high-cost inputs, including inorganic fertilizers, pesticides, machinery, credit and water regulation. These technical innovations were then implemented in the best-favoured agroclimatic regions and for those classes of farmers with the best expectations of a means for realizing the potential yield increases (Conway and Barbier, 1990). As a result, average cereal yields have roughly doubled in 25 years. The remaining production growth has been met through a 20 per cent expansion of the agricultural area.

Yet in many ways the most difficult challenges are just beginning. The world population is not thought likely to stabilize until there are between 8 and 13 billion people. Even at the lowest estimates, and given current inequitable access and rights to resources, there will be a need for agricultural production to increase substantially if current levels of nutrition are to be maintained. Without very considerable growth the prospects for many people in poor countries and regions of the world are bleak. Given the extraordinary success of the Green Revolution, many believe that this model of development continues to provide the most effective and efficient prospect for all people of the South.

However, not only have many people missed out on the benefits of this revolution but there have been hitherto hidden costs that, once taken into account, make the previous measures of efficiency less attractive.

Characteristics of High- and Low-External Input Systems

By focusing on the import to farms of new seeds or animal breeds, the Green Revolution has encouraged the development of two distinctly different types of agriculture in countries of the South. The first type has been able to respond to the technological packages, producing high-external input (HEI) systems of agriculture. These tend to be endowed with good soils and adequate supply of water, through either stable rainfall or irrigation systems, and access to marketing infrastructure, modern farm inputs, machinery, transport, agroprocessing facilities and credit.

HEI systems are found in the large irrigated plains and deltas of the southern, southeastern and eastern parts of Africa, and parts of Latin America and North Africa, but also in patches in other regions. They tend to be focused upon monocrops and mono-animal enterprises, and geared for sale. So they include lowland irrigated rice, wheat and cotton; plantations of bananas, pineapples, oil palm and sugar cane; market gardening near to urban centres; and intensive livestock rearing and ranching.

Table 4.1 Internal and External Resources for Agrosystems

Internal Resources	External Resources
Sun: source of energy for plant photosynthesis	*Artificial lights*: used in greenhouse food production
Water: rain and/or small scale local irrigation schemes	*Water*: large dams, centralized distribution, deep wells
Nitrogen: fixed from air, recycled in soil organic matter	*Nitrogen*: primarily from applied synthetic fertilizer
Other nutrients: from soil reserves recycled in cropping system	*Other nutrients*: mined, processed and imported
Weed and pest control: biological, cultural, mechanical and locally available chemicals	*Weed and pest control*: synthetic chemical herbicides and insecticides
Seed: varieties produced on farm	*Seed*: hybrids or certified varieties purchased annually
Machinery: built and maintained on farm or in community	*Machinery*: purchased and replaced frequently
Labour: most work done by the family living on the farm	*Labour*: most work done by hired labour
Capital: source is family and community, reinvested locally	*Capital*: external indebtedness, benefits leave community
Management decisions: information from farmers and local community	*Management decisions*: from input suppliers and crop consultants
Varieties of plants: thrive with lower moisture and fertility	*Varieties of plants*: need high inputs to thrive

Sources: Rodale (1985) and Francis (1989).

The second type comprises all the remaining agricultural and livelihood systems which, in terms of area, are in the great majority. These are the low-external input (LEI) systems and they are located in drylands, wetlands, uplands and near deserts, mountains and hills. Farming systems in these areas are complex and diverse, and rural livelihoods are dependent on wild resources as well as agricultural produce. Agricultural yields are low, and the poorest countries tend to have higher proportions of these agricultural systems. Diversity means that what is appropriate for one farmer may not be for a neighbour; they are remote from markets and infrastructure; they are located on fragile or problem soils; they have very low productivity; they are less likely to be visited by agricultural scientists and extension workers; and they are much less likely to be studied in research institutions.

The number of people directly supported by LEI systems is enormous, probably some 1.4 billion, yet "most agricultural development assistance . . . has emphasized external resources" (OTA, 1988). They can neither afford to sustain the use of external resources, nor produce them in their own economies; the alternative lies in LEI systems, as for most poor countries no viable alternative exists (Wolf, 1986; OTA 1988, Chambers, Pacey and Thrupp, 1989; Horwith et al, 1989).

The proportion of major crops currently planted to MVs varies widely across continents. In Asia, 45 per cent of rice is planted to MVs, but in Africa the proportion is only 5 per cent. Where HEI systems occur, in almost every case external inputs have been substituted for the internal sources, rendering them less powerful (Table 4.1). HEI systems produce up to five times more food per unit area. The result is rice yields of 4 tonnes/ha in Indonesia, where 83 per cent of the rice land is planted to MVs and 63 per cent irrigated compared with only 1.1 tonnes /ha in Cambodia, where the use of MVs is 71 per cent but only 11 per cent of the land is irrigated (Lipton with Longhurst, 1989).

The direct economic benefits of HEI systems are clear: more food per hectare and per farm worker. Yet despite these returns, and considerable investment in research and extension, why have more farmers and countries not adopted HEI systems for agriculture?

Farmers' Views of Modern Varieties (MVs)

Using the conventional criterion of productivity, agricultural development judges HEI systems as successes. Yet farming households do not always see the modern varieties and associated package of external inputs in the same way as researchers and extension workers. Their criteria for evaluating and making choices are frequently so different that the best products of research services are sometimes rejected, while others judged as inappropriate are chosen by farmers as favourable.

In Colombia, farmers rejected a high-yielding variety of bush bean because its variable colour made marketing difficult; another variety (rejected by researchers for its small bean size) was acceptable because, as one farmer put it, "it is good for consumption purposes because it swells to a good size when cooked — it yields in the pot" (Ashby, Quiros and Rivera, 1987). In the Philippines, sweet potato varieties bred for high yield and sweet taste were rejected by upland farmers who preferred rapidly vining varieties that prevented weed growth and rain-induced soil erosion. They also selected varieties tolerant to weevil damage during the underground storage phase, as this meant the potatoes could be harvested only as required (Acaba et al, 1987).

Taste is one of the factors in the failure of maize MVs to be adopted widely in Malawi, formerly one of Africa's Green Revolution successes (Kydd, 1989; Barbier and Burgess, 1990). From the 1960s, agricultural research in Malawi has focused on "dent" varieties that have soft starch which is easier for modern rollers to handle to produce flour. But rural people prefer "flint" varieties for their taste and high starch content, and because they are less subject to insect damage during storage. Researchers accepted these drawbacks, but suggested that further new technologies would solve the problems. This would comprise the promotion of insecticides to control storage pests, and mechanical mills to overcome the difficulties of hand-milling dents. But the package was too costly and risky to farmers. By the beginning of the 1990s, only 5 per cent of the maize area was being planted to modern dent varieties.

Adopting the Whole Package

The Green Revolution begins on the research station, where scientists have access to all the necessary inputs of fertilizers, pesticides and labour at all the appropriate times. But when the package is extended to farmers, even the best-performing farms display the now well recognized yield gap. For example, rice yields on the International Rice Research Institute (IRRI) station are usually 1 tonne/ha better than the best-performing farmers, who in turn yield at 1–1.5 tonne /ha more than the average adopting farmers (Barker and Herdt, 1983). Differences in soil fertility, water control, insects, weeds, cultural practices, access to inputs, labour risk awareness and credit availability experienced by farming households explain the difference in yields.

If one element of the package is missing, the seed delivery system fails or the fertilizer arrives late, or there is insufficient irrigation water, then yields may not be much better than those for traditional varieties. Farmers with access to plentiful irrigation achieve steadily increasing yields of rice for each additional increase in applied nitrogen fertilizer, yet those applying nitrogen with a poor or variable supply of water produce steadily falling yields (Barker and Herdt, 1983). For high productivity per hectare, farmers need access to the whole package: MV seeds, water, labour, capital or credit, fertilizers and pesticides. This is not always possible.

Farmers Prefer Biodiversity

The introduction of MVs often displaces traditional methods and varieties. Over the past 25 years genetic stock has been greatly narrowed, and yields monocropped to single varieties are common. This is in marked contrast to the patchy mixtures that small farmers traditionally promote in the interest of minimizing risk of crop failure, a central element of most small farmer strategies. The diversity on fields and farms can be extraordinary. In one field in the Andes in Peru, some 36 potato varieties were recorded growing in 13 rows (Rhoades, 1984). Altogether some 10 000 traditional varieties are still grown by Andean farmers.

Contrary to the strategies of researchers, who have simplified and standardized agriculture, farmers of LEI agricultural systems still select for a diversity of crops and varieties. Very few fields and farms are monocropped, and for good reason — mixed cropping systems can be less risky and more productive. Farmers of LEI systems utilize intercropping and multiple cropping widely. In Africa, more than 80 per cent of all cereals are intercropped, producing in some cases highly complex patterns on the ground, with up to 20 species grown in close proximity (OTA, 1988). In Latin America, about 60 per cent of maize is intercropped, and 80 to 90 per cent of beans are grown with maize potatoes (Francis, 1986).

The Hidden Costs of HEI Systems

The agricultural production increases brought about by HEI packages have brought great benefits. Without them many people would be worse off than they are now; many others might have died of starvation. But in order to assess the true net benefits of HEI packages, it is important also to investigate some of the hidden costs.

Intensification of agriculture means greater use of inputs and a tendency to specialize operations. The inputs of nutrients and pesticides, though, are never used entirely efficiently by the receiving crops or livestock and, as a result, some are lost to the environment (Conway and Pretty, 1991). Some 30 to 80 per cent of nitrogen and up to 2 per cent of pesticides are lost to the environment to contaminate water, food and fodder and the atmosphere. These costs to national economies and environments are growing, particularly in industrialized countries but also in developing countries.

In Tanzania, for example, US $75 million of Canadian aid has been spent over 20 years to develop 40 000 hectares of monocropped wheat farms on the dryland Hanang Plains. Yields are comparable with those on the Canadian Plains, and the farms supply nearly half of the national wheat demand. Yet the scheme has displaced local Barabaig pastoralists from their prime grazing lands, disrupted their complex rotation patterns, destroyed cultural sites and induced ecological damage in the form of soil erosion and siltation of lakes (Lane and Pretty, 1990). From the viewpoint of the farms, they are financially profitable. But if these wider impacts are accounted for, then the picture changes. The financial resources spent developing an HEI system in an LEI region would have been more efficiently used by buying wheat in the world market.

Continuing the Dependency on External Inputs

HEI agricultural systems will continue to be immensely important for Third World farmers and economies. However, the potential for marginal improvements in growth in HEI systems is not clear. All countries where the Green Revolution has had a significant impact saw average annual output growth rates in the agricultural sector fall during the 1980s compared with the post-revolution period of 1965–80 (World Bank, 1991). For example, annual growth rates fell in the Philippines from 4.6 to 1.8 per cent, in Mexico from 3.2 to 1.2 per cent, in Indonesia from 4.3 to 3.2 per cent and in Syria from 4.8 to 0.5 per cent. There is also evidence that returns to MVs grown on the same land are now declining, despite technological advances. On IRRI farms, rice yields are now falling, and more inputs will be required to maintain current levels of productivity (Flinn and De Datta, 1984). This evidence, together with that indicating natural resource damage from pollution and depletion from over-use, indicates that many HEI systems are at or above sustainable levels of production. It will be difficult to achieve further benefits that are not outweighed by the marginal costs.

Opportunities may come with new biotechnology and genetic manipulation techniques. This may produce crops and animals that are more efficient converters of nutrients and more resistant to pests and diseases; it may succeed in incorporating nitrogen-fixing nodules to the roots of cereals; and it may produce better slow-release fertilizers containing nitrification inhibitors. All of these techniques will still be part of a package that must be supplied to farmers and paid for, however. Although offering great potential, they are likely simply to foster even greater dependency on external resources and systems. Those low-income countries that are poorly endowed with natural resources and infrastructure and where population growth is high are unlikely to benefit (Hobbelink, Vellve and Abraham, 1990).

Regenerating Agriculture through Low External Inputs

There is enormous potential in LEI systems. Productivity is certainly far below potential levels, unlike in the Green Revolution areas. The key question is now: how can this potential be partly of fully unlocked? An alternative and regenerative agricultural strategy is quite different to that of the HEI approach exemplified by the Green

Revolution (NRC, 1989; Conway and Pretty, 1991). Sustainable LEI agriculture pursues the following goals:

- more thorough incorporation of natural processes such as nutrient cycles, nitrogen fixation and pest-predator relationships;
- reduction in the use of external, off-farm inputs with the greatest potential to harm the environment or the health of farmers and consumers;
- greater productive use of biological and genetic potential of plant and animal species;
- improvement of the match between cropping patterns and the productive potential and physical limitations of agricultural lands to ensure long-term sustainability of current production levels.

Evidence is now growing that the result of such a regenerative strategy will be the creation of more productive and sustainable systems that emphasize the use of available resources, do not damage the environment and avoid the dependency on external and locally uncontrollable resources and systems. Despite the diversity of LEI systems and the range of research and extension efforts developed for them, there are certain common elements critical for their successful development. These are:

- building on local knowledge of pest management, soil and nutrient conservation, water conservation and harvesting, waste recycling and irrigation;
- building on local social organization and management systems;
- using process-oriented approaches for projects to permit sequential and adaptive planning and development.

Building on Local Knowledge and Agroecological Processes
In rural areas the livelihoods of poor households are diverse, commonly relying on a mix of agricultural produce, wild plants and animals, remittances and trading. Over generations, people have developed a wealth of detailed knowledge about the quality and quantity of natural resources, and the means to manage and exploit them. This knowledge is a resource commonly neglected by agricultural projects, yet is critical to the success and improvement of LEI systems. The first component of success requires taking the detailed knowledge as a starting-point and building upon it. Where agricultural development has done this, the economic benefits are remarkable. When development planning ignores this rule not only may goals not be met, but greater environmental and social damage may arise.

Provided groups or communities are involved in identification of technology needs, the design of testing and experimentation, the adaptation to their own conditions and finally the extension to others, then sustainable and cheaper solutions can be found. Development focusing on appropriate agroecological pest, nutrient and water management practices can lead to at least a 50 per cent increase in the yields of crops, livestock and trees.

Pest Management Strategies
Agricultural pests and pathogens are thought to destroy some 10 to 40 per cent of the

world's gross agricultural production. It is this potential for damage that has driven the search for synthetic pesticides and resulted in their widespread use. Pesticides, though, are not a perfect answer to controlling pests and pathogens. They can be dangerous to human health and damage natural resources and the environment. But more importantly to the farmer, pesticides are often inefficient at controlling pests (Conway and Pretty, 1991). They can cause pest resurgences by also killing off the natural enemies of the target pests. They can also produce new pests by killing off the natural enemies of species that hitherto were not pests. Pests can become resistant to pesticides, so encouraging further applications; there are some 470 pest species known to be resistant to at least one product (NRC, 1984). Finally, pesticides provide no lasting control, and so, at best, have to be repeatedly applied. LEI systems make use of the agroecological processes of predation, competition and parasitism in six broad strategies of pest control:

• emphasizing natural enemies of pests and pathogens;
• breeding crop plants or livestock for resistance to pests or pathogens;
• using locally available insecticidal compounds to reduce pests;
• increasing agroecosystem diversity to reduce pest or pathogen numbers;
• disrupting pest reproduction;
• the selective use of pesticides, with low toxicity and little environmental hazard.

Integrated pest management (IPM) is the integrated use of some or all these pest control strategies in a way that not only reduces pest populations to economically acceptable levels but is sustainable and non-polluting. It is by no means a new approach. LEI farmers have long used combinations of these technologies to provide a degree of pest control. All IPM successes begin by understanding local practices and agroecological processes and building upon these. One traditional technique on citrus trees has been to encourage populations of predatory ants that feed on various insect pests. In China, bamboo bridges have from some 1700 years been placed between branches to encourage movement of citrus ants from tree to tree, and whole orchards are colonized by securing a nest on one tree and then connecting this to others with the bamboo strips (Huang and Pei Yang, 1987).

Although IPM is a more complex process than, say, scheduled spraying of pesticides, the large-scale IMP for rice programmes in the Philippines, Indonesia and Thailand shows that ordinary farmers are capable of rapidly acquiring the principles and approaches (Kenmore et al, 1987; Craig and Pisone, 1988; Kenmore, 1989). This is producing a 50 per cent reduction in insecticide use, a 10 per cent increase in profits and a reduced variance of profits. The 50 per cent reduction in pesticide use represents savings of US \$5–10 million each to Thailand and the Philippines, and US \$50–100 million to Indonesia.

Nutrient Conservation Strategies

It is virtually impossible to maintain crop production without adding nutrients. When crops are harvested, nutrients are invariably removed and so have to be replaced. There are a variety of sources: the mobilization of existing nutrients in the soil and parent rocks; the fixing of nitrogen from the atmosphere; or the supply of organic or inorganic fertilizer. The options for nutrient conservation include improving the efficiency of fertilizers, using alternative sources of nutrients and environmental manipulation.

The application of fertilizer, ideally, should closely match the needs of crops; but often farmers, for reasons of cost, will apply fertilizer only once. Fertilizer is often applied in excess of need, so some nutrients are lost from the farm as nitrates to surface or ground water, or as ammonia or nitrous oxide to the atmosphere. Efficiency of uptake is influenced by the crops themselves, the solid type and the timing and appropriate placement of fertilizers.

Farmers who can neither afford nor rely on a regular supply of inorganic fertilizers must find alternative organic sources of nutrients. Livestock manures have been the traditional key to maintaining agricultural productivity in LEI systems, replenishing nutrients and improving solid structure. Composting is a technique of similar long standing that combines the use of animal manures, green material and household wastes. The impact of legume grown together with or before a cereal crop can further reduce and sometimes eliminate the needs for nitrogen fertilizers. Symbiotic bacteria present in specialized nodules that develop on the roots of legumes can fix a considerable amount of nitrogen from the atmosphere. In a well-noduled and managed stand of legumes, fixation can be about 50 to 100 kg N/ha/year (NRC, 1989; Young, 1989; Sarrantonia, 1991). The cultivation of cereals and legume crops together can improve both total yields and stability of production. Bushes and trees with nitrogen-fixing capacity also have beneficial effects on plants growing with or after them.

Nutrients are supplied when vegetation is incorporated in the solid as a green manure. This technique has been practised for a long time; the Romans grew lupins and ploughed them in before sowing cereals more than 2000 years ago. Quick-growing legumes are popular green manures for LEI systems. In Honduras, the introduction of the velvet bean as a green manure on poor soils has raised yields of maize from 850 to 2500 kg/ha (Bunch, 1990). and in Rwanda, *Tephrosia* has increased cereal yields fivefold (Kotschi et al, 1989).

Blue-green algae are another important source of nitrogen, the most widely exploited being the alga *Anabaena azollae*. This fixes atmospheric nitrogen while living in cavities in the leaves of a small fern, *Azolla*, that grown on the water of rice fields. In one year, *Azolla* can fix more than 400 kg/ha, a rate in excess of most tropical and subtropical legumes. In the Philippines, *Azolla* increased rice yields by 12 to 25 per cent; and in India, wheat crops following rice with *Azolla* have also been shown to produce improved yields (Wantabe et al, 1977; Kolhe and Mitra, 1987).

Interventions that help to conserve solid and water are powerful techniques for nutrient conservation. Soil nutrients can be conserved by a wide range of physical structures of varying scale. Most of these are designed to check the surface flow of water, and thus perform the dual role of soil conservation and water harvesting and retention. If successful they can minimize the need for fertilizer application. The simplest approach is to construct earth bunds across the slope that act as a barrier to runoff. They are suitable on shallow slopes and are often used on tropical smallholding together with contour planting. Sometimes the earth bunds are reinforced with vegetation such as crop stalks or trees. Such vegetative bunds are partly permeable, so crops planted in from the bund also benefit from water runoff. More elaborate are various forms of retention and bench terraces, which raise crop yields by some 30 to 50 per cent over those on non-terraced slopes. A lower-input alternative is to plant crops along contours. Water flow is slowed as it meets rows of plants growing perpendicular to the flow, thus improving infiltration. In strip cropping the main row crop is grown along the contour in wide strips alternating with strips of protective crop, such as grass or a legume. Contour bunding and contour ploughing in Gujarat, India, more than doubles millet yields by improving moisture and nutrient retention (Shah, Bharadwaj and Ambastha, 1991). Soil, water and nutrient conservation is also furthered by the uses of mulches or cover crops. Organic or inorganic material is spread on the soil surface to provide a protective physical cover, the mulch, for the topsoil. Erosion, desiccation and excessive heating are reduced, thus promoting optimal conditions for the decomposition and mineralization of organic matter. The cheapest and easiest method is to use plant residues from previous crops, from nearby perennials or from wild areas, such as reeds from swamps (Kotschi et al, 1989).

These low-external input options for farmers comprise a wide range of interventions that will reduce the losses of nitrogen to the environment and act as alternatives to inorganic fertilizers. They are usually integrated on farms to give a finely timed strategy specific to the biophysical and socio-economic conditions of individual farmers. As with IPM, integrated nutrient conservation successes have all begun with building on technologies that farmers are already using and with which they are already familiar.

In all parts of the world where farmers' knowledge about local complexities is built upon by outside projects and programmes, the impacts on agricultural production alone can be significant (Craig, 1987, Fujisaka, 1989; Bunch, 1990, Kerkhof, 1990; Poffenberger, 1990; Pretty, 1990, Shah, Bharadwaj and Ambastha, 1991). In all cases, yield increases of 50 to 100 per cent, and sometimes more, were achieved without the addition of inorganic fertilizers. However, access to inorganic fertilizers, even in very small quantities, will improve yield even further.

Water Conservation and Harvesting

Where rainfall is unreliable, inadequate and distributed erratically, water shortages often severely limit crop production. Water conservation and harvesting can carry crops over an otherwise disastrous dry period, can stabilize and increase production and can even make agricultural production possible for the first time. Water harvesting systems are used in arid and semi-arid regions where runoff is intermittent, and with water storage an essential component; they include a runoff-producing and a runoff-using area; water is not usually transported over long distances; and harvesting is carried out on a relatively small scale in terms of area, volume and capital investment (Reij, Muller and Begemann, 1988, Reij, 1991). Water harvesting systems can be found in all parts of the world, including the Middle East, South Asia, China, North America and sub-Saharan Africa.

Water harvesting systems from short slopes are simple and cheap. One very old system of microcatchment use is *meskat* in Tunisia, where fruit trees are fed by runoff from upper slopes in a 200 to 400 mm rainfall area. The *zay* system in Burkina Faso is another example, involving the digging of small pits, local application of manure and construction of stone bunds to catch runoff. The concentration of both water and nutrients has made *zay* a method to rehabilitate degraded land. Yields from these areas can be 1000 kg/ha or more, in areas where average yields are only 400 to 500 kg/ha. For water harvesting from long slopes semi-permeable stone contour lines and bunds are used. Water runoff is slowed down, rather than concentrated, and so has more time to infiltrate below the stones. Half-moon shaped bunds are used to concentrate water, almost always for forest or fodder trees.

Floodwater harvesting in the streambed, whether a valley bottom or floodplain, blocks the water which flows intermittently and often in flash floods. In North Africa and the Middle East *wadi* floors are blocked and fill with water from the adjacent slopes and the main watercourse. Many local variations of this basic principle have been documented, from Mexico, India, Pakistan, Burkina Faso and elsewhere. On the central plateau of Burkina Faso, low semi-permeable dams of loose rock are constructed in the gullies to slow the after flow and push water out of the gullies on to the floodplain. Soil is also conserved in the process, with rapid formation of terraces between the dams. Sorghum yields are 200 to 300 per cent higher on fields connected to the dams than on unimproved fields (Reij, Muller and Begemann, 1988; Critchley, 1991; Scoones, 1991).

Building on Local Social Organization and Management Systems

Individuals and Cooperatives

A common element of successful implementation of agroecological technologies has been the attention paid to local social organization. Success measured in the form of change sustained over long periods has been achieved through either building on existing patterns of organization (formal or informal) or the development of new institutions. Yet this has not always been so in agricultural development. There have been two quite different approaches, both with the same goal of widespread adoption of charges. The first ignores existing local formal and informal institutions by dealing with individual farmers or households. These are chosen partly for their likelihood to adopt new technologies and are expected to induce further adoption in their community through a demonstration effect. At the other extreme is the approach of building community-wide cooperatives or collectives, whose action is governed by members and whose impact is expected to be positive on all members.

There is growing evidence to suggest that both approaches are flawed. At best only a few people benefit, and the gap between the poorest and the relatively wealthy grows. At worst the technologies are only adopted under the close supervision of external officials, the departure of whom often signifies the end of the effective use of the technology.

In the individual approach, the contact farmers are usually selected on the basis of literacy, wealth, readiness to change and progressiveness. This often sets them apart from the rest of the community. This approach is exemplified by the training and visit (T & V) system of extension widely adopted in the South over the past 10 to 15 years (Howell, 1988; Moris, 1990). Extension agents receive regular training to enhance their technical skills, which they then pass on to farmers through regular contact with the selected contact farmers. This technical advice and knowledge are then supposed to diffuse from the messages. However, this has been much less successful than predicted and adoption rates are commonly very low among non-contact farmers (Chapman, 1988; Mullen, 1989).

Despite the intention of involving the whole community directly, the community or collective approach to extending technologies to rural people has resulted in inequitable development, with benefits being captured by the relatively well-off. Large cooperatives, in which the needs of different members vary enormously and which are too large for widespread participation, have to be managed by small groups, usually comprising the most wealthy, to whom decision-making has been delegated. They are thus inevitably less effective in meeting the needs of the poor (Ramaprasad and Ramachandran, 1989).

Small Entrepreneurial Groups

The alternative lies in the middle with small groups of households with a common interest in resource management and control. Sometimes these are existing formal or informal groups, such as traditional leadership structures, water users' groups, neighbourhood groups, youth groups, housing societies, grazing management groups, and so on. On other occasions they are groups formed with outside facilitation to take charge of and manage a new resource, such as water users' associations for irrigation, credit groups for loans access or water-point committees to manage pumps. These groups promote incentives and enforce rules and penalties aimed at eliciting behaviour conducive to rational and effective use of resources (Kottack, 1985; Cernea, 1987 and 1991; *Environment and Urbanization*, 1990; Jodha, 1990; Murphy, 1990; Uphoff, 1990; Shah, Bharadwaj and Ambastha, 1991).

It is widely believed that taking social considerations into account results in greater costs. The concrete economic evidence, however, suggests quite the opposite. One study of 25 multilateral projects, conducted five to ten years after project completion, found the flow of benefits to have risen or remained constant where institutional development had been important (Kottack, 1985; Cernea, 1987). Where it had been ignored, economic rates of return declined markedly, and in some cases had become negative.

The benefits can have a wider social and environmental significance. Groups commonly pass through several phases. First the group establishes agreed rules for management and decision-making. These are then used by members as a vehicle to channel information or loans to individual members. As confidence grows with success, and resource bases expand, group activity evolves to an entrepreneurial stage where common action projects and programmes are initiated (Rahman, 1984; Ramaprasad and Ramachandran, 1989; D'Souza and Palghadmal, 1990; Shah, Bharadwaj and Ambastha, 1991). An example is provided in Box 4.1.

Box 4.1 MYRADA SMALL CREDIT GROUPS IN SOUTHERN INDIA

The work of the NGO Myrada of Bangalore has shown that small-group formation or strengthening mobilizes resource flows. Seven years of concentration upon credit supply via nationalized banks and local cooperatives were heterogeneous, too large for effective shared decision-making and bound by rigid rules. One large society, built up with a great deal of external effort, broke into 14 small groups. Myrada agreed to lend money, with positive results: "Not only was the money managed more carefully, there was a far greater commitment and respon-

---

sibility from the group towards repaying the amount of money, something that had not unduly bothered them when they were part of the cooperative."

It was realized that members of small groups participated more, had common concerns and needs and, after developing their own rules and decision-making, expanded their resource base and took up common action programmes. Myrada has now helped establish 1700 groups containing 48 000 families in southern India, to whom Rs 16 million have been loaned in 100 000 separate loans.

No two groups are completely alike, though all groups encourage members to save; all hold money in a common fund; all advance loans for consumption as well as production purposes; all can engage in income earning to expand their resource bases; all can engage in providing or running community services; all evolve their own set of rules and regulations; and all agree that leadership responsibility must be shared. Each group decides its own interest rates to members as well as the types of loan it will permit. What is particularly significant is that the majority of loans are taken out for consumption purposes, and many of these for less than Rs 100. Rather than borrowing money from a moneylender to meet consumption or contingency needs, such as for a funeral, marriage or pre-harvest food shortage, now rural households are able easily to borrow small amounts of money. Without such groups, the rural poor inevitably get caught up in the cycle of indebtedness.

Success of Myrada's credit group programmes in two parts of Tamil Nadu, India

Number of groups	72	58
Number of members	1754	1569
Fund size (Rs)	470 000	904 000
Total advanced (Rs)	1.5 million	1.2 million
Number of loans advanced	9871	6515
Total overdue (Rs)	21 000	no data
Proportion of money advanced overdue	1.4%	no data
Proportion of loan for consumption (mostly food)	77%	82%
Proportion of loans for less than Rs500	98.5%	no data
Proportion of loans for less than Rs100	38%	no data
Proportion of food loans for less than Rs100	no data	94%

The success of this programme rests on three points: the groups have the flexibility to make their own decision and so know the priorities of members much better than a bank; the poor are not a single group; and when confidence grows with skills and knowledge, groups turn towards community-wide development.

(*Source*: Ramaprasad and Ramachandran, 1989)

The next phase comprises inter-group cooperation as several groups might come together to federate and pool resource and knowledge. This opens up economies of scale that bring greater economic and ecological benefits. Lastly, the emergence of groups and federated groups makes it easier for government and non-governmental organizations (NGOs) to develop direct links with the poor (Bebbington, 1991). This results in greater empowerment of poor households, as they draw down on public services. It also permits more efficient passing of socially important messages relating to family planning, adult education, sanitation and so on (Rahman, 1984).

Groups Sometimes Fail

Not all groups are successful. In general, external institutions find social change much less easy to promote than technical and economic change. In the Hill Resource Management Programme of Haryana, India, users' groups for natural resource management were established to fill the gap left by the decline and near disappearance of indigenous management systems. After early success, the state forestry department took over implementation. But only in 30 per cent of these communities have they successfully established management societies. Technology has outpaced attention to social factors and in the long run the whole effort may be jeopardized as local people become less and less involved in planning and management (Chopra, Kadekodi and Murthy, 1990; Poffenberger, 1990).

Groups are often more effective in their early years. As they grow in confidence and become empowered, so the action taken can bring them into new conflicts (Murphy, 1990). The ZOTO people's organization in Manila began with a successful first four to five years. It was much less successful, however, as a growth in demand for concrete results caused members to neglect the formation of a secondary leadership, and local people paid to become organizers tended to dominate. Ideology came to dominate, too, and the leadership failed to see that the government was making concessions. The members observed this and left to take the compromises offered (Honculada in Murphy, 1990).

Growth in size can also threaten effectiveness. As interest and enthusiasm spreads, so more people become interested in joining. Group sizes in the Kenya Woodfuel Development Project grew from 12 to 40, making it hard for extension workers to maintain a personal approach, and allowing social hierarchies to dominate (Chavangi and Ngugi, 1987; Huby, 1990).

Innovative Approaches Adopted by Projects and Institutions

Incorporating Local Knowledge

As has been repeatedly shown, farmers and rural households in complex, diverse environments are fully capable of contributing to development research, planning and implementation and monitoring. Agricultural development emphasizing both HEI and LEI strategies is littered with spectacular failures where local perceptions and needs have not been understood. Where these local factors are not involved, projects are less effective as fewer people adopt the new technologies, and these are often not sustained. This can mean expensive development efforts wasted for want of critical information. In Nigeria, for example, research scientists at the International Institute for Tropical Agriculture spent several years trying to break the seed dormancy of yams. Between one-quarter and one-half of the edible portion of the crop has to be set aside for replanting, yet if yams could be grown from seed then food yields would dramatically improve. The research failed when the first generation tubers were always found to be small. Yet farmers knew this already; some had been conducting their own experiments on this in the late 1930s (Richards, 1985).

There are many more examples of farmers informing the agricultural research and development process. In many cases this local knowledge has been discovered by individuals or institutions working in a participatory mode with rural people. This does not mean farmers participating in doing what outsiders want them to do, or think is best for them. Participation means that outsiders learn with rural people and are willing to change their activities and direction in the light of locally articulated needs and knowledge. As Yves Cabannes, co-ordinator of the habitat section of the Groupe de Recherche et d'Échanges Technologiques, Paris has said "Given the chance, poor communities hold the key to the solution of their own problems" (Cabannes, 1988).

Box 4.2 SMALL-SCALE IRRIGATION IN THE PHILIPPINES

The Institute of Philippine Culture compared two types of NIA-assisted communal projects: those that NIA developed through its participatory intervention methods, and those assisted through its traditional approach. A pilot participatory approach gives attention to the development of the irrigators' association months before project construction starts. The key mechanism used to develop these associations is farmers' involvement in the planning and constriction of the irrigation system. Full-time organizers reside in the project area and prepare the association to work with the engineers.

The incorporation of local knowledge into design made a large difference. Farmers provided information on the behaviour of the proposed water source and on the location of more stable river banks; they pointed out alternative canal routes to avoid low-lying or sandy areas; they indicated routes that would include distant fields of farmers who had shown great interest in the project; they indicated where a canal would consume too much of small farmers' land; and they suggested structures across streams that would serve their needs. As De los Reyes and Jopillo (1986) noted: "NIA's judicious use of the farmers' knowledge of their environment resulted in more functional systems".

The NIA participatory approach was successful in producing larger irrigated areas, greater productivity, stronger associations, improved water distribution, better compliance with government policy and an improved relationship between farmers and government. NIA achieved this because it had a policy framework supportive of local involvement, the presence of a supportive bureaucracy and a new and appropriate attitude to programme implementation.

Comparison of participatory and non-participatory irrigation system developed with the support of the NIA, Philippines (1983–85)

Indicators	Participatory	Non-Participatory
(1) Size of irrigation systems (ha): Design area	205	246
Irrigated Area: wet season	104	149

dry season	76	123
(2) Cost per hectare of actual irrigated land (pesos)	15 150	15 599
(3) Proportion of NIA-built structures assessed by farmers as defective	13%	20%
(4) Proportion of NIA-built canals abandoned or rerouted by farmers	9%	18%
(5) Proportion of systems in which farmers' suggestions were incorporated in system layout and design	83%	27%
(6) Rice yields wet season: before NIA	2.84	2.59
after NIA	3.05	2.65
(7) Rice yields dry season: before NIA	2.56	2.57
after NIA	3.11	2.54
(8) Farmers' per hectare contribution to costs (pesos)	357	54
(9) Remittance of amortization payments due to NIA (by 1984–85)	82%	50%
(10) Number of group works held per association	32	14
(11) Person-hours contributed by each system user	67	28
(12) Measure of financial management capacity of irrigators' associations	5.11	2.45

(*Source*: De los Reyes and Jopillo, 1986; Bagadion and Korten, 1991)

Participatory Methods

In recent years participatory methods have spread at a remarkable pace through NGOs and government organizations around the world. A large number of approaches for collaborative research, planning, implementation and monitoring have been developed, including rapid rural appraisal, participatory rural appraisal and other similar techniques (Farrington and Martin, 1988; McCracken, Conway and Pretty, 1988; *RRA Notes*, 1988–91; Gueye and Schoonmaker Freundenberger, 1991; Mascarenhas et al, 1991). Once exposed to the culture of learning from and with rural people, more organizations are trying out various methods, inventing their own and developing variations. Already this had produced a wealth of practical field experience. Where the attitudes of outsiders are appropriate and rapport and accountability are good, it has repeatedly been shown that villagers know a great deal, and this itself helps to drive innovations.

With the devolution of planning and monitoring to villagers, people in rural communities are no longer seen simply as informants, but as teachers, extensionists, activists and monitors of change. These specialists include village para-professionals, village extensionists, experts, village game wardens, women veterinarians, and so on (Huby, 1990; Cernea, 1991; Shah, Bharadwaj and Ambastha, 1991). An emphasis on village specialists integrates marginalized groups more readily, so allowing their skills and knowledge to influence development priorities. In this way local people are able to monitor changes and articulate local demands for support.

Participatory methods have now been used by sufficient numbers of institutions that it is possible to evaluate their impact in comparison with situations where no such methods have been used. One significant case study is the irrigation development conducted by the National Irrigation Authority (NIA) in the Philippines (Box 4.2).

Project Flexibility

The most successful institutions are those that start their projects small and cheaply. They promote uncomplicated design and do not try everything at once. Technologies promoted tend to be low risk to farmers, easy to teach and demonstrate and tested under local conditions, and tend to offer the prospect of learning, large, on-site benefits in the coming season or year. Paternalism in the form of financial or food incentives to encourage short-term adoption is avoided as it created dependency and so threatens the long-term commitment of local people (Bunch, 1990; Lobo, 1990; .Reij, 1991). After initiation, projects may stay small (Goethert and Hamdi, 1988; Uphoff, 1990) or be combined into larger programmes once the participatory procedures and processes have been fully elaborated (Cernea, 1983 and 1987).

It is impossible to predict the results of participatory planning and development without sustained contact with potential beneficiaries. A common feature of successful projects has been an early period of experimentation and continuous dialogue that allows outsiders to learn, return to the drawing board and replan. Investing in appropriate human resource development is also vital, which includes improving the skills of outsiders in facilitating development, and fostering multidisciplinary and multisectoral working. Many successful projects have changed priorities and adapted practices following the incorporation of people's needs and priorities. After a survey, the Kenya Woodfuel Development Project, planning to teach tree planting and raising as a major activity, discovered that 30 per cent of farms already has agroforestry micro-nurseries, and project managers were able to make a drastic change in the project design (Chavangi and Ngugi, 1987; Huby, 1990). Elsewhere in Kenya, a project in Turkana used theodolites and other complicated equipment to design water harvesting technologies for sorghum gardens for pastoralists, but social factors were overlooked as food for work was used to persuade the pastoralists to participate (Critchley, 1991). When the project realized the reasons for the ensuing lack of success, design was turned over to the Turkana people, who designed modified and simple water harvesting that has produced reliable crop yields.

The length of time for which external agencies are willing to commit funds is also critical to success. For real social and natural resource change, development projects must be of realistic lengths. Projects of less than five years' duration have a much greater chance of failure than those of five to ten or more years (Hudson, 1989; Uphoff, 1990). This need to give sustained support is increasingly being recognized. Just as local communities take a long-term and sequential view of resource use and management, so must projects and governments.

Farmer-to-Farmer Extension

Where there has been successful extension of LEI agroecological technologies to new communities, farmers have always been involved in the transfer of their expertise. This farmer-to-farmer extension takes many forms. Most common are farmer exchange visits, in which farmers are brought to the site of successful use of technologies, where they are able to observe benefits and costs and discuss them with adopting farmers. Project staff can play the role of bringing interested groups together and facilitating the process of information exchange. For farmers "seeing is believing", and the best educators of farmers are other farmers. Such farmer-to-farmer extension has resulted in the spread of *Leucaena* contour hedgerows in the Philippines (Fujisaka, 1989); management innovations for irrigation systems in Nepal (Pradan and Yoder, 1989); velvet beans for green manuring in Honduras (Bunch, 1990); and a range of watershed protection technologies in India (Mascarenhas et al, 1991; Shah, Bharadwaj and Ambastha, 1991). These all have shown that farmer-to-farmer extension is a low-cost method of motivating farmer groups to change habits and practices. It also provides crucial leadership experience for villagers and provides role models that they can reasonably aspire to emulate.

Conclusions

The experiences documented in this chapter suggest that agricultural production in LEI systems can be improved by 50 per cent or more. Yield improvements through sustainable intensification would be accompanied by further indirect economic benefits. There would be no need for extensification into uncultivated areas, so ensuring that non-agricultural plant and animal species with value to the local livelihoods would be sustained. Non-use benefits would also be preserved, such as locally valued cultural sites and globally valued biodiversity and ecosystems, both of which are threatened when cultivation expands. There would be reduced contamination and pollution of the environment, so reducing costs incurred by farming households, consumers of food and national economies as a whole. Migration patterns could also be reversed as economic growth based upon agricultural regeneration occurs. In the long run the benefits will extend to reduced population growth rates as rural people become better off and less in need of large supportive families.

When people's ideas and interests, not just their labour, are sought and incorporated fully in development projects and programmes, then conventional indicators of development success are all met. Effectiveness is improved as people feel an ownership of the developmental change and are willing to contribute to maintenance; and efficiency is better as cost recovery improves. Where the appropriate incentives are applied by national government in the form of enabling institutional, economic and legal frameworks, then the potential for widespread sustainable agricultural developments can be fulfilled.

References

Acaba, M, D Apura, J Cabiling, R De Pedro and C Lightfoot (1987) *A Study of Farmers' Evaluation of Camote Varieties*, Farming Systems Development Project, Eastern Visayas, Visayas State College of Agriculture, Leyte, Philippines

Ashby, J A, C A Quiros and Y M Rivera (1987) *Farmer Participation in On-Farm Trials*, ODI, London

Bagadion, B U and F F Korten (1991) "Developing Irrigators' Organizations: A Learning Process Approach", in M M Cernea (ed) *Putting People First*, 2nd edn, Oxford University Press, Oxford

Barbier, E B and J Burgess (1990) *Malawi: Land Degradation in Agriculture*, report to the World Bank Economic Mission on Environmental Policy, IIED, London

Barker, R and R Herdt (1983) *The Rice Economy of Asia*, Resources for the Future, Washington, DC

Bebbington, A (1991) *Farmer Organizations in Ecuador: Contributions to Farmer First Research and Development*, Sustainable Agriculture Programme Gatekeeper Series no 26, IIED, London

Bunch, R (1990) *Low Input Soil Restoration in Honduras: The Cantarranas Farmer-to-Farmer Extension Programme*, Sustainable Agriculture Programme Gatekeeper Series no 23, IIED, London

Cabannes, Y (1988) "Human Settlements", in C Conroy and M Litvinoff (eds), *The Greening of Aid*, Earthscan, London

Cernea, M M (1983) *A Social Methodology for Community Participation in Local Investments*, Staff Working Paper no 598, World Bank, Washington, DC

—— (1987) "Farmer Organizations and Institution Building for Sustainable Development", *Regional Development Dialogue*, 8, pp1–24

—— (1991) "Social Actors of Participatory Afforestation Strategies", in M M Cernea (ed) *Putting People First*, 2nd edn, Oxford University Press, Oxford

Chambers, R, A Pacey L A and Thrupp (1989) *Farmer First: Farmer Innovation and Agricultural Research*, Intermediate Technology Publications, London

Chapman, N (1988) "The Impact of T & V Extension in Somalia", in J Howell (ed) *Training and Visit Extension in Practice*, ODI, London

Chavangi, N A and Ngugi, A W (1987) "Innovatory Participation in Programme Design: Tree Planting for Increased Fuelwood Supply for Rural Households in Kenya", paper for Workshop on Farmers and Agricultural Research, Institute of Development Studies, University of Sussex.

Chopra, M, G K Kadekodi and M V Murthy (1990) *Participatory Development: People and Common Property Resources*, Sage Publications, New Delhi

Conway, G R and Barbier, E B (1990) *After the Green Revolution*, Earthscan, London

Conway, G R and J N Pretty (1991) *Unwelcome Harvest, Agriculture and Pollution*, Earthscan, London

Craig, I A (1987) "Pore-Rice Crop Green Manuring: A Technology for Solid Improvement under Rainfed Conditions in NE Thailand", NERAD Project, Tha Phra, Khon Kaen, Thailand

Craig, I A and U Pisone (1988) *A Survey of NERA Promising Processes: Methodologies and Technologies for Rainfed Agriculture in NE Thailand*, NERAD Project, Tha Phra, Khon Kaen, Thailand

Critchley, W (1991) *Looking After Our Land: New Approaches to Soil and Water Conservation in Dryland Africa*, Oxfam, Oxford and IIED, London

D'Souza, E R and T J Palghadmal (1990) *Sustainable Water-Use System: A Case Study of Sase-Gandhalewadi Lift Irrigation Project*, Social Centre, Ahmendnagar, India

De los Reyes, R and Jopillo, S G (1986) *An Evaluation of the Philippines Participatory Communal Irrigation Programme*, Institute of Philippines Culture, Quezon City

Environment and Urbanization (1990) "Community Based Organizations: How they Develop, What they Seek and what they Achieve", 2, 1, IIED, London

Farrington, J and A Martin (1988) *Farmer Participatory Research: A Review of Concepts and Practices*, Agricultural Research and Extension Network Paper no 19, ODI, London

Flinn, J C and S K De Datta (1984) "Trends in Irrigated Rice Yields under Intensive Cropping at Philippine Research Stations", *Field Crops Research*, 9, pp1–15

Francis, C A (1986) *Multiple Cropping Systems*, Macmillan, New York

—— (1989) *Internal Resources for Sustainable Agriculture*, Sustainable Agriculture Programme Gatekeeper Series no 8, IIED, London

Fujisaka, S (1989) *Participation by Farmers, Researchers and Extension Workers in Soil Conservation*, Sustainable Agriculture Programme, Gatekeeper Series no 16, IIED, London

Goethert, R and Hamdi, N (1988) *Making Microplans: A Community Based Process in Programming and Development*, Intermediate Technology Publications, London

Gueye, B and Schoonmaker Freudenberger, K (1991) *Introduction à la Méthode Accelerée de Recherche Participative: Quelques Notes Pour Appuyer une Formation Pratique*, IIED, London

Hobbelink, H, R Vellve and M Abraham (1990) *Inside the Bio-Revolution*, IOCU, Penang, and GRAIN, Barcelona

Horwith, B J, P N Windle, E F MacDonald, J K Parkers, A M Ruby and C Elfring (1989) "The Role of Technology in Enhancing Low Resource Agriculture in Africa", *Agriculture and Human Values*

Howell, J (ed) (1988) *Training and Visit Extension in Practice*, ODI, London

Huang, H T and Pei Yang (1987) "Ancient Culture of Citrus Ant as Biological Agent", *Bio Science*, 37, pp665–71

Huby, M (1990) *Where You Can't See the Wood for the Trees*, Kenya Woodfuel Development Programme Series, Beijer Institute, Stockholm

Hudson, N (1989) *A Study of the Reasons for Success or Failure of Soil Conservation Projects*, FAO Soils Bulletin 64, Rome

Jodha, N S (1990) *Rural Common Property Resources: A Growing Crisis*, sustainable Agriculture Programme Gatekeeper Series no 24, IIED, London

Kenmore, P (1989) "IPM means the Best Mix", *MAPPS Newsletter*, 11, p38

Kenmore, P, J A Litsinger, J P Bandong, A C Santiago and M M Salac (1987) "Philippine Rice Farmers and Insecticides: Thirty Years of Growing Dependency and New Options for Change", in E J Tait and B Napoment (eds) *Management of Pests and Pesticides: Farmers' Perceptions and Practices*, Westview Press, London

Kerkhof, P (1990) *Agroforestry in Africa, A Survey of Project Experience*, Panos Institute, London

Kolhe, S S and B N Mitra (1987) "Effects of Azolla as an Organic Source of Nitrogen In Rice–Wheat Cropping System", *Journal of Agronomy and Crop Science*, 159, pp212–15

Kotschi, J, A Waters-Bayers, R Adelhelm and U Hoesle (1989) *Ecofarming in Agricultural Development*, GTZ, Eschborn

Kottack, C P (1985) " When People Don't Come First: Some Sociological Lessons from Completed Projects", in M M Cernea (ed) *Putting People First*, Oxford University Press, Oxford

Kydd, J (1989) "Maize Research in Malawi: Lessons from Failure", *Journal of International Development*, 1, pp112–44

Lane, C and J M Pretty (1990) *Displaced Pastoralists and Transferred Wheat Technology in Tanzania*, Sustainable Agriculture Programme Gatekeeper Series no 20, IIED, London

Lipton, M with R Longhurst (1989) *New Seeds and Poor people*, Unwin Hyman, London

Lobo, C (1990) *Watershed Development: A Participatory Development Approach to Resource Mobilization*, Social Centre, Ahmednagar, India

McCraken, J, G R Conway and J N Pretty (1988) *An Introduction to Rapid Rural Appraisal for Agricultural Development*, Sustainable Agriculture Programme, IIED, London

Mascarenhas, J, P Shah, S Joseph, R Jayakaran, J Devavaram, V Ramachandran, A Fernandez, R Chambers and J N Pretty (eds) (1991) *Participatory Rural Appraisal: RRA Notes 13*, Sustainable Agriculture Programme, IIED, London

Moris, J (1990) *Extension Alternatives in Tropical Africa*, ODI, London

Mullen, J (1989) "Training and Visit System in Somalia: Contradictions and Anomalies", *Journal of International Development*, 1, pp145–67

Murphy, D (1990) "Community Organization in Asia", *Environment and Urbanization*, 2, pp51–60

NRC (1984) *Pesticide Resistance Strategies and Tactics for Management*, National Academy Press, Washington, DC

—— (1989) *Alternative Agriculture*, National Academy Press, Washington, DC

OTA (1988) *Enhancing Agriculture in Africa: A Role for US Development Assistance*, US Government Printing Office, Washington, DC

Poffenberger, M (1990) *Joint Management of Forest Lands: Experiences from South Asia*, Ford Foundation, New Delhi

Pradan, N C, and R Yoder (1989) *Improving Irrigation Management through Farmer-to-Farmer Training: Examples from Nepal*, Working Paper no 12, International Irrigation Management Institute, Katmandu

Pretty, J N (1990) *Rapid Catchment Analysis for Extension Agents: Notes on the Kericho Training Workshop for the Ministry of Agriculture*, Kenya, IIED, London

Rahman, M A (ed) (1984) *Grass-roots Participation and Self-Reliance*, Oxford University Press, Oxford, and IBH Publication Company, New Delhi

Ramaprasad, V and V Ramachandran (1989) *Celebrating Awareness*, Myrada, Bangalore, and Foster Parents International, New Delhi

Reij, C (1991) *Indigenous Soil and Water Conservation in Africa*, Sustainable Agriculture Programme Gatekeeper Series no 27, IIED, London

Reij, C, P Muller and L Begemann (1988) *Water Harvesting for Plant Production*, Technical Paper no 91, World Bank, Washington, DC

Rhoades, R E (1984) *Breaking New Ground: Agricultural Anthropology*, International Potato Centre, Lima, Peru

Richards, P (1985) *Indigenous Agricultural Revolution*, Hutchison, London

Rodale, R (1985) " Internal Resources and External Inputs: The Two Sources of all Production Needs", Rodale Institute Research Centre, Kuztown, Pa.

RRA Notes, (1988–91) Issues 1–14, Sustainable Agriculture Programme, IIED, London

Sarrantonia, M (1991) *Soil Improving Legumes: Methodologies for Screening*, Rodale Institute Research Centre, Kuztown, PA

Scoones, I (ed) (1991) *Wetlands in Drylands: The Agroecology of Savanna Systems in Africa*, Drylands Programme, IIED, London

Shah, P, G Bharadwaj and R Ambastha (1991) "Participatory Impact Monitoring of a Soil and Water Conservation Programme by Farmers, Extension Volunteers, and AKRSP", in J Mascarenhas et al (eds) *Participatory Rural Appraisal: RRA Notes 13*, Sustainable Agriculture Programme, IIED, London

Uphoff, N (1990) "Paraprojects as New Modes of International Development Assistance", *World Development*, 18, pp140–1

Wantabe, I, C R Espinsa, N S Berak and B V Alimango (1977) *Utilization of the Azolla–Anabaena Complex as a Nitrogen Fertilizer for Rice*, Research Paper Series no 11, IRRI, Los Baños, Philippines

Wolf, E C (1986) *Beyond the Green Revolution: New Approaches for Third World Agriculture*, Worldwatch Paper no 73, Worldwatch Institute, Washington, DC

World Bank (1991) *World Development Report 1991*, Oxford University Press, Oxford

Young, A (1989) *Agroforestry for Soil Conservation*, CAB International, Wallingford

Economic and Political Consequences of the Green Revolution in India
Utsa Patnaik

The inception of India's "new agricultural strategy" from 1961 followed the visit of a team of experts from the Ford Foundation, whose report on "India's Food Crisis" evidently greatly influenced government policies. Under the new strategy the Intensive Agricultural Development Programme (IADP) was started in 15 districts selected from the availability of irrigation and absence of acute tenurial problems. High-yielding cereal seed varieties already developed in Mexico and Taiwan, along with fertilizers, pesticides and credit to farmers, were made available at subsidized rates. The high-yielding varieties programme was subsequently extended to all 324 districts in the country.

Government policy documents of that time bear the stamp of ideas of "modernizing" agriculture such as those of T W Schultz (1965). Policy documents stressed the need to "transform traditional agriculture" by introducing an entirely new, imported technology package, while the need to reform land-holding structure and tenurial relations receded to the background.

Two Phases of the Green Revolution: The Uneven Expansion of Output

The first phase of the Green Revolution from the early 1960s to the mid-1970s was primarily concentrated on wheat and was associated with a substantial rise in both yield per unit area and total output, especially in north India. In this phase foodgrains prices were rising faster than prices of either manufactured inputs into agricultural production, or final consumption goods. Thus, it took less wheat output, for example, to buy fertilizers or fuels in 1974 than it had before the start of the Green Revolution in 1963. The barter terms of trade moved sharply in favour of the agricultural sector. At the same time, real earnings of rural labour were declining. The profitability of producing cereals rose significantly, especially in wheat where the new varieties gave a substantial yield grain under field conditions. Considerable capitalist investment was visible, especially in the wheat-growing region of north India (comprising Punjab, Haryana and

Uttar Pradesh), in the form of irrigation pumpsets, threshers and tractors in addition to higher working capital outlays on the new inputs and on wages. On the other hand the relative profitability of pulses (which provides the main source of foodgrain protein for the rural poor) fell and a declining trend of pulse production per capita set in.

In the primarily rice-growing coastal and river delta areas of high rainfall and canal irrigation, the new varieties were found to be less successful in terms of yield rise. Water management problems and high atmospheric humidity during long periods of cloud cover raised costs and limited yields in the field by promoting pest infestation. Capitalist investment was much lower than in the wheat-growing regions and widespread petty tenancy continued. In north India, however, there were several rounds of tenant evictions by landowners switching to direct cultivation with hired labour, and the proportion of hired labour in the rural working population rose sharply.

During the second phase of the Green Revolution, from about 1975 to the present, despite the advocates of the new strategy anticipating that the new techniques would be generalized wholesale to rice-producing areas, this has not happened. Instead, high-yielding rice has emerged as a second crop grown primarily for sale in the traditionally wheat growing region of north India, which had already benefited the most from the first round of technical change. Over 90 per cent of the Punjab rice crop today is sold, compared to barely one-third to two-fifths in the traditional rice growing areas where it is also the staple foodgrain of the producers. Since 1975, the rate of increase in foodgrain prices compared to manufactured goods prices has slowed down. In non-foodgrains of commercial importance, such as cotton and sugar cane, the price rise even during the first phase had been much less than in foodgrains; the recent unfavourable shift in the terms of trade has hit producers of these crops particularly hard. Waves of peasant agitation for higher crop prices have erupted during the last decade.

National Self-Sufficiency Combined with Mass Poverty
The new strategy has been in operation for over three decades and it is now clear that the unevenness of growth has been accentuated at multiple levels. Gains have been concentrated in particular crops, regions and social groups (they have not been spread evenly through society). Total output of foodgrains has registered an impressive expansion, trebling from 50 million tons in 1951 to 150 million tons by 1983/4 (however, it fell below this level in the following years with a sharp dip in the drought year of 1987/8). In terms of production and availability per head of population, however, the picture is disappointing in that the well-documented decline in grain production during the half-century preceding independence has not been made up. While the average Indian consumed 200 kg of grain on the eve of the First World War, this had dropped to 150 kg by independence. In the subsequent 35 years per capita foodgrain availability rose by less than 10 per cent to around 166 kg. These levels are inadequate to meet minimum nutritional requirements when there are large income disparities. A more populous and initially equally poor neighbour, China, started with a higher per capita availability in 1951 and by 1984 had raised it still further to achieve a 50 per cent higher level (about 250 kg, using comparable concepts) than India. Rural income distribution is known to be considerably less unequal in China than in India. Further, the nutritional balance of the average Indian's food intake has worsened, with a fall in the share of pulses relative to cereals.

For a quarter-century after the inception of planned development, from 1951 to 1975, India produced less foodgrains than were consumed, the balance being imported (mostly from the USA). In the decade 1975 to 1984, however, domestic production exceeded consumption, the difference going into building up food stocks and a small volume of exports. India thus became "self-sufficient" in foodgrains during this decade; indeed, the government's buffer stocks had amounted to an unprecedented level of nearly 30 million tins by 1984/5, which is 20 per cent of the peak annual output.

The concept of "self-sufficiency", defined by zero food imports or positive exports, is, however, a tricky one: it need not mean that people are not going hungry. "Self-sufficiency" in a market economy has to be understood in relation to effective demand. It is quite possible for foodgrains to be exported while famine prevails, as happened during the great Bengal famine of 1943/4. At that time, nearly four million of the rural poor died as a consequence of the British colonial government's policy of printing money to finance its war expenditure. This policy sent rice prices soaring ahead of the buying capacity of the rural masses. In contemporary India there is no famine, but there is widespread and persistent unemployment and poverty, especially in rural areas. This has led many observers to conclude that the excess-supply situation, which enabled the government to build up large food stocks by 1984, even with stagnant and inadequate levels of per capita consumption, was the outcome of the lack of purchasing power of the undernourished, combined with burgeoning marketable surpluses in the hands of the minority of capitalist farmers.

Macroeconomic indicators relating to incomes and employment tend to support this conclusion. There has been a process of profit-inflation in the economy. The official National Accounts Statistics show that total property income, that is profits, rent and interest, as a proportion of total income generated by agriculture and mineral extraction, rose steadily from 8.7 per cent in 1978/9 to 12.5 per cent by 1984/5. On the other hand, the real value of the rural wage bill has remained level during this period, even though the number of rural employees has gone up by nearly 20 per cent. A constant level of real income shared among larger numbers of wages workers implies declining real earnings per head. Analysis of the variation between states shows that the largest declines are in the relatively stagnant regions of western, central and southern India. Labourers and poor peasants make up some three-fifths of the rural population; the contraction or stagnation of their income restrains their food consumption even though their food intake is nutritionally inadequate; the obverse of this fall is the rise in the real income of the propertied minority, whose food consumption is already at satiation levels, and who therefore spend a much lower proportion of their higher incomes on food. This shows at the aggregate level (given the substantial share of this minority in total expenditure) as a small decline in the proportion of total consumption expenditure going on food, or an Engel effect incorrectly integrated by some observers as indicating a rise in the general standard of life.[*]

The Green Revolution strategy has implied a standardization of cereal crop varieties and a narrowing of the earlier traditionally diversified genetic base of crop types. Combined with the dependence on these new dwarf varieties on irrigation, this has

---

[*] In the nineteenth century, Ernst Engel discovered that as family incomes rose, the proportion of their budget spent on food declines. This effect has come to be known as Engels' Law.

contributed to an increase in output fluctuations compared to the period before the mid-1960s. If the rains are good and irrigation water available at the right time, yields from the dwarf varieties are high, but either drought or water-logging makes them plummet. In traditional practice, by contrast, some insurance was provided by sowing part of the areas to lower-yield but drought-resistant varieties and part to tall, flood-resistant varieties. Second, the proportion of cultivated area under effective irrigation is just over one-quarter, with rainfed and dryland agriculture relatively neglected: over 100 districts, or nearly a third of the total area, is now declared to be drought-prone. The reliance placed by the new strategy on giant state-financed irrigation projects on the one hand and on private tubewell-pumpset irrigation projects on the other, has also led to a sharp decline in traditional small- to medium-scale water conservation systems maintained in the past by community labour. (These systems can still be seen in operation in the few remote parts of the country relatively little ravaged by the inroads of capitalism.) These problems have been compounded by rapid deforestation contributing to solid erosion and degradation as well as a lowering of the sub-soil water table.

The Regional and Class Concentration of Growth

India can be divided into three groups of states: a fast-growing region in the north (Punjab, Hayana and Uttar Pradesh), a stagnating region in the east and south (Gujarat, Rajasthan, Maharashtra, Andhra Pradesh, Karnataka, Kerala and Tamil Nadu), and the rest of India. These groupings are very rough and there are many high-growth irrigated sub-regions in the second category just as there are some low growth areas in the first. Between 1974/5 and 1985/6, the second phase of the Green Revolution, the area of north India in total food output rose steadily from 29 to 36 per cent; the area of west and south India declined from 37 to 32 per cent; while the share of the rest of India changed marginally from 34 to 32 per cent, with some fluctuation. Thus the region of north India, which initially had the lowest share of the three in total output, accounts for the highest share today; while a far vaster region in terms of area and population, which initially contributed the highest share of total food output, today accounts for the lowest share.

While the region of stagnating production registered a mere 16 per cent rise in food output in the 1983/4 to 1985/6 period compared to the 1974/5 to 1976/7 period, the region of dynamic growth by contrast has registered a 67 per cent rise in output. Population has grown everywhere by about one-fifth, so it is clear that per capita food output has been falling in most of the country while rising fast in north India. A comparison of the all-India sample surveys on employment relating to 1972/3, with later rounds in 1977/8 and 1983, shows a rise in unemployment in rural areas.

No less striking is the class concentration of gains in the areas experiencing the Green Revolution. A cross-sectional study of farms in Jaryana indicates that investment in new techniques was strongly concentrated in the larger-scale, labour-hiring farms while the majority of families, who were self-employed or hired out their labour, failed to reach the poverty line. A comparison of the agricultural censuses of 1981 and 1971 shows that in the Punjab the number of smallholdings below two hectares fell, owing mainly to the cessation of some 0.8 million petty tenancies; land concentration increased and the average holding size went up. At the same time Punjab has registered a steep rise in the proportion of labourers in the agricultural workforce (from 32 to 38

per cent), completing the classic scenario of capitalist development in agriculture leading to the displacement of small producers and to proletarianization.

The importance of food stocks procured and operated by the government becomes
evident. On the one hand, large procurement is possible because the well-to-do surplus
farmers in the fast-growing regions sell almost their entire crop; on the other hand, the
distribution of food at subsidized rates protects the non-rural consumer against inflation, and provides the rural landless and land-poor employment — albeit on a limited
scale — under various food-for-work programmes. Nevertheless, the real incomes of
the rural poor are declining alarmingly in the low- and negative-growth regions.

The Green Revolution region of north India not only accounts for one-third of total
foodgrain production: it contributes 97 per cent of the government's procurement of
wheat and 65 per cent of its total rice procurement. Within the region, the state of
Punjab alone accounts for 61 per cent and 44 per cent respectively of total wheat and
rice purchased by the government. In recent years this granary of India has seen an
unprecedentedly violent movement, albeit supported only by a minority, for secession
from the Indian union.

Reference
Schultz, T W (1965) *Transforming Traditional Agriculture*, Yale University Press, New Haven, CT

■ Pricing Policy and Sustainability in Indonesia
Gordon Conway and Edward Barbier

The case of Indonesia clearly illustrates that governments can dramatically influence incentives for sustainable agricultural development. Policies on commodity prices, farmer incentives and input subsidies all have significant implications for erosion, pollution and the use of scarce resources (Ackerman et al, 1987).

Commodity Prices

Agricultural markets in Indonesia are complex and, though government management is pervasive, the level of intervention varies significantly from market to market for the various crops cultivated. Some crops are protected; others are not. The market for rice, for instance, is highly regulated, with the government of Indonesia's (GOI) procurement agency, BULOG, maintaining floor and ceiling prices by accumulating and controlling inventory stocks and imports. BULOG has also been active in the markets for sugar, corn, soya beans and wheat, though mainly to restrict imports. In addition, extremely high and effective protection rates exist for fruits, vegetables and dairy products as a stimulus to domestic production, which for the most part are not traded internationally. The rate has been as high as 200 per cent (Glassburner, 1985). Cassava, too, has been supported. Prices doubled in 1985 and again in 1987, largely reflecting the GOI's targeting objectives of overcoming domestic shortages and procuring sufficient supplies to meet the EEC export quota. By contrast, there has been little government intervention in the markets for the mostly non-tradable non-grain staples (apart from cassava) like groundnuts and minor legumes (mungbeans, pigeon peas).

Examination of the ratio of domestic producer prices to border prices (the nominal protection rate or NPR) suggests that despite the varying degrees of market intervention, prices for rice, corn and cassava have not been significantly distorted. But the mainly positive NPRs for soya beans and sugar between 1972 and 1985 indicate that import controls have lifted domestic prices well above world levels. For export crops the long-term decline in world commodity prices has significantly eroded the nominal and real incentives to domestic producers, but recent devaluations have somewhat restored Indonesia's competitiveness.

The overall effect of these interventions has been to reinforce the profitability of horticultural crops and, to a lesser extent, soya beans and livestock products. Protective pricing together with rigid import controls and stringent area-targeting have also resulted in expanded small-holder sugar production on Java. And there has been a steady increase in rice production, though this is less a function of producer prices, which have been declining in real terms, than of input subsidies. This, however, has had the effect of depressing prices for the less desirable staple substitutes produced mainly on rainfed lands, such as corn and root crops. They are strong substitutes for rice, especially among the rural poor.

Pricing and the Environment

What have been the environmental implications of this agricultural pricing structure, particularly in the uplands of Java? The most notable effect arises from the dramatic increase in terms of trade for horticulture and livestock products. These appear, over the long term, to be encouraging upland agricultural production to move from less profitable cultivation of relatively inelastic, basic starch staples to more profitable, income-elastic commodities such as fruits, vegetables, milk and meat. This may constitute an important incentive for upland farmers to invest in soil conservation measures and improved land-management techniques, although increased profitability alone may not be sufficient (Carson, 1987; Barbier, 1988). However, the increased profitability of vegetable crops also means that farmers are encouraged to cultivate them on steeply sloped volcanic soils, where water run-off and hence soil erosion are enhanced (World Bank, 1987a). Furthermore, as the average returns increase to these and other highly commercialized and input-intensive crops, such as sugar cane, then share tenancy and absentee ownership become more common. If these tenancy arrangements are insecure or if the objective of absentee owners is short-term profit maximization or land speculation, then the incentives for long-term investments in improved land management may be greatly reduced.

Finally, the recent and rapid rise of cassava prices is worrying, as some upland farmers are switching back from more protective farming systems, based on livestock rearing, agroforestry and multi-cropping, to growing cassava alone on highly erosive soils.

Farmer Investments

To what extent are farmers making long-term investments? Improvements in terms of trade may not be directly benefiting farmers who need to make these investments. Although in the last few years the relative competitiveness of agricultural exports has improved due to devaluations, the considerable market power of exporter associations, licensed exporters and approved traders and other marketing intermediaries ensures that upland farmers are receiving relatively few of the benefits (World Bank, 1987b). In general, farmers growing crops on marginal lands tend to have lower producer margins than farmers growing crops on the irrigated lowlands. For example, farmers receive 80–85 per cent of the retail price for rice, 70–75 per cent of the retail price for soya beans and only 60–65 per cent of the final price for corn, which is predominantly a dryland crop (World Bank, 1987b). Farmers on marginal lands are less likely to engage in marketing activities and more prone to price discrimination by marketing intermediaries. In the Citanduy River Basin, west Java, only 10–20 per cent of clove and peanut farmers perform marketing activities, such as drying or transporting the commodities to sub-district sellers (Irawan, 1986).

In addition, while pricing policies can encourage sustainable agricultural practices they are rarely, by themselves, sufficient to ensure that new appropriate farming systems for marginal lands are adopted. For instance, on steep upland, livestock- and agro-forestry based systems are likely to be more sustainable than the cultivation of annual crops, while on acidic swamplands coconut-based systems may be more appropriate than irrigated rice. Yet if diversified small-holder production systems such as these are to be viable on marginal lands, improvements are needed in the quality and marketing of small-holder production, particularly of potentially tradable crops and import substitutes. As an example, improved drying of coconut would increase the value of copra by at least Rp 25/Kg, but for small-holders this requires knowledge of better techniques (such as using the coconut shell for drying and not using the coconut husk for fuel) and collective investment, such as farmers' groups sharing the costs of more efficient drying kilns (GOI, 1987).

Input Subsidies

What are the effects of such subsidies on sustainable practices? In Indonesia, input subsidies totalled about US $725 million in 1985. The current effective subsidy for fertilizers to farmers is about 38 per cent of the farmgate price (68 per cent of the world price); and for credit it is an implicit rate of 8 per cent.

This policy of heavily subsidizing agricultural inputs was one of the hallmarks of the rice self-sufficiency strategy of the 1960s and 1970s, and thus most of the subsidies have benefited the lowland, irrigated, mainly rice-producing areas of Java, south Sumatra, south Sulawesi and Bali. The effects have been dramatic; the area of higher yielding varieties (HYVs) has expanded from 0.8 to 6.8 million hectares, and on Java the average area planted with HYVs has reached 94 per cent. The irrigated area increased from 3.7 to 4.9 million hectares. Distribution of subsidized fertilizers rose from 0.2 to 4.1 million tonnes, and of subsidized pesticides from 1080 to 14 210 tonnes (World Bank, 1987b).

Now, with a new emphasis on agricultural diversification, these subsidies are increasingly being used to stimulate production of other crops — notably sugar, cassava, maize, palm oil and soya beans. Assuming no change in input policy, the total cost of the subsidies is anticipated to increase, as they are gradually extended to agricultural cultivation on marginal lands. For example, rainfed crops on Java, with the exception of high-valued vegetables, fruits and estate crops, still tend to use relatively fewer subsidized inputs than irrigated rice and sugar, but use relatively more organic fertilizers. This will change, but not necessarily for the better.

Although the yields and net returns of intensive irrigated rice on Java are substantially higher than for rainfed crops, this does not imply greater efficiency in use of inputs. For instance, despite the larger applications of chemical fertilizer and pesticides on intensive irrigated paddy, their use on non-intensive irrigated paddy and on the predominantly rainfed staple crops, apart from maize, appears to incur lower per-unit costs. This suggests that subsidies are encouraging overuse of these inputs in intensive rice cropping. Similarly, per-unit irrigation costs for rice are strikingly low, given that irrigation accounts for 91 per cent of the water use on Java (World Bank, 1987a). Efficiency of input use is thus likely to decline and be accompanied by a greater and more widespread environmental impact, particularly from fertilizers and pesticides.

Fertilizers

Overuse of fertilizers is already a substantial problem in lowland irrigated areas. In some areas of Indonesia, applications of urea can reach between 200 and 250 kilograms. Since fertilizer comprises less than 10 per cent of the production cost of rice and the largest production response is achieved at relatively low levels of application, the current high rice–fertilizer price ratio of 1.5–2 will continue to encourage inappropriate application and waste, with little stimulation to rice output (Barbier, 1988). Moreover, providing subsidized fertilizers to cultivators on marginal lands may be counter-productive in that farmers will apply relatively cheap fertilizers to increase yields, rather than consider more expensive but environmentally sound methods such as green manuring, mulching and using compost to maintain soil fertility. For example, in Ngadas, east Java, farmers are presently using over 1000 kilograms of subsidized chemical fertilizers per hectare to produce two ten-tonne potato crops. Yields are declining and, as experiments have shown, are less than one half of what could be attained with improved soil management and green manuring techniques. Recently, the farmers have come to realize that increased fertilizer use was not offsetting yield reductions and have begun to use more organic fertilizer (World Bank, 1987a).

Pesticides

The government has recently banned the use of 57 pesticides and is undertaking an integrated pest-management training programme with the World Bank and the Food and Agriculture Organization (FAO). Nevertheless, the current subsidy levels will most likely continue to encourage inappropriate and excessive use. In fact, the pesticide ban was a belated response to that latest plague of rice brown planthopper, which was associated with the misapplication of pesticides that have wiped out natural enemies of pests. Pesticide subsidies tend to discourage traditional methods of eradicating pests and make integrated and biological pest control methods relatively less attractive to farmers. Subsidized pesticides encourage farmers to treat fields preventively even before an economically damaging insect population is present, causing natural enemies to be killed and releasing pests (such as brown planthopper) from natural control. Even rice varieties normally resistant to brown planthopper, such as IR–36, have been known to be "hopperburned" (severely damaged from brown planthopper feeding) when treated too often with insecticides. For example, in northern Sumatra, the population density of brown planthopper (between 0.5 and 40 per plant) rose directly as the number of reported insecticide applications increased; in five areas experiencing hopperburn farmers were treating fields between six and twenty times in four to eight weeks without any success (Kenmore, 1986). Recently there have been attempts to reduce pesticide subsidies. But while fiscal outlays for the subsidies have been reduced, preliminary indications suggest that the costs of these subsidies are being shifted from the official budget to the operations of parastatal producers, who are financing the cost burden through additional borrowing.

Irrigation

The high level of subsidy for irrigation — US $401 million spread over approximately four million hectares — is also causing problems of overuse. With total operation and maintenance spending being reduced by budget cuts, the failure to recover any significant amount of irrigation costs is also jeopardizing the supply network. In the long run, failure to maintain the irrigation network will translate into losses of agricultural productivity, which will be exacerbated by any water scarcity problems caused by overuse. Allocation of scarce water supplies will become a pressing problem on Java in the near future, as municipal and industrial uses continue to expand.

Credit

Credit is of crucial importance in furthering adoption of improved soil-conservation and land-management technique on marginal lands. For example, investments in bench terracing require a medium-term loan for at least two years and short-term loans for succeeding years. Agroforestry requires long-term loans for at least seven years. Different rates and terms are required for various private small-holder investments in marketing, transport facilities, post-harvesting technologies and quality improvements (World Bank, 1987a).

Yet despite implicit subsidies, public liquidity credit is estimated to meet only 15 per cent of the demand for credit by farmers. The other 85 per cent is obtained informally at an interest rate of around 60 per cent. Small farmers, particularly those outside lowland irrigated areas, are especially dependent on high cost, informal sources of funds. And, despite the fact that over 50 per cent of the subsidized liquidity credit goes to sugar production, it accounts for only 3.3 per cent of the value of total crop production in Indonesia. There is also concern that certain subsidized and liquidity credit-financed priority programmes, such as in the major tree-crops sectors, may distort the capacity of small-holder producers to become financially viable. These distortions in the credit market, and the general lack of multi-purpose credit at affordable rates with medium- and long-term payback periods, are major constraints on the sustainable development of agricultural lands.

Alternative Policies

How can existing policies be improved or replaced? Since producer prices for the major food crops in Indonesia — rice and corn — have generally followed the underlying trend in world market prices, there seems little need to change these. But for upland soya bean and other higher valued upland crops, improved quality and yields may in the long term be a more effective way of increasing farmer incomes than the current practice of maintaining domestic prices well in excess of world levels. There is a particularly strong argument for reducing the very high effective protection rates for vegetables and sugar production, since these are not conducive to improved soil conservation practices in upland areas, and may in fact benefit the richer farmers more than poorer upland farmers.

It may be necessary to continue some restrictive import controls for perennial fruits and animal husbandry products so as to encourage the spread of agroforestry and livestock-based forage systems, particularly in the uplands of Java. But over the long term, Indonesia will need to develop export markets for certain products, such as tropical fruits, which will require a gradual dismantling of protectionist policies. In general, for all export crops vital to sustainable upland development (for example, coffee, cloves, tea and cocoa), not only does international competitiveness need to be maintained by an effective exchange-rate policy but monopolistic trading practices must be removed to allow the benefits of improved terms of trade to reach upland small-holders.

Perhaps the major change is most needed in those policies — particularly input subsidies and investment strategies for research, extension and infrastructure — which are still largely biased towards lowland irrigated agriculture, especially rice cultivation. These result in an under-investment of resources in other agricultural areas that are currently absorbing labour and could potentially yield higher growth and incomes. They also artificially overvalue the contribution of the lowlands to agricultural development. Furthermore, high input subsidies encourage wasteful use which is the direct cause of serious environmental problems (for example, pest outbreaks, over-fertilization) and act as disincentives for proper management of land and water resources. With Indonesia now producing rice surpluses — resulting in additional high costs for storage of excess stocks and for subsidized exports — there is a case for introducing a phased reduction of these subsidies and reallocating funds towards higher priority agricultural investments for sustainable agricultural development in non-rice growing areas.

Reducing or eliminating input subsidies and reallocating research and extension funds could, in the short term, release US $275 million annually for investment in more sustainable agriculture. Assuming a complete phase out over time of the fertilizer subsidy and a fourfold increase in both research and extension budgets, this could increase to as much as US $525 million a year. Such funds could be used, effectively, for:

- integrated pest management (IPM), for brown planthopper control, to be gradually extended to IPM for other pests;
- increasing the availability of general rural credit, particularly to marginal farmers, at affordable rates and with multiple terms;
- research and extension to develop and support new farming systems and land-management techniques appropriate for the marginal (mainly dryland and swamp-land) sedentary agriculture in the outer islands and uplands of Java, as well as shifting cultivation. This would include the development and dissemination of new varieties appropriate to diverse agroecological conditions, research into pest and disease outbreaks, and improvements in small-holder estate crop systems; and
- investment in: (a) further improvements in farming systems for specific agro-ecological zones; and (b) improvements in the physical infrastructure serving these zones, including rural transport, integration of markets, credit facilities, post-harvest technology and processing, and produce quality.

We have discussed the particular case of Indonesia in some detail because it clearly illustrates the manner in which government policies interact with one another to inhibit sustainable agricultural development. As we have tried to demonstrate, policies can be changed, and in ways that not only further sustainability but improve efficiency.

The next question is how to translate such policies into workable programmes and projects that affect the livelihoods of small farms.

References

Ackerman, R, E Barbier, G R Conway and D Pearce (1987) "Environment and Sustainable Economic Development in Indonesia: An Overview Report", in *Indonesia — Fava Watersheds: Fava Uplands and Watershed Management*, World Bank, Washington, DC

Barbier, E B (1988) *The Economics of Farm-Level Adoption of Soil Conservations Museums in the Uplands of Java*, IIED, London

Carson, B, with the assistance of the East Java KEPAS Working Group (1987) *A Comparison of Soil Conservation Strategies in Four Agroecological Zones in the Upland of East Java*, Malang, KEPAS, pp32–7

Glassburner, B (1985) "Macroeconomics and the Agricultural Sector", *Bulletin of Indonesian Economic Studies*, vol 21, no 2

GOI, Ministry of Agriculture, DG of Estates (1987) "Coconut Processing and Marketing", *Feasibility Study, Smallholder Estate Crops Development Project*, vol 8, pp8–18

Irawan, B (1986) "Executive Summary: Marketing Analysis for Dryland Farming Development in Citanduy River Basin", USESE, Ciamis, Indonesia

Kenmore, P E (1986) "Status Report on Integrated Pest Control in Rice in Indonesia with Special Reference to Conservation of Natural Enemies and the Rice Brown Planthopper (*Nilaparvata lugens*)", FAO, Indonesia

World Bank (1987a) *Indonesia — Fava Watersheds*, Washington, DC

—— (1987b) *Indonesia — Agricultural Policy: Issues and Options*, Washington, DC

Chapter 5 | INDUSTRIAL-
IZATION and
POLLUTION

Industrialization is important in the achievement of sustainable development for two reasons: first, as part of the development process and second, as a threat to the health of people living near industrial plants. Nick Robins and Alex Trisoglio draw attention to these positive and negative aspects of industrialization, noting that both in high rates of resource consumption and in creation of pollution, much of manufacturing industry is unsustainable. They call for an eco-industrial revolution in both the North and South. Later in the chapter, they discuss the obstacles to achieving sustainable industrial development: the traditional view of environment as a "free good", the pressure of competition, misdirected government policies, overestimates of the costs of prevention, financial short termism, the weak environmental capacity of small businesses, institutional weaknesses, conservation, linear rather than circular approaches and closed decision making processes. They then examine the changes necessary to the achievement of the eco-industrial revolution.

Indira Jaising and C Sathyamala review the Bhopal disaster in which thousands of people were killed and several million permanently disabled. They identify a number of failures in the legal and medical responses to the event. As David Weir shows, such accidents are likely to recur, particularly in the Third World where, as Jorge Hardoy and David Satterthwaite explain, many hazardous industries are now located and to which toxic and hazardous waste are exported from "environmentally sensitive" developed countries. Matthias Koch and Michael Grubb summarize the UNCED Agenda 21 recommendations for the management of toxic chemicals and hazardous wastes.

Restructuring Industry for Sustainable Development
Nick Robins and Alex Trisoglio

The Need for an Eco-Industrial Revolution

In the debate on how to achieve sustainable development, industry plays a paradoxical role. On the one hand, it is one of the major productive and wealth-creating sectors of society, contributing on average one-third of measured national income. However, industry is also a major polluter, both directly through its production processes and indirectly through the product it sells. The challenge for companies, governments and the public at large is, how can industry both produce products to meet needs and generate wealth in ways that do not degrade the environment or exacerbate growing global inequality? As the World Commission on Environment and Development stated in 1987: "Industry has the power to enhance or degrade the environment; it invariably does both" (WCED, 1987).

Industry is also an elusive and ever-changing sector of the economy. Currently, the traditional division between manufacturing and services is becoming blurred as products and processes become redefined in the light of the shift to a global, information-based economy. Environmental impacts are also changing in intensity and location as some regions deindustrialize and others go through rapid industrialization. But the basic expansionary drive that has led to a sevenfold increase in manufacturing output since 1950 remains. Indeed, WCED projected a further five- to tenfold expansion of production by the time the world population stabilizes some time in the next century.

But WCED, like countless other government or business analyses of the problems related to industry and sustainability, declined to assess whether an expansion at the rate predicted was either desirable or feasible, given the accelerating depletion of national "capital stocks". Furthermore, there has been no serious attempt to pursue to its logical extent the Brundtland Report's objective of "meeting needs" of current and future generations in the industrial context. In a world of increasing poverty and inequality, this would mean questioning the continuing concentration of industrial process and product development funding in the saturated markets of the North, which the "green consumer" movements of Europe and North America have scarcely begun to challenge.

Since sustainable development is essentially a global concept, as far as industry is concerned it means the ability of production and consumption patterns to be universalized so that needs are met and environmental integrity guaranteed for the future. However, the dominant industrial model of the North is far from sustainable. In the USA, for example, hazardous waste generation is growing at an annual rate of 7.5 per cent, considerably more than the rate of economic growth. Energy and materials consumption levels remain excessive, although some progress towards greater efficiency was made during the 1970s, particularly in Japan. And despite considerable improvements in environmental awareness and, in some cases, performance, industry remains resistant to the restructuring that will be required, for instance, to reduce fossil fuel consumption and phase out toxic substances.

The Eco-Industrial Revolution

Maurice Strong, the secretary general of UNCED, has spoken of the need for an "eco-industrial revolution". Its purpose would be to redefine the goals of industrialization and the tools and technologies used to achieve them. This process of industrial restructuring for sustainable development would have two main priorities:

- The first priority would be to redirect corporate energies to satisfy the broader human aspects of development. This would mean refocusing product and process development to ensure that basic human needs are met on a global basis, establishing formal commitments to transparency and community access to decision-making, and collaborating in the creation of sustainable livelihoods for the growing labour force of developing countries.
- The second priority would be to maximize long-run efficiency in the use of environmental resources in the production and consumption of useful goods and services. This would involve a move to industrial ecosystems that are increasingly "closed" in environmental terms, with increasing bias in favour of renewable or recyclable resources.

Unlike previous industrial revolutions, the restructuring needed to achieve sustainable development will require conscious and deliberate changes in corporate goals, business practice and regulatory frameworks. Sustainable development cannot be left to the market, since markets fail to internalize social and environmental costs and to reflect the full range of human choices. But neither can it be planned or driven solely by governments. Instead, both industry and governments need to become more open and accountable, and develop effective partnerships with stakeholders, whether citizens, employees or consumers. In the particular case of governments, without the active support of both industry and society, state action to promote sustainable industry will be futile. Governments need to provide an empowering framework and, within this, stimulate, cajole and sometimes force a long-term shift in industrial behaviour. This will involve the application of a range of policy tools at different levels from the global to the local.

The concept of an "eco-industrial revolution" has only just emerged, and the possible scope, timescale and contours of the required changes remain unclear. This section seeks to fill some of these gaps. It begins by examining structural changes in industry that have occurred since the UN Conference on the Human Environment in Stockholm in 1972, and then looks at some of the ways that industry has moved to improve its environmental performance. The key obstacles to further improvement are then discussed, leading to an outline of some of the main priorities for an eco-industrial policy.

Stockholm to Rio: Structural Change in Industry, 1970–90

Industry has historically been a significant consumer of energy and raw materials, as well as a major generator of pollution and wastes. But industry is also a dynamic and constantly changing sector of the economy. As Ruprecht Vondran, president of the German Steel Federation, said at the Second World Industry Conference on Environmental Management in April 1991: "The history of industrialization is the history of constant structural change, without which economic growth would not have been possible" (WICEM, 1991). Often change comes in waves, characterized by new technologies, energy sources, transport systems and social arrangements.

Since the late 1960s there has been a "volatile and turbulent transitional period" towards a new pattern of industrial development (Gruber and Nowotny, 1990). This has changed the balance of industry around the world and brought a shift towards relative "dematerialization" of production in the North, in which the volume of raw materials and energy needed to generate added value is reduced. There has also been rapid industrialization in some parts of the South. However, this period of structural change has not reduced the total burden of industry on the environment, and there is growing concern about the environmental implications of high-consumption lifestyles.

The Changing Balance of Industry

In the OECD, industry's share of gross domestic product has fallen from an average of about 40 per cent to about 30 per cent. During this process of restructuring one-third of the "*Fortune* 500" list of leading industrial companies has disappeared through merger or closure. In the developing world, the trend has been the reverse; in China, for example, industry now accounts for almost 50 per cent of GDP, compared with less than 40 per cent in 1965. The changes are particularly marked in Nigeria, where industry grew from 13 per cent to 44 per cent of GDP over the same period. Thus as the economies of the OECD become increasingly dominated by the service sectors, many developing countries are developing proportionately larger industrial sectors.

"Dematerialization" in the North

The Brundtland Commission and others have noted a number of environmental benefits flowing from this shift to a "post-industrial, information-based era" in the developed world (WCED, 1987). One of the most notable aspects of these changes has been the relative "dematerialization" of production in the OECD region. Following the two oil crises of the 1970s, a drive for efficiency improvements ensured that while the output of the chemicals industry has more than doubled since 1970, its energy consumption per unit of output has fallen by 57 per cent (OECD, 1991). A recent study by the International Monetary Fund has shown that improved resource productivity is a long-term trend: "raw material requirements for a given unit of output have fallen by an average of 1.25 per cent a year since the start of the century" (OECD, 1991). Companies have found that they can deliver the same or a better service with fewer materials; for example, the average weight of a car has declined by nearly 400 kilograms since 1975, through improved design and the partial substitution of plastics for steel.

Despite the often considerable "environmental gratis" effects of increasing production efficiencies, these improvements have to be placed in context (see Simonis, 1990). Although average energy intensity — the amount of energy used to generate one unit of GDP — in the OECD has fallen, total energy consumption has increased by over 30 per cent in the last 20 years. Despite all the regulatory efforts to date, no country has yet managed to fill the gulf between the social and environmental costs externalized by industry and other sections of society, or to delink economic growth from the production of waste. For example, in Germany total spending on environmental protection reached 1.5 per cent of GDP in the mid-1980s. However, the costs of pollution have been estimated to be in the region of 10 per cent of GDP (Weizsacker, 1991). Similarly, in France, every 1 per cent of growth generates 2 per cent extra waste. Continued growth has meant that add-on technical solutions to pollution problems, such as catalytic converters for auto emissions, have been overwhelmed. In addition, from the middle of the 1980s falling oil prices have removed the stimulus for conservation. As a result, the positive trend decoupling economic growth from energy growth has actually been reversed. Finally, while relative dematerialization has occurred in the OECD in certain sectors, to a significant degree this has been brought about by the net transfer of energy- and resource-intensive industries to the developing world, in effect displacing rather that solving the environmental problems of production.

Industrialization in the South

Developing countries' proportion of global industrial production has increased from 9.3 per cent to 13.2 per cent, although most of this increase occurred during the 1970s. In particular, there has been a marked redeployment of traditional industries such as textiles, leather, iron and steel, industrial chemicals and petrochemicals from North to South. Unfortunately, most of these industries are heavily polluting; and, in the absence of adequate financial resources and management practices, "such structural change could lead to increased environmental pressures in the South unless clean and efficient technologies are adopted on a large scale" (UNIDO, 1990). Among the newly industrializing countries (NICs) of east Asia such as Taiwan, Thailand and South Korea, the output of waste is beginning to reach levels in the OECD (Hirschhorn and Oldenberg, 1991) (see Table 5.1).

In Thailand, "the share of hazardous waste generating factories has increased from 29 per cent in 1979 to 58 per cent in 1989. The trend towards more hazardous waste producing industries is expected to continue during the next 15 to 20 years" (Phantumvanit and Panayotou, 1990); only one area in Thailand has adequate treatment facilities (Phantumvanit and Panayotou, 1990). But as happened earlier in the OECD region, industrial accidents are generating a mounting wave of public outrage at corporate environmental performance. For example, in South Korea, the environment minister was dismissed in February 1991 following national protests after an affiliate of the giant Doosan group had dumped 30 tons of phenol in the Naktong River.

The trend to dematerialization in the OECD has also had important economic impacts. The increasing use of synthetic substances (such as artificial sweeteners for sugar) or new materials (such as fibre optics for copper) is undermining the competitive basis of resource-based developing economies, often resulting in increased exploitation of natural resources to compensate for reduced market prices and although the consumption of raw materials and energy has continued to increase in the OECD, the relative decline in importance of resource inputs has been reflected in declining real prices for commodities. Between 1980 and 1988 the real prices of non-fuel commodities from developing countries declined by 40 per cent; fuel prices declined by 50 per cent in the same period (UNCED, 1991b). The full-scale entry of the resource-rich former Soviet Union into world markets will increase the supply of commodities, depressing prices even further. These trends have reinforced the urgent need for developing countries to industrialize.

Table 5.1 Hazardous Waste Generation

Country	Tons per capita	GNP per capita (US$)
Japan (1983)	0.01	16 000
West Germany (1988)	0.1	15 000
UK (1988)	0.1	8 000
Taiwan (1986)	0.2	3 000
South Korea (1985)	0.01	2 000
China (1987)	0.004	250

Source: Hirschhorn and Oldenberg (1991).

However, developing countries' efforts to diversify their economies have been severely hampered by increasing trade and technological protectionism within the OECD, a lack of industrial know-how and a shortage of financial resources to purchase or develop the necessary technology, exacerbated by the debt crisis. Furthermore, according to the United Nations Economic Commission for Latin America and the Caribbean, there has been an "erosion of traditional competitive advantages", with information technology and flexible automation undermining the attraction of cheap labour and natural resources for multinational corporations (ECLAC, 1991). In some cases, this has meant that industry has begun to return to the developed world. For example, Fairchild Semiconductors, one of the pioneers of offshore manufacturing, has returned its assembly operations back to the USA after automating the welding of semiconductor chips and the inventory tracking system (Bellow, 1990).

Although "human capital" is now held to be the key to economic progress in the 1990s, this is not labour as traditionally conceived, but the highly sophisticated application of relatively few skilled workers together with costly hardware. Management, organization and information management skills are rapidly becoming the basis of competitiveness. This contrasts with the growing number of low-skilled and unskilled workers in the developing word, where underemployment and unemployment now affect half a billion people out of a total working population of 1.8 billion —as many as the entire workforce of the industrialized world (UNCED, 1991c). Many developing countries are in any case afflicted by a "brain drain" of their more skilled workers and scientists to the developed world.

The trends in foreign investment during the 1980s reflected this changed balance of competitive advantage. Although total foreign investment increased faster than the growth in world trade, four-fifths of this was between North America, western Europe and Japan. Developing countries' share of global investment declined from 25 per cent in the first half of the 1980s to 18 per cent in the second half. Furthermore, about 75 per cent of foreign investment in developing countries was accounted for by only ten countries, with close links to the markets of the OECD, whereas during the second half of the decade, the least developed countries received only 0.7 per cent (UNCTC, 1991). These trends highlight the difficulty of achieving what the United Nations Centre on Transnational Corporations has identified as one of the key criteria for sustainable industrial development, "the diversification of appropriate production activities around the planet".

Developing countries appear to be faced with a no-win situation. Without industrial development, they will continue to be plagued with poverty-induced environmental degradation and plummeting competitive advantage in the world market. But industrialization, when it does occur in developing countries, is often repeating all the environmental mistakes of the developed world.

Consumerism and the Environment

In this context, the environmental performance of the "post-industrial" economies offers only a limited guide. Indeed, Maurice Strong has commented that "the livelihoods of the rich are the real security risk and greatest threat to our common future". In the North, new environmental problems are emerging, linked to high-consumption lifestyles, and the focus of concern is shifting from industry's production processes to the environmental impact of its products. An analysis of the total lifecycle of a car, for instance, shows that 90 per cent of energy consumption and pollution occurs during use, and only 10 per cent during production. Managing the consumption habits of millions of individual consumers, however, poses new problems for governments. The problem has been accentuated by the shift from mass production to mass customization, where advanced manufacturing techniques are able to produce products tailored individually to consumer demands. This has greatly increased the number and variety of products: "if present trends continue, 50 per cent of the products which will be used in 15 years' time do not yet exist" (OECD, 1991).

The profitability of industry relies on constantly growing consumption relentlessly promoted through the marketing and advertising of unsustainable lifestyles. By contrast, sustainable development requires "a concerted approach at remoulding the consumer's sovereignty, and steering wants in the direction of environmentally benign activities" (Goodland et al, 1991). Furthermore, a number of consumption patterns are also "inherently dissipative" in their use of dangerous substances, such as mercury in disposable batteries (Ayres, 1991). One of the clearest symbols of environmentally dissipative lifestyles has been the rise in packaging; in the last 40 years, the amount of packaging in the municipal waste stream of Paris has increased from 13.5 per cent to 61.8 per cent (McCarthy, 1991). But packaging has also been at the forefront of government and consumer efforts to establish effective recycling schemes and reduce the unnecessary consumption of scarce resources. In the Netherlands, for example, the government decided in the mid-1980s that plastic containers for soft drinks could only be used if efficient recycling was adopted. Countries have found that the only effective way to deal with dissipative uses of toxic substances is to develop "sunset" policies to phase out their use (for example, lead in petrol). But because of industry resistance, the elimination of toxic substances remains the exception rather than the rule. Unfortunately, too, new substances that are toxic in even small amounts continue to be developed at a rate that exceeds the possibilities of testing and regulation (UNCED, 1991a).

The Partial Greening of Business

Across the world, company responses to environmental issues have mostly been driven by legislative demands, with "probably no more than 100–200 companies worldwide having made environmental performance one of their top concerns" (Cairncross, 1990). By the late 1980s a number of multinationals in environmentally intensive industries, such as chemicals, had begun to develop a kind of "corporate environmentalism". As well as individual company efforts, industry associations have introduced numerous codes of conduct to exert peer pressure and improve public image. This has coincided with the emergence of new market-driven pressures on companies from the "green consumer" movement. For developing countries, however, a prime concern has been how to ensure that multinational corporations do not abuse their weak regulatory regimes by operating according to double standards.

If companies have been largely reactive, this mirrors the behaviour of society at large, which has often only been galvanized into action following major accidents, such as the release of dioxin at Hoffman La Roche's Seveso plant in Italy in 1976 and the disaster at Union Carbide's plant at Bhopal in India in 1984. But behind these incidents have been two noticeable waves of environmental concern, the first of which peaked in the early 1970s, when some major multinationals such as Philips and IBM introduced corporate environmental policies. The second "green" wave, which grew in strength through the 1980s, was marked by a significant broadening of the industrial base affected by tightening regulation and public scrutiny. But the diffusion of new ideas and clean technologies has been highly erratic, with the developing countries suffering from a weak "trickle down" of best practice from the developed world.

Company actions on the environment have been shaped by predominantly regulatory requirements. Industrial unwillingness to consider fundamental changes in processes or products, and government desires for a quick fix to pollution problems, has resulted in unsystematic and "end-of-pipe" solutions. Wastes have been disposed of through dilution, dispersion and dumping. Emissions to different environmental media have generally been treated separately, leading to the transfer of pollution from one medium to another (such as from water to land). Nevertheless, government regulation focusing on pollution control has spawned a rapidly expanding pollution control and waste management industry which, rather than being "green", relies on the continued growth in pollution for its profitability.

It was not until the late 1980s that the common-sense concepts of resource conservation, risk reduction and pollution prevention (or waste minimization), which had been pioneered almost two decades before with initiatives such as the "Pollution Prevention Pays" programme at 3M, became more widely accepted by both government and industry. In the USA, for example, Congress passed a Pollution Prevention Act, requiring companies to detail their efforts to reduce pollution. These concepts have now been integrated under the single heading of "cleaner production" by the United Nations Environment Programme's Industry Office (UNEP, 1991). Rather than focusing simply on "clean technology", UNEP stresses the importance of effective management and organization, and the need for constant improvement in performance (thus cleaner rather than clean). Nevertheless, as the 3M and other cases show, good environmental practice is good for business, and the payback of investment is often short. Furthermore, companies have barely begun to take advantage of the low- or no-cost prevention options. In the USA, the Office of Technology Assessment estimated in 1986 that 50 per cent of all industrial waste could be prevented using current technologies (quoted in Hirschhorn and Oldenberg, 1991), while the Dutch Prisma Project concluded that "a substantial part (an estimated 30–60 per cent) of pollution caused by industry can be reduced by the prevention of waste and emission, keeping within business economic conditions, by using existing management techniques, and by employing today's technology" (Prisma, 1991) (see Table 5.2). The same potential for cleaner production exists in developing countries. Fritz Balkau of UNEP's Industry and Environmental Office believes that "a general industrial rule of thumb for old plant is that 50 per cent of pollution abatement can be achieved by better operation and minor plant modifications" (Balkau, 1990). In the Hong Kong textile industry, for example, the amount of waste water has been substantially reduced by relatively simple "good housekeeping" practices, such as the "shutting off of water supply to equipment not in use, installing automatic shut-off valves in hoses and supplying only the optimum amount of water to the machine". But companies can quickly reach a plateau of such "good housekeeping" improvements. Further measures require investments in time, training, technology and know how, which many companies do not have.

Table 5.2 Good Environmental Practice — Good Business Practice

Industry	Method	Reduction of wastes	Payback
Pharmaceutical production	Water-based solvent replaced organic solvent	100%	< 1 year
Equipment manufacture	Ultrafiltration	100% (solvent/oil) 98% (paint)	2 years
Automotive manufacture	Pneumatic process replaced caustic process	100% (sludge)	2 years
Organic chemical production	Adsorption, scrap condenser, conservation vent, floating roof	95% of cumene	1 month
Photographic film processing	Electrolytic recovery ion exchange	85% (developer) 95% (fixer, silver and solvent)	< 1 year

Source: Huisingh (1987).

By necessity, environmental efforts have been greatest in environment-intensive industries, such as petrochemicals, where most of the large US, European and Japanese multinationals have now established specialized environmental departments, introduced regular internal monitoring and auditing procedures and inaugurated company-wide programmes to reduce environmental impacts. Successful corporate programmes have relied on strong support from senior management and significant reforms in organization and management structures to allocate responsibility and provide effective incentives for reducing environmental impacts.

This more positive approach to environmental management in leading companies is reflected in a survey carried out by the management consultancy McKinsey of 290 senior executives during 1991, 12 per cent of whom were from the Third World. The survey found "a positive, growing awareness"; 80 per cent of those surveyed belonged to companies that had published an environmental policy statement, and 25 per cent carried out evaluations of their suppliers' environmental performance to minimize the waste they received (McKinsey & Company, 1991). The survey found that on average companies spent 3 per cent of sales on environmental protection; this was expected to increase to 5 per cent by 2000. A survey of 12 000 managers by the *Harvard Business Review* found that companies now accept that solving environmental problems is the responsibility of those that create them (Kanter, 1991).

A few companies have declared their intention to go beyond current requirements and anticipate future regulations, thereby hoping to exercise greater control over their environmental destiny. This more active stance has not come from altruism, but from a recognition that the scale of government and public expectations has turned the environment into an issue. For example, the UK chemical company ICI has stated that "unless we treat environmental matters seriously, we are not going to survive as a company" (Robins, 1990). ICI subsequently announced that it will reduce waste by 50 per cent by 1995, and require all new plants to be built to standards that anticipate future regulations "in the most environmentally demanding country" in which it operates that process. The change towards an anticipatory approaches was shown by reference to ICI's operations in Taiwan. Local opposition to the marine dumping of wastes forced the closure of a plant producing acrylic intermediates in 1984. The same year, ICI announced the opening of a new plant to produce terephthalic acid, which will produce little or no waste.

Corporate Environmentalism?

In the USA, the shock produced by the Bhopal disaster and the passage of the Superfund Amendment and Reauthorization Act (SARA) stimulated a similar response. A number of chemical companies such as Dow, Dupont and Monsanto introduced company-wide programmes to minimize waste and reduce risks. Enhanced liability laws and rapidly rising waste disposal costs made waste minimization programmes increasingly attractive, and also necessary. The new mood was exemplified by Edgar Woolard, chief executive of Dupont, who coined the phrase "corporate environmentalism" in a speech in London in May 1989. By this he meant "an attitude and a performance commitment that place corporate environmental stewardship fully in line with public desires and expectations". Dupont believes that an environmental management paradigm shift is under way, so that, rather than regarding environmental quality as an added burden for business, it is now considered a vital part of a company's competitive advantage. Instead of the traditional reactive response to pollution problems, seeking to comply with regulations and no more, the aim is now to prevent pollution at source and aim for "environmental excellence".

Collaborative Efforts

From the beginning of the first wave of environmental concern individual company initiatives to improve environmental performance have been supplemented by collective efforts at the sectoral, national and international levels. Industry has come to realize that it is judged by the performance of its worst member. Codes of conduct and statements of principle can help to exert pressure on these companies and can provide the framework for technology and know-how transfer to pull up standards. A good example of this is the chemical industry's "Responsible Care" initiative, started by the Canadian Chemical Producers' Association in the late 1970s, and since adopted by industry associations in Australia, Europe and the USA.

Responsible Care requires companies to make a formal commitment to continuous improvement in performance as a condition of membership. This commitment is detailed in a series of binding codes of conduct, such as on process safety, community awareness, emergency response and pollution prevention. In the USA, each company has to complete an annual self-evaluation form for each code, from which public reports on progress will be released. Furthermore, in a number of countries, an advisory panel has been established to act as a formal conduit for public concerns about the chemical industry. The mandatory nature of the programme marks a new stage in voluntary agreements by industry, and provides a vital mechanism for providing peer pressure and assistance to chemical companies that are performing below acceptable standards. Although Responsible Care is operated by nationally based industry associations, the aim is to spread the programme throughout the global chemicals industry. In the developing world, industry associations in India, Mexico and Taiwan have programmes under preparation.

As with individual company programmes, collective efforts need to be more than statements of good intent to be effective; they need to be followed up with detailed commitments and plans of action. However, in most cases industry codes have stopped at the formulation of principles. This is the case with the Business Charter for Sustainable Development, issued by the International Chamber of Commerce (ICC) at the Second World Industry Conference on Environmental Management in April 1991. The charter details 16 principles for environmental management, ranging from giving the environment "corporate priority" to adopting the precautionary principle regarding environmental risks. The charter has been supported by over 500 companies and business associations; but unlike the Responsible Care programme, or the rival Valdez Principles launched by the US environmental investment group CERES in 1989 (see CERES, 1990), the ICC has chosen not to require companies to report on the integration of the principles into daily practice. This lack of rigour in the implementation of the charter has raised a number of doubts about its effectiveness.

The Green Consumer Pull

In addition to the regulatory "push" and voluntary initiatives, companies now face a market "pull" for cleaner products and processes. The advent of the "green consumer" movement in Europe and North America in the late 1980s was in some sense a reflection of growing popular dissatisfaction with the slow pace of environmental improvement according to the traditional regulatory model. It built on a number of environmentalist product boycott campaigns, most notably against CFC-powered aerosols and natural fur coats. Initially, many of the company responses to this new environmental challenge were inept, leading to the establishment of the "Green Con" award by the UK branch of Friends of the Earth in 1990. However, companies have become increasingly sophisticated at analysing the environmental implications of their product portfolios and redesigning them to reduce impacts. In some sectors, the result has been dramatic. For example, consumer pressure rather than government regulation has led to considerable reductions in the use of phosphate-based detergents in Europe. Many supermarket chains have introduced own-brand ranges of "green" products to satisfy niche market demand. The green consumer movement has the potential to go far deeper into the corporate psyche than regulatory compulsion, for the basic reason that it affects the primary aim of companies in a consumer economy, to provide products to meet demand. For this to happen, however, consumers will need greater access to objective information about the relative environmental impacts of difference products. False claims by companies have led to considerable scepticism. But current "eco-label" schemes, such as Germany's "Blue Angel" and Canada's "Environmental Choice", only scratch the surface of the immensely complex interactions between a product and the environment. A handful of companies have begun to apply life cycle analysis to explore the relative environmental merits of different product options (such as between plastics and steel for cars, or between cloth and paper for diapers). For these to be credible, the public must be given access to the data upon which materials and technology choices are made. Furthermore, standardized methodologies need to be developed so that different eco-balances can be compared.

Avoiding Double Standards

For developing countries, a prominent issue is to ensure that multinational companies do not operate according to double standards, abusing the often weak regulatory and enforcement regimes in these countries. Multinational companies often have a better environmental record than local companies, largely because of their visibility and exposure to pressure and because of their superior access to finance, know-how and clean technologies. As one observer has commented: "even if multinational corporations do use a double standard, their performance looks good by comparison" (Gruber, 1991). None of the 98 US multinationals surveyed by Tufts University's Centre for Environmental Management in 1991 set standards that met or exceeded the requirements in place in all countries of operation (Rappaport and Flaherty, 1991). In fact, 40 per cent of the respondents agreed that one of the reasons US corporations locate abroad is because of weak regulatory systems.

Research undertaken by the Thailand Development Research Institute shows that between 1987 and 1989 the proportion of foreign investment projects that would produce significant amounts of hazardous waste, and which attracted incentives from Thailand's Board of Investment, rose from 25 per cent to 55 per cent (Phantumvanit and Charnpratheep, 1991). The consequences for the local environment can be

■ *Nick Robins and Alex Trisoglio*

profound, as shown by the impacts of Mexico's border industrialization programme, which has encouraged major multinationals and local operators to establish *maquiladora* (assembly) plants for the US market. The US $3 billion in foreign exchange earnings produced by the *maquiladoras* is second only to Mexico's oil and gas exports. But this is produced at a cost of 20 million tons of hazardous waste, with inadequate treatment facilities and no incentive for waste minimization (Ladou, 1991). The approach of legislation to establish a free trade area between the USA and Mexico has, however, led to efforts to clean up the border zone. Many companies now recognize that the establishment of a tough code of conduct for multinationals could provide a basis for minimizing the damage done by "free riders", exploiting the differences between the developed and the developing world (McKinsey & Company, 1991).

References

Ayres, R U (1991) *Eco-Restructuring: Managing the Transition to an Ecologically Sustainable Economy*, IIASA, Vienna
Balkau, F (1990) "Tanning and the Environment in the 1990s", *Journal of the Society of Leather Technologists and Chemists*, no 74
Bellow, W (1990) *Brave New Third World*, Earthscan, London
Cairncross, F (1990) "Cleaning Up: The Economist Survey of Industry and the Environment", *The Economist*, 9 September
CERES (1990) *The 1990 Guide to the Valdez Principles*, CERES, New York
ECLAC (1991) *Sustainable Development: Changing Production Patterns, Social Equity and the Environment*, ECLAC, Santiago
Goodland, R, H Daly, S El Sarafy and B von Drost (1991) *Environmentally Sustainable Economic Development: Building on Brundtland*, UNESCO, Paris
Gruber, M A (1991) *Sustainable Development in the Pacific Rim*, National Wildlife Federation, Washington, DC
Gruber, A and Nowotny, H (1990) "Towards a Fifth Kondratiev Upswing", *International Journal of Technology Management*, vol 5, no 4
Hirschhorn, J S, and Oldenberg, K U (1991) *Prosperity without Pollution*, Van Nostrand Reinhold, New York
Huisingh, D (1987) *Good Environmental Practices, Good Business Practices*, WZB, Berlin
Kanter, R M (1991) "What Does it Mean to be Green", *Harvard Business Review*, July–August, pp38–47
Ladou, J (1991) "Deadly Migration", *Technology Review* (MIT), July
McCarthy, J E (1991) "Environmental Regulation of Packaging in OECD Countries, Packaging and the Environment, Lund University, Lund, Sweden
McKinsey & Company (1991) *The Corporate Response to the Environmental Challenge*, McKinsey & Company, Amsterdam
OECD (1991) *Technology in a Changing World*, OECD, Paris
Phantumvanit, D and K Charnpratheep (1991) *The Greening of Thai Industry: Producing More with Less*, Thailand Development Research Institute, Bangkok
Phantumvanit, D and T Panayotou (1990) *Industrialization and Environmental Quality: Paying the Price*, Thailand Development Research Institute, Bangkok
Prisma (1991) *Prevention is the Winning Option!*, Prisma Project, The Hague
Rappaport, A and, M Flaherty (1991) "Multinational Corporations and the Environment: Context And Challenges", *International Environment Reporters*, 8 May
Robins, N (1990) *Managing the Environment: The Greening of European Business*, Business International, London
Simonis, U E (1990) *Beyond Growth*, Edition Sigma, Berlin
UNCED (1991a) *The Relationship between Demographic Trends, Economic Growth, Unsustainable Consumption Patterns and Environmental Degradation*, A/CONF 151/PC/46, UNCED, Geneva, August

—— (1991b) *The International Economy and Environment and Development*, A/CONF 151/PC/47, UNCED, Geneva, August

—— (1991c) *Poverty and Environmental Degradation*, A/CONF 151/PC/45, UNCED, Geneva, August

UNCTC (1991) *The Triad in Foreign Direct Investment*, UNCTC, New York

UNIDO (1990) *Industry and Development: Global Report 1990–91*, UNIDO, Vienna

WCED (1987) *Our Common Future: Brundtland Report*, Oxford University Press, Oxford

Weizsacker, E U (1991) "Sustainability is a Task for the North", *Journal of International Affairs*, Winter

WICEM (1991) *WICEM II: Conference Report and Background Papers*, ICC, Paris

Legal Rights ... and Wrongs: Internationalizing Bhopal
Indira Jaising and C Sathyamala

The disastrous event on the night of 2 December 1984 in Bhopal, in which more than 40 tons of a deadly mixture of toxic gases from the Union Carbide factory escaped into the atmosphere, has been misleadingly termed an accident. In fact the disaster, which killed thousands and injured several million permanently, could almost have been predicted. In the late 1960s, a decision was taken at the Union Carbide Corporation (UCC) headquarters in the USA to set up a factory for the manufacture of pesticides in a populous section of the city of Bhopal, capital of the state of Madhya Pradesh in India. The nature of the product, the process of manufacturing, the secrecy surrounding all procedures, the double standards in safety maintained by the transnational company, the measures taken by the management to cut costs, the run-down condition of the plant, all added up to create the right mix for a massive environmental disaster.

That it was just waiting to happen had been noted by a Bhopal-based journalist, Raj Kumar Keswani, three years before December 1984. In a series of articles printed in September/October 1982 in *Saptahik Report* (The Weekly Report), a local Hindi newspaper, he wrote, "Save! Please Save the City", "Bhopal on the Mouth of a Volcano", and "If you don't understand you will be wiped out". Again in June 1984, barely five months before the disaster, he underlined his warning in an article published in a Hindi daily, *Jansatta*. Today, the corpses of the dead and the suffering of millions stand in mute testimony to the prophetic nature of his warning, which was based on a study of the total absence of safety mechanisms in the manufacture of a deadly chemical.

The Bhopal disaster had the potential for changing the entire chemical industry and for challenging the need for technologies that can cause grave and irreversible damage to the environment and to people. That it has not, only demonstrates the utter contempt industry has for life in its all-consuming pursuit of profit. An analysis of the response to the disaster will help to unravel the nexus between a transnational corporation and a national government and its agencies in their combined effort to suppress and underplay the magnitude and consequences of the event. It is almost as if they have succeeded in erasing the event from human memory and public consciousness.

The Failure of Transnational Corporations

The catastrophe demanded from the Union Carbide Corporation, the organization responsible for the accident, a response that was humane and in keeping with the image that industry wishes to project, that of a concerned partner. The immediate task was to provide medical relief to the thousands of exposed victims who flooded the hospitals in Bhopal. As people were brought in, the management of the factory maintained that the gas was non-poisonous, that it was "just like tear gas" and that its effect on the eyes could be relieved by washing with water. Medical experts flown in by Union Carbide assured the Bhopal victims that recovery was almost certain and that there would be no long-term effects from the exposure.

Further, the Union Carbide Corporation refused to reveal the composition of the gases in the gas cloud, the toxicological information on these gases, the nature of injuries that could be caused by exposure and the antidote or specific treatment which needed to be prescribed. Even Dr Bipin Awasi, medical director and toxicologist at the UCC plant in the USA, retracted his earlier statement about the possibility of cyanide poisoning. It was only when it became clear that UCC was not going to respond positively that a litigation strategy began to be worked out.

The Failure of Legal Mechanisms

The first legal response came from American lawyers who flew down to Bhopal and obtained thumb impressions from the victims, authorizing the lawyers to file suits on the victims' behalf in the USA. Some of these attempts were so crude that there were reports of authorizations being available at a price. Based on these authorizations, suits were filed in different states in the USA, and all were subsequently transferred to the southern district of New York to be judged by Judge Keenan. It was at this point that the Indian government woke up to the situation and attempted to formulate a legal strategy. Its response was to enact a law which gave the government the sole authority to litigate on behalf of the victims. Armed with this new act, the Bhopal Gas Leak Disaster (Processing of Claims) Act (1985), the Indian government filed a suit in the southern district of New York, to be heard along with all the others. Even while these suits were pending, negotiations had begun on settling the dispute, well before anyone had had an opportunity to estimate the nature and extent of injury, the number of dead and injured and the long-term consequences of the disaster. The American lawyers proposed a settlement of US $350 million; although there was no rational basis for this amount, Judge Keenan was invited to accept it as fair. Reports say the Union of India (UOI) refused to accept the settlement not because it was opposed to it in principle, but because it was dissatisfied with the amount. It is not clear why it opposed it, nor is there any record of whether it had proposed an alternative figure for consideration.

In the absence of consent to the settlement on the part of the Union of India, Judge Keenan had to proceed with the hearings. At this stage, UCC made an application on the court that the suits be dismissed on grounds of forum and convenience. Simply stated, what was being argued by UCC was that the USA was an inconvenient forum in which to decide the suit, the inference being that it should be tried in India since all the evidence and witnesses were located there. The hidden agenda was, quite clearly, UCC's wish to avoid paying the levels of compensation ordinarily awarded by US courts in tort litigation; secure in their assumption that life in India was cheap they were confident that an Indian court would make much lower awards. Judge Keenan accepted the arguments of UCC and transferred the case to India on condition that UCC submit to the jurisdiction of the Indian courts, which they willingly did. His decision reflects the political reluctance of the American legal system to deliver justice to people of Third World countries who have been the victims of American transnational corporations. It seems clear that neither the voluntary groups in India, who strongly favoured conducting the litigation in the USA, nor the UOI had anticipated this decision. As a result, both were caught off-guard, fumbling to formulate a strategy for pursuing the litigation in India.

By this time the American lawyers had already lost interest in the case, and the pitch was therefore clear for the Indian government to become the sole representative of the victims within the authority of law. Strangely enough, none of the groups of victims that had been formed by then realized the enormous implications of surrendering vital decision-making powers to the UOI, which now assumed the role of *parens patriae* vis-à-vis the victims. No attempt was made to challenge the exclusivity of the government's right to represent the victims; they now lost round two of the legal battle, this time to the Union of India.

One solitary petition was filed in the Supreme Court in early 1986 by Rakesh Shroti, an advocate, a resident of Bhopal and a victim of the tragedy, who challenged the validity of the act, claiming the right to be represented by lawyers of his own choice and stating his apprehension that conceding exclusive powers to the government would mean giving them the right to settle or negotiate the claims with UCC, without the knowledge of the victims.

Meanwhile, the suit was being litigated in the district court of Bhopal, with UCC doing everything in its power to delay the proceedings. At this point, one of the victims' organizations, Zahreeli Gas Khand Sangharsh Morcha (Forum Against Toxic Gas Poisoning) made an application for interim relief to be provided to the victims; it was supported by the UOI but vehemently opposed by UCC. However, even this application did not contain any details of a realistic estimate of the number of people injured and the nature and extent of their injuries.

The Failure of the Medical System

The logical consequence of the legal appropriation of the disaster was its medical appropriation as well. Government research units such as the Indian Council of Medical Research (ICMR), the Defence Research Development Establishment, the Industrial Toxicology Research Centre and others were given an exclusive right to conduct epidemiological surveys and toxicological research and to suggest possible lines of treatment. They failed to associate voluntary organizations or any victim groups with this effort. As a result, the medical aspects of the disaster were gradually, almost deliberately, shrouded in secrecy. All information was made confidential under the Official Secrets Act. Because of the monopoly on medical information, it was virtually impossible to keep vested interests in check, and the consequences of this appropriation were a minimizing of the nature and extent of injury and a failure to come up with the required line of treatment for the victims. The ICMR took almost three months to suggest that a course of sodium thiosulphate injections (NATS) be given to the victims. NATS is a specific antidote in cyanide poisoning and had been suggested by Dr Bipin

Awasi, the medical director of UCC in the period immediately following the disaster. It was opposed by UCC and a section of the medical community in Bhopal, which maintained that the effects of the gas were felt only in the eyes and lungs and that NATS would provide no symptomatic relief. Although this debate was posed as a medical controversy, a conflict between two contradictory medical opinions, it was in fact political. While it is true that the ICMR failed to provide further proof of the efficacy of NATS, the debate had more to do with demarcating the extent of injury. Accepting NATS as a treatment would have meant acknowledging the toxic gases had indeed crossed the lung-blood barrier to cause systemic damage. The controversy ultimately led to the withholding of NATS from the victims and now it is too late to determine whether it would have provided any relief to them had they received it in the early exposure period.

The State: Protector of Victims versus Mediator of Foreign Investment.

The appropriation of medical information meant that the medical consideration was subordinated to the political one. There was a clear conflict of interest between the demands for justice for the victims, and the need of the Indian government for foreign capital. A proper epidemiological study, which could have been the turning point in establishing the nature and extent of injury, was not undertaken and, until today, no proper scientific survey of the entire exposed population exists. The confusion about treatment was never resolved. The teratogenic, carcinogenic and mutagenic potential of the gases was denied without adequate proof. Thus, even at the point when the Indian government filed its suit for three billion dollars in the USA, no valid survey of the gas victims was available. So the government gave arbitrary figures for the number of those injured, and these ultimately became the basis for the interim order passed by the Bhopal district court for Rs 350 crores (approximately US $115 million) to be paid by UCC; the High Court later reduced this to Rs 250 crores (approximately US $85 million). It was this interim order that UCC challenged in the Supreme Court of India, exposing their strategy of delaying monetary relief with the sole purpose of arm-twisting the victims into an unfair settlement.

For five years no monetary relief from any source was made over to the victims. Then, on 14 February 1989, they were told that a settlement had been reached; the Union of India and Union Carbide had agreed on a figure of US $470 million in settlement of claims past, present and future, and to quash all criminal charges against UCC. This settlement created national and international outrage at the blatancy of its disregard for the injury caused to the victims, and at the Indian government's sell-out to a transnational corporation.

The Supreme Court of India gave its endorsement without even adjudicating on the validity of the Bhopal Act under which the government had arrived at a settlement. Realizing this blunder, in March 1989 it was decided to hear the petition challenging the Bhopal Act, while the settlement itself was held in abeyance. Union Carbide, aware that there was a strong national sentiment against the settlement, quickly transferred the US $470 million to India so as to present the court with a *fait accompli*. In the meantime, review petitions were filed by organizations such as the Bhopal Gas Peedith Mahila Udyog Sanghathan (The Association of Women Victims of Bhopal) and several others, challenging the settlement. Even at this stage, UCC's strategy was to sidestep the

issue, but it was ultimately directed by the court to continue to submit to the jurisdiction of Indian courts until the validity of the act and the settlement were decided.

Ultimately, in December 1989, the court delivered its judgement by upholding the
act and the power of the government to settle the dispute, but made a very important
contribution to the cause of the victims by stating that they had a right to be heard
before any settlement could be arrived at, and acknowledging the fact that they had not
yet been heard. It also said that the UOI was obliged to pay interim relief to the victims
since they had assumed the responsibility of litigation on their behalf.

It was while the interim relief petitions were being heard that the victims were
confronted by the gross underestimation of the nature and extent of injury and the
number of those injured, as assessed by the Madhya Pradesh government.

Conflicting Assessments of Injury

In January 1987, two years after the disaster, the Madhya Pradesh government, in order
to provide medical documentary evidence for all the claimants in the case against the
UCC, initiated the process of assessing personal injuries for approximately 600 000
persons who had filed compensation claims. Two years later, in 1989, after the process
of medical evaluation had been initiated, less than 10 per cent of the claimants had been
assessed. When, therefore, in February 1989, the Supreme Court gave its blessing to the
settlement between UOI and UCC, the compensation amount was not based on an
assessment of all 600 000 claimants, nor on epidemiological evidence, but on totally
mythical figures. The Supreme Court simple accepted a figure of 30 000 for those
injured permanently and another 20 000 injured temporarily, based only on hospital
records.

The Madhya Pradesh government presented its figures of numbers of injured, as
assessed, in August 1989. According to them, of the total of 123 560 claimants, barely
800 were found to have permanent disability; extrapolating a figure in relation to the
600 000 claimants would have meant that only 4000 were to be considered permanently disabled. In October 1989, a critique by an independent group of researchers
found that the gross underestimation had resulted from faulty methodology, which
used arbitrary scores for assessing injury, claimed to identify disability in the absence of
relevant information, did not carry out complete investigations, and relied on the production of records by the victims as proof of their exposure. By assessing a small sample
population of the injured, using the diagnostic method followed in clinical practice,
independent researchers could prove that more than 70–80 per cent of the gas-exposed
population in the seriously affected municipal wards of Bhopal were permanently and
seriously injured. This works out to approximately 300 000 to 400 000 victims suffering from serious medically diagnosable injury today.

In December 1989, with the change in national government, several groups representing the victims' interests came together to demand from the National Front
government that interim relief be paid to the victims on the basis of residence on the
night of 2 December 1984 and the consequent exposure to toxic gases. They also
insisted that the personal injury evaluation followed by the Madhya Pradesh government should not form the basis for deciding the amount of interim relief. The
government accepted this argument and decided to pay Rs 200 (US $6.50) per month,
per person, to all those resident in the 36 municipal wards of Bhopal who had been

declared as directly exposed on the night of 2 December 1984. However, a major question still remained, i e on what basis was the settlement to be challenged? The National Front government announced that it proposed to support the efforts of the victims in reopening the settlement; however, in court, its major emphasis was on the dropping of criminal charges against UCC. No effort was made seriously to question the level of compensation. But as a concession on the victims, the National Front government decided to relax the Official Secrets Act and released pertinent research findings of the ICMR and other research organizations to the victim groups.

From this information it became clear that the toxic gases had caused multi-systemic injury to those exposed to them. The damage caused was both irreversible and led to progressive deterioration. Exposure had also damaged the immune system, so that previously asymptomatic persons were exhibiting symptoms at a later date. The possibility of later effects and unsuspected complications arising could not be ruled out, and there was a grave possibility of carcinogenic and mutagenic changes in the population.

While the information provided by the ICMR presented a serious scenario, the Madhya Pradesh government's estimate underplayed the nature and extent of injury. The court was confronted with two contradictory sets of information, both provided by government establishments: while that provided by the ICMR was on a small sample population, the Madhya Pradesh government claimed to have individually examined each claimant. In the absence of any scientifically valid assessment, one alternative was to identify the number of persons exposed in a given geographical area. The victims argued that all those exposed constituted an identifiable group that had been placed at increased risk. They argued further that the government had categorized the victims on the basis of an arbitrary scoring system, and that no effort had been made to diagnose and assess the injury and disability of each individual victim. Given the magnitude of the disaster and the nature of the injury, it was not reasonably possible to diagnose each and every victim or to assess the risk of future injury. Hence, the only rational method of arriving at an estimate of the number of persons injured would be to consider every exposed person as injured or potentially injured. This would be approximately 400 000. As against this, the figure agreed to by UOI and UCC had seemed absurdly low. Quite apart from the gross underestimation of the number of persons injured, the actual amount agreed to be paid as compensation was unacceptable — ranging from Rs 10 000 to Rs 2 000 000 each (approximately between US $350 and US $6500).

On 3 October 1991, the Supreme Court pronounced its judgement in the review petition: it held that the settlement was beyond challenge, that in the event of a shortfall in the compensation payable to the victims, the government of India was liable to make good the shortfall, and that the criminal prosecution against UCC and UCIL (Union Carbide India, Ltd) be dropped and its officials restored. The battle on behalf of the victims was already lost. The court refused to go into the question of the numbers of victims or the nature of the injury caused. As a result, the government's own estimates of the number of those injured has been accepted without question, leaving out of consideration the thousands of victims whose injuries remain unrecognized.

Bhopal: A Global Challenge

The extraordinary nature of this disaster and the unique circumstances of the litigation and judicial process over a period of seven years, raise some fundamental issues regarding rights jurisprudence itself, and the question of liability across international boundaries. It also compels us to reconsider the definition of compensation when long-term consequences are feared, and the scope of responsibility and liability when potential hazardous substances are involved.

For Bhopal was not an isolated incident. A study of the Agent Orange case reveals striking parallels. The Vietnam veterans who were exposed to Agent Orange, a herbicide used in the Vietnam war, had to accept a settlement very unfavourable to them, against their will and through a legal process. Medical information was suppressed and the medical community took refuge behind the near impossibility of doing a proper epidemiological study. If this is so, the intriguing question is: would the Bhopal settlement have been different if the case against UCC had been tried in the USA? Perhaps not, because the political compulsions of the Indian government, which was the sole representative of the victims, would have been the same as the political compulsions exhibited by the American legal system in other disasters. Until today, the American transnational has not disclosed the chemical composition of the mixture of gases that leaked into the atmosphere in December 1984. When specifically asked to disclose these, they pleaded trade secrecy and took shelter behind patent laws.

In cases such as the Bhopal disaster, where the damage is latent and long-term, the invisible nature of the crime makes it possible for the court to evade the real issues because the law is so structured as to deal with the immediate and individual claim. In view of such cases, this may be an appropriate moment to look at the prevalent legal discourse on rights.

An analysis of the Bhopal case reveals that the origin of rights continues to spring from ownership of property rather than from a recognition of the needs of individuals. When the law looks at individuals it does so only in their capacity as political beings; hence, it confers political rights such as the right to freedom of speech, the right to vote, the right to form associations and so on. These rights inhere in individuals rather than in communities. It follows that there is no recognition of the right to protection of the environment, for such a right would by definition recognize collective control over common resources and a common heritage. For the first time, in 1986, motivated by the Bhopal disaster, the government of India passed the Environment Protection Act, which vests powers in the state to prevent the destruction of the environment, but unfortunately, even in this law, the conceptual framework of rights remains the same. The state continues to be both the enforcing agency, and the owner of all natural resources, so that the beneficiaries are still marginalized and have little or no role to play in the management and control of their own environment. The hallmark of all political formations after the Second World War is that the management and control of rights rests in the state. In a manner of speaking there is an unbroken link in the structure of legal control between colonial and post-colonial societies; only the managers of power have changed.

A significant function of the fact that ownership of property alone gives birth to rights is that all rights are then capable of, and liable to, being monetized. What then is the measure of loss of rights? If one is measuring monetary loss, then the claim is reduced to the loss of earning capacity; thus a working-class man or woman would have lost his or her daily wage and will be compensated for that loss, whereas a businessman would lose his earning capacity, running probably into many millions, for which he will be compensated in millions. Unequal treatment is thus built into the structure of the law. The value of life is reduced to the value of its productive capacity measured in economic terms alone. Hence in the Bhopal case there is a total absence of a recognition of the violation of the right to dignity, the right to live in a healthy environment and the right to access to community resources. There is a corresponding absence of a recognition of the need to nurture and restore human life and ecosystems.

Run into the Wind
David Weir

If a [phosgene] leak occurred today, people would die. It would enter their houses; they would notice a sweet-sour smell, but bearable . . . go to sleep and die.

(A former Bayer supervisor)

The people living down wind and down river from the massive Bayer industrial complex in the Belford Roxo district, some 20 miles from downtown Rio de Janeiro, know a lot about chemicals. Inside the mammoth German-owned industrial site are more than a dozen separate factories, manufacturing everything from acids and chrome salts to dyes and resins, from pharmaceuticals and emulsifiers to phosgene and isocyanates closely related to MIC, plus a long list of pesticides, including ethyl and methyl parathion, the nerve gas derivatives that originated in the German laboratories of the Second World War.

Approximately 1800 people work in the complex, many living among the tens of thousands who exist "mainly in poor and even shantytown neighbourhoods", according to David Hathaway, author of an upcoming book on the pesticide industry in Brazil. The workers from the dye plants come home a different colour each day, "sometimes yellowish, other days blue or red — depending on the pigment in use" (Fullgraf, 1985).

The wives and mothers of workers in the plants get used to the products their husbands and sons work with. "There is a lot of pollution and a bad smell, a chemical smell that comes at certain times of the day," explains Maria das Gracas, who lives near the Sarapui River flowing beside the plant. "I know the smell because my husband works in the laboratory with chemicals for dyeing clothes and I am familiar with all kinds of chemical smells." Das Gracas spoke with documentary producer Frederico Fullgraf in June 1985 about the pollution coming from the Bayer plant. "There are certain hours when they let out that smell, about ten in the morning and again around six or seven in the evening. . . . It is an acid smell that burns. This very morning I woke up with my eyes irritated; they are not red, but they burn. And my daughter's eyes are actually red" (Fullgraf, 1985). Das Gracas says the river by the factory "turns red, real red. . . . Sometimes it stays red for three, four days. And it stinks!" Another resident, Rafael Luis says, "It looks like they threw blood into the river" (Fullgraf, 1985).

"Ever since (the Bayer complex) came, we have been having these problems," says das Gracas. "This river had fish in it, but not any more, none at all. My mother used to fish in this river, and it's been years now that the fish are gone." Besides pollution from Bayer and other chemical factories in the area, residents throw trash and garbage in the river, compounding the problem into a serious public health menace. "They say the garbage truck comes by, but it never does," explains das Gracas. "And we have no storm sewers on the street. This whole riverbank area floods, the water flows from up there and right into our houses, full of pollution from the river. And when people step in it their feet get full of sores, and that water is rotten."

The area, which was once quite pleasant (residents used to swim in the river during the 1950s), now seems barely habitable to das Gracas. "When the sun comes out," she says, "you smell the chemicals mixed with the smell of rot coming out of the river mud. I lock myself into the house because I can't stand being outside with that horrible smell."

In the midst of this poor, underdeveloped community, Bayer's modern chemical works churns out a large share of the company's $265 million (in 1983) worth of Brazilian products, which, though impressive, represents less than 2 per cent of the multinational's global sales (ANDA, nd). "Bayer is one of the most internationalized companies in the world, garnering 79 per cent of its total sales from overseas business" (Lukomski, 1985). Pesticides account for a little over 11 per cent of the group's total sales and hit the $1.5 billion mark in 1983, meaning that Bayer alone controls almost 10 per cent of the world pesticide market (Wood, MacKenzie & Company, 1984). In Brazil, pesticides are produced for cotton, tomatoes, potatoes, coffee, soy, wheat, green vegetables, citrus and other fruit, tobacco, corn, cocoa, rice, cucurbitaceae, rubber, and many other crops (ANDA, nd).

Sebastian Richard, Bayer's manager for environmental affairs at Belford Roxo, rejected residents' claims that the company's complex is responsible for pollution in the area. Interviewed by David Hathaway in December 1985, Richard stated that Bayer opened an $8 million biological treatment plant in October 1984 to control all solid and liquid effluent from the plant (Hathaway, 1985). According to Richard, only treated liquid wastes flow into the river now, and all solids are deposited in a 60-acre landfill lined with clay and polyurethane. As to the red colour of the river, "that I can say is technically impossible," Richard stated. "There is only one single outlet for all our (treated) wastes. So there is no technical possibility of any given plant in the (complex) bypassing the treatment station."

References
ANDA (nd) Associacão Nacional de Defensivas Agricoles, Brazil; written statement
Fullgraf, F (1985) Personal Interview, Nova Iguacu, Brazil, June
Hathaway, D (1985) Personal Interview, Belford Roxo, Brazil, 19 December
Lukomski, J (1985) "Bayer Profits Jump on Gains Abroad", *Journal of Commerce*, 8 May
Wood, MacKenzie & Company Agrochemical Service (1984); written statement

Environmental Problems
Jorge Hardoy and David Satterthwaite

Toxic/Hazardous Wastes

In the Third World, as in the West, one sees the familiar list of pollution problems: the heavy metals (which include lead, mercury, cadmium and chromium), oxides of nitrogen and sulphur, petroleum hydrocarbons, particulate matter, polychlorinated biphenyls (PCBs), cyanide and arsenic as well as various organic solvents and asbestos.

Some of these and certain other industrial and institutional wastes are placed in a special category of "hazardous" or "toxic" waste because special care is needed for disposal, so they are isolated from contact with humans and stored in ways which prevent them polluting the environment. If such wastes are buried, great care must be taken that they could not contaminate underground water sources. If stored in drums, great care must be taken that the drums do not corrode. Most toxic wastes remain toxic so simply sorting them does not solve the long-term problem.

Most toxic wastes come from chemical industries, although several others such as primary and fabricated metal and petroleum industries, pulp and paper industries, transport and electrical equipment industries and leather and tanning industries also produce significant quantities of hazardous wastes.

There are many different kinds of hazardous wastes. Some are highly inflammable, such as many solvents used in the chemical industry. Some are highly reactive and can explode or generate toxic gases when coming into contact with water or some other chemical. Some have disease-causing agents: for instance, sewage sludge or hospital wastes often contain bacteria, viruses and cysts from parasites. Some wastes are lethal poisons, such as cyanide, arsenic and many heavy-metal compounds; and many are carcinogenic (cancer inducing).

The scale of the problem of hazardous wastes and the potential danger to people's health has only been recognized for 15 years. The USA, for example, industrialized rapidly, giving little consideration to the safe disposal of hazardous wastes. Now it is faced with some 50 000 land-sites where hazardous wastes may have been dumped without control, and without provision to ensure that the wastes do not pollute groundwater. The cost of dealing with the backlog created by inadequate or non-existent control runs into tens of billions of dollars (Anandalingam and Westfall, 1987).

Box 5.1 EXAMPLES OF TOXIC CHEMICALS, THEIR USE AND THEIR POTENTIAL HEALTH IMPACTS

ARSENIC	pesticides/some medicines/ glass	dermatitis/muscular paralysis/ damage to liver and kidney/ possibly carcinogenic and teratogenic
ASBESTOS	roofing insulation/air conditioning conduits/ plastics/fibre/paper	carcinogenic to workers and even family members
BENZENE	manufacture of many chemicals/gasoline	leukaemia/chromosomal damage in exposed workers
BERYLLIUM	aerospace industry/ceramic parts/household appliances	fatal lung disease/lung and heart toxicity
CADMIUM	electroplating/plastics/ pigments/some fertilizers	kidney damage/ emphysema/ possibly carcinogenic, teratogenic and mutagenic
CHROMATES	tanning/pigments/corrosion inhibitor/fungicides	skin ulcers/kidney inflammation/ possibly carcinogenic/toxic to fish
LEAD	pipes/some batteries/paints/ printing/plastics/gasoline additive	intoxicant/neurotoxin/affects blood system
MERCURY	chloralkali cells/fungicides/ pharmaceuticals	damage to nervous system/kidney damage
PCBs	electric transformers/ electrical insulator	possibly carcinogenic/nerve, skin and liver damage
SULPHUR DIOXIDE	sugar/bleeding agent/ emissions from coal	irritation to eyes and respiratory system/damage to plants and buildings
VINYL CHLORIDE	plastics/organic compound synthesis	systemically toxic/carcinogenic

(*Source*: Krishnamurthi, 1987)

Today, most toxic wastes are either dumped in liquid wastes which run untreated into rivers, streams or other nearby water bodies, or are dumped on land-sites with few safeguards to protect those living nearby or nearby water sources from contamination.

Very few Third World nations have effective government systems to control the disposal of hazardous wastes; indeed, in most, there are no regulations dealing specifically with such wastes, let alone the system to implement them. Such systems need a competent well-staffed regulatory authority with the ability to make regular checks in each industry using or generating toxic chemicals, and with power to penalize offenders. This authority needs the backing of central government and the courts. For the control of toxic wastes to be effective, industries must keep rigorous records of the kinds and quantities of waste they produce and the dates and methods by which these are disposed of. Businesses that specialize in collecting and disposing of these wastes must be very carefully monitored; so too must the specialized facilities which need to be created to handle toxic wastes. Since the safe disposal of toxic wastes is extremely expensive, there are enormous incentives to cheat in any regulatory system.

Reports of problems arising from the careless disposal of chemical compounds with heavy metals (including mercury, cadmium, lead, nickel) are increasingly frequent. The problem of mercury contaminated wastes being discharged into water bodies, which received such publicity through the hundreds of deaths and disablements it caused in Minamata, Japan and which has caused serious problems in many North American water bodies, has also been noted in Bangkok, Perai (Malaysia), Bombay, Managua, Alexandria, Cartegena and in various Chinese cities (Phantumvanit and Liengsharernsit, 1989; Ruddle, 1983; Centre for Science and Environment, 1983; IRENA, 1982; Street, 1981; Hamza, 1983; Lopez, 1988; Smil, 1984). Significant build-ups of mercury, lead, cadmium, copper and chromium have been reported in recent years in almost every industrializing nation in Southeast Asia (Jimenez, 1984; Leonard, 1984). The Kalu River which runs through two of Bombay's industrial suburbs receives the liquid effluents of over 150 industrial units and these include heavy metals. This causes dangerously high levels of mercury and lead in the water near the village of Ambivali and the villagers are slowly being poisoned as heavy metals enter the food chain through cattle browsing on the river bank vegetation (Centre for Science and Environment, 1983). On the southeast Pacific coast of Latin America, heavy metals have been detected in practically all areas that receive industrial and municipal wastes and worryingly high concentrations of mercury, copper and cadmium have been found in some fish species (UNEP/WHO, 1987). Lead and cadmium concentrations in drinking water were found to exceed the guideline values in about a quarter of the 344 stations that monitor water pollution within the Global Environmental Monitoring Network. In Jakarta, 13 children were reported to have died of mercury poisoning in 1981 after eating fish caught in the waters of Jakarta Bay tributary, while mercury levels in the water polluted by nearby factories were found to have dangerously high concentrations (Leonard, 1984). Jakarta Bay remains the source of much of the fish consumed in the city.

Reports from China in 1980 and 1981 note "some astonishingly high cadmium and mercury concentrations in rivers and underground waters" (Smil, 1984). For instance, downstream from Jilin, a major industrial city with a high concentration of chemical industries, the Songhua Jiang River had organic mercury pollution for a stretch of more than 20 kilometres. The concentration reached between 2 and 20 mg per litre which is between 2000 and 20 000 times the concentration recommended for inland surface waters by the European Commission. Fish in the Zhaoyuan Jiang River have a mercury content of 5.35 mg per kilograms body weight, 18 times the maximum concentration level set by the European Commission (Smil, 1984).

One final kind of toxic waste which deserves special attention is radioactive wastes. The problems are best illustrated by an accident in Goiania, Brazil where a scrap-metal dealer broke up an abandoned cancer-therapy machine and released the radioactive chemical caesium-137 from inside it. Because the powder and some of the metal glowed in the dark, the scrap dealer and his family and friends handled it. Around 240 people were contaminated and several people have died; many of those who survive will probably develop cancer (Anderson, 1988). Even for nations that have no nuclear power stations, radioactive chemicals are widely used in other activities. Wherever governments seek to develop waste disposal sites for these or other toxic wastes, local citizens are likely to mount strong protests. For instance, there was a long battle in Malaysia between a firm called Asian Rare Earth and local residents (aided by environmental groups) over the siting of a dump for radioactive wastes near their town (Consumer Information and Documentation Centre, 1988).

Transferring the First World's Pollution to the Third World

Since governments in the North enforced more stringent regulations on pollution control and on the disposal of hazardous wastes, many companies from the North have tried to transfer the problem to the Third World. In some instances, dirty industries have been transferred; in others, the hazardous wastes have been transferred.

To take first the transfer of production; there has been a trend towards the relocation of industries manufacturing asbestos from the USA to Latin America, with Brazil and Mexico as the most frequent recipients. Asbestos textile imports into the USA from Mexico, Taiwan and Brazil grew rapidly between 1969 and 1976 and Taiwan and South Korea have been displacing Japan as a source of asbestos textiles for the USA as new regulations on this industry have been introduced in Japan (Castleman, 1979). There has been a comparable transfer of production by Japanese and North American subsidiaries in other dirty industries with Taiwan, South Korea, the Philippines and Thailand being among the recipients (Castleman, 1979; El-Hinnawi, 1981). For instance, the Nihon Chemical Company closed its polluting factory in Tokyo and constructed a replacement in Ulsan, South Korea and many Japanese companies have invested in petrochemical industries in Southeast Asia (Nishikawa, 1982).

To meet demand for the products of certain dirty industries in Japan, western Europe or North America, multinational corporations may increasingly transfer production to Third World nations to avoid the costs associated with meeting workplace safety and pollution standards. Arsenic production, lead refining and battery manufacture, metal smelters and biocide production are among the industries where this transfer may increasingly take place. This transfer, allied to increasing dirty industry production in Third World cities to meet local and regional demand, has serious implications for the health of city populations both now and in the future. The lessons learnt in the West over the last 15 to 20 years on the enormous health costs associated with the uncontrolled disposal of toxic wastes by certain industries do not seem to be heeded by government, and are often being ignored by the industrial sector.

The case of mercury pollution in Managua illustrates this problem. In 1980, an investigation by Nicaragua's new government found that Electroquimica Pennwalt (Elpesa), an affiliate of a Philadelphia-based multinational, was responsible for mercury contamination of Lake Managua from where some of the drinking water for the capital city is drawn. The lake, more than 1000 square kilometres in size, has been a major source of fish for city inhabitants. But the problem was not only the contamination of the fish and drinking water source. Workers at the factory were also affected. An inspection in 1980 found the level of mercury in the air was 12 times the recommended safety level by the US National Institute of Occupational Safety and Health and that the workforce had not been warned about possible health hazards. An examination of workers found that 37 per cent had evidence of mercury contamination (IRENA, 1982; Street, 1981).

Box 5.2 THE WEST'S EXPORT OF TOXIC WASTES

BANKGOK: Large quantities of chemical wastes have been stored in Bangkok's main port, Klong Tuey. Most came from unknown shippers in Singapore although some also came from the USA, Japan, west Germany and Taiwan. Officials from the government's National Environment Board have expressed fears that the barrels may contain PCBs or dioxin which can only be destroyed in high temperature incinerators which Thailand does not possess.

BENIN: European firms were seeking a contract to send five million tons of wastes each year from Sesco, a company registered in Gibraltar. It was reported that Benin was to receive $2.50 for each ton received while Sesco would charge firms up to $1000 a ton or more to dispose of the wastes. Benin is one of the poorest nations in the world and lacks virtually all the infrastructure and the government system needed to handle and manage even a small fraction of the 5 million tons a year proposed.

GUINEA-BISSAU: It was reported that Lindaco, a firm based in Detroit, applied to the US government to ship up to six million tons of chemical waste to Guinea-Bissau, one of the world's poorest nations. Other contracts have been signed for importing chemical and industrial wastes from Western nations.

GUINEA: A Norwegian firm dumped some 15 000 tons of burnt or partially burnt industrial waste and incinerator ash from the USA and Norway on the island of Kassu, near the capital Conakry. Toxic wastes could filter down to pollute ground-water supplies used by the islanders and into the sea to damage fisheries.

NIGERIA: 3800 tons of European chemical wastes were dumped by Italian ships in the southern port of Koko on the Niger River with a payment to the landowner of the equivalent of around $100 a month; the cost of disposing of these in Europe would be of the order of $350 to $1750 a ton. The wastes are stored in 45-gallon (around 200-litre) drums, many of them leaking and most in poor condition. Many drums have volatile chemicals, which in a hot climate present a serious risk of a spontaneous fire or explosion.

PERU: Negotiations were reported between a Peruvian company and a US company to dispose of barrels of toxic wastes from US industries — solvents, burnt oils and chemical wastes.

VENEZUELA: In October 1987, 11 000 barrels of chemical wastes were returned to Italy after a private Italian company had tried to store them in a warehouse in Puerto Cabello; local inhabitants claimed that some barrels leaked and caused various diseases.

(*Source*: Consumer Information and Documentation Centre, 1988; Kone, 1988; MacKenzie and Mpinga, 1988; Phantumvanit and Liengcharernsit, 1989; Secrett, 1988)

There is also the issue of the export of hazardous wastes to the Third World, which recently gained a lot of attention in the press, as it was discovered that certain European or North American businesses were dumping toxic wastes in certain Third world nations with little or no provision to protect the people living there. It also became evident that the scale of this exporting operation was likely to grow very rapidly, since the cost of transporting and dumping toxic wastes to Third World nations was only a fraction of the cost of safely incinerating or storing them in the West and meeting government regulations in doing so.

Box 5.2 gives some examples of this export trade; the publicity coming from press coverage has helped mobilize environmental groups and some governments both in the West and in the Third World to guard against this. There are reports of this problem having existed for some years — especially in northern Mexico with the illegal dumping of toxic wastes produced by US firms, which have been shipped across the border. But a lot more attention needs to be given to the dumping of toxic wastes in exactly this same manner by branches of multinational firms or by domestic industries within Third World nations. Most Third World nations do not have the special facilities needed to store such wastes safely. It is likely that most toxic wastes are currently dumped on land-sites with no provision to ensure these remain isolated from contact with plants, animals and humans or simply dumped in sewers, drains, wells or nearby water courses — rivers, lakes, estuaries.

References

Anandalingam, G and G Westfall (1987) "Hazardous Waste Generations and Disposal: Options for Developing Countries", *Natural Resources*, vol 11, no 1, pp37–47

Anderson, I (1988) "Isotopes from Machine Imperil Brazilians", *New Scientist*, 15 October

Castleman, B I (1979) "The Export of Hazardous Factories to Developing Countries", *International Journal of Health Sciences*, vol 9, no 4, pp569–97

Centre for Science and Environment (1983) *The State of India's Environment: A Citizen's Report*, Delhi, India

Consumer Information and documentation Centre (1988) *Consumer Currents*, International Organization of Consumers Unions, March–April, pp5–6

El-Hinnawi, A (1981) "Three Environmental Issues", *Mazingira*, vol 5, no 4, pp26–35

Hamza, A (1983) "Management of Industrial Hazardous Wastes in Egypt", *Industry and Environment*, no 4, pp28–32, UNEP, Paris

IRENA (1982) *Taller International de Salvamento y Aprovechamiento Integral del Lago de Managua*, vol 2, no 2

Jimenez, R D and Velasquez, A (1984) "Metropolitan Manila: A Framework for its Sustained Development", *Environment and Urbanization*, vol 1, no 1, IIED, London

Kone, S (1988) "Stop Africa from Becoming the Dumping Ground of the World", *The Siren*, no 37, pp2–3, July

Krishnamurthi, C R (1987) "Toxic Chemicals", *State of the Environment: Some Aspects*, National Committee on Environmental Planning, New Delhi quoted in G Anandalingam and Mark Westfall, "Hazardous Waste Generation and Disposal: Options for Developing Countries", *Natural Resources Forum*, vol 11, no 1, February

Leonard, J H (1984) *Confronting Industrial Pollution in Rapidly Industrializing Countries: Myths, Pitfalls and Opportunities*, Conservation Foundation

Lopez, J M (1988) "The Caribbean and Gulf of Mexico", *The Siren*, no 36, pp30–1

MacKenzie, D and Mpinga, J (1988) "Africa Wages War on Dumpers of Poisonous Waste", *New Scientist*, pp3–31, 23 June

Nishikawa, J (1982) "The Strategy of Japanese Multinationals and South-east Asia", *Development and Environment Crisis: A Malaysian Case*, Consumer's Association of Penang

■ *J Hardoy and D Satterthwaite*

Phantumvanit, D and Liengcharernsit, W (1989) "Coming to Terms with Bangkok's Environmental Problems", *Environment and Urbanization*, vol 1, no 1, IIED, London

Ruddle, K (1983) "Inshore Marine Pollution in Southeast Asia", *Mazingira*, vol 7, no 2, pp23–44

Secrett, C (1988) "Deadly Offer Poor Countries Find Hard to Refuse", *The Guardian*, July

Smil, V (1984) *The Bad Earth: Environmental Degradation in China*, M E Sharpe, New York

Street, A (1981) "Nicaraguans Cite Pennwalt, US Company has Poisoned its Workers and Lake Managua", *Multinational Monitor*, vol 2, no 5, pp25–6

UNEP/WHO (1987) *Global Pollution and Health — Results of Health-Related Environmental Monitoring*, Global Environment Monitoring System

Agenda 21
Matthias Koch and Michael Grubb

Environmentally Sound Management of Toxic Chemicals Including Prevention of
International Traffic in Toxic and Dangerous Products
Risks associated with the handling and use of chemicals require assessment and regulation "to ensure the environmentally sound management of toxic chemicals". Only
about 100 000 commercial chemical substances are yet assessed for their risks to human
health and the environment, and much effort on international risk assessment of
chemicals is still to be undertaken. Major pollutants should be assessed by the year
2000. Guidelines should set acceptable human and environmental exposure limits.
Existing programmes on chemical risk assessment, like the International Programme on
Chemical Safety (IPCS),[*] should be expanded. Collaboration among governments,
industry, academia and NGOs is to be strengthened. Data should be provided by the
industry and/or generated by the existing international programmes. A system of
priority setting for the assessment of chemicals should be established. Research on
alternatives to toxic chemicals and on methods to replace animal testing should be
strengthened. To make handling and use of chemicals safer globally, a harmonized
hazard classification and labelling system should be established by the year 2000.
Material safety data sheets and easily understandable symbols should be developed.

The exchange of information on chemical safety, use and emissions should be
strengthened. Prior Informed Consent (PIC) procedures should be adopted, as
introduced in the London Guidelines[**] and the FAO international pesticide code of
conduct.[***]

Risk reduction programmes aim to eliminate unacceptable risks and to substitute
toxic chemicals by less harmful substances. The entire life cycle of products should be
analysed. Governments should *inter alia* adopt producer liability principles, preventive
measures against accidents and emergency response procedures. Industry should

---

[*] Jointly organized by UNEP, ILO and WHO in 1980, "to assess the risks that specific chemical
pose to human health and the environment" (UNEP, 1992).

[**] London Guidelines for the Exchange of Information, UNEP Governing Council, 1989.

[***] International Code of Conduct on the Distribution and Use of Pesticides, FAO, 1989.

establish a code of principles on chemical trade, adopt a "responsible care" approach and should consider community-right-to-know programmes. International cooperation on risk reduction should be strengthened.

International measures for chemical safety rely on adequate national capacities and capabilities, that is legislation, effective implementation and enforcement. National systems for environmentally sound management of chemicals should be established by the year 2000. Institutional mechanisms are to be established and adequate coordination of all relevant parties is to be achieved. Preparedness for accidents should be ensured, including emergency response centres and emergency plans. International cooperation should support the effort of developing countries on chemical safety rules. International principles for accident prevention should be promoted.

Transboundary movement of toxic products is of international concern. Measures for detection and prevention of illegal international traffic should be undertaken. National capacities including regulatory measures and enforcement programmes are to be strengthened. Developing countries are to be assisted in their effort. National alert systems, regional monitoring and assessment and arrangements for international exchange of information on the movement of toxic products should be established.

The central concerns of this chapter are the problems posed by the lack of adequate information for assessing the risks posed by toxic chemicals, and the problems of preventing illegal traffic in them. Difficult negotiations in the PrepComs led to a chapter that was accepted without difficulty at Rio.

Environmentally Sound Management of Hazardous Wastes Including Prevention of Illegal International Traffic in Hazardous Wastes

Hazardous wastes are produced in increasing amounts; its management and disposal need appropriate national institutions and international cooperation. Transboundary movements are of increasing international concern, particularly its illegal traffic. The global Basel Convention[*] and African Bamako Convention[**] should be ratified and implemented.

The most environmentally sound way to deal with hazardous wastes is to prevent or at least to minimize its generation. National strategies should aim to stabilize the generation of hazardous wastes and to reduce its hazardous characteristics as an intermediate stage and to reduce the amount in a long-term programme. Governments should promote recovery of materials, cleaner production methods and technology assessments. They should establish domestic hazardous waste treatment and disposal facilities and strengthen transfer of relevant technologies to developing countries. Industry should deal with hazardous wastes at the source of generation and should establish environmental management systems. Information on cleaner production should be disseminated internationally.

Many problems of hazardous waste and its transboundary movement can be related to the lack of institutional capacities. Governments should adopt legislation on

---

[*] Basel Convention on the Control of Transboundary Movements of Hazardous Wastes and their Disposal, 22 March 1989, Basel, Switzerland.

[**] Bamako convention on the Ban on the Import into Africa and the Control of Transboundary Movement of Hazardous Wastes within Africa, OAU, Bamako, Mali, 1991.

environmentally sound management of hazardous wastes and establish comprehensive research programmes. Awareness of the public and of workers should be strengthened on hazardous waste issues through education and training programmes. Endogenous capacities in developing countries should be improved. Assessments and inventories on human exposure and health risks should be promoted.

International cooperation on hazardous waste management should be strengthened, including control of transboundary movement. Export to countries which do not have appropriate treatment or disposal facilities should be prohibited. Transboundary movement for recycling and recovery should be controlled. Criteria and guidelines for hazardous waste management should be harmonized and strengthened internationally.

Illegal transboundary movement of hazardous wastes should be prevented; effective monitoring and appropriate penalties are required. Institutions should be strengthened to detect and halt the illegal import of hazardous wastes; assistance should be given particularly to developing countries on issues of illegal traffic. Regulatory measures should be adopted to prevent illegal import and export of hazardous wastes; detection of violations should be strengthened. Exchange of relevant information, networks and alert systems should be promoted.

A total ban on exports of hazardous wastes to developing countries was not adopted. Instead, language from the Basel Convention was introduced. The G77 countries would not agree that financial resources should be provided to economies in transition. References to military establishments were questioned by the USA, but compromise language was found to recognize them as an important source of waste and consequently on the need for them to "conform to their nationally applicable environmental norms in the treatment and disposal of hazardous waste".

Reference
UNEP (1992) *Saving Our Planet: Challenges and Hopes, The State of the Environment 1972–1992*, UNEP, Nairobi

Chapter 6 | URBANIZATION and HEALTH

At present about half of the population of the world live in large settlements. In the last generation, the population of large settlements has tripled: in the Third World it has quadrupled. These exploding cities create a huge local demand for resources, especially food, water, fuel and building materials. They are also characterized by desperate environmental conditions for much of their populations. One third of the population of Third World cities live in informal/squatter settlements; many others live in more traditional slums. The planning system has been unable to cope with the rapidity of urban growth and associated ill health. Jorge Hardoy and David Satterthwaite provide an introduction to the problems of urban growth. Irene Dankelman and Joan Davidson provide more details of environmental issues in Third World cities, concentrating on women's living conditions. Jorge Hardoy and David Satterthwaite show how one family succeed in building and improving their house over a period of 26 years. In a different source, with Sandy Cairncross, they examine the health problems of children in both urban and rural areas of the Third World. They include a list of the world's major diseases, indicating those where reduction could be cheaply achieved by creation of a better environment. These diseases are particularly common in the Third World. Their concluding section compares different ways of spending $20 million in improving housing and living environments: clearly the most effective investment is in support to community based organizations.

Urban Growth as a Problem
Jorge Hardoy and David Satterthwaite

Most governments have identified urban growth as a problem and many have used repressive measures to control it. For instance, in Senegal in 1977 there was a major effort to remove beggars and small traders from the streets of Dakar while in Nigeria in 1983, there was a massive "clean up" of urban traders (Stren, 1989). In Tanzania, in 1983, elaborate administrative machinery was established for the "transfer, training and rehabilitation of unemployed (urban) residents" (Stren, 1989), which led to thousands of arrests in Dar es Salaam. In Manila in 1982, Mrs Marcos ordered the creation of a special commission "to prevent and control the entry of squatters in Metro Manila" with the powers and the equipment to remove squatter families immediately and drive them to a relocation site (Concerned Citizens for the Urban Poor, 1982).

Other governments have sought to control migration to cities in other ways. For example, an attempt was made in Indonesia in 1970 to control migration to Jakarta. All migrants had to obtain a residence card to be allowed to remain in the city and, to qualify for the card, they had to prove they had a job, accommodation and permission to leave their destination. They also had to make a deposit, equivalent to their return fare. In addition, attempts were made to exclude hawkers and street sellers from certain districts (Drakakis Smith, 1981). In South Africa, one of the various aims of the apartheid system is to control the migration of black citizens by providing the legal basis to deny them the right to live in cities. In certain centrally planned economies, large-scale programmes to force people out of cities and into the countryside have been implemented (Kirkby, 1985).

Such policies usually derive from the mistaken belief that poor people flood into cities attracted by the lure of the bright lights. As late as 1976, a UNESCO Expert Meeting on Urban Problems talked of "the ever increasing migratory movement — in practice beyond control — of families from rural areas attracted to the glitter and fallacious promises of consumer society", with the migrants described as "potential parasites" (Moser and Satterthwaite, 1988). But numerous case studies have shown that most people come to cities because that is where economic opportunities are concentrated or survival is more certain. People's movements to or from cities are logical responses to the pattern of economic opportunities across the nation. Most decisions to move to cities are based on careful, logical and rational judgements; many result from information from people in the cities about job opportunities there. Such judgements are more solidly based on an understanding of economic change than government programmes that try to control population movements, and migrants are not parasites; indeed, the prosperity of cities often largely depends on the jobs that they do for very low pay with long hours and very poor working conditions. Thus, government attempts to control city growth by trucking the poor out to the countryside, or to control movement into the city through some form of licence, are simply addressing the effects, not the causes.

Governments might decry the fact that a city is growing rapidly but they rarely ask why — or consider the extent to which their own policies are one of the main causes. Nor do they look at why people are leaving their original homes. In many cases, the migrants are small farmers forced off their lands or agricultural labourers whose livelihood has disappeared because of soil erosion, low crop prices or the increasing concentration of land ownership, with consequent changes in crops and the means of producing them. Many other migrants came from smaller urban centres whose economies stagnate and whose potential for development is stifled by inappropriate government policies. These are causes about which governments could take action, if they wanted to slow migration to cities.

But it is also possible to question whether population growth or the "flood" of migrants is in fact the problem. Most of the Third World's urban centres are not growing very rapidly, and the natural increase in population as children are born to parents already residing in urban areas contributes much more to urban population growth than new people coming into the city.

Many of the cities that have grown most rapidly during the last 20 to 30 years have done so because their booming economy attracted a large number of people. Many others grew rapidly because they were the location of most new investments and job opportunities within the nation, even if the national economy was not growing rapidly. In theory, government should have been able to recapture some of the profits from such expanding city economies to pay for infrastructure and services for both the inhabitants and for city businesses. In this way, government could not only tackle the problems but also provide the basis for continuing economic expansion. Of course, there are also many cities that grew rapidly because they became the homes of those fleeing drought, floods or war, or those pushed off the land that had provided their livelihood; rapid city growth was thus not necessarily associated with an expanding city economy. But this should not disguise the fact that many city problems could have been greatly reduced if governments had more effectively drawn resources from expanding economic activities to provide the capital needed for infrastructure and service investments.

Many Western cities grew at rates comparable to most of the Third World's fast-growing large cities, which shows that it is possible for governments to deal with rapid city growth. For example, the population of the Los Angeles–Long Beach urban agglomeration has grown more rapidly than Calcutta's since 1900 and the population of the Tokyo agglomeration has, in recent decades, grown on a scale comparable to that of Mexico City. While there are serious housing problems in both Los Angeles and Tokyo, they do not compare with those in Calcutta or Mexico City. Nor is their population growth associated with comparable levels of poverty, malnutrition and disease.

The problems for Third World cities are not the result of rapid population growth itself, but of growth within the context of a legal and institutional structure unable to cope with the needs of the population and the tasks of providing and running city services. Central to this is the weakness of municipal and city government. More recently, problems have been further compounded by declining public investment capacity, the giving of low priority to investments in basic services, and inappropriate models of public intervention. As Otto Koenigsberger commented, "rapid population growth does not create poverty; it merely makes poverty more visible" (Koenigsberger, 1976).

There is evidence is recent years that some governments are beginning to appreciate the gap between their plans and the reality around them — perhaps partially as a result of conferences, projects, better knowledge and closer ties between researchers and community leaders. But more effective pressure on governments has come directly from community groups formed by the poor, even if these usually receive neither official recognition nor representation within government.

References
Concerned Citizens for the Urban Poor (1982) *Wretched of the Earth*, series no 2, Manila

Drakakis Smith, D (1981) *Urbanisation, Housing and the Development Process*, Croom Helm, London

Kirkby, R J R (1985) *Urbanization in China: Town and Country in a Developing Economy AD 1949–2000*, Croom Helm, London and Sydney

Koenigsberger, O (1976) "The Absorption of Newcomers in the Cities of the Third World", *ODI Review*, no 1

Moser, C O N and Satterthwaite, D (1988) "The Characteristics and Sociology of Poor Urban Communities", paper presented to the workshop on community Health and the Urban Poor, Oxford, July

Stren, R E (1989) "Administration of Urban Services", in R E Stren and R E White (eds), *African Cities in Crisis*, Westview Press, USA

■ Human Settlements: Women's Environment of Poverty
Irene Dankelman and Joan Davidson

"By the turn of the century, almost half the world will live in urban areas — from small towns to huge megacities."

(WCED, 1987)

Since the beginning of this century, the world's population has grown from 1600 million to more than 5000 million. By the year 2000, the UN predicts a global population of 6000 million. Growth rates are especially high in the Third World: here populations have been expanding more than twice as fast as those in developed countries.

Poverty and Urbanization

Most of the world's people still live in rural areas, and the majority are poor. FAO estimates that 70 per cent of rural people in the Third World (excluding China) live on small farms or are landless (World Resources, 1986). With some 1400 million people living in abject poverty, more and more are migrating to urban areas, attracted by the projects of employment and a better standard of living. Others leave their villages to join a relative, find a spouse or escape from a difficult family situation: for young people especially, as the "Child from Delhi" case study illustrates, the city seems to offer freedom.

Rapid urbanization is not caused only by migration from the countryside: Third World cities have high rates of natural population increase. At the start of this century, less than 14 per cent of the world's people were urban dwellers; by 1985, the proportion was 42 per cent, with over half living in the cities of the Third World. The largest agglomerations have shown a spectacular expansion. Since 1950, the populations of cities such as Abidjan, Dar es Salaam and Nairobi have increased sevenfold. It is estimated that by the end of the century some 439 cities will have more than a million people, and nearly 100 may have more than four million each. Beijing, Buenos Aires,

Cairo, Mexico City, São Paulo and Shanghai already have populations over 10 million. Although some commentators advise caution in projecting the future patterns of urbanization in the Third World, especially for large cities, the trend is clear: increasing numbers of poor people, coupled with diminishing resources to cope with their needs and expectations (Hardoy and Satterthwaite, 1986a).

Some countries are now promoting the development of small and intermediate centres in their settlement strategies, but this offers little hope of alleviating the appalling and deteriorating conditions in most Third World cities.

Environments of Poverty

Half the inhabitants of some cities in the South live on vacant lots in the urban centre or as squatters in the slums and "popular settlements" at their margins. Here, people provide their own shelter, often illegally, and frequently on land that is unfit for housing and prone to severe environmental damage. To avoid eviction, the poor build on land of low commercial value. Homes are constructed upon unstable hillsides or on land subject to flooding by sea and river. In Mexico City, about 1.5 million people live on a dry lake bed, which floods in winter and creates dust storms in summer. Houses may be located on sandy desert land or in heavily polluted areas close to industry.

In such overcrowded, makeshift settlements, there are few if any services save those organized by the slum-dwellers themselves. Often there is no water supply, sewerage, garbage removal or electricity; roads and transport facilities are poor, medical care is inadequate and there are few schools. Debt and the other economic crises faced by Third World countries ensure that there is little or no investment in construction, basic infrastructure or social services.

The World Commission on Environment and Development describes conditions in India:

> Out of India's 3119 towns and cities, only 209 had partial and only 8 had full sewage treatment facilities. On the River Ganges, 114 cities each with 50 000 or more inhabitants dump untreated sewage into the river every day. DDT factories, tanneries, paper and pulp mills, petrochemical and fertilizer complexes, rubber factories, and a host of others use the river to get rid of their wastes. The Hoogly estuary (near Calcutta) is choked with untreated industrial wastes from more than 150 major factories around Calcutta. Sixty per cent of the city's population suffer from pneumonia, bronchitis and other respiratory diseases related to air pollution.
>
> (WCED, 1987)

Those who live in these "environments of poverty" (Hardoy and Satterthwaite, 1984) suffer three kinds of environmental degradation — the constant danger of industrial pollution, the effects of minimal basic services and the cumulative deterioration of the urban hinterland.

Industrial Pollution

Many popular settlements are located in environmentally vulnerable or dangerous places, thus increasing the chance of catastrophe. And, as the industrial accidents of the last decade show, the danger is ever present and profound. In 1976, dioxin released in

Italy's Seveso disaster poisoned thousands. Mexico City's poor San Juanico neighbourhood was devastated by an explosion of liquefied petroleum gas in 1984: 452 were killed, 4240 were injured and more than 31 000 were made homeless. At least 2500 people were killed by the methyl isocyanate gas which leaked from a pesticides plant in Bhopal, India, in 1984. The vapour which escaped into Bhopal's slums has left many others permanently damaged. A Third World nuclear accident on the scale of the Chernobyl explosion in May 1986 would bring much greater devastation.

Many industrial plants in the South fail to meet the strict safety standards required in the North. Most are located in dense population centres (UNEP, 1985). Not only is there a continual risk of explosions, but also industries are a permanent source of pollution in these areas, for the rapid industrialization of the South is marked by the transfer of "dirty industries" from the North. Air pollution from noxious emissions and water pollution caused by waste dumping in local waters have serious health implications, both directly within neighbourhoods and farther away, beyond city boundaries. And there are other consequences: in India, Malaysia and elsewhere, river and coastal fisheries (and therefore livelihoods) are destroyed by industrial effluents. The soils surrounding industrial plants, on which slums are built and food may be grown, often contain high concentrations of heavy metals.

Poor Services

The lack of clean water, sanitary systems and solid waste removal means that most informal settlements have no option but to pollute themselves. Millions literally live on city garbage dumps. Their health is directly affected: intestinal diseases flourish and are rapidly transmitted in the cramped living conditions. The high levels of air pollution from traffic (especially from old and badly maintained engines), as well as industry, cause serious respiratory problems. In Jakarta and Mexico City, for example, respiratory ailments are legion.

Human settlements have a major impact upon the environment of their hinterlands: they can destroy the soils, crop and forest lands which support life, provide energy and sustain incomes in the informal economy. Around the cities of the South, deforestation, overcropping and overgrazing often result in permanent degradation of the soil, which is followed by erosion, flooding or the encroachment of desert.

Refugee Camps

Some of the worst environmental effects of human settlements are found at the margins of refugee camps, where people who may already be victims of natural disasters — such as the Sahelian drought — are desperately trying to meet their basic needs. Around the camps, demands for fuel as well as increased "slash and burn" practices to grow subsistence crops can bring total environmental degradation. In camps in Somalia, fuel became more valuable than food, and a "fuel-for-work" programme (as opposed to food-for-work) had to be introduced to allow the forest to recover (Cecelski, 1985).

Where refugees are moved to new regions or countries, the clash over scarce resources can be profound:

> In Pakistan, nearly three million Afghan refugees have settled, many with their animals, in the already semi-desertic North West Frontier and Baluchistan

provinces. Bare hills now surround most of the camps, and conflicts between the armed Afghans and local Pakistani villagers over forest resources have been a constant point of friction.

(Cecelski, 1985)

Effects on Women

"We sit here day after day worrying what will happen. I wonder if the rest of my life is going to be like this. We don't have a real life here, we just survive. I would like to go home, where we can grow our own food" (Sara, an Ethiopian refugee of 14 living in a Somalian camp).

Women make up a slight majority of the global population and a visible majority of the poor. A large proportion of the world's homeless — about 1000 million people — are women (Celik, 1985). And of the world's ten million refugees, women and children make up, in some areas, 90 per cent.

As home-makers and child-rearers, women are directly affected by the place in which they live (Kudat, 1986). The prospects for their children are slender: poor people in parts of many cities can expect to see one in four of their children die of malnutrition before they are five. Just as the lack of sanitation in the home affects women most strongly, so the destruction of water resources and fuelwood around settlements hits them hardest. The environment, both inside and outside the home, has everywhere a greater significance for women — a fact which is reinforced by cultural patterns.

In some areas it is still a woman's task to supply the building materials. In Ghana, for example, rural women haul mud for walls and thatch for the roof, and often carry out the final plastering (UNCHS, 1986; Agarwal, 1983). But there have been few studies of the nature and size of the burden women face in providing shelter. Clearly, some groups are especially disadvantaged, including the old and the growing number of women heads of household. Women now make up 90 per cent of single parents.

These groups are commonly excluded from shelter programmes, for women suffer here, as on other issues, from general discrimination. With little or no formal education and training, it is harder for them to be employed outside the home. When they are, their incomes are low. As elsewhere, their access to land and credit is limited. Although traditionally, in many cultures, women have been the main builders and maintainers of the family home, men dominate the modern approach to shelter planning and construction.

Inside the Home

Women spend more time at home than men, much of it is maintenance and repair. Their daily domestic tasks — cooking, washing and child care — confine them to the environs of the house. Women in seclusion, particularly in Islamic countries, must remain inside most of the time. Yet the internal environment of the home is often dangerous: fumes from open wood and charcoal fires damage eyes and lungs. Household accidents are common where there is little protection from unguarded stoves and heaters, and where perhaps seven or more live in one room.

Environmental disasters, too, can affect women more severely, although their perspective is rarely studied. In the aftermath of Bhopal, many suffered menstrual and other gynaecological problems; pregnant women gave birth to deformed babies; some of the infants were blind. In the demonstrations which followed the gas leak, women were especially active in protesting against the damage to their families (Butalia, 1985).

Women at Work

Often the workplace is no better than the home. Increasingly, multinational firms are employing young women in the South to work in electronics and textile factories. These women have few legal rights — and even fewer rights in practice — and have little power with which to fight workplace hazards. Often they work with toxic chemicals, or damage their eyesight by continuous use of microscopes. Lighting and ventilation are inadequate and there is usually no protection from machinery, dust and noise. The hours are long; rarely is there a right to refuse overtime. Where employers provide living quarters, as in many Asian countries, women live in cramped company dormitories, sharing beds in tiny rooms. Worldwide, women workers are among the lowest paid and least organized in unions, which makes them vulnerable to these kinds of exploitation and unable to secure better living and working conditions for themselves.

Responses to the Problems

Shelter is now officially recognized as a basic need. More and more local housing organizations are encouraging community participation and are aware of the need for legal access to land, building materials, credit without collateral and incomes to sustain investment in better housing (Hardoy and Satterthwaite, 1986b). The inhabitants of informal settlements display extraordinary vitality and resourcefulness in providing shelter and services for themselves and in generating incomes. In the poor districts of many cities, communities are transforming their environment through self-help.

But they cannot continue to do so without supportive policies and legislation. Outdated by-laws prevent the poor from getting access to affordable shelter and from earning a living in the informal economy (in some cities, petty traders are hounded like criminals). Strict application of outmoded regulations limits the adoption of more appropriate technologies. For example, costly sewers instead of latrines are installed in areas where there is no water for flushing. Roads are built but then not maintained. Jorge Hardoy of the International Institute for Environment and Development argues that most present shelter priorities in the south are misguided: money spent on expensive housing and service schemes should go instead to support comprehensive and affordable self-help shelter schemes organized by NGOs. Governments and aid agencies need to assist the poorest by granting them legal tenure or plots to build their homes, by providing building materials (and promoting their local production) and by increasing access to credit. "People," says Hardoy, "are themselves a resource."

> *"Site and service" and settlement upgrading projects adopt this philosophy. Even here, however, the needs of women can be ignored. Moser (1985) observes that housing projects often use a gridiron layout that does not allow women to work in their house and at the same time keep an eye on their own or their neighbours' children. House designs and plot sizes rarely consider the fact that many women will want to use their houses as workshops or as shops to sell goods — such enterprise is often forbidden in low-income housing projects. Hosken (1987) argues that housing managers as well as international financiers must start to recognize*

women's vital contribution in building new communities and maximize the oppor-
tunities for them to be full partners at every stage of the work.

Local Action

In Indonesia, the traditional artisan self-help system among rural women combines basic housing, financed by government, with improvements (bathrooms and latrines) financed by the women themselves. In Jamaica, few projects are designed specifically to help women, but there is one exception: the Women's Construction Collective, which has trained young unemployed women in building skills and found them jobs. In a similar project in Panama, launched with support from the Ministry of Housing in 1981, poor women (half of them single parents) aim to construct 100 homes. They receive land, building materials, training and a small monthly wage. By minimizing labour costs and bringing new skills to the participants, the scheme appears to have served both the government and the women well (UNCHS, 1986).

When the chance is offered, it is clear that women are anxious to respond. In two low-cost housing projects in Zimbabwe, the majority of participants in the workshops on community issues were women. They now play an important role in the design and management of their houses and in the shape of the overall settlement programmes. In Kenya, the Mabate Women's Groups are among a number of active self-help building cooperatives, and the Kenyan Women's Finance Trust intends to start up a loan-guarantee scheme to help women finance shelter improvements.

Nor is construction the only sector in which women can influence their living environment. In Mexico, they played a crucial part in adopting and promoting an integrated system for recycling wastes (SIRDO), a scheme that now controls sanitary conditions and offers the local community the possibility of earning an income. Pakistan's Baldia project has transformed the prospects for women. And they are involved in the provision of clean water.

Urban Agriculture

While women remain largely excluded from the benefits of the formal economy of cities, their position in the informal sector is improving. They play a dominant role, for example, in selling "street foods" (Tinker and Cohen, 1985). In Senegal, women constitute some 53 per cent of vendors, although both the food and the place of sale are completely sex segregated. In the Philippines, women control 79 per cent of street food enterprises and, in the 7 per cent that are owned by couples, are the major decision-makers. With as much as 20 per cent of the food budget being spent on street foods, according to a worldwide study conducted by the Equity Policy Centre, these small business centres can be an important source of income for women. By creating demand for locally-grown produce, they also provide income to rural farmers, particularly to women farmers, with whom women street vendors often collaborate.

Where low-income families can cultivate a vegetable garden, the crops can contribute substantially to the family diet and supplement the family income. Urban gardens are a priority for many women, especially when incomes are low. Urban agriculture is beneficial on several counts: it provides fresher, cheaper food, more green space, and scope for recycling household wastes, all attributes highly valued by women as the providers of food and the ensurers of good health in the family.

Much more vacant urban land (there are large amounts in some Third World cities, especially in Africa) could be cultivated if more women were granted legal title or access to sites and supported in other ways, for example with seed, tools, water and fertilizers, storage space, advice and credit for improved production and marketing. Demonstration plots and training schemes are needed, but few settlement projects have the staff, funds or institutional capability to incorporate such developments (Davidson, 1985).

In many ways, urbanization offers a unique opportunity for women to change their lives and escape from some of the oppressive traditions of the past and of village life which have excluded them from positions of control and stifled their initiative (Hosken, 1987). Living in the city offers women the prospect of education and self-development, of learning new skills, of earning an income. Information about health care, family planning and women's rights is more likely to be available. But as a priority, women's access to all these aspects of urban life must be improved.

It is clear from the success of some local projects that community based organizations and NGOs do well when they are helped and encouraged to involve women in the provision of shelter, and in the development activities that flow from it. The World Commission on Environment and Development argues for a much larger proportion of development assistance to be channelled through these organizations (WCED, 1987).

Box 6.1 A CHILD OF DELHI

Urmila is 14 years old. Five years ago, she moved with her family from a poor village in Uttar Pradesh to India's capital. Now she is a child of the city, and very unwilling to return to her village.

"I don't want to go back," she says. "There is more entertainment here — TV, video — and we have better food."

Not that families like Urmila's live in very attractive conditions. Old Delhi is a labyrinth of small streets studded with mosques, temples, monuments, bazaars and wandering cows. There are about 4000 people per square kilometre, and 40 per cent of the population live in slums — the bastis.

Urmila's family came to Delhi because her father was sick with asthma and it was thought he would get better medical treatment in the city. Urmila, who was nine when they arrived; her 13-year-old sister and her 10-year-old brother immediately looked for work. They spent every day running errands, washing utensils or carrying goods through the narrow streets. Their day began about 6 o'clock in the morning when their mother started to prepare the day's meal. By 8.00 a m they would all have left for work, except the father, who was ill and stayed home to look after the baby.

At 6.30 in the evening they returned. Then the hut was lit by a paraffin lamp and food was cooked on a charcoal stove (the girls collected unburnt coal from the railway station nearby). By 9.30 p m they were all asleep.

After two years the routine was broken by the father's death and the family split up. Urmila's elder sister returned to the village to marry; the baby was sent to a relative; Urmila, her mother and younger brother all went to work in Delhi as *domestic servants. They now live with their employers and rarely see each other. Urmila earns Rs 150 (about US $20) a month in the home of a wealthy industrialist. She looks after the young children, plays with the older ones, cleans, sweeps, dusts and cooks. Her day begins at 6.30 a m and ends at 10 p m. But Urmila feels she is much better off — and healthier — than she was in the village, although she would like to see her family. The only thing she does not like about the city is the traffic.*

Urmila has less in common now with her mother, for she has been learning the language of her employers while her mother still speaks the village dialect. But Urmila knows that she may well have to return to the village to marry. "If my mother forces me to, I'll have to go, there would be no choice."

(Singh, 1986)

We estimate that at least 600 million people living in urban areas of the Third World live in what might be termed life and health threatening homes and neighbourhoods. Perhaps as many (if not more) have inadequate access to effective health care — though again, official statistics provided by governments claim much better coverage (some as much as 99–100 per cent) than that known to exist in reality.

Virtually all the homes and neighbourhoods of poorer groups share two characteristics with serious impacts on health: the presence in the environment of pathogenic micro-organisms (especially those in human excreta) and crowded, cramped housing conditions. A lack of readily available drinking water, of sewerage connections (or other systems to dispose of human wastes), of garbage collection and basic measures to prevent disease and provide health care ensure that many diseases are endemic: diarrhoea, dysenteries, typhoid, intestinal parasites and food poisoning among them. These combined with malnutrition so weaken the body's defences that measles, pneumonia and other common childhood diseases become major killers.

Most urban centres in Africa and Asia — including many cities with a million or more inhabitants — have no sewerage at all. Rivers, streams, canals, gullies and ditches are where most human excrement and household wastes end up, untreated. For those cities with a sewerage system, it is rare for more than a small proportion of the population — typically the richer, residential, government and commercial areas — to be served. Garbage collection services are inadequate or non-existent in most residential areas; an estimated 30–50 per cent of the solid wastes generated within urban centres is left uncollected. It accumulates on streets, open spaces between houses and wasteland, causing or contributing to serious health problems. And poorer households suffer most because it is overwhelmingly the poorer areas that have no services to collect garbage or service levels are very inadequate. Box 6.2 illustrates these inadequacies in water, sanitation and garbage collection in different cities.

This health goal is neither revolutionary, utopian nor unfeasible. Each provision is a current objective of health workers and society in general. It should be recognized that most communities currently have acceptable experience with at least some of the listed provisions, and the shortcomings, although enormous in a global sense, are also within humanity's long-term capability.

Box 6.2 INADEQUACIES IN WATER SUPPLY, SANITATION AND
GARBAGE COLLECTION

Bangkok: *About one-third of the population has no access to public waste and must obtain water from vendors. Only 2 per cent of the population is connected to a sewer system; human wastes are generally disposed of through septic tanks and cess pools and their effluents — as well as waste water from sinks, laundries, baths and kitchens — are discharged into stormwater drains or canals. In 1987, around a quarter of solid wastes generated in the city remained uncollected and were dumped, mostly onto vacant land or on canals and rivers.*

Calcutta: *Some 3 million people live in bustees and refugee settlements which lack potable water, endure serious annual flooding and have no systematic means of disposing of refuse or human wastes. Some 2.5 million others live in similarly blighted and unserviced areas. Piped water is only available in the central city and parts of some other municipalities. The sewerage is limited to only a third of the area in the urban core. Poor maintenance of drains and periodic clogging of the system have been made flooding an annual feature.*

Dakar and Other Senegalese Towns: *Senegalese towns have no provision for the removal of household and public waste. Of the five urban centres with sewerage systems, generally only the inner urban population has access to these facilities. In Dakar, the capital, a 1980/1 survey found that 28 per cent of households have private water connections while 68 per cent rely on public standpipes and 4.2 per cent on buying water from carriers. A survey in Pikine, the outer part of Dakar, found an average of 696 persons per standpipe with 1513 in one neighbourhood. In Dakar, nearly one-sixth of all human faeces are dumped outside proper toilet facilities.*

Dar es Salaam: *From a survey of 660 households drawn from all income levels in 1986–7, 47 per cent had no piped water supply either inside or immediately outside their houses while 32 per cent had a shared piped-water supply. Of the households without piped water, 67 per cent buy water from neighbours while 26 per cent draw water from public water-kiosks or standpipes. Only 7.1 per cent buy water from water sellers. The average water consumption is only 23.6 litres per person per day. Only 13 per cent of the dirty water and sewage produced is regularly disposed of. Of the 660 households, 89 per cent had simple pit-latrines. Only 4.5 per cent had toilets connected to septic tanks or sewers. Most households have to share sanitary facilities. Overflowing latrines are a serious problem, especially in the rainy season, and provision to empty septic tanks or latrines is very inadequate. Only in a quarter of the city is refuse collected.*

Jakarta: *Less than a quarter of the city's population has direct connections to a piped water system; some 30 per cent depend solely on water vendors with water costing five times that of piped water. The city has no waterborne sewerage. Septic tanks serve about 25 per cent of the city's population; others use pit-latrines, cesspools and ditches along the roadside. Much of the population had to use drainage canals for bathing, laundering and defecation. Around 30 per cent of the garbage is not collected and ends up in canals and rivers and along the roadsides where it clogs drainage channels and causes extensive flooding during the rainy season.*

Karachi: Potable water has to be brought more than 160 kilometres from the Indus and is available for only a few hours a day in most areas. One-third of households have piped water connections and most slum dwellers and squatters must either use public stand-posts or buy water from vendors at inflated prices. Only one-third of the solid wastes produced in the city are being removed.

Khartoum: The systems of water supply, sewage disposal, refuse disposal and electricity supply are all inadequate both in the coverage of the urban area and the maintenance of the service. The water supply system is working beyond its design capacity while the demand continues to rise. The coverage is poor, with the low-income groups in squatter settlements suffering the cost of all through paying the most for water, often bought from vendors. Breakdown and cuts in the supply system are common. The municipal sewerage serves only about 5 per cent of the Khartoum urban area. Even that system is susceptible to breakdowns when waste is discharged either directly into the river or onto open land. For most people in the low-income areas, there is no system of sewage disposal.

Kinshasa: There is no sewerage in Kinshasa. Around half the urban population (some 1.5 million people) are not served by a piped-water network. High income areas are often 100 per cent connected while many other areas have 20–30 per cent of houses connected: essentially those along the main roads. The sale of water flourishes in areas far from the network — in these areas water is usually obtained from wells or the river. Household waste is only collected from a few residential areas. In the rest of the city, household waste is dumped on roadsides, on illegal dumps, in stormwater drains or buried in open spaces.

Madras: Only 2 million of the 3.7 million residential consumers within the service area of the local water supply and sewerage board are connected to the system. On average, they receive some 36 litres per capita per day. The rest within the service area must use public taps which serve about 240 persons per tap. Another million consumers outside the service area must rely on wells — but supplies are inadequate here too because of falling groundwater levels. The sewerage serves 31 per cent of the metropolitan population and raw sewage flows freely into the metropolitan area's natural watercourses at many points.

Manila: Only 15 per cent of the population of Metro Manila is served with sewers or individual septic tanks. Some 1.8 million people lack adequate water supplies — as well as educational, community, health and sanitary services. Inadequate collection of domestic wastes also means that garbage blocks canals and drains and makes flooding problems much more serious.

São Paulo: Of the more than 13 million people living in the metropolitan area, 64 per cent lived in households not served by the sewerage system in 1980, and very little sewage was treated. One-third of the population live in areas with no service to collect household wastes.

(Hardoy and Satterthwaite, 1989)

The short term outlook for health in housing is bleak. Conservative estimates indicate that more than one billion people in cities throughout the world live in grossly inadequate housing bordering on squalor, and more than 100 million have no housing whatsoever. The major developmental trends that could influence this situation are also unfavourable, namely global population growth, rapid urbanization and debilitating debt in many Third World countries. These are times that call for courage and determination on the part of all people working for social and economic development and improvement of the living environment. Over the years we have found a note of encouragement wherever we have had the opportunity to visit low-income communities. It seems that no matter how desperate the economic or environmental situation, there are always a few resourceful individuals and families who are able to make a clean and welcoming human refuge, and that groups of people, working together, can create a pleasant community. There is always something that can be done by conscientious self-reliant people to improve their home environment. Governments and societies in general can and must do more to support the natural inclinations of people everywhere to improve and use their housing environment so that its health potential can be realized to the full.

References

Agarwal, A (1983) *Mud Mud*, Earthscan, London

Butalia, S (1985) "Bhopal: Women Bear Brunt of Environmental Disaster", *Women and the Environmental Crisis*, Report of the Proceedings of the Workshops on Women, Environment and Development, Environment Liaison Centre, Nairobi, 10–20 July

Cecelski, E (1985) *The Rural Energy Crisis, Women's Work and Basic Needs: Perspectives and Approaches to Action*, Rural Employment Policy Research Programme, ILO, Geneva

Celik, A (1985) "Human Settlements: A Critical Factor", *Women and the Environmental Crisis*, Report of the Proceedings of the Workshops on Women, Environment and Development, Environment Liaison Centre, Nairobi

Davidson, J (1985) "Human Settlements: Building a New Resourcefulness", *Habitat International*, vol 9, nos 3/4

Hardoy, J E and D Satterthwaite (1984) "Third World Cities and the Environment of Poverty", *Geoforum*, 15

—— (1986a) "Urban Change in the Third World", *Habitat International*, vol 10, no 3

—— (1986b) "Shelter, Infrastructure and Services in Third World Cities", *Habitat International*, vol 10, no 3

—— (1989) *Squatter Citizen: Life in the Urban Third World*, Earthscan, London

Hosken, F (1987) "Women, Urbanization and Shelter", *Development Forum*, May

Kudat, A (1986) *Women and Shelter*, UNCHS, Nairobi

Moser, C O N (1985) *Housing Policy: Towards a Gender Awareness Approach*, Working paper no 71, Development Planning Unit, London

Singh, A (1986) *A Child of Delhi*, UNFPA, Geneva

Tinker, I and Cohen, M (1985) "Street Foods as a Source of Income for Women", *Ekistics* 310, January/February

UNCHS (1986) *Report of the Advisory Seminars on Women and Shelter. Vienna, 9–17 December*, UNCHS, Nairobi

UNEP (1985) *Sustainable Development and Peace*, Report prepared by the United Nations Environment Programme, Conference of the UN Decade for Women, Nairobi, 15–26 July

WCED (1987) *Our Common Future*, Oxford University Press, Oxford

The Search for Shelter
Jorge Hardoy and David Satterthwaite

"The Value of My House — 26 Years' Struggle"

Box 6.3 tells the story of the Ramirez family's search for shelter; this story was used on a United Nations poster to illustrate the struggle of a family of recent rural migrants to find a home in a large metropolis. It illustrates the kinds of political, environmental, cultural and economic problems that the family had to overcome. After 20 years of struggle and the loss of one of their children (who died after drinking contaminated water), the Ramirez family finally obtained their goal of a conventional house in a legal urban development with basic services. As one householder in the squatter settlement Brasilia Teimosa said, "the value of my house — 26 years' struggle".

Box 6.3 THE SEARCH FOR SHELTER

Below is the text of a poster printed by the United Nations during the International Year of Shelter for the Homeless in 1987.[*] It illustrates the difficulties faced by a poor family in finding a decent house in the city. Their struggle for shelter is presented in the form of a series of steps which the family have to move through. It was designed in the form of a game known in English as Snakes and Ladders; each player would start at the beginning and take turns to move through the steps, after throwing a dice. Below is a slightly shortened version of the text taken from the game.

BACKGROUND: Mr Ramirez (31), his wife Ines (25) and their children Carlos (8), Clara (5) and Rosa (3) find that they cannot survive on their rented farmland. The rains have been poor and the one hectare plot they farm has been producing

---

[*]This text was written by Jorge E Hardoy and David Satterthwaite for a poster prepared at the request of the United Nations Centre for Human Settlements (Habitat) for the International Year of Shelter for the Homeless in 1987; Pat Crooke designed the poster and both he and John F C Turner helped develop the text.

less each year. Ramirez decides to go to the city to see if he can find a job. His cousin Juan moved to the city two years earlier and has offered to help Mr Ramirez

Ramirez says goodbye to his family and catches a bus to the city

Arrives at the bus-station; cousin Juan not there; sleeps on a bench in the bus station

Arrives at the bus station, cousin Juan meets him

Looks for Juan; finds that he has left the city for a week and so sleeps on waste-land until Juan returns

Ramirez sleeps on the floor of Juan's shack

Ramirez finds a temporary job on night shift at a factory

Ramirez works with Juan selling fruit

Juan's son is sick: Ramirez gives the money to provide medicine

Crop tended by Ines destroyed by drought. Ines and the children join Ramirez in the city and stay with Juan

The family find a room for rent in an inner-city tenement

Ines finds work as a maid which allows better diet for the family

Ramirez purchases a plot of land in an illegal sub-division on the edge of the city with a loan from a money lender using the land as security

Rosa (the youngest daughter) burnt in a household accident; funds have to be found to treat her burns and time taken off work to take her for treatment

Carlos (the eldest child) finds discarded wood on the city dump; the family builds a temporary shack

Ramirez hears from friends of a squatter invasion being planned; he joins the organization of the invasion

Private firm which sells water to those in the illegal sub-division from a tanker raises prices

The family takes part in an invasion of land; on the plot of land they occupy; then build a makeshift shack

Rise in the price of bus-fares increases cost of travel to work

Ramirez loses his job; cannot pay the

Police suppress the invasion and destroy the Ramirez shack

loan used to purchase the land and so they have to sell the land

The family return to a room rented in an inner-city tenement

The family acquire another plot of land either through a squatter invasion or by buying another illegal subdivision and manage to hold onto it and built a shack

A flood inundates the site of their house which delays construction and means they live in a plastic tent

A candidate for Mayor of the city promises that if elected, he will give Ramirez and others in their settlement legal tenure

Ines buys a second hand sewing machine; the extra income from selling the clothes she makes, and which Rosa helps deliver, helps speed up house construction

Clara goes to school; extra cost for family for books and clothes delays house construction

Carlos drops out of school to work as a builder; extra income helps speed up house construction

Candidate for Mayor who promised legal tenure wins election and after lengthy negotiations between the community organization formed by the residents of Ramirez's neighbourhood, they receive legal tenure

A group of people in the newly legalized settlement for a cooperative and apply for a loan to the national housing bank

The Ramirez have a fourth child

The cooperative receive the loan from the housing bank and Ramirez, as members of the cooperative, receive a loan to allow them to purchase materials to build a permanent first storey to replace the wooden shack

Neighbours help the Ramirez family to pour and form the concrete for the first storey

The youngest child dies of dysentery because the water supply is polluted

Ramirez contracts TB which slows down the construction of the house

Clara qualifies as a teacher and finds a job teaching; she contributes to the family income and this allows the construction of a second storey to the house

The City Council provides piped water to the settlement with a public tap installed close to the Ramirez house

Clara gets married and moves out; the family rent out a room in the house to obtain extra income

THE END: The Ramirez family finally have a safe, well-built home of their own; it has taken them 20 years of struggle to do so, since they moved to the city. Ramirez is now 51 years old while Ines is 45, Carlos 28, Clara 25 and Rosa 23.

The Scale of the Problem
Sandy Cairncross, Jorge Hardoy
and David Satterthwaite

Most poor people die young in the Third World. Half of all deaths are infants or children; in many poor communities, half of all deaths are children under five years of age (Morley and Lovel, 1986). In western Europe, North America and other prosperous regions, 80 per cent of the population live for over 65 years; in the South, only a quarter live to this age. In the Third World, poor people's lives are characterized by almost continuous ill-health; a high proportion are also disabled (for instance by polio or from injuries arising from household or workplace accidents which receive inadequate treatment) (WHO, 1989).

Certain statistics give an idea of the severity of these problems. In many Third World nations, a child born today is 15 to 20 times more likely to die before the age of five than a child born in a prosperous western nation (Tabibzadeh et al, 1989). Among many poorer households in Third World nations, a child is 40 to 50 times more likely to die before the age of five than a child born in the West (WHO, 1989). A woman born poor in the Third World is 150 times more likely to die in pregnancy or childbirth that a woman in Europe or North America (Stambouli, 1990). Infants and children in the Third World are several hundred times more likely to die from diarrhoea, pneumonia and measles than those in Europe or North America; these are the most common causes of child death in the Third World. In 1986, an estimated 14.1 million children under five years of age died; 98 per cent were in the Third World (UN/WHO/UNICEF, 1987).

In many of the poorest Third World nations, between a quarter and a third of all children die before the age of five; among the poorer families within these nations, one child in two may die before the age of five. This compares with a rate of less than 1 child in 100 dying before the age of five in the richest nations.

For the rich, rates of infant and child mortality in Third World nations are often as low as those in western nations. But amongst poor families, for every child who dies, many more live on in hunger and ill-health; on average, children in these families under five have survived ten attacks of diarrhoea (Morley and Lovel, 1986). Around a quarter of the Third World's children are malnourished, which reduces their energy, stunts their growth, lowers their resistance to disease and impairs their intellectual attainments (Morley and Lovel, 1986). Their nutritional weakness is often exacerbated by parasitic worm infections which afflict more than a quarter of the world's population.

Other statistics give an idea of how many people suffer. One estimate suggests that some 2.2 billion people live in poverty in the Third World (Jancloes, 1990). Nine out of ten of them have no access to safe drinking water, most have no primary health care service and one child in four is of low birth weight (Jancloes, 1990). In the absence of sophisticated equipment and highly trained medical personnel, a high proportion of low birth-weight children die before the age of one. Fewer than half the mothers receive adequate care from qualified personnel during their pregnancy and only one child in seven will receive vaccinations which protect them from such common childhood killers as diphtheria, tenanus and whooping cough (UN/WHO/UNICEF, 1987). Some 500 000 women die each year from pregnancy-related causes, 99 per cent of them in the Third World (Morley and Lovel, 1986). More than 750 000 newborn babies (and many of their mothers) die of neonatal tenanus each year — virtually all of them in the Third World. A measure as simple as immunizing women against tenanus would considerably reduce both infant and maternal deaths.

Poor people in Europe and North America also suffer more ill health and premature death than richer groups. But in the Third World, the problem is of a much larger scale and severity; a far higher proportion of the population are poor and their health problems are much more severe. In around two-thirds of all Third World nations, the poor are the majority as a result of their lack of income, capital resources or productive land. This means that they use virtually all their resources on daily necessities (especially food) and have a very limited capacity to pay for housing or basic services (including health services). But even in most of the wealthier Third World nations, between a quarter and a half of the population are also too poor to be able to spend much on such necessities. If the government does not ensure that there is an effective preventative and curative health care system — and that every one can find accommodation with piped water, sanitation, cooking and washing facilities and sufficient space — the poorer groups will continue to suffer from easily preventable disease, disablement and premature death. Table 6.1 (page 217) lists the 48 most prevalent diseases worldwide.

Those marked with an asterisk could be enormously reduced at a relatively low per capita cost through improved housing and living conditions, better nutrition and comprehensive coverage of primary health care. For instance, vaccinations could radically reduce the number of deaths and infections from tuberculosis, measles, whooping couch, tenanus, polio and diphtheria — together saving each year several million lives and tens of millions of people from ill health. Improved water and sanitation and the wider availability of simple, inexpensive oral rehydration salts would cut enormously the number of people who die or suffer regularly from diarrhoeal diseases. Improved water and sanitation would greatly reduce the incidence of most parasitic worms — including schistosomiasis, hookworm and roundworm — especially if combined with treatment (it is common for half or more of the population in low income settlements to have one or more intestinal parasite). Pneumonia, one of the main causes of child death in the Third World, can be reduced with better nutrition, immunization against other childhood diseases (since these often combine with pneumonia to cause death) and by equipping mothers with the knowledge of how to diagnose it (Shimouchi,

1989). If no action is taken to address these most serious health problems, in the next ten years 200 million people may die prematurely from preventable causes.

Table 6.1 The World's Most Prevalent Diseases

Diseases	Number of People Infected
Vaccine-preventable diseases	
Turberculosis*	1700 million
Measles*	49 million
Whooping cough (Pertussis)*	46 million
Tetanus*	1.5 million
Polio*	200 000
Diphtheria*	>23 000
Tropical diseases	
Malaria*	270 million
Schistosomiasis*	200 million
Filariasis*	90 million
Chagas' Disease*	15–18 million
River Blindness*	18 million
Leishmaniasis*	12 million
Leprosy*	10–12 million
Guinea worm*	5–10 million
African sleeping sickness (new cases)	>20 000
Diarrhoeal diseases	
Amoebiasis*	480 million
Giardiasis*	200 million
Typhoid*	1 million
Cholera*	>40 000
Sexually transmitted diseases (new cases)	
Trichomoniasis	120 million
Genital Chlamydia	50 million
Genital Papillomavirus	30 million
Gonorrhoea	25 million
Genital herpes	20 5–10 million
Syphilis	3.5 million
Endemic Treponematoses	2.5 million
Chancroid	2 million
Other infectious and parasitic diseases	
Hepatitis B	2000 million
Ascariasis*	700 million
Hookworm*	700–900 million
Trichuriasis*	500 million
Dengue*	30–60 million

Toxoplasmosis	420 000
Rabies*	35 000
Yellow Fever*	10 000–25 000
Endocrine and nutritional diseases	
Iodine deficiency*	200 million
Diabetes (Third World)	40 million
Vitamin A deficiency*	40 million
Others	
Cardiovascular diseases (deaths)	12 million
Pneumonia (deaths)*	4.8 million
Anaemia*	1500 million
Mental disorders	200 million
Drug abuse	>85 million
Trachoma*	6–9 million
Cancer (new cases)	6.4 million
Meningococcal Meningitis	>65 000
Brucellosis	>80 000

Source: WHO (1990). *Note*: Many people are infected with multiple diseases; turberculosis infects 1.7 billion but only 20 million are sick. From the 5–10 million people infected with the AIDS virus, only some 400 000 are sick with AIDS.

With few exceptions, the causes of diseases and death in the Third World are no less a factor in urban areas than they are in the countryside. While average rates of disease, malnutrition and death for many cities are lower than in the surrounding rural areas, they are held down by the presence in such cities of a high proportion of the nation's middle and upper income classes who enjoy a relatively good standard of health. By contrast, the poor in urban areas generally live in overcrowded tenements, cheap boarding houses or illegal housing and usually suffer comparable or even higher rates of disease and death than their rural counterparts. The close proximity of large numbers of people, in an environment which provides no protection from the pollution caused by their own and other city wastes, creates conditions very favourable to the rapid spread of a variety of infectious diseases, often in disastrous epidemics.

Box 6.4 DIFFERENT OPTIONS FOR A GOVERNMENT SPENDING $20 MILLION ON IMPROVING HOUSING AND LIVING ENVIRONMENTS

Option 1: $20 million spent on the construction of two-bedroom "low cost" housing units "for low-income groups". The cost of each unit is some $10 000, once the land has been purchased, the site prepared, the contractor paid for building the units and the infrastructure and the units allocated. Thus 2000 households or 12 000 people receive a good quality house — if we assume that on average, there are six persons per household. Cost recovery would be difficult if these were from among the poorer households.

Option 2: *$20 million is spent on a serviced-site project, so that more households can be reached than in public-housing projects. Knowing that poorer households need to live close to the main centres of employment, a relatively central site was purchased for $12 million with the other $8 million spent on site preparation and installing infrastructure and services. At a cost of $2000 per plot, 10 000 households (or 60 000 people) could benefit. It would be easier to recover some costs than in the public-housing project but for the poorer households, $2000 for a site on top of the cost of having to construct their own house would be too much.*

Option 3: *Local government makes available to any residents' organization formed by the majority of the inhabitants of an area the sum of $100 000 for site improvements. These residents' organizations have considerable flexibility as to how they choose to spend these funds and who they turn to for technical advice. For instance, they can use local NGOs for technical advice, as long as certain basic standards are met. Although what can be achieved with such a sum will vary greatly depending on site characteristics, local costs and the extent to which residents contribute their skills and labour free, within an area with 500 households. It should be possible to reblock the site to allow better paved access road and also greatly to improve site drainage, water supply and sanitation. Support could be given to local artisans to fabricate the materials, fixtures and fittings that are most cheaply and effectively made on site — for instance, a carpenter's cooperative to make doors and windows or cheap building block fabrication. Of the $100 000, an average of $150 is spent per household on improved infrastructure and services with $10 000 spent on technical advice and $15 000 on support for local businesses. The reblocking of the site also frees up sufficient land to allow 50 more housing plots to be developed within the existing site or on adjacent as yet undeveloped land, and the cost of providing these with infrastructure and services and of building a community health centre is paid for by selling them.*

With $100 000 provided to 150 community organizations with an average of 500 households (3000 people) the total cost was $15 million and the whole programme reached 150 × 3000 people: 450 000 people. Since an average of 50 new housing plots were produced in each reblocking, not only did 450 000 people benefit from improved housing, infrastructure and services but 7500 new plots with services were developed and new health centres constructed in each site. The possibility of cost recovery was much better than for Options 1 and 2 since most households could afford to pay $200 — or take out a loan which allowed repayment over a few years. Spending $15 million in this way still left $5 million from the original $20 million which could be used to improve some city-wide service — for instance, training community health workers to run health clinics and health campaigns in each settlement.

(*Source*: Hardoy and Satterthwaite, 1989)

■   *Sandy Cairncross, Jorge Hardoy and David Satterthwaite*

References
Hardoy, J E and D Satterthwaite (1989) *Squatter Citizen: Life of the Urban Third World*, Earthscan, London
Jancloes, M (1990) "More than a Billion ...", *World Health*, WHO, Geneva
Morley, D and Lovel, H. (1986) *My Name is Today: An Illustrated Discussion of Child Health, Society and Poverty in Less Developed Countries*, Macmillan, London
Shimouchi, A (1989) "Controlling Pneumonia in Children", *World Health*, WHO, Geneva
Stambouli, F (1990) "Born Underprivileged", *World Health*, WHO, Geneva
Tabibzadeh, I, A Rossi-Espagnet and R Maxwell (1989) *Spotlight on the Cities: Improving Urban Health in Developing Countries*, WHO, Geneva
UN/WHO/UNICEF (1987) *The State of the World's Children 1987*, Oxford University Press, Oxford
WHO (1989) *World Health Statistics 1989*, WHO Publications Unit, Geneva
—— (1990) *Global Estimates for Health Situation Assessment and Projects 1990*, Division of Epidemiological Surveillance and Health Situation and Trend Assessment, Geneva

| THE COMMONS

Common property resources and open access resources — those to which access is not controlled — have been widely discussed ever since Hardin (1968) suggested that common property resources would inevitably be overused since no user had an incentive to moderate their demands when others were tempted to maximizing their use of the resource. The classic example in Hardin's "The Tragedy of the Commons" is the incentive to pastoralists to maximize their personal herd on common land since the cost in degradation of the grazing is paid by all the herders. Kevin Gray examines the complex issue of entitlement to access to resources. He shows that, in fact, purely private resources are rare and that multiple rights in property — common rights — are widespread. The poorest members of a society depend disproportionately on common resources because they own few private posessions. But, as *The Ecologist* explains, the process of development has historically led to the enclosure of common resources, both of land and of intellectual property. From the Middle Ages, common land was enclosed in Britain and the theft of land continued in colonial and post colonial times through the actions of powerful elites and more recently by transnational corporate activities. *The Ecologist* sees the challenge to be the reclamation of the privatized commons.

Christopher Stone gives a lawyer's view of the problems of protecting the atmosphere and the oceans against pollution and against the over-consumption of resources. Later in the chapter he outlines a response to the degradation of these resources. Global common guardians — UN agencies and selected NGOs — would monitor environmental quality, act as disinterested intervenors on behalf of degraded global commons and be able to sue the degraders. A global commons trust fund raised through taxes on the use of global common resources would be responsible for maintenance and repair. Other responses to the degradation of the global commons are covered in the sections on environmental economies, biodiversity and energy and climate.

Though the greens have recently concentrated on the crisis of the global commons, particularly concerned by the threats of human-generated climate change, loss of biodiversity and pollution, others have been concerned to examine the place of common resources in the local management of development. *The Ecologist* cites examples of success in local management of the commons. Camilla Toulmin, Ian Scorer and Joshua Bishop show that the local management of wildlife on common resources can provide a sustainable income for local people. Alan Grainger discusses 'scientific' attempts to improve the management of African grasslands. These attempts have been unsuccessful in stopping degradation of grasslands.

The Ambivalence of Property
Kevin Gray

Property is Not a Thing

The beginning of truth in this area is the realization that "property" is not itself the thing or resource that is "owned". "Property" is instead the term used to describe a legally (because socially) endorsed concentration of power over things and resources. Use of the term "property" is a coded shorthand reference to a quantum of socially permissible power exercisable in respect of a socially valued resource. Thus, property is not a thing but a power relationship. "Property" is what we have in things, not the things that we think we have. (Jeremy Bentham would have had no doubt on this point.) It was he who emphasized long ago that "in common speech in the phrase 'the object of a man's property', the words 'the object of' are commonly left out; and by an ellipsis, which, violent as it is, is now become more familiar than the phrase at length, they have made that part of it which consists of the words 'a man's property' perform the office of the whole" (Harrison, 1948, p337).

On this basis, then, one may rightly claim to have "property" in a motorcar or "property" in a stamp collection and so on. And at this point it becomes possible to concede, as did Coke almost four centuries ago, that the notion of "property" in a resource is not absolute, but relative. There may be gradations of "property" in a resource, and it becomes feasible to measure or calibrate the quantum of "property" we have in a particular resource at a particular time.

The concept of "property" is, accordingly, not static, but dynamic. I may have "property" in a resource today, but not tomorrow. Such is the case, for instance, with patents, copyrights and other forms of intellectual property, whose expiration is governed by a statutorily authorized "sunset clause" (ownership of a copyright normally expires 50 years after the death of the author). Again, it is never permissible to do exactly as I wish with things or resources that are supposedly "mine". There are distinct limits, practical, moral and social, upon the amount of property I may claim in any resource. There may be a significant quantum of social "property" in "my" resource, which outweighs the value of my own claim of "property" in that resource. For instance, I cannot build a skyscraper on my suburban block of land, any more than I may use "my" meat cleaver or "my" axe to make large holes in my neighbour's head.

Perhaps most important, it becomes rapidly apparent that I can have "property" even in resources that are supposedly "owned" by someone else. This proposition has been recognized for centuries in English law, an excellent example being provided by the restrictive covenant over land, such a covenant itself constituting one of the earliest means of environmental protection in respect of the natural world. If I enjoy the benefit of a restrictive covenant over my neighbour's land, English law has no difficulty in saying that I have thereby been allocated some of the "property" in that land — in the sense that I am now in a position to control (or at least influence) activities on the land. I can stop my neighbour from further building development or from engaging in trade, business or industry and so on. Nor is it mere metaphor to say that since, in modern times, the law of private restrictive covenants has very largely been socialized through the medium of planning legislation, all citizens can now, in some quite important sense, claim a certain quantum of "property" in everyone else's land.

The conclusion of this approach is that the concept of "ownership" in respect of any particular resource dissolves into differently constituted aggregations (or "bundles") of power over that resource. "Ownership" breaks down, as it were, into distinct quantums of "property" in a resource, which are then distributed variously to perhaps a vast range of persons. The concept of "ownership" is thus reduced to a concealed form of per-centage game, in which the winner — with the predominating percentage of quantum of "property" in a particular resource — is collectively awarded the titular attribution of "owner". But, despite the utility of this shorthand reference to "ownership", we should all be sneakily aware of the misleading, and ultimately worthless, nature of the attribution. Careless talk about "ownership" only superficially hides the comprehensive interpenetration of "property" in the earth's resources. "Property" references have about them an utterly interdependent quality.

Before we lay aside the heavy conceptualism of "property", we must pick up one last corollary which follows from the almost infinitely gradable quality of the "property" notion. There is no inevitability about the existence of a clear threshold between having "property" in a resource and not having "property" in it. Propertiness — if I may use this phrase — is perhaps best represented by a continuum along which varying kinds of "property" status shade finely into each other. The amount of "property" I may claim in any resource thus varies — along some sort of sliding scale — from a minimum value to a maximum value. It does not follow that there are any resources in the world in which I (or anyone else) may claim a total or 100 per cent quantum of "property". Correspondingly — although less obviously — there is no resource in the world in which my "property" stake is reduced to a zero sum. It may be almost true to say that the earth contains no resource from the "property" in which I am entirely and in all circumstances excludable.

Now, all of the foregoing analysis sits very uncomfortably beside the conventional notions of property with which most of us are brought up. For each of us, property is — literally or metaphorically — something with six sides and two holes in the middle, which we can pick up and look at. And it belongs either to me or to you. So how do we reconcile this uncompromising everyday view with the amorphous, almost anarchic, concept of property I have just outlined? The key lies in the slowly emerging ambiv-alence of the property concept, and it is the realization of this ambivalence that promotes the cutting edge in contemporary property jurisprudence.

It was Professor C B Macpherson who pointed famously to the tension between property as the right to exclude and property as a right of access. In Macpherson's view the notion of "property" consists not so much in the Blackstonian right to exclude strangers from privately owned resources, as in the assertion of public rights to share in a number of socially valued resources which enable us to lead fulfilled and dignified lives. Thus, in Macpherson's view, the idea of property is constantly being broadened to secure the right of the citizen to "that kind of society which is instrumental to a full and free life", and therefore to "a set of power relations that permits a full life of enjoyment and development of one's human capacities".

It is precisely this tension between private rights of exclusion and public rights of access which lies today at the heart of a multi-levelled debate about the dominant ideology in property thinking. It is the interrelation between exclusion and access which indeed provides the pivot of the contemporary property reference and it is precisely the ambiguity of this interplay which I wish to develop here.

The juxtaposition of ideas of exclusion and access already indicates that the "property" concept has both a private and a public dimension. The distinction between these two dimensions or axes falls roughly at the boundary of what historically has been called the "commons". A moment's thought will confirm that not all of the earth's human and economic resources are allowed to be subjected to the peculiarly intense reach of exclusory claims of private property. Not every resource is, in this sense, privatized. Not every resource — to use another ugly but effective phrase — is "propertized". Indeed, contrary to popular perception, the vast majority of the world's human and economic resources still stands completely outside the threshold of private property and therefore remains immune to claims of private exclusory power. These "unpropertized" resources remain by definition in the commons, available for use and exploitation by all. Historic examples include, of course, the high seas and the upper stratum of navigable airspace. Both of these resources survive effectively as part of the original commons, and, in enjoying immunity from self-interested claims of property, both remain available to facilitate the commerce and intercourse of humanity. Both resources constitute what an American judge once called "free territory . . . a sort of no-man's land". Neither resource belongs to any individual or state, yet, in some paradoxical way, both assets belong to the world. It is precisely upon this ambivalence that Sir Julian Oswald alights in his invigorating plea for new thinking in his chapter.

There is thus a public "property" in the commons which is no less significant in that the "property" which may be claimed in those resources is privatized or propertized. And it is this double-edged aspect of the "property" concept which has vital explanatory power in elucidating the common heritage of humankind. For perhaps the essential truth in the Macpherson thesis is that the role of the "property" concept is not simply to guarantee the private ownership of certain goods, but also to stop others more powerful than ourselves from propertizing all the goods of life and thereby precluding general access. In this way, "property" is a bivalent concept, operating just as significantly (if more silently) to assure us of our continuing vested rights in the natural and social goods which remain in the commons.

The range of the world's resources in which exclusory "property" may be claimed is indeed much more limited than we might imagine. Only a relatively small part of the total field of economic facility and human capacity is at present permitted to be the subject of private property. The withholding of private "property" in certain crucial resources is what gives a new and invigorated content to the assertion that property jurisprudence is ultimately concerned with claims of access to natural and social goods — of access to a common heritage of humankind.

Reference

Hardin, G (1968) "The Tragedy of the Commons", *Science*, 162, pp1243–8

Harrison, W (ed) (1948) *An Introduction to the Principles of Morals and Legislation*, Oxford University Press, Oxford

The Commons: Where the Community has Authority

The Ecologist

An Everyday Reality

For many people in the West, the word "commons" carries an archaic flavour; that of the medieval village pasture which villagers did not own but where they had rights to graze their livestock. Yet, for the vast majority of humanity, the commons is an everyday reality. Ninety per cent of the world's fishers rely on small inshore marine commons, catching over half the fish eaten in the world today (Ostrom, 1991, p27). In the Philippines, Java and Laos, irrigation systems are devised and run by villagers themselves, the water rights being distributed through rules laid down by the community (Cruz, 1989). Even in the North, there are communities which still manage their forests and fishers jointly (lobster harvesters in Maine, for example, or forest communities in many areas of Finland), bestowing on themselves the power to divide up what they regard as "their" patches of sea or soil among their own communities and kin (Acheson, 1987). Moreover, new commons are constantly being born, even among what might seem the most fragmented communities. In the inner cities of the USA black communities' dialects express concepts that the language taught in state schools cannot touch. At toxic dump sites and around proposed nuclear plants in France, Switzerland, and elsewhere, people have insisted on their "rights" to keep the earth and air around their communities free from the threat of poisonous and radioactive substances, damning the economic and "public" rationality which dictates that their homes are "objectively" the best locations for waste sinks. For them, the sentiments expressed by an elder of a Brazilian tribe, despite the religious language in which they are couched, cannot be completely unrecognizable: "The only possible place for the Krenak people to live and to re-establish our existence, to speak to our Gods, to speak to our nature, to weave our lives, is where God created us. We can no longer see the planet that we live upon as if it were a chess-board where people just move things around" (WCED, 1987, p114).

The Commons: Neither Public Nor Private

Despite its ubiquity, the commons is hard to define. It provides sustenance, security and independence, yet (in what many Westerners feel to be a paradox) typically does not produce commodities. Unlike most things in modern industrial society, moreover, it is neither private nor public: neither commercial farm nor communist collective, neither business firm nor state utility, neither jealously-guarded private plot nor national or city park. Nor is it usually open to all. The relevant local community typically decides who uses it and how (Ostrom, 1991, p27).

The unlimited diversity of commons also makes the concept elusive. While all commons regimes involve joint use, what they define access to is bewilderingly varied: for example, trees, forests, land, minerals, water, fish, animals, language, time, radio wavelengths, silence, seeds, milk, contraception and streets.

Trying to find some order in this field, some theorists claim that the commons are "resources for which exclusion is difficult" and boundary-setting not worthwhile, or which "are needed by all but those whose productivity is diffuse rather than concentrated, low or unpredictable in yield, and low in unit value": for example, seasonally inundated swamplands in Borneo, moorland in England, semi-arid rangements in Botswana or Ethiopia, and scrubby *maquis* or *garrigues* in France and Spain (McCay and Acheson, 1987). Yet smaller, more easily divisible, and more highly productive and defensible arable lands are often also treated as communal property. In traditional Malaysia and Laos as well as Ethiopia and much of the rest of contemporary Africa, plots have been traditionally allocated to individuals by the community, which nevertheless reserve the authority to redistribute them if they are not used for subsistence. In such cases of usufruct, common rights can be defined as the right not to the land or the soil, which rests with the community, but the right to what the soil brings forth over a particular period.

Other theorists suggest that the commons are jointly-used resources whose use by one person may subtract from the welfare of the next, and which are thus potentially subject to crowding, depletion and degradation. Yet while this may be true of a great range of cases, genetic diversity or knowledge of contraception (to cite just two examples of "resources" often maintained by commons regimes) are not "subtractible" in this way.

Social Organization is the Key

More fruitful than such attempts to define commons regimes through their domains are attempts to define them through their social and cultural organization: for example, local or group power, distinctions between members and non-members, rough parity among members, a concern with common safety rather than accumulation, and an absence of the constraints that lead to economic scarcity. Even here, however, it would be a mistake to demand too much precision. For example, what does the "local" in "local power" mean? In Shanxi province in China, communal forests were owned by villages, several villages together, or clans. In India the relevant bodies may be caste groups, while for Switzerland's city forests, it is "citizenship" (election to a given community) that counts (Fortmann and Bruce, 1988).

Similarly, what does the "power" in "local power" consist in? Sometimes it is the power to exclude outsiders or to punish them if they abuse the commons. Often this power lays the foundation for an additional structure of internal rules, rights, duties and beliefs which mediates and shapes the community's own relationship with its natural surrounds. In Maine, for example, it is only in strongly defended territories that lobster harvesters have successfully enacted informal and formal regulations on the numbers of traps used, and elsewhere in North America there have been clear "post-fur-trade linkages between the existence of viable hunting territories and intentional conservation measures" (McCay and Acheson, 1987). Sometimes the meshes of power internal to commons regimes give rise to notions of "property" or "possession", but in many cases the relevant group does not regard itself as owning, but rather as owned by, or as stewards of, water or land.

Perceptions of Scarcity

A further characteristic often ascribed to the commons is that, unlike resources in the modern economy, it is "not perceived as scarce". This is not only because many things available as commons, such as silence, air or genetic diversity, will renew themselves continually until deliberately made scarce by the encroachment of outside political actors. More importantly, the needs many commons satisfy are not infinitely expanding. They are not determined by a growth-oriented external system producing goods and services, but rather are constantly adjusted and limited by the specific commons regime itself, whose physical characteristics remain in everyone's view. Without the race between growth and the scarcity growth creates, there can thus be a sense of "enoughness". Even where produce from the commons is sold, the "needs" defined by consumerism and external market demand for goods and services will be subject to external revision.

The Worldly Commons

Despite their resolutely local orientation and resistance to being swallowed up by larger systems, commons regimes have never been isolated in either space or time. Nor have their social organizations ever been static. Commons regimes welcome, feed upon and are fertilized by contact, and evolve just like any other social institution (Norgaard, 1988; Illich, 1982). Communities maintaining commons often work out arrangements over larger geographical areas with other groups. For example, intervillage commons boundaries are acknowledged by villagers in the Munglori area of Tehri Garhwal: each village has a recognized "turf" and encroachment by other villages, for fodder-collection is likely to provoke objections (Moench, 1988). In the Philippines, competing claims to water rights among different *zanjaras*, or communal irrigation societies, have customarily been decided by inter-village councils composed of *zanjara* officers and family elders in the community (Cruz, 1989).

Systems of common rights, in fact, far from evolving in isolation, often owe their very existence to interaction and struggle between communities and the outside world. It is arguably only in reaction to invasion, dispossession or other threats to accustomed security of access that the concept of common rights emerges. Today, such rights are evolving where access to seeds, air and other resources previously taken for granted are being challenged through commoditization, legal enclosure or pollution.

Existing commons regimes, too, vary continuously with changes in their natural or social environment. Property-rights systems can shift back and forth in long, short or even seasonal cycles from communal to private and back again, depending on struggles among prospective beneficiaries, ecological change and shifts in social relationships.

For example, common-field systems are instituted in some new or revived villages in Ethiopia to attract labour and people; where this succeeds the tenure system may be switched to one based on inheritance. Later on, villages may revive communal tenure (Bauer, 1987).

Defining Oneself

Each commons regime may be as different culturally from the next as all are from, say, a factory. But it is not only their cultural diversity that makes such regimes difficult to "capture" in technical or universal terms. Ivan Illich makes this point when he says that the "law establishing the commons was unwritten, not only because people did not care to write it down, but because what it protected was a reality much too complex to fit into paragraphs" (Illich, 1983). This is somewhat inexact; commons rules are sometimes written down; and where they are not, this is not so much because what they protect is complex as because the commons requires an open-endedness, receptiveness and adaptability to the vagaries of local climate, personalities, consciousness, crafts and materials which written records cannot fully express. But Illich's point is important. What makes the commons work, like the skills of wheelwrights, surgeons or machinists, cannot easily be encoded in written or other fixed or "replicable" forms useful to cultural outsiders. These forms can make some of the workings of commons regimes "visible" to moderns but have generally functioned to transfer local power outside the community.

In this and other respects, the concept of the commons flies in the face of the modern wisdom that each spot on the globe consists merely of coordinates on a global grid laid out by state and market: a uniform field which determines everyone's and everything's rights and roles "commons" implies the right of local people to define their own grid, their own forms of community respect for watercourses, meadows or paths; to resolve conflicts their own way; to translate what enters their ken into the personal terms of their own dialect; to be "biased" against the "rights" of outsiders to local "resources" in ways usually unrecognized in modern laws; to treat their home not simply as a location housing transferrable goods and chunks of population but as irreplaceable and even to be defended at all costs.

No Free-for-All

For many years, governments, international planning agencies (and many conservationists) have viewed commons regimes with deep hostility. Nothing enrages the World Bank more, for example, than the "Not-In-My-Back-Yard" or "NIMBY" mentality, which so many communities display in defending their commons against dams, toxic waste dumps, polluting factors and the like (World Bank, 1992, p15). Many UNCED delegates and conservationists, similarly, view local control over land, forests, streams and rivers as a recipe for environmental destruction. The only way to secure the environment, they say, is to put a fence around it, police it and give it economic value through development.

In defence of such views, development agencies have played upon two related confusions. The first, promulgated most famously in the 1960s by Garrett Hardin and others, is the myth of the "tragedy of the commons". According to Hardin, any commons (the example he used was a hypothetical rangeland) "remorselessly generates tragedy" since the individual gain to each user from overusing the commons will always outweigh the individual losses he or she has to bear due to its resulting degradation (Hardin, 1968). As many critics have pointed out, however, and as Hardin himself later acknowledged, what he is describing is not a commons regime, in which authority over the use of forests, water and land rests with a community, but rather an *open access* regime, in which authority rests nowhere; in which there is no property at all; in which production for an external market takes social precedence over subsistence; in which production is not limited by concentrations of long-term local abundance; in which people "do not seem to talk to one another" (McEvoy, 1990), and in which profit for harvesters is the only operating social value.

Tending the Commons

The difference is critical. Far from being a "free-for-all", use of the commons is closely regulated through communal rules and practices. In Canada, for example, the peoples of the Wabigoon Lake Ojibway Nation of Ontario still harvest wild rice as a commons, despite efforts by the state government to impose modern management methods. The rice grows in Rice Lake and until the 1950s was harvested entirely by hand from canoes, but recently machine harvesting has also been introduced. Both machine harvests and canoe harvests are regulated through community meetings in which harvesting rights are allocated. Depending on the will of the meeting, certain areas (generally those which have been recently seeded or which are more remote) may be set aside for machine harvesters, or else machines are allowed to enter into certain areas for a limited period "only after the customary canoe harvesters have been allowed to exercise their rights to the extent decided upon at the community meeting" (Chapeskie, 1988, p18). Violations of harvest allocations by machine harvesters are dealt with at community meetings: a recent case resulted in one machine harvester being denied harvest rights for the rest of one season. For each canoe harvest area, the community agrees upon a "field boss" whose responsibilities are to regulate the harvest cycle according to custom, and to arbitrate in any disputes. Where harvesting rules are breached, the offender may be "grounded", one person in a recent harvest being told to "relearn the Indian way to sitting on the shore and watching" (Chapeskie, 1988, p18).

Amongst the Barabaig, a semi-nomadic pastoralist group in Tanzania, rights of use and access to land are variously invested in the community, the clan and individual households. As Charles Lane (1990, p7) explains:

> *The Barabaig recognize that, to make efficient use of resources, access to grazing needs to be controlled to prevent exploitation beyond the capacity to recover. Although surface water is universally accessible to everyone, its use is controlled by rules . . . water sources must not be diverted or contaminated. . . . A well becomes the property of the clan of the man who digs it. Although anyone may draw water for domestic purposes from any well, only clan members may water their stock there.*

Whether land is privately or collectively owned, there are rules ensuring that the use made of it is not detrimental to the community as a whole, while certain species of tree are regarded as sacred for the same reason. Disputes, which are rare, are resolved by a public assembly of all adult males, though sometimes in the case of a particularly difficult issue a special committee is formed. There is a parallel council of women, who also have property rights over land and animals, and occasionally may be the head of a family. Women have jurisdiction in matters concerning offences by men against women and in matters concerning spiritual life. Lane describes how recently a women's council upbraided the men for ploughing sacred land. At a regional level, a similar council oversees the movement of herds and people to ensure that there is no overgrazing.

A third example comes from Torbel in Switzerland, a village of some 600 people, where grazing lands, forests, "waste" lands, irrigation systems and paths and roads connecting privately and communally-owned property are all managed as commons. Rights to these commons are not open to all but are conferred by existing commoners who have the power to decide whether or not an outsider should be admitted as "citizens" in the community. Under a regulation that dates back to 1517, which applies to many other Swiss mountain villages, no one can send more cows to the communal grazing area than they can feed during the winter, a rule that is still enforced with a system of fines. As Elinor Ostrom (1991) reports: "This and other forms of 'cow rights' are relatively easy to monitor and enforce. The cows are all sent to the mountain to be cared for by the herdsmen. They must be counted immediately, as the number of cows each family sends is the basis for determining the amount of cheese the family will receive at the annual distribution". Once again, the commons are administered by a council, in this case consisting of all local cattle-owners. Besides grazing rights, it assigns timber for construction and fuel, arranges the distribution of manure, and is responsible for the upkeep of fences, huts and so on.

The Tragedy of Enclosure

A second confusion that muddies the debate over the commons is between environmental degradation that can be attributed to the commons regimes themselves and that which typically results from their breakdown at the hands of more global regimes. As many authors have pointed out, "tragedies of the commons" generally turn out on closer examination to be "tragedies of enclosure" (Bromley, 1991). Once they have taken over land, enclosers, unlike families with ties and commitments to the soil, can mine, log, degrade and abandon their holdings, and then sell them on the global market without suffering any personal losses. It is generally enclosers rather than commoners who benefit from bringing ruin to the commons.

In the mid-north region of Brazil, for example, poverty has sometimes been blamed on dependence on the babacu palm in secondary forests, but can be more accurately attributed to the placement of the babacu commons by commercial forces. The palm has long been revered by local forest dwellers as a "tree of life" and was used to furnish leaves for shelter, husks for fuel and fodder for animals. Following a period of open access when the region was first colonized, common property rights to the palms were established informally, and many peasants depend partly on sales of babacu products harvested from trees growing on agricultural land. When large-scale investors moved into the area to produce sugar, alcohol and cellulose, much land previously covered with babacu stands was cleared. Ranchers have also cleared large areas for pasture. Peasants who gather babacu fruits from this pastureland are castigated as trespassers and blamed for "starting wild fires, cutting fences and leaving behind fragments of fruit husks that can cause injury to the hooves of cattle", justifying further cuttings which lead to deeper impoverishment.

Commons Regimes and Their Natural Surroundings

None of this is to suggest that all commons regimes are always capable of preventing degradation of forests, fisheries or land indefinitely. But as Martin Khor of Third World Network puts it, "local control, while not necessarily sufficient for environmental protection, is necessary, while under state control the environment necessarily suffers" (Khor, 1992).

One reason why local control is essential is that, as Richard O'Connor has argued, "the environment itself is local; nature diversifies to make niches, enmeshing each locale in its own intricate web. Insofar as this holds, enduring human adaptations must also ultimately be quite local (O'Connor, 1989). Biological diversity, for example, is related to the degree to which one locale is distinct from the next in its topography and natural and human history. It is best preserved by societies that nourish those local differences — in which the traditions and natural history of each area interact to create distinctive systems of cultivation and water and forest use.

This local orientation is displayed *par excellence* in small commons regimes. As Elinor Ostrom (1985) notes:

> *Small-scale communities are more likely to have the formal conditions required for successful and enduring collective management of the commons. Among these are the visibility of common resources and behaviour toward them; feedback on the effects of regulations; widespread understanding and acceptance of the rules and their rationales; the values expressed in these rules (that is, equitable treatment of all and protection of the environment); and the backing of values by socialization, standards, and strict enforcement.*

A second reason why local control is important is that where people rely directly on their natural surroundings for their livelihood, they develop an intimate knowledge of those surrounds which informs their actions. The Barabaig, for example, fully understand that if cattle were to be kept permanently on pastures near local water sources, the land would quickly become degraded.

> *As herds of livestock are brought to the river margins every day, whatever the season, they know that the forage there is needed by those who are watering their stock. If others are allowed to permanently graze it, this forage would soon be depleted and not available to those who go there to draw water. This would ultimately result in destruction of the land through over-grazing and damage from concentration of hoof traffic. The Barabaig, therefore, have a customary rule that bans settlement at the river margins and denies herders the right to graze the forage if they are not there to water their stock.*

> (Lane, 1990, p7)

Similarly, the many diverse systems of agriculture evolved by peasant farmers around the world have not evolved randomly but reflect a "thorough understanding of the elements and interactions between vegetations and soils, animals and climate" (Altieri, 1991, p93). They are both dynamic and innovative, evolving out of a continuing dialogue with the land. Because each technique used is evaluated above all for its long-term local impact, the lore which governs commons regimes, unlike modern science, tends not to split itself into rigid disciplines which pretend to have application in all circumstances. Instead, it tends to focus on a "set of constraints which [help] conserve the social and physical environment for generations" (McCorkle et al, 1988). Indeed, the notion that present generations are merely stewards who hold the land of the ancestors in trust for future generations is one held by many local communities, particularly in the South.

That notion is not simply an ideal but, where commons regimes still hold sway, informs and influences day-to-day behaviour. Some commons, for example, are totally protected against even substance harvesting: for example, the *iiri* groves of the Mbeere of East Africa, where even fallen timber could not be gathered. In Nigeria around Yoruba villages, and around Akha villages in Yunnan, Burma and Thailand, traditional rings of thick forest used for defence, where cultivation was not permitted, were also sites of shrines to village deities. In the Himalayas, too, it is through a mix of religion, folklore and tradition that peasants draw a "protective ring around the forests" (Guha, 1993), and in British Columbia, conscious management and ceremonial life alike "dictated a period of abstention from fishing so that adequate escapement of salmon to their spawning grounds up the rivers and to other upriver groups was ensured" (Pinkerton, 1987, p347).

Checks and Balances

The remarkable success of local commons in safeguarding their environments is well documented in a detailed study of Japanese common land (*iriaichi*) by M A McKean, who, for example, was unable to find a single example of a "commons that suffered ecological destruction while it was still a commons" (McKean, 1987). In Pakistan, even the official National Report to UNCED 1992 ranks traditionally managed *shamilaat* communal forests as more effective in environmental protection than forests owned and managed by the state.

But that success depends on more than local knowledge of the environment, respect for nature or indigenous technologies. The extent to which sanctions against environmental degradation are observed depends greatly on the extent to which members of a community rely on their natural surroundings for their long-term livelihood and thus have a direct interest in protecting it. Once that direct interest is removed — once members of the community look outside the commons for their sustenance and social standing — the cultural checks and balances that limit potential abuses of the environment are rendered increasingly ineffective. The authority of commons regimes declines.

In that respect, the key to the success of commons regimes lies in the limits that its culture of shared responsibilities place upon the power of any one group or individual. The equality that generally prevails in the commons, for example, does not grow out of any ideal or romantic preconceived notion of *communities* any more than out of allegiance to the modern notion that people have "equal rights". Rather, it emerges as a by-product of the inability of a small community's elite to eliminate entirely the bargaining power of any one of its members, the limited amount of goods any one group can make away with under the others' gaze, and the calculated jockeying for position of many individuals who know each other and share an interest both in minimizing their own risks and in not letting any one of their number become too powerful in contemporary Laos. For example:

> *Relations among the villagers may seem strikingly egalitarian, but this is not due to explicit ideology. . . . For the Lao, no one's survival should be put at risk by someone else in the community: instability could endanger the survival of the entire village. In a natural economy barely providing sustenance, everyone knows this primary rule, so no one pushes. Older families can sometimes gain influence in a village, but only if the villagers see it as enhancing their chance of survival. Clientage of this sort does not last for long since the environment is not stable. Influence eventually disappears as a family's branches fade, move elsewhere, or experience bad weather. . . . No one is in charge — although sometimes there is a village elder who helps make decisions, and who must work just as hard as everyone else. . . . Everyone works hard, eats adequately, and gets along well together.*
>
> (Anon, 1991, p8)

Where everyone has some degree of bargaining power, no one is likely to starve while others are comfortable. As in Indonesian or medieval European village society, any hardship must be shared. (This helps explain why exclusion from the group is still regarded as tantamount to a death sentence in many societies in which the commons plays a central role.) In many such societies, commoditization of food is often perceived as a threat, since it takes power over subsistence out of the hands of the less well-off.

Changes in the power base of a local elite or increases in effective community size entailed by integration into a global social fabric can rapidly undermine the authority of the commons. The sense of shame or transgression so important to community controls, as well as the monitoring of violations themselves, is diluted or denatured by increase in numbers, while envy of outsiders unconstrained by those controls flourishes. At some point "the breakdown of a community with the associated collapse in concepts of joint ownership and responsibility can set the path for the degradation of common resources in spite of abundance" (Berkes and Feeny, 1990, p50).

It is precisely this process that development fuels. The expansion of the modern state's international and market institutions entails a shrinking space for the commons. Today, virtually all "human communities are encapsulated within or fully integrated into larger sociopolitical systems" as are their "local systems of resource use and property rights" (McCay and Acheson, 1987), making enclosure an ever-present threat. As political, social and ecological boundaries are erased, control is centralized or privatized, skills are made obsolete, people put at the service of industry or made redundant, and land is commercialized or placed under management. As their environments are destroyed or degraded, their power eroded or denied, and their communities threatened, millions are now demanding a halt to the development process. As the social activist Gustavo Esteva writes, "if you live in Rio or Mexico City, you need to be very rich or very stupid not to notice that development stinks. . . . We need to say 'no' to development, to all and every form of development. And that is precisely what the social majorities — for whom development was always a threat — are asking for" (Esteva, 1992). For them, the struggle is to reclaim, defend or create their commons and with it the rough sense of equity that flows from sharing a truly common future.

References

Acheson, J M (1987) "The Lobster Fiefs Revisited: Economic and Ecological Effects of Territoriality in Maine Lobster Fishing", in B McCay and J Acheson (eds), *The Question of the Commons: The Culture and Ecology of Communal Resources*, University of Arizona, Tucson, pp37–65

Altieri, M A (1991) "Traditional Farming in Latin America", *The Ecologist*, vol 21, no 2, March/April

Anon (1991) "The Lao Alternative", *Rain*, vol 14, no 1

Bauer, D (1987) "The Dynamics of Communal and Hereditary Land Tenure Among the Tigray of Ethiopia", in B McCay and B J Acheson, *The Question of the Commons: The Culture and Ecology of Communal Resources*, University of Arizona, Tucson, pp217–232

Berkes, F and D Feeny (1990) "Paradigms Lost: Changing Views on the Use of Common Property Resources", *Alternatives*, vol 17, no 2

Bromley, D W (1991) *Environment and Economy: Property Rights and Public Policy*, Blackwell, Oxford

Chapeskie, A J (1988) *Indigenous Law, State Law and the Management of Natural Resources: Wild Rice and the Wabigoon Lake Ojibway Nation*, July

Cruz, M C J (1989) "Water as Common Property: The Case of Irrigation Water Rights in the Philippines" in F Berks (ed), *Common Property Resources: Ecology and Community-Based Sustainable Development*, Belhaven Press, London, pp218–235

Esteva, G (1992) "The Right to Stop Development", *NGONET UNCED Feature*, 13 June, Rio de Janeiro

Fortmann, L and J W Bruce (1988) *Whose Trees? Proprietary Dimensions of Forestry*, Westview, Boulder

Guha, R (1993) "The Malign Encounter: The Chipko Movement and Competing visions of Nature", in T Banuri and F Apffel-Marglin (eds), *Who Will Save the Forests?*, Zed Books, London and New Jersey

Hardin, G (1968) "The Tragedy of the Commons", *Science*, no 162, 13 December, pp1243–8

Illich, I (1982) *Gender*, Pantheon, New York

—— (1983) "Silence is a Commons", *Co-evolution Quarterly*, Winter, pp5–9

Khor, M (1992) Presentation at World Rainforest Movement meeting on land insecurity and tropical deforestation, 1 March, New York

Lane, C (1990) *Barabaig Natural Resource Management: Sustainable Land use under Threat of Destruction*, Discussion Paper 12, UN Research Institute for Social Development, Geneva

McCay, B and J Acheson (1987) *The Question of the Commons*, University of Arizona, Tucson

McCorkle, C M et al (1988) *A Case Study on Farmer Innovations and Communication in Niger*, Academy for Education Development, Washington, DC

McEvoy, A (1990) "Toward an Interactive Theory of Nature and Culture", in D Worster (ed) *The Ends of the Earth: Perspectives on Modern Environmental History*, Cambridge University Press, Cambridge

McKean, M A (1987) *Management of Traditional Communal Lands (Iriachi) in Japan*, Duke University Press

Moench, M (1988) "Turf and Forest Management in Garhwal Hill Village, in L Fortmann and J Bruce, *Whose Trees? Proprietary Dimensions of Forestry*, Westview, Boulder, pp127–36

Norgaard, R (1988) "The Rise of the Global Exchange Economy and the Loss of Biological Diversity", in O Wilson (ed), *Biodiversity*, National Academy Press, Washington, DC

O'Connor, R (1989) "From Fertility to Order", *Siam Society, Culture and Environment in Thailand*, Siam Society, Bangkok, pp393–414

Ostrom, E (1985) "The Rudiments of a Revised Theory of the Origins, Survival and Performance of Institutions for Collective Action", Working Paper 32, *Workshops in Political Theory and Policy Analysis*, Indiana University, Bloomington

—— (1991) *Governing the Commons: The Evolution of Institutions for Collective Action*, Cambridge University Press, Cambridge

Pinkerton, E (1987) "Intercepting the State: Dramatic Processes in the Assertion of Local Co-management Rights", in B J McCay and J M Acheson, *The Question of the Commons*, University of Arizona, Tucson

WCED (1987) *Our Common Future*, Oxford University Press, Oxford

World Bank (1992) *World Development Report 1992: Development and the Environment*, Oxford University Press, New York

■ Defending the Global Commons
Christopher D Stone

Across the world, the environment is in peril. Forests are being stripped, stressed and burned. Natural habitats are vanishing. Deserts are advancing. Croplands suffer from waterlogging in some regions, overgrazing and salinization in others. The atmosphere and ozone shield are under assault. The oceans are being loaded with pollutants and swept of marine life. We are sullying the polar regions, perturbing the climate and eradicating species.

All these alarms, and more, have been widely sounded. There is no reason to belabour them: what we need are answers. I have two to put forward: a system of global guardianships, and a global commons trust fund. They alone will not solve our complex environmental predicaments (Stone, 1993), but together they would constitute a major stride forward, a foundation for an appreciable "greening" of international law.

To understand these proposals, a good start is to mark the distinction in outlook between the scientist, on the one hand, and the international lawyer and statesperson, on the other. Scientists — such as geophysicists, geochemists and the like — "have the luxury of contemplating the planet from the grand panorama of astronauts". From such a removed state, national boundaries fade and the mind can be struck by the marvellous wholeness of the Earth and the interconnection of globe-spanning phenomena that sustain its tenants: one great swirling envelope of atmospheric gases, the great body of ocean, and the broad globe-spanning belts of weather and vegetation.

International lawyers and statespersons operate from a more cramped and mundane vista. Ours is an inherited world in which all that grand unity has been disrupted into political territories. We all know that most of these pencilled borders have little to do with the great natural processes that the scientist is drawn to; that they are often the legacies of chance, intrigue, vanity, avarice, and military battles that could have gone either way. But for all their caprice and impermanence, the boundaries that mark the diplomats' world, hardened as they commonly are, by pronounced cultural, religious and socioeconomic differences, are no less to be reckoned with than carbon.

Broadly speaking, the diplomats' maps (the foundation for received international law) divide the world into two sorts of regions: those which fall under territorial sovereignty, and those that lie outside the political reach of any nation state — the global commons.

In this view of things, the territorial sovereignty that each nation enjoys is co-extensive with its geographic boundaries, extends upwards through its air traffic space, and, in the case of the many nations with coastal borders, extends across an exclusive economic zone (EEZ) running 200 nautical miles seaward (UN, 1982; Greenville and Wasserstein, 1987, p498).

The global commons refers to those portions of the planet and its surrounding space that lie above and beyond the recognized territorial claims of any nation. That includes the atmosphere, outer space and the high seas, together with the potentially valuable seabeds and subsurfaces that have yet to be "enclosed" by any coastal state as part of its territorial extension. On some accounts, much the same commons status does, or should, apply to the resource-rich Antarctic, which comprises 10 per cent of the planet's land mass, and whose ownership is currently in limbo (Kimball, 1993).

Viewed within the constraints of traditional international law, this twofold division into national territories and commons area has crucial significance for all efforts to defend the environment. Within its sovereign territory, a nation can, by and large, do whatever it wants. Each nation, and it exclusively, has the right to pull up its forests, bulldoze habitats, wipe out species, fish, farm, and mine — and not have to answer to any "outside" authority for any repercussions on its own environment (UN, 1972).

If the "outside" world wishes to influence a country's internal behaviour to constrain deforestation, for example — its recourse is limited. International organizations can try to persuade a developing country's leaders of the long-term benefits of a scale and pace of development that is environmentally kind. Funding sources, pre-eminently the World Bank, can withhold support from massive projects that are environmentally disruptive (Plater, 1989, p204; Wirth, 1990; Rich, 1990, p322; Scott, 1992; Guyett, 1992). Wildlife groups have been known simply to pay a country to set aside an exotic habitat as a wildlife reserve, often arranging so-called "debt-for-nature swaps" (Post, n d). However, as long as a nation is chewing up only its own insides, it is not, in the eyes of international law, doing anything for which it can be sued. It is true there are declarations that all the environment, including internal environments, are to be valued (UN, 1990); but they are consistently undermined by conflicting declarations that a nation's use of its own resources is a matter of sovereign prerogative (Kuala Lumpur, 1992). The counterbalance could be resolved in a "seen" direction: that is, conceivably, grave damage to internal environments could someday come to be considered as sort of "ecocide", and, likened to human rights violations, made a violation of international law. Unfortunately, such a development does not appear imminent. In the meantime, "outside" influence is constrained to such tactics as bargaining, loan conditions, and perhaps trade pressures. As we know all too well, desertification and deforestation continue, and thus far neither these tactics nor any others have been able to arrest the degradation of internal environments.

As frustrating as one finds it to have an effect on "internal" scenarios, the situation in the commons areas is, in many regards, even worse. All the nations of the world are faced with deterioration of their internal environments, with the result that resources required for cleaning up the commons have to compete with resources required to clean up internal environments. This is a competition in which the domestic demands have a clear advantage. When a country's interior deteriorates — as urban areas become smoggy, or fish die in lakes — there is at least a political constituency of directly aggrieved voters to focus pressure on whichever government — state, federal or local — to provide relief. In contrast, when we turn to the commons, the areas lack, by definition, their own "citizens" to complain, and those who do in fact have complaints cannot locate a competent authority to which to complain.

However, the plight of the commons reflects more than a jurisdictional vacuum. Important economic and bargaining considerations reinforce the inclination to give the commons short shrift. When a nation turns its attentions inward, it can select the most pressing problem on its own political agenda, be it water quality or soil treatment. Since a nation has full control over its domestic programmes, it can arrange to fund only those projects for which it receives at least a dollar benefit for each dollar it spends. However, suppose we were to ask the same nation to invest a million dollars in mending the commons — to restrict carbon emissions, for example, and thereby reduce the risks of climate change. In expenditures to clean up the commons, the nation stands to capture some fraction of benefits (the reduced risks of climate change). But most of the benefit will be diffused among all 180 or so members of the world community, some of whom will fail to shoulder their proportionate share of the burden.

One can put the point in familiar public finance terms: the maintenance of the commons is a public good, and efforts to provide for the public good are notoriously dogged by the manoeuvres of those who wish to "free ride" on those who contribute. Of course, domestic governments face the same problem when they undertake any public finance project: parks, police and so on. The problem is that combatting strategic behaviour and securing cooperation in the international arena are considerably more difficult than overcoming the analogous obstacles in domestic contexts. In domestic democratic societies subject to majority rule, dissenters — potential free riders — can be simply forced to pay their share by law. In the international community, however, a corollary of sovereignty is that no nation can be forced into any agreement to which it does not assent: in essence, unanimity, not majority, is the collective choice rule. As a consequence, every country is wary of getting drawn into a fragile multilateral agreement in which it may find itself under pressure to pay out a larger share of the costs than its benefits warrant. (This is one reason for the USA's reluctance to put teeth into a climate change convention.) Each nation may incline to mend its own local disorders even when it would make more sense overall (if cooperation could be ensured) for all the nations of the world to turn their joint attention to more ominous problems they face in common.

This "no man's land" feature of the commons has important implications for the design of institutional remedies. The fact that the degraded area lies outside anyone's exclusive jurisdiction presents impediments to monitoring deterioration, and presents even more serious obstacles to securing legal and diplomatic relief.

Invasion of Territories

Speaking realistically, international law does not enter the picture until something a nation does — releasing a radioactive cloud, for example — sweeps across its boundaries and damages a neighbouring country. In those circumstances it is generally agreed, at least it is universally verbalized, that the injured neighbour has grounds for diplomatic and legal remedies. In the 1940s the USA successfully sued Canada over sulphur fumes from a Canadian lead smelter that were wafting across the boundary into the state of Washington (RIAA, 1941). The USA once even acquiesced to a Mexican diplomatic demand that it eliminate offensive transboundary odours that were blowing south from a US stockyard (Springer, 1983, pp150–2). Such results in transboundary contexts are rare; but relief is at least a theoretical option that potential polluters have to consider in the design of factories.

When fumes blow across a frontier, not into a neighbouring nation but up into the commons region of higher atmosphere or out across the sea, however many soft declarations may denounce it (UN, 1972) resort to law becomes appreciably more problematic. In a typical nation-to-nation transboundary conflict, such as the US–Canada case referred to, one can assume there are officials of the injured state on hand at the site of the harm to inspect the damage and determine from where it is coming. In that dispute the fumes could be characterized as an "invasion" (however modest) of US sovereignty, the sort of thing international law has customarily sought to mend.

By contrast, when the open sea or the atmosphere is degraded, who is on hand to keep watch? Are significant loadings of heavy metals working their way into the deep seas and seabed? If so, are the levels dangerous and are they insinuating their way into the food cycle? Who is responsible for cleaning them up? To answer these questions, even to gather the relevant facts in a scientifically and internationally credible way, goes beyond any single nation's ordinary motivation and competence; it practically necessitates a multinational coordinated effort.

Even then, if the appropriate institution could be established, and the monitors could identify substantial and worrisome changes in the environment and pin down their source, there would remain judicial obstacles of legal interest and standing. If someone should come into your yard and steal your pet turtle from your pond, you would have a suit because it would be a trespass and injury to your property. But if some nation's fleet of fishing vessels, sweeping the high seas with nets, obliterates scores of rare sea turtles or dolphins, customary international law — that is, international law as it stands absent of some specially-tailored treaty — it is unlikely to grant a remedy to any nation that objects (UN, n d). Who can prove that the destroyed creatures would have been captured by the objecting nation? On the high seas, because the turtles do not belong to anyone, it is unclear that anyone has the legal interest which the law requires to complain. Besides, what is the market value (the law would want to know) of turtles and dolphins? Where was the legal damage?

Who is Responsible?

One should understand that the liberty of each state to impair the commons is not a principle that is condoned. There are, in fact, any number of lofty declarations of international conferences and commentators that solemnly (although usually with saving double-speak qualifications) renounce abuse of the commons areas. There are even scraps of legal doctrine from which a suit to protect the commons areas might be constructed. Some government could argue that a country responsible for a massive injury to the commons had committed a wrong *erga omnes* (crime against the community of nations), a notion historically invoked to legitimate the power of any nation to punish piracies on the high seas. But the fact is, aside perhaps from the special case where the complaining nation was able to show that the offender violated an express agreement (such as a treaty), no claim arising out of commons despoliation has yet to be pressed, and the prospects of such a suit would have to be regarded at present as rather doubtful (PCIJ, 1927).

Thus, whatever lip service environmental diplomats will pay the commons areas at great Earth summits, nations still find it expedient to let vast proportions of their pollutants simply blow away into the global atmosphere or run off untreated into the open sea. Each year, humankind pumps into the atmosphere over eight billion tons of carbon, together with hundreds of millions of tons of nitrogen oxides, sulphur dioxide, particulate, and other such airborne junk. Into the oceans, their marine life already pillaged by modern fishing technology, go hundreds of millions of tons of sewage, dredge spoils, agricultural run-off and industrial wastes. To this we add millions of tons of marine litter — no longer your ordinary biodegradable garbage, either. Each year, tens of thousands of marine mammals, turtles, and seabirds die from entanglement with or ingestion of plastics and abandoned fishing gear ("ghost nets"), some of which will not disintegrate for centuries.

Some of the stuff that has been dumped is even worse. Sitting on the seabed right now are hundreds of thousands of tons of Second World War munitions, including unfired chemical weapons (Simon, 1992), to which we have more recently added untold canisters of nuclear waste that were deposited in the sea for "safe storage", which are already showing signs of fatigue (Anon, 1990; Holliday, n d, pp56–9). An ex-Soviet official recently admitted that for nearly 30 years the Soviet military had been jettisoning its nuclear wastes (including thousands of canisters, 12 old reactors and one damaged submarine) into the Arctic Sea in the most heedless way imaginable (Tyler, 1992). The important thing now is, no one is responsible for cleaning up the whole mess.

This does not mean that the commons are utterly undefended. While no nation can be compelled to protect the commons, various protective conventions and declarations have garnered the cooperation of enough countries to monitor the rate of deterioration. The 1985 Vienna Convention on Substances that Deplete the Ozone Layer is achieving a dramatic reduction in the release of ozone-depleting agents. The 1991 UN General Assembly Resolution against Driftnetting is, technically, no more than that, a legally nonbinding "resolution". Yet, the announced willingness of the major driftnetting nations, Japan, Taiwan and Korea, to respect it is a promising development of some significance. Also there is a whole patchwork of other conventions in other areas, each with its own aspirations and attainments. These include the ban on weapons testing in space, the International Whaling Commission (IWC), the Antarctic treaty system, and the London Convention on the Prevention of Marine Pollution by Dumping of Wastes. The present picture can best be summarized as this: if one looks behind the various lofty declarations and examines the prevailing practices — the law in action — one finds that, aside from a few areas provided for by special treaty, much of the commons is only partially and feebly protected. In essence, since the commons are available for purposes of wealth exploitation — anyone can sweep it for fish or scoop up deep seabed minerals without answering to the world community — questions about the pollution of the commons are going unanswered. What is to be done?

A Voice for the Environment: Global Commons Guardian
One approach is to negotiate more and stronger multinational treaties specially tailored

to protect designated portions of the commons, along the lines of the ozone agreements, and the more recent, still nebulous, framework conventions on climate change that emerged from the Earth Summit at Rio. Those efforts deserve further support.

Yet, there is another approach, in some ways bolder, and in some ways integral and supplementary to the treaty efforts. As we saw, one of the reasons for over-exploitation of the commons is the lack of a plaintive clearly qualified to demonstrate both standing and injury. Hence, the first proposal; to establish a system of guardians who would be legal representatives for the natural environment. The idea is similar to the concept of legal guardians (sometimes "conservators") in familiar legal systems. Presented with possible invasions of the interests of certain persons who are unable to speak for themselves as such, unrepresented infants, the insane and the senile, courts are empowered to appoint a legal guardian to speak for them. So too, guardians can be designated to be the legal voice for the otherwise voiceless environment: the whales, the dolphins, important habitats, and so on.

The guardians could either be drawn from existing international agencies that have the appropriate focus, such as the United Nations Environment Programme (UNEP) and the World Meteorological Organization (WMO), or from the many non-governmental organizations (NGOs), such as Greenpeace or the World Wide Fund for Nature (WWF). Certainly the guardians would not be given plenary and unreviewable powers to halt any activity of which they disapproved. Rather, the guardian would be built into the institutional process to ensure that environmental values were being identified and accounted for. Take the oceans, for example. To ensure that oceanic ecosystems were being adequately accounted for, an ocean guardian might be designated to, perhaps, the Joint Group of Experts on the Scientific Aspects of Marine Pollution (GESAMP), with supplementary legal staffing.

As guardian, its first chore would be to monitor. It would review ocean conditions not just to gather facts "scientifically", but with a specific eye towards assuring compliance with conventions already in place. One weakness of the 1972 London Dumping Convention (LDC) and many fishing agreements is that compliance depends almost entirely on "self-monitoring", without any independent effort to survey the activities of signatories. The guardian could provide that monitoring. By doing so, it would improve the willingness of every state to comply, since each country will no longer feel hesitant that if it observed the rules, it would be the only nice, law-abiding "sucker". Everyone would benefit from the mutual assurances.

Second, the guardian would exercise legislative functions, not as a legislative body, but as part of the complex web of global policy-making institutions. In exercising the monitoring function it would undoubtedly come across problems uncovered by existing agreements, which would prompt it to recommend and stimulate formation of new multinational agreements. The guardian could appear before international agencies and even the domestic legislatures and administrative agencies of nations considering ocean-impacting actions to counsel moderation and to suggest alternatives on behalf of its "client".

Third, it could be authorized to appear as a special intervenor — counsel for the unrepresented environmental "victim" in a variety of bilateral and multilateral disputes. For example, whenever there is a proposal to dam an international river, one or more of the nations along the river may initiate international negotiations to assure the fair division of the water flow, electric and irrigation benefits. However, we have learned, often too late and to our chagrin, that such dam projects inevitably affect the environment, including life in the oceans to which they feed. The ocean guardian would appear as a "third party" before the appropriate body to assure, not necessarily that the viability of the ocean environment was the conclusive issue, but at least that it was raised in the most effective manner possible. *

The final function simply takes the intervenor concept one step further. International treaties should endow the guardian with standing to initiate legal and diplomatic action on the ocean ecosystem's behalf in appropriate situations; to sue at least in those cases where, if the ocean were a sovereign state, the law would afford it some prospect of relief. The law could be arranged so that even if a violating nation refused to appear, the guardian could secure a declaratory judgment that the conduct in question was indeed unlawful. Such a judicial pronouncement is far less steely than an injunction, but is not the sort of thing members of the world community would simply brush off either.

The notion of legal standing for nature is hardly far-fetched. Indeed, many guardianship functions are currently recognized in US environmental laws on a more modest scale. For example, under Superfund Legislation, the National Oceanic and Atmospheric Administration (NOAA) is designated trustee for fish, marine mammals, and their supporting ecosystems within the US fisheries zone. NOAA has authority to institute suits to recover restoration costs against any party that injures its "ward" (CRF, 1990). A major law suit is presently proceeding in a federal court in southern California, in which NOAA attorneys are suing local chemical companies allegedly responsible for seepage of PCBs and other chemicals into the coastal water ecosystem (UN, 1990). There is no reason why such a system could not be replicated internationally.

References

Anon (1990) "Atomic Waste Reported Leaking in Ocean Sanctuary off California", *New York Times*, 7 May
CFR 40 (1990) SS 300.600, 300.615(a)(1)
Greenville, J and B Wasserstein (1987) *The Major International Treaties Since 1945*, Methuen, New York
Guyett, S C (1992) "Environment and Lending", 24 *International Law and Politics*, pp889–919
Holliday, F G T (n d) "The Dumping of Radioactive Waste in the Deep Ocean", in D Cooper and J Palmer (eds), *The Environment in Question*, Routledge, New York, pp51–64
Kimball, L (1993) "Environmental Law and Policy in Antarctica", in P Sands (ed) *Greening of International Law*, Earthscan, London
Kuala Lumpur (1992) "Declaration on Environment and Development", article 4, no 22, *Environmental Policy and Law*, pp266–7
PCIJ (1927) *SS Lotus (France v Turkey)*, PCIJ, Ser A no 10
Plater, Z (1989) "Multilateral Development Banks, Environmental Diseconomies and International Reform Pressure on the Lending Process", *Boston College Third World Law Journal*, no 9, pp169–215
Post, M (n d) "The Debt for Nature Sway: A Longterm Investment for the Economic Stability of Less Developed Countries", *International Lawyer*, no 24, pp1071–98
RIAA (1941) *Trail Smelter (US v Canada)*, RIAA
Rich, B (1990) "The Emperor's New Clothes", *World Policy Journal*, 305–29

---

* PCIJ (1920) NGOs were invited to make submissions to early human rights cases.

Scott, D J (1992) "Making a Bank Turn", *The Environmental Forum*, pp21–5

Simon, S (1992) "Fears over Nazi Weapons Leaking at Bottom of Baltic", *Los Angeles Times*, 18 July

Springer, A (1983) *The International Law of Pollution*, Qurom Books, Westport

Stone, C D (1993) *The Gnat is Older than Man: Global Environment and Human Agenda*, Princeton University Press, Princeton

Tyler, P E (1992) "Soviets' Secret Nuclear Dumping Causes Worry for Arctic Waters", *Los Angeles Times*, 4 May

UN (n d) General Assembly Resolution on Driftnetting

—— (1972) Conference on the Human Environment, Chapter II, Principle 1, *International Legal Materials*, pp1416–69

—— (1982) "Convention on the Law of the Sea", *International Legal Materials*, pp1261–1354

—— (1990) *United Nations v Montrose Chemicals*, Dkt No CV 90–3122 AAH, DCD, Cal

Wirth, D A (1990) "Legitimacy, Accountability and Partnership", *Yale Law Journal*, vol 100, no 265/6, pp2647–8

Improving Livestock Raising
Alan Grainger

Regulating Nomads

Nomadic grazing is a sound technique for using scarce pasture resources in dryland areas, where rainfall fluctuates widely from place to place and mobile herds have freedom to search for areas where rain has fallen and grass has grown. For example, Maine-Sora in southeast Niger has an average rainfall of 43 mm per annum. In 1949, it received 230 mm of rain, but only 67 mm fell at Diffa, 50 kilometres further east. Herds would have suffered if government grazing regulations had prevented them from moving out of Diffa that year.

Mobility also means better nutrition: if herds can arrive in a place when the grass is still green, digestibility is of the order of 70 per cent compared with 43 per cent for dry grass. Without mobility, herds would gain ever poorer feed value from the pasture as its digestibility decreased throughout the season. Cattle that annually trek more than 1000 kilometres between the Malian Delta and the Mauritanian Sahel return in better physical condition than the milking cows and calves that remain in the village throughout the year.

Despite the advantages of nomadic grazing there have been continuing attempts by governments and aid agencies to regulate it, mainly by reducing herd mobility. Some attempts arise from a desire for a more "scientific" approach to livestock raising which, it is hoped, will prevent overgrazing. Others result from a determination by governments to bring these wandering peoples more under their control, whether for altruistic reasons such as providing education and health facilities or merely to tax them more easily. There have been four main types of interventions: (1) grazing controls; (2) sedentarization; (3) establishment of ranches; and (4) stratification.

Grazing Controls

Despite strenuous efforts over the last 30 years, most attempts to control grazing have failed. This is largely due to the ignorance of "experts" or the neglect of traditional grazing controls exerted by pastoralists. It may be imagined that because grazing lands are communal they are also unregulated, but this is not usually the case. Michael Horowitz, a social anthropologist at the State University of New York at Binghampton, writes: "There is an emerging awareness among scientists . . . that strict regulation of access to scarce resources (water and grass) and limits on herd size may well be the rule rather than the exception among herding societies in semi-arid lands" (Horowitz, 1979).

Why do governments wish to control what has previously been self-regulated by nomadic peoples! "With the exception of Mauritania in the Sahel and Somalia in East Africa," writes Horowitz, "the ruling elites of these states are drawn from groups which are not only not pastoral, but which have historically viewed pastoral peoples with ambivalence at best, and often outright hostility." The dominance of the farming peoples in such countries was confirmed by the colonial powers, forcing the herdsmen to retreat in the face of constantly expanding cultivation. "The final insult was the implantation of deep wells open to all comers, leading to chaotic competition for grazing land" (Horowitz 1979).

The imposition of grazing controls by governments has therefore aroused resentment and resistance. One type of control is the grazing fee, which, while not limiting the herd's freedom of movement, has the motive of forcing the herdsmen to dispose of non-productive animals.

Enthusiasm for the notion of a grazing fee should not be anticipated, however, especially from the owners of relatively large herds of cattle. Paying for a resource that has such a long and culturally embedded history of being freely available (or at least free, even if not always available) is an innovation that is likely to have its legitimacy seriously questioned. Grazing fees were an integral part of a number of grazing schemes in the colonial period, and they undoubtedly generated considerable antipathy

Another type of control is the division of a region into blocks of rangelands. These are then used successively as part of a rotational scheme in which each block is left for a fallow period during which pasture regenerates. One way to manage such a scheme would be to turn off or physically remove the pumps from water-holes in a particular block where forage is approaching exhaustion. This, as has been seen above, could provoke violent reactions on the part of the herdsmen. When tried out in Kenya among the Pokot and Samburu, the block system failed dismally. Like enforced sedentarization, it limits freedom of movement, one of the key components of the nomadic life.

Sedentarization

The sedentarization (settlement) of nomadic herdsmen is one opinion for improving livestock raising in semi-arid areas, but in practice it is difficult to consider it in isolation from the strong political pressures against nomads (described above) which in some countries have led to forcible sedentarization. This is not to say that sedentarization is always forced or even planned. Many nomads, such as some of the Fulani people in Mali, settled spontaneously in the aftermath of the 1968–73 phase of the Sahel drought. They saw it as a temporary measure until their herds built up again, but many have not returned to their former way of life.

Sedentarization has a number of disadvantages in practice. The increased concentration on livestock around a village often degrades nearby pastures. This degradation may be exacerbated by an increase in herd size as the settled nomads tend to become more dependent upon grain, require less meat and milk, and therefore kill fewer animals. Resettlement schemes in Sierra Leone, Burkina Faso and Nigeria have not been very successful because animals have suffered health problems in the new locations and conflicts have arisen between the nomads and local peasant farmers owing to planners' failure to recognize the previous range of uses of project sites. Nomads used to travelling longer distances have experienced particular difficulties in adjusting to being settled in one place, and some pastoralists resettled by the Senegal government after the 1968–73 drought began to neglect their cattle, even though tubewells were provided. with the result that the herds increased in size and became vulnerable to disease (Oxby, 1984; Santoir, 1983).

One of the few really successful examples of sedentarization is that involving the Fulani in central Nigeria who combine livestock raising with cropping. Each household crops an average of about 0.9 hectares, with sorghum and maize (either alone or together) accounting for 70 per cent of the total area. Forage crops are grown and the fields are manured by cattle, though most Fulani also use some chemical fertilizers. Crop residues are another valuable source of fodder. However, because the area being settled was previously underpopulated, and the climate is less arid than in other African countries with large nomad populations, the example might not be generally applicable (Powell and Taylor-Powell, 1984).

Nomads may suffer a drop in income when they are sedentarized, according to Mustafa Mohamed Khogali, of the Department of Geography at the University of Khartoum in Sudan, who has estimated that the average annual returns of (unsettled) nomads may exceed those of rainfed cultivators by at least 30–50 per cent. Khogali thinks that nomads should be encouraged to settle if they want to, but that planners who urge them to become cultivators without animals have failed to understand the nomad mentality, since settlement may require just too much of a break from past traditions (Khogali, 1983).

Ranching

The introduction of intensive livestock ranching to developing countries has rarely been a success. After the Second World War, "development" usually meant transferring Western technology without adaptation to developing countries, and many aid agencies essentially tried to take Texas to the Sahara. The president of Niger and other Sahelian heads of state talked of exporting beef all over the world. Reality has proved less rosy.

According to the Club du Sahel (1980): "Results on the whole have not been satisfactory: the investments called for were too heavy; the farms, placed in regions poor in resources, resulted in mediocre productivity; and finally, marketing of production was hampered because the ranchers were too far from the large commercial centres."

Under colonial rule, Europeans appropriated land and established commercial ranches, showing little regard for the welfare of the indigenous people. The ranches tended to be effective when established in areas with favourable soil and climatic conditions. After countries gained independence, their governments sometimes replicated the actions of the colonizers. In the 1960s, the World Bank promoted commercial cattle ranching in southwest Uganda with the construction of over 100 ranches, each of several thousand hectares. The political elite of Uganda took control over the lands and succeeded in establishing themselves as absentee landowners of large tracts of Uganda's grasslands.

The "group ranch", so-called because it is run as a cooperative by several families, was supposed to be more democratic and give a wider spread of benefits than a strictly commercial ranch. The government of Kenya established 14 group ranches in the late 1960s, each averaging 19 000 hectares and 100 families settling the people and registering land ownership. The Maasai agreed to participate in these ranches, less out of enthusiasm than in fear of what the government might do if they refused. As one elder said: "If there is rain in Kenya and people have ranches there, I cannot move my cattle into that place." Some of the Maasai arranged to have family members registered in different ranches so that they could still move to more favourable lands when drought threatened their own grazing lands. The experiment was not very successful. The cooperative has improved marketing and the availability of cattle dips, sprays and the like, but the ranches are still run basically on traditional subsistence lines and the lands have often been invaded by outsiders, leading to armed clashes.

In Tanzania the government has tried for many years to integrate pastoralists into its Ujaama (socialist community) villages. After various incentives and even coercion had failed, in 1973 the government tried (with the help of USAID and the World Bank) to establish cooperative (group) ranches, but with communal herds. Members could bring their own cattle if they wanted, but people have been loath to do this and unwilling to accept government-subsidized communal cattle because this ran contrary to their basic belief in self-reliance.

The government of Botswana tried to curb overgrazing near villages and increase beef production by opening up new rangelands in the western Kalahari to grazing. It established 25 ranches near Ncojane in Ghanzi district, drilled boreholes and erected fences, and leased them to the owners of large cattle herds from adjacent villages. The project ran into problems because most of the new owners were absentee ranchers who only visited their herds occasionally and did not have much interest in taking care of their rangelands (UNEP, 1985).

Game ranching, in which wild game rather than traditional domestic livestock are raised, has been widely advocated as a both profitable and more ecological form of livestock husbandry. However, one evaluation of the relative merits of game or cattle ranching on Kenyan savanna lands receiving less than 600 mm of rainfall annually found that, at current costs and prices, neither activity would be economically viable if projects had to start from scratch and all land, facilities and equipment had to be purchased (McDowell et al, 1953). Higher prices would be needed to make game ranching profitable, and it was unlikely that it would improve the protein intake of local low-income families because they would never be able to afford to buy game meat.

Stratification

Stratification is a far more elaborate form of reorganization of livestock management than the types already mentioned. Proposed for West Africa by the World Bank and FAO since the end of the 1960s (Mayer et al, 1983), the basic idea was that calves would be reared, as at present, on arid rangelands in the north but then moved south to the more humid pastures for fattening, either by peasants looking after small numbers of animals or on large intensive feedlots where animals would be kept in stalls and given concentrated feeds. Finally, they would be sold in the cities and on the coast. This was the basis of the SOLAR project (Stratification of Livestock in Arid Regions), which was adopted as one of six transnational projects that were part of the UNCED Plan of Action.

With a few very local exceptions, stratification has been a failure. The lifestyle and culture of nomadic pastoralists severely limit the rate of offtake from the herd, and herdsmen have been unwilling to sell large numbers of young stock for fattening. The planned reduction in herd sizes has not been achieved and there has been no improvement in living conditions for nomadic people. On the contrary, the majority of nomads involved in stratification schemes have probably suffered a reduction in their quality of life because the schemes did not take account of crucial aspects of nomadic cultures. Stratification requires nomadic pastoralists to make a severe cultural transition, and considerable efforts will be necessary in future schemes of this kind to prepare them for a change of which the psychological and social implications may not always be fully appreciated by planners from the developed world (Baumer, 1981).

Nor has stratification proved to be an economic proposition so far. Dozens of abattoirs in the more humid "fattening zone" of sub-Saharan Africa have either been abandoned because they were unprofitable, or operate at only a fraction of their maximum capacity. It has been estimated that the cost of feed and supplements needed to fatten the cattle in this grain-deficient region is two or three times the value of the gain in livestock weight. Intensive fattening would increase the price for which livestock could be sold, but since beef is imported into West Africa, linking the Sahel with world markets, there is an upper limit on local livestock prices.

Some success has been obtained with attempts to stratify the Kenyan beef industry by breeding herds and producing store cattle on dryland ranges and then finishing animals for slaughter on intensively managed pastures on better lands or in special feedlots. The feedlots increased income and employment, but because they were owned by large farmers or state enterprises the benefits were not widespread, especially since European cross-breeds were used for fattening. When it was shown the Boran cattle raised in northern Kenya could be economically fattened in feedlots, pastoralists became convinced of the potential benefits. High-quality beef was produced and the project helped to stimulate more government support for foot-and-mouth disease control programmes. However, the rate of growth of feedlots has been disappointing, mainly due to government controls on meat prices.

The Prospects for Livestock Development

Can livestock raising in the Sahel ever be improved? Walter Goldschmidt (1981) concludes: "The picture that emerges is one of almost unrelieved failure." Michael Horowitz (1979) talks of "the almost unblemished record of project non-success in the Sahelian livestock sector". Ibrahima Toure, a UNESCO range management expert based in Dakar states: "There have been many livestock projects since the drought, but few very positive results. Things go wrong in implementation. Planners don't have an overall view of the problem."

The lack of success is not surprising. Nature does not run like clockwork in the Sahel or other arid areas, and it would be difficult if not impossible to devise a block grazing scheme which was flexible enough to give levels of productivity and insurance against poor rainfall similar to those of the traditional system. Michael Horowitz (1979) recommends that: "Range management interventions can and should be based, where possible, on the system of controls already practised by the people." Instead, schemes are devised on the basis of inappropriate and inadequate policies, and very often it is these, rather than the actions of pastoralists or poor project administration, which result in failure (Haldeman, 1985).

Such experience has left its mark. Planners and overseas aid agencies now feel they cannot do anything to improve livestock raising. Only 5 per cent of all development aid to the Sahel goes to this sector, even less than the 9 per cent for rainfed cropping (Club du Sahel, 1981). Decades of failure have also made pastoralists suspicious of all government attempts to intervene in their practices. For their part, governments tend to label nomads as stubborn and inflexible. There are elements of truth in both views.

Even if perfect management could be assured there is no guarantee that the results obtained would be any better. A study by a team from the Institut d'Économie Rurale in Bamako, Mali, and the University of Wageningen in the Netherlands concluded that failure to appreciate the effects of low soil fertility on pasture growth in the Sahel has meant that the potential for improving livestock production has been overestimated and traditional pastoral systems have been greatly undervalued (Breman and de Wit, 1983).

In principle, it should be possible to improve livestock production in ways which do not result in overgrazed rangeland and which are compatible with the traditions and wishes of the pastoralists. However, major problems still await solution in terms of achieving the right balance between conservation of the environment and the constraints of land tenure; balancing the individual and communal interests of pastoralists; overcoming the cultural and economic conflict between pastoralism and commercial beef production; and deciding what is the best path — for the "development" of the livestock sector (Haldeman, 1985).

Pastoral Associations: The Last Hope?

A promising new initiative now being tested in the Sahel gives some cause for hope. A number of projects in Mali, Senegal and Niger, funded by the World Bank and USAID, are promoting the formation of pastoral associations. Instead of trying to regulate pastoralists from outside, these projects try to adapt the traditional self-regulation of nomadic herders to modern conditions. Groups of closely connected families are encouraged to form a pastoral association which is given responsibility for managing a borehole or watering point and the surrounding rangelands, and is eligible to receive benefits such as low-cost drugs, vaccinations and other animal health measures.

The idea of pastoral (or herders') associations in West Africa developed in the early 1970s from the concept of group ranches tried previously in East Africa. USAID sponsored an extensive study of pastoralism in central Niger between 1978 and 1983 before formulating the practical second phase of its project, but as a result of the good relations project personnel formed with local people 10 pastoral associations were established before the first phase ended. The follow-up (second phase) project, covering 4 million hectares in an area bounded by the towns of Agadez, Tahoua and Tanout, began in January 1984 and was intended to increase the number of associations to at least 110. Instead, it failed dismally, though more as a result of poor project implementation than of any fault in the basic concept. In the transition from the first to the second phase project personnel with whom the pastoralists were acquainted left the area. This, together with a variety of difficulties in relating the project to local government bureaucracy, made the pastoralists disillusioned with the scheme and prevented it from being extended as planned (Aronson, 1982; Swift, 1984; Abdou et al, 1985).

World Bank experts are cautiously optimistic about the future of their projects. In Mali up to ten pastoral associations, each consisting of 30 to 50 families, have been formed around existing watering points. In Niger 18 associations have been formed in an area to the southeast of the USAID project in the departments of Maradi, Zinder and Diffa. The most promising example of pastoral associations is in Senegal, where Fulani herders who are already well settled have formed 52 associations. The concept is now also being tested in Burkina Faso and Mauritania.* Experience in Lesotho, on the other hand, casts some doubt on the effectiveness of pastoral associations, suggesting that self-managed associations of herders may not be able to take unpopular decisions and that some external influence may be required after all. A grazing association established in the Sehelabathebe area to improve range management and animal health covers 11 villages and accounts for 96 per cent of all livestock in that area. Farmers already perceive benefits in the form of better rangelands, animal quality, and facilities for wool shearing and dip tanks. The association enforces the grazing and livestock regulations, and is managed by a committee of village chiefs together with two elected members from each village. However, a detailed evaluation of the project has stated that:

> because of the sensitivity of the issues involved, grazing association members often cannot act decisively or agree among themselves. . . . Field technicians often decide for the grazing association, thus relieving its members of the responsibility of making unpopular decisions on controversial issues. . . . Although the local chief-tainship structure is incorporated into the grazing association, the project represents externally imposed decision criteria for exercising systematic control over resources in ways not previously done. The project becomes a kind of adversary, forcing unpopular but necessary decisions that grazing association leaders, by virtue of their identity with village society, find it impossible to impose. At present there is no institution that can play this adversarial role after the technical assistance team is withdrawn.

The report concludes that for this reason the grazing association may well not last beyond the end of the project unless there is some external leadership which can take the blame for unpopular decisions (Warren et al, 1985).

The Livestock Dilemma
Technically, it would seem quite simple to control desertification caused by over-grazing, either by reducing the number of animals or by improving the quality of rangelands. All attempts to do this, however, have so far met with little success, and these experiences illustrate the importance of social controls over resource use and what can happen when attempts are made to replace or circumvent them. Whether the new pastoral associations will put Africa's livestock sector on a sounder footing remains to be seen, but in general projects that work with the people should have more chance of succeeding than those — all too frequent in the past — that work against them. Reducing the extent of overgrazing will also require a greater recognition by govern-ments of the importance of pastoralism in dry areas, and corresponding action to

---

* Sihm, personal communication.

prevent the incursion of rainfed cropping on to marginal rangelands, which reduces the area available to herds and is a major indirect cause of overgrazing.

References
Abdou, N, M Keita, G Kaka, H Hamadous, J Erikson, C Beal, B Skapa and G B Greenwood (1985) *The Niger Integrated Livestock Project: A Mid-term Evaluation*, USAID, Washington, DC
Aronson, D (1982) *Towards Development for Pastoralists in Central Niger: A Synthesis Report of the Work of the Niger Range and Livestock Program*, Niamey, USAID, Republic of Niger
Baumer, M (1981) "Livestock Stratification: Help or Hindrance to Arid Land Pastoralism", *Magingira*, no 5, pp72–80
Breman, H, and C T de Wit (1983) "Rangeland Productivity and Exploitations in the Sahel", *Science*, no 221, pp1341–7
Club du Sahel (1980) *The Sahel Drought Control and Development Programme, 1975–1979: A Review and Analysis*, OECD, Paris
—— (1981) *Official Development Assistance to CILSS Member Countries 1975–1980*, OECD, Paris
Goldschmidt, W (1981) "The Failure of Pastoral Development Projects in Africa", in J G Galaty, D Aronson, P C Saltzman and A Chouinard (eds) *The Future of Nomadic People*, International Development Research Centre, Ottawa
Haldeman, J M (1985) "Problems of Pastoral Development in Eastern Africa", *Agricultural Administration*, no 18, pp199–216
Horowitz, M M (1979) "The Sociology of Pastoralism and African Livestock Projects", AID Programme Evaluation Discussion Paper no 6, USAID, Washington, DC
Khogali, M M (1983) "The Grazing Resource of the Sudan", in Jin Bee Ooi (ed) *Natural Resources in Tropical Countries*, Singapore University Press, Singapore
McDowell, R E, D G Sislev, E C Schermerhon, J D Reed and R P Bauer (1983) "Game or Cattle for Meat Production on Kenyan Rangelands?", Cornell International Agricultural Development Mimeograph, no 101, Ithaca, Department of Economics, New York State College of Agriculture, Cornell University
Mayer, H et al (1983) "The Pastoral-Nomadic Subsistence Sector in Africa: Causes and Consequences of Economic and Social Changes", *Africa Spectrum*, no 18, pp295–304
Oxby, C (1984) "Settlement Schemes for Herders in the Sub-humid Tropics of West Africa: Issues of Land Rights and Ethnicity", *Development Policy Review*, no 2, pp217–33
Powell, J M and E Taylor-Powell (1984) "Cropping by Fulani Agropastoralists in Central Nigeria", *ILCA Bulletin*, no 19, pp21–7
Santoir, C (1983) "Raison pastorale et politique de developpement: Les problemes des peul Senegalais face aux ainenagements", *Travaux et Documents de L'ORSTROM*, no 166, Office de la Recherche Scientifique et Technique Outre-mer, Paris
Swift, J (ed) (1984) *Pastoral Development in Central Niger: Report of the Niger Range and Livestock Project*, Niamey, USAID, Republic of Niger
UNEP (1985) "Promotion of Exchange of Information and Expertise on Desertification Control and Technology in Africa", *Actions*, vol 1, UNEP, Nairobi
Warren, M, G Hondale, S Montsi and B Walter (1985) *Development Management in Africa: The Case of the Land Conservation and Range Development Project in Lesotho*, AID Evaluation Special Study no 31, USAID, Washington, DC

■ The Future of Africa's Drylands
Camilla Toulmin, Ian Scorer
and Joshua Bishop

Local Control over Wildlife in Zimbabwe

Most of Zimbabwe's small-scale farming population lives in the dry, marginal communal lands of the country. Many of these are far from urban centres, transport routes and marketing facilities. Some are on the edge of the major wildlife areas of the country, where elephants and other large animals regularly damage the crops during the growing season. In such areas, wildlife are usually regarded as pests by the local inhabitants. However, an approach to wildlife management pioneered by the Zimbabwe government and various NGOs attempts to offset the costs of wildlife by turning them into a resource for exploitation and for local revenue earning.

In marginal areas, with a high population of existing wildlife resources, the returns from wildlife use can potentially be higher than alternative options of dryland agriculture and extensive cattle rearing. High economic returns from wildlife are attained if safari operations, particularly trophy hunting, are established. Large-scale commercial farmers in many parts of the country have also switched to wildlife enterprises over the past 20 years as returns from beef ranching have proven less attractive (Child, 1988).

The CAMPFIRE (Communal Area Management Programme for Indigenous Resource Exploitation) project was launched in 1986, but had various antecedents dating back over the previous decade. Its aims, as outlined in the original project document (DNPWM, 1986) include:

- the introduction of group ownership with defined rights of access to natural resources for the local communities;
- the provision of appropriate institutions under which resources can be managed and exploited for local benefit;
- the provision of technical and financial assistance to communities.

For local resource management schemes to be successful, it became increasingly evident that a clear legal framework for their operation needed to be established; local institutions needed to be strengthened with real power devolved to them; financial mechanisms for revenue extraction and redistribution needed to be established; and technical, managerial and administrative support for emergent local groups had to be supplied. The comparative success of the CAMPFIRE schemes in the late 1980s and early 1990s has been based on this analysis.

Nyaminyami Council, situated in the Zambezi valley, was the first of several local councils legally to establish a wildlife trust, which since late 1988 has been supported by a local NGO. Several safari operations on short contracts provided much of the income during the first year of operation, with revenue supplemented by a number of game culls. The trust has shown a significant operating profit, even after aid subsidies are accounted for. The revenues are received directly by the trust and can be redistributed by the council. The first revenues were shared among the many wards in the district for the support of community development projects (Jansen, 1990).

A number of the problems faced by early schemes have been overcome. No longer does money get diverted to the central treasury, local claims have priority. A local institution is the prime authority and the scheme is not imposed from outside. The lack of technical and managerial capacity at council level is compensated for by the support provided by NGOs and government departments.

However, challenges still remain. How sustainable and replicable is the Nyaminyami experience? A next stage must include the development of capacity within local councils either to provide services themselves or to contract in the technical support they require.

Long-term financial control and involvement by the local institution in wildlife utilization operations must be ensured if these schemes are to be sustainable. The degree of long-term investment and financial security is limited by the short-term nature of many of the agreements reached to date. However, new financial arrangements are being sought. Joint venture agreements are being worked out where local councils have a direct share in the operation, resulting in increased control and greater opportunities for long-term investment. The distribution of benefits within the community poses certain questions. In the past, wildlife revenues have been shared at the ward level by elected committees and spent on projects considered by the community to be a priority. But is this sufficient incentive to ensure the commitment of individual people?

The devolution of responsibility over wildlife requires a realistic assessment of the conflicting claims of different groups at national and local levels. For local control and proprietorship to become a reality, effective legal and institutional frameworks need to be in place, lest the acquisitive desire for resources and power of central government takes precedence over local priorities.

References
Child, B (1988) "The Role of Wildlife Utilization in the Sustainable Economic Development of Semi-Arid Rangelands in Zimbabwe", D Phil thesis, University of Oxford
DNPWM (1986) *Communal Areas Management Programme for Indigenous Resources (CAMPFIRE)*, Branch of Terrestrial Ecology, DNPWM, Government of Zimbabwe, Harare
Jansen, D (1990) *Sustainable Wildlife Utilization in the Zambezi Valley of Zimbabwe: Economic, Ecological and Political Trade-Offs*, Worldwide Fund for Nature, Harare

Chapter 8 | # ENVIRONMENTAL SECURITY and ENVIRONMENTAL INSTITUTIONS

The concepts of environmental security and environmental conflict have been increasingly discussed during the last few years, This is partly because the threat of global military conflict appears to be reduced with the decline of communism in eastern Europe, partly because the environment may become relatively more important as a cause of conflict. Conflict may become war within a state or between states. Alternatively, even if fighting does not occur, there may be trade wars, or a breakdown of cooperation between different groups of people. The tensions between nations of the North and the South, for example, at UNCED, reduced the possibility of reaching international agreements on environmental issues.

Environmental institutions such as those of the UN, among others, may help to reduce environmental conflict. Environmental and developmental institutions may play a large part in achieving sustainable development. But as the environmental and development agendas change, institutions too need to change.

Philippe Sands discusses environmental security and ways in which problems of security may be resolved at the international scale. His particular concern is the international legal system. Josef Vavrousek examines the case for redesigning international institutions to better respond to environmental conflict. He proposes a modification of the UN system that would strengthen environmental interests. Jacob Werksman considers changes in the Bretton Woods institutions, particularly the World Bank, as they have responded to rising concern about environmental matters. David Pearce and fellow authors outline the political and institutional challenges of sustainable development, indicating a possible path towards it.

Enforcing Environmental Security
Philippe Sands

Humanity stands at a defining moment in history. We are confronted with a perpetuation of disparities between and within nations, a worsening of poverty, hunger, ill health and illiteracy, and the continuing deterioration of the ecosystems on which we depend for our wellbeing.

(UN, 1992a)

The emerging importance of environmental concerns to international security (Tuchman, 1989, p163) was emphasized in a January 1992 statement by the 15 members of the United Nations Security Council, declaring that "non-military sources of instability in the economic, social, humanitarian and ecological fields have become threats to peace and security" (UN, 1992a). Six months later, the majority of the world's nations gathered in Rio de Janeiro for the UN Conference on the Environment and Development (UNCED), which had, as one of its major objectives, to assess the capacity of the UN system to assist in the prevention and settlement of disputes in the environmental sphere and to recommend measures in this field, while respecting existing bilateral and international agreements that provide for the settlement of such disputes (UN, 1989).

Implicit in the international legal instruments adopted at UNCED is the recognition that the members of the international community must act together to address global environmental challenges and to prevent the occurrence and escalation of international environmental conflicts (UN, 1992b).

In this broader security context, states' compliance with their international environmental obligations has become a more critical issue in international affairs than ever before. This is evident from the attention the subject received during UNCED as well as the negotiation of recent landmark environmental treaties, including the 1987 Montreal Protocol on Substances that Deplete the Ozone Layer and the 1992 conventions on Climate Change and Biological Diversity.

Three factors underlie this increased concern with compliance. First, the growing demands and needs of states for access to and use of natural resources, coupled with a finite, and perhaps even shrinking, resource base, lay the groundwork for increasing interstate tension and conflict. Second, as international environmental obligations increasingly affect national economic interests, states that do not comply with their environmental obligations are perceived to gain unfair competitive economic advantage over other states. Finally, the nature and extent of international environmental obligations have been transformed in recent years as states assume greater environmental treaty commitments.

Despite the recent emergence of the concept of environmental security, the challenges it poses are not new to the international legal order. Indeed, the legal issues facing the international community today in relation to the environment are remarkably similar to those addressed 100 years ago (Fur Seal Arbitration, 1983). Over the past century, the international legal system has developed institutions, mechanisms and techniques for preventing and resolving international environmental disputes that have emerged as certain natural resources diminish. The controversial issues include transboundary air pollution, the diversion of international rivers, conservation of fisheries resources, national import restrictions adopted to enforce environmental objectives and responsibility for rehabilitation of mined lands (UN, 1941, p755). The existing institutions that deal with environmental security are the United Nations, regional and other organizations established by UNCED and earlier environmental agreements. Furthermore, in the last two decades since the 1972 Stockholm Conference on the Human Environment — which was the precursor of today's environmental movement — the international community has created a large body of international environmental law to establish standards and procedures on handling disputes. The current dispute between Hungary, the Czech Republic and Slovakia over the diversion of the Danube, illustrates the range of enforcement and dispute settlement options available: Hungary is seeking to prevent further dam construction by taking the case to the International Court of Justice (ICJ), as well as to arbitration and the emergency procedures of the Conference on Security and Cooperation in Europe (CSCE) (Anon, 1992).

Although the legal mechanisms for ensuring compliance and resolving environmental disputes have developed significantly, these mechanisms are still used infrequently and have yet to be tested by a major conflict.[*] In the absence of clear rules establishing acceptable global and regional standards of environmental behaviour with regard to such areas as atmospheric emissions, waste disposal and production of hazardous substances, interstate disputes will occur with increasing frequency. Similarly, the failure to comply with minimum standards of good neighbourliness — carrying out transboundary environmental impact assessments, exchanging information or consulting on projects likely to have transboundary effects — will cause significant tension. It is unclear whether the international legal system has the resources to meet these and other imminent challenges to environmental security. UNCED provided an opportunity to develop stronger enforcement mechanisms, but it now appears that this opportunity was not fully utilized. Achieving international environmental security thus demands setting firmer standards and procedures to enforce compliance with these obligations. Non-compliance by states and international institutions limits the overall effectiveness of environmental treaties, undermines the international legal process and

---

[*] Non-compliance with international environmental obligations can occur for a variety of reasons, including a lack of institutional, financial or human resources, and differing interpretations as the meaning or requirements of a particular obligation.

contributes to conflict and instability in the international system. Non-compliance raises three separate, but interrelated, legal questions regarding implementation, enforcement and conflict resolution:

1. What formal or informal steps must a state or international institution take to implement its international legal obligations?
2. Who may seek to enforce the international environmental obligations of a state or international organization?
3. What techniques and bodies exist under international law to settle disputes over alleged non-compliance with international environmental obligations?

This extract briefly considers these three questions, and then identifies some of the more critical issues that are likely to face the international legal system in the near future. Case examples highlight possible techniques to resolve those disputes. The extract concludes with a brief assessment of UNCED and the capacity of the international legal system to respond effectively to growing threats to environmental security. The discussion notes that although considerable precedents exist with regard to environmental law, the international legal system does not yet have the institutional capacity to deal with new environmental challenges that transcend national boundaries and require a supranational response. Recent developments, however, suggest that the international community recognizes this problem and is preparing to address it.

Challenges to Environmental Security
Today, international law is concerned with environmental challenges at national, regional and global levels. Whereas international environmental law was developed to address additional concerns such as the protection of flora and fauna, the conservation of fisheries resources and oil spills — all of which had a somewhat localized interest — the fundamental challenges of the late twentieth century are of a different order. The Rio declaration and Agenda 21 (so called for its prescriptions for the next century) advocate the integration of environmental considerations into all development activities, thus creating an enormous new agenda for international environmental law. The number of environmental disputes undoubtedly will rise as the international community seeks to reconcile the conflicting demands of economic growth and environmental protection.

Atmospheric issues are now at the top of the agenda, as scientific evidence mounts about the consequences of the depleting ozone layer and increased atmospheric concentrations of greenhouse gases to human health and the environment. In addition, the massive loss of biological diversity, deforestation, increased soil degradation, drought and desertification are issues now considered to be the common concern of all states and peoples, and thus ripe for international action.

Moreover, hazardous substances and activities, including pesticides and nuclear power, are matters demanding increased international attention and new regulatory treaties. Minimizing the generation and international transport of waste will require new legal instruments; and, as international legal prohibitions on dumping at sea and incineration begin to take effect, techniques for the disposal of waste must be found. Finally, and perhaps most challenging of all, the adverse environmental consequences caused by activities within the international trading system and multilateral development banks require the so-called greening of such institutions as the General Agreement on Tariffs and Trade (GATT). These challenges threaten to place immense strains on the existing international legal system.

On a more positive note, however, there now exists a sufficiently well-developed body of precedent to suggest that the international legal system does have available a number of mechanisms to deal with environmental disputes that constitute a threat to international peace and security. The following cases illustrate the availability of certain international institutions and implementation techniques that may offer the most optimism in addressing new challenges.

Indicative Cases

An important and long-standing source of international tension between North and South is the belief of people in many less-developed countries (LDCs) that their former colonial occupiers were responsible for the plunder of natural resources, and thus are obligated to rehabilitate lands and restore natural resources that were damaged or removed during colonial occupation. The ICJ has now been called upon to resolve a dispute between the island nation of Nauru and the trustee governments who managed Nauru's affairs prior to its independence in 1968. The dispute concerns damage to the territory of Nauru caused by the mining of phosphates on a massive scale, an act that has made more than one-third of the island uninhabitable. The claim is based, in part, on the principle of general international law that a state responsible for the administration of a territory must not bring about changes in the condition of the territory that will cause irreparable damage to the legal interests of a future successor state. Nauru is seeking a declaration of its legal entitlement to the proceeds of the phosphate sales, and to reparation for losses due to breaches of international legal obligations. The claim presents the ICJ with an important opportunity to consider, *inter alia*, the environmental responsibilities of an administering state, and to lay down principles that could be applied to similar disputes between other states. The ICJ could also lay down principles of more general application, concerning states' responsibilities relating to the environment and natural resources.

The Nauru case is potentially important in determining responsibility for environmental damage in the newly independent states of east-central Europe, and whether — and to what extent — the governments of the Commonwealth of Independent States might be responsible for environmental damage in the former Soviet satellites. Similarly, this case may help ascertain the liability of the United Kingdom for the effects of nuclear tests that were performed in Australia prior to independence.

With regard to ozone depletion and climate change — another critical environmental issue — new environmental treaties have begun to establish environmental standards that have significant economic implications for signatory states. The 1987 Montreal Protocol, as amended, requires the total phase-out in production and consumption of certain ozone-depleting substances. This was the first time that the international community had banned the production and consumption of any product. The 1992 Climate Change Convention now requires industrialized countries to return their emissions of greenhouse gases to 1990 levels by the year 2000 — a move that has significant implications for transport and energy sectors. The fear of the effects wrought by non-compliance with those obligations, and the consequential economic benefits to be gained from ignoring obligations, has led to the establishment of important new techniques for ensuring compliance.

In June 1990 the state parties to the Montreal Protocol established an Implementation Committee to consider and report on submissions made by one or more states concerning reservations about another state's implementation of its obligations under the protocol (UNEP, 1990). The committee is required to try to secure "an amicable resolution of the matter on the basis of respect for the provisions of the Protocol" (UNEP, 1990) and report to the Meeting of the Parties, which may decide upon and call for steps to bring about full compliance with the protocol. In November 1992 the non-compliance procedure under the Montreal Protocol was amended to include an indicative list of measures that might be taken by a Meeting of the Parties with respect to non-compliance with the protocol (UNEP, 1992).

In another significant move, the 155 signatories to the 1992 Climate Change Convention created a subsidiary body for implementation to help assess and review state implementation of the convention. It also provided for the possibility of establishing a "multilateral consultative process" for the resolution of implementation questions, to be available to the parties on their request (Articles 10 and 13). These important and innovative developments are evidence of a broadly held belief that compliance mechanisms need to be strengthened to make these treaties workable. The participation of NGOs in the negotiation of these treaties also suggests that they could be an important source of information on non-compliance; indeed, the reluctance of states to engage in whistle-blowing will require international institutions or NGOs to play a greater role in enforcement.

The impact of trade on the environment has also become a growing source of conflict among states. In the absence of international environmental standards for products and manufacturing processes, states will resort to unilateral measures of environmental protection, including import bans on products that they consider to be environmentally harmful or produced by environmentally harmful processes. Given the often severe economic consequences that result from such bans, those states whose products have been subject to an import ban have considered such an act to be an unwarranted incursion into their internal affairs.

In August 1990 the USA imposed a ban on the importation of yellow-fin tuna and yellow-fin tuna products from Mexico and intermediary nations that had been caught with purse-seine fishing nets. Use of these nets resulted in the incidental killing of dolphins in excess of US standards. In January 1991 Mexico requested the GATT to establish a dispute settlement panel to examine the compatibility of the import prohibition with the GATT rules on free trade. The following September, the panel ruled in Mexico's favour that the import ban contravened the GATT, since it amounted to the extra-jurisdictional application of US law; the measures had not been shown to be necessary; the US had not exhausted all options reasonably available to it to pursue its dolphin protection objectives, neglecting negotiation through international cooperative arrangements; and finally, the measures taken were too unpredictable (Fur Seal Arbitration, 1983).

Although the USA has not yet complied with the ruling of the panel — which is not legally binding — the ruling provided Mexico with important leverage for subsequent negotiations and an eventual solution between the two countries. In effect the panel, which fulfilled the role of conciliator, provides another example of a mechanism available under international law for defusing environmental tensions between states.

Establishing international standards, such as trade bans, also leads to conflict, as evidenced by attempts to reduce the threat to the survival of the African elephant. This has been a controversial issue for a number of years. The main institutional forum for resolving disputes over measures to restrict international trade in ivory has been the Conference of the Parties (COP) to the Convention on International Trade in Endangered Species (CITES), which meets every three years. In 1989 NGOs played a key role in the decision to ban international trade in ivory: environmental NGOs for many years raised public consciousness about the issue and — relying on international law, including their observer status at CITES — forced the issue on to the international agenda. The World Wide Fund for Nature (WWF) dismissed the argument that the proposed ban would amount to a retroactive application of law or constitute a wrongful interference with the legitimate expectations of existing ivory stockpile holders. The WWF did this by obtaining, and then circulating to all 103 states present at the CITES meeting in Lausanne, an independent and formal legal opinion challenging the basis of the "retroactivity and legitimate expectation" arguments (Fur Seal Arbitration, 1983). While the effect of WWF action cannot be quantified with certainty, it is interesting to note that following the circulation of the legal opinion, those legal arguments did not reappear. A former member of the CITES secretariat has indicated that this outcome was a direct result of WWF action.

The complex legal saga of the attempt to save the African elephant did not, however, end with the overwhelming vote of the COP to CITES. On 17 January 1990, shortly before the 90-day period for entering reservations to the CITES amendment had expired, the United Kingdom entered a reservation excluding the application of the ban to the territory of Hong Kong. The task was left to environmental NGOs to consider the legality of that reservation under English law, under CITES and EC law. Immediately after the reservation was entered, a group of US environmental NGOs, led by Greenpeace, obtained an independent and formal legal opinion from another NGO. On 25 April 1990 they formally petitioned the US secretary of the interior to certify that China, the United Kingdom (on behalf of Hong Kong) and Zimbabwe were "diminishing the effectiveness" of the CITES programme for the protection of the African elephant (Sands and Bedecarre, 1990). If it had been successful, President Bush would have been required to impose appropriate economic sanctions against the named countries. In July 1990 the reservation expired and was not renewed, bringing the issue to a close and illustrating the effective use of informal legal opinions and NGO advocacy.

UNCED and Beyond
Whereas the 1972 Stockholm Conference did not address the issue of state compliance in any depth, the subject was clearly an important one for the preparations for UNCED in 1992 — yet this task was only partially fulfilled. The Rio declaration goes part way toward identifying some of the inadequacies in the institutional and legal arrangements for the maintenance of environmental security. The declaration calls on states to provide "effective access to judicial and administrative proceedings, including redress

and remedy," to "enact effective environmental legislation" and to "resolve all their environmental disputes peacefully, by appropriate means and in accordance with the Charter of the United Nations" (UNCED, 1992). Agenda 21 goes even further. It recognizes the limitations of existing arrangements, including inadequate implementation by states of their obligations, the need to involve multilateral organizations in the implementation process, and gaps in existing dispute settlement mechanisms.

Agenda 21 also recognizes the role of various international institutions as central to the maintenance of environmental security. The UNEP is called upon to promote the general implementation of international environmental law, while the UNDP will play a lead role in supporting the implementation of Agenda 21 and capacity building at country, regional, interregional and global levels (UNCED, 1992). The newly created UN Commission on Sustainable Development will evaluate information supplied by states with regard to their progress in implementing environmental conventions (UNCED, 1992). The role of the UN General Assembly and other agencies concerned with international environmental issues will continue to expand. Moreover, the World Bank will become an increasingly dominant presence through the activities of the Global Environment Facility, which now serves as the interim financial mechanism to disburse resources under the climate change and biodiversity conventions. Regional organizations, including the EC and the regional development banks, have also signalled their intention to promote activities that will contribute to the maintenance of environmental security. The effectiveness of these organizations, however, will ultimately depend on the extent to which states are willing to cede sovereignty in the establishment, monitoring and enforcement of international standards.

The international community must study and consider ways in which the capacity of current enforcement mechanisms can be broadened and strengthened to promote the prevention and peaceful settlement of environmental disputes (UNCED, 1992). Agenda 21 does not provide any details about such mechanisms, yet it does address the need for mechanisms and precedents to improve the exchange of data and information, notification and consultation regarding situations that might lead to disputes with other states. This is particularly important in the field of sustainable development and for effective peaceful means of dispute settlement in accordance with the Charter of the United Nations including, where appropriate, recourse to the ICJ, and their inclusion in treaties relating to sustainable development (UNCED, 1992).

Will UNCED make a difference? Certainly, it helped to secure a place for environmental security on the international agenda. The international legal and institutional responses to deal with challenges to environmental security will be channelled principally through the General Assembly as well as through the Commission on Sustainable Development. As discussed in this extract, however, there are many limitations inherent in the ability of international arrangements to ensure widespread compliance with international environmental obligations.

Conclusion

Developments in international law alone will be insufficient to overcome the political, economic and social reasons underlying non-compliance. Nevertheless, the law itself, legal processes and institutions can make a difference, and recent developments suggest strong recognition of the need to make changes in the very structure of the traditional international legal order. To begin with, the provision of technical, financial and other assistance to states, particularly LDCs, will internationalize the domestic implementation of international environmental obligations. In addition, the expanded role granted to international institutions and, to a lesser extent, NGOs in setting international standards, monitoring and enforcement, broadens the scope of actors formally entitled to identify and remedy violations. This should facilitate early warnings of activities that pose significant threats to environmental security. Finally, the establishment of a wider range of mechanisms for dispute settlement suggests an important and growing role for independent international adjudication. These are all important developments and — however inadequate they might appear — should be welcomed as a basis for further efforts toward environmental conflict resolution.

References

Anon (1992) "Danube Dam Threatens to Open Floodgates of Hostility", *Financial Times*, 29 October

Fur Seal Arbitration (1983) "Great Britain v United States", in *Moore's International Arbitration Awards*, vol 1, p755

Sands, P and A Bedecarre (1990) "CITES: The Role of Public Interest Non-Governmental Organizations in Ensuring the Effective Enforcement of the Ivory Trade Ban", *Boston College Environmental Affairs Law Review*, no 17

Tuchman, J (1989) "Redefining Security", *Foreign Affairs*, no 68

UN (1941) "Trail Smelter Arbitration, *Canada v United States*", *United Nations Reports of International Arbitration Awards*, vol 3, no 1

—— (1989) General Assembly Resolution 44/228, 20 December

—— (1992a) "The Responsibility of the Security Council in the Maintenance of International Peace and Security", *UN Doc S/23500*, 31 January

—— (1992b) Agenda 21, UN Doc A/CONF 151.26, I, II, III, New York

UNCED (1992) *Rio Declaration*, Principles 10, 11 and 26

UNEP (1990) "Decision 11/5 (non-compliance) of UNEP", *Report of the Second Meeting of the Parties to the Montreal Protocol on Substances that Deplete the Ozone Layer*, UNEP Doc OzL Pro 2/3, 29 June

—— (1992) *Report of the Fourth Meeting of the Parties to the Montreal Protocol*, UNEP DOc OzL Pro 4/.15, 25 November

Institutions for Environmental Security
Josef Vavrousek

There are three weighty justifications for building new international environmentally-oriented institutions. They also show why new global institutions, expressing the global as distinct from the lowest common denominator of different national interests, must be built too.

The first is quite clear. Without the dedicated and systematic coordination of regional and national environmental protection and restoration activities we face the very real threat of global environmental disaster. No single country or group of countries can avoid it by sole action, regardless of how intensive their efforts are or should be.

There is then a second justification for supranational environmental institutions. This is that we have to avoid the danger of possible severe political, racial or military tensions between different regions, states, or even blocks of countries which could have their roots in environmental degradation: trans-regional and trans-boundary air pollution; dirty rivers poisoning distant seas; CFCs and carbon dioxide emissions from sources located mainly in the rich North destroying the protective ozone layer and changing the global climate with severe adverse impact especially on the vulnerable countries of the South, and many others. There are also potential conflicts between neighbouring countries because of controversial dams such as the Gabcikovo-Nagymaros dams on the Danube, nuclear power-plants, agricultural practices or other conflicting issues. So we urgently need efficient mechanisms to enable us to identify and prevent, or to solve peacefully, these environmentally based problems. Such mechanisms should include, *inter alia*, also global environmental legislation setting up basic rules and international institutions able to identify existing or emerging environmental problems; to find generally acceptable solutions; and prevent further environmental degradation. Otherwise the future can bring old-new types of international tensions or even wars: fighting for water, for air, for the right to live in a healthy, safe environment. History knows many of these "eco-wars".

The third justification for international and global environmental institutions is, however, maybe the most important. The need is to establish the natural basis for a future reintegration of human society. We are living in a transitional, risky but also very promising period. The old global international system, which was formed after the Second World War, is melting down. I think that this is partly because it was unable to prevent or solve many of the interlinked problems that create environmental insecurity. These are, in my opinion, primarily the consequence of abundant consumption in some countries and deep poverty in many others; of the demographic *tsunami** of exponentially growing population, to use Commander Cousteau's arresting image for it; of the rapid erosion of genetic potential; of too much, too rapid and too careless exploitation of natural resources; of extensive pollution, and deterioration of the natural and the man-made environment; of the steep decrease in the "cultural diversity" of humankind and growing tensions and local wars in many different parts of the world. This, I believe, is common cause with one of the most important and constant themes of this book, shared by many authors.

But the Cold War order ended also because the overall nature and balance of the political, economic and military condition changed fundamentally. More than 100 new states, independent at least in name, have emerged in the former colonies, and after the inevitable — and desirable — collapse of the Soviet empire there are no longer "three worlds". The former "Second World" is still experiencing the savage disintegrative forces which are evident also in central and eastern Europe, all of which stands in contrast to the hesitantly continuing unification of the western part of Europe through the Maastricht process. After the downfall of COMECON (Council for Mutual Economic Assistance) and the Warsaw Treaty Organization, the countries of central and eastern Europe live, to all intents and purposes, in an "international institutions vacuum". The UN Economic Commission for Europe operates only in some areas, CSCE (the Helsinki process) is not very efficient, unable to solve the Yugoslavian, Caucasian and many other problems. There is a serious lack of effective international platforms for the coordination of national activities in central and eastern Europe, which leads often to unsatisfactory solutions and to the dangerous strategy of each man for himself: "save your own nations; do not care about others". It is a sad paradox that the two successor states of former Czechoslovakia — the Czech Republic and the Slovak Republic — emerged on 1 January 1993, just at the moment when the European Community and EFTA countries had made another big step towards integration.

We have to search for new platforms for the future political reunification of the European continent as well as of the world community. There are not too many options, I am afraid. Economic interests — at least short-term ones — are often quite contradictory. The creation of common markets needs long-term preparation if the free market shock is not to be deadly for the weaker economies. Narrow-minded national and ethnic interest and religious beliefs could hardly become the basis for real international or global cooperation. On the contrary, they are actually dividing many states into foreign and sometimes even hostile and cruelly fighting tribe-like societies. Former Yugoslavia is an infamous example: but I think that tribal grouping is probably not only the consequence of "time bombs" (unsolved problems inherited from history and sometimes very old); it is primarily an atavistic reaction of many living through a

---

* *Tsunami* is the Japanese name for the huge tidal wave which may be created by a submarine earthquake.

difficult transitional phase of development when the old system has disappeared and the new one has not yet emerged or works badly. Hostility is the typical reaction to adaptional crises, well known by ethnologists from the studies of animal behaviour under stress. Nationalism, religious intolerance and racism as ritual "fixed points", provide in such situations temptation for deluded people to believe that their uncertainties, economic and other problems and despairs can be treated by a few simple medicines. This is the opportunity for dogmatism, fanatics and strong men of all orientations, as has occurred within the "international institutional vacuum" of the countries of central and eastern Europe.

In this very difficult and risky situation, common concern about our common natural heritage and vital environmental interests is possibly the most promising starting point for further international cooperation at the European as well as the global scale. It is in the basic interests of all human beings to have clean air and water, unspoiled soils, healthy forests and conserved natural resources, biological diversity, the beauty of harmonious landscapes and many other gifts of nature. And this is also our responsibility, not only for future generations of humanity, but for all living beings as well as non-living elements of nature. The sooner we realize it the better. It is an enormous challenge for humankind but also a great opportunity which should not be missed. We may not have another chance.

Towards a More Efficient and More Environmentally Oriented United Nations System
Humankind has to solve many global problems that are mutually dependent. This is why there is no real chance that they can be solved separately or by the effort of individual countries. The need for coordinated global scale action is thus becoming more and more urgent.

The United Nations system has played a very important role in the prevention or solution of worldwide as well as local problems during the last decades, and with the end of the Cold War, we have a chance to activate its full potentialities for the first time. This is timely because at the same moment new problems have emerged, among which environmental insecurity is prominent. At the global scale, it is composed of uncontrolled population growth, unbalanced economic development leading to excessive consumption in some countries and deep poverty and even starvation in orders, rapid deterioration of the human environment and vast depletion of nature, weakening some of its crucial life-protecting systems.

The UN system is the natural framework within which to tackle these global security issues, but it needs considerable reform and improvement. The charter framework of the UN system, established in San Francisco in 1945 just after the end of the Second World War, has proved to have remarkable durability although no mention of the environment appears in it: the issue simply was not salient at that time. Within it new institutions have been created, one of which was the United Nations Environmental Programme (UNEP), established in 1972. This add-on approach widened step by step the scope of UN operations and thus, on the one hand, allowed the organization to adapt to new situations, but on the other led to the creation of too many different institutions with very small — if any — mutual links. The existing UN structure is thus too ineffective and also too expensive in my opinion. The traditional approach of extending the list of UN agencies and other institutions seems to be inefficient.

Disappointment with performance has contributed to support for the dictum "no new institutions within the UN", which now prevails.

The vast new challenges for the UN system need new solutions, however. One possible blueprint for such a deep change in the UN structure I proposed in the context of the Rio Earth Summit. I believe that the moment is ripe to reshape the UN system and to focus it upon the new security agenda. The revised UN structure should be both more decentralized, and therefore better able to tailor solutions to specific problems, and also more efficient. I think that the future structure of the UN system should have four specialized subsystems, which would form its primary structural framework (see Table 8.1) to increase the efficiency of the UN system without creating a highly centralized bureaucracy with a monopoly on power. I suggest the following criteria to inform the new structure:

Table 8.1 *Main Pillars of the UN System and their Interactions*

Main relations: the interaction of influences	(a) UN security system	(b) UN economic system	(c) UN social system	(d) UN environment system
(a) UN security system		influence of instability on economic development	influence of instability on the social human culture	influence of instability on the quality of the environment
(b) UN economic system	influence of economic crises on security		influence of economic crises on human culture and health	influence of economic crises on the environment
(c) UN social system	influence of social unrest on security	influence of education on economic development		influence of human value in relation to Nature
(d) UN environmental system	influence of environmental deterioration on security	influence of environmental deterioration on the efficiency of economy	influence of environmental deterioration on human culture and health	

- balanced awareness of the spectrum of global problems competing for consideration in the UN system; and
- precise division of functions and responsibilities within the UN system, (similar functions in the present system should be integrated and unnecessary ones should be terminated);

- decentralization of the activities; decisions should be made as close to the problems as possible so that they may be based on knowledge of the specific conditions while at the same time being based on a common policy set by the General Assembly; and
- efficient feedback built into the system to allow the early identification and correction of problems that may arise during the planning and conduct of a UN operation.

The four sub-systems are:

1. A UN security system seeking to prevent or resolve peacefully international conflicts, governed by the UN Security Council;
2. A UN economic system promoting balanced global economic development through appropriate financial, trade and other measures governed by a UN Economic Council;
3. A UN social system concentrating on the support of culture, education, health care, social security and similar activities headed by a UN Social Council; and
4. A UN environment system focusing on the protection and restoration of nature in general and the human environment in particular, headed by a UN Environment Council.

Each of these four specialized pillars should be autonomous as they each concentrate on a different aspect of the sustainable development of our planet. At the same time they must work closely together since all real problems are mixtures of these areas. However, this tension between working together and maintaining their own point of view will increase the probability of optimal decisions when they confront the complex problems of the world. It will also promote efficient implementation of the decisions by specialized institutions once a course has been decided upon.

Anyone familiar with the UN will recognize that my plan is evolutionary rather than revolutionary: (1) exists already, and under Marrack Groulding's leadership, peace-keeping is in vigorous development; (2) and (3) involve boosting and dividing the functions of the present ECO SOC (Economic and Social Committee); while only (4) is really new.

Splitting the Economic and Social Council would help solve the complex problems with inner structures that are so interrelated that they require the distinctive points of view of the four separate pillars to analyse and solve them synergistically.

The new UN environment system (4) would subsume the existing UN Environment Programme, and be much enhanced in status: accorded equality with the other UN pillars. In fact, one of the most urgent reasons for the amplification of this office is to provide a counterbalance to the other three parts in the UN system. This organization should have a working institute on the ground as the place in which to debate environmental policy: a sort of environmental staff college for the member states. My new UN structure would absorb the majority of the existing UN organs, programmes, organizations and institutions.

The requirement to decentralize the UN system activities and thus to increase their efficiency on the basis of precise knowledge of the situation in different parts of our planet, leads me to propose a secondary "cross" structure of the system. This secondary structure should be organized on a continental or regional basis, following a well recognized principle in the UN Charter, and would be developed from the existing regional commissions. But I would increase their number. There should be UN commissions for Africa, Europe, North America, South America and the Caribbean, eastern and western Asia, Australasia and Antarctica. Each of these commissions would concentrate on the four principal themes: security, economy, social affairs and the environment, corresponding to the four pillars of the primary structure of the UN system. The two different structures would form a robust "matrix" structure, which would enable it to respect the global consequences of specific problems as well as their geographic dimensions (see Table 8.2).

Table 8.2 *The Main Areas of Cooperation Between Two Proposed Structures of the UN System*

Primary Structure	Secondary Structure		
	UN African system	UN European system	Overall mission
(a) UN security system	African security	European security	Global security
(b) UN economic system	African economic development	European economic development	Global economic development
(c) UN social system	African social, cultural development and health care	European social, cultural development and health care	Global social and cultural development and health care
(d) UN environmental system	African nature protection, and environmental restoration	European nature protection and environmental restoration	Global nature protection and human environmental restoration
Overall mission	Sustainable African development	Sustainable European development	Sustainable planetary development

There are several ways to strengthen the "fourth (environmental) pillar" of the proposed UN system. The most promising would be to establish a UN World Environment Organization (UNWEO) to coordinate environmentally oriented efforts on a global scale. The future UNWEO could be based on the existing UNEP structures. The blueprint for UNWEO should adopt a "flat" institutional network with a comparatively small coordinating centre which could be developed from the existing UNEP secretariat in Nairobi. It would relate to autonomous continental environmental centres following the same general "planetary" strategy which could in turn be fashioned out of a merger between UNEP's regional offices and the UN economic commissions for each continent. The scope of activities of different continental environment organizations could be very distinctive — probably broader in continents divided into a large number of countries (such as Europe), and narrower in the continents with a smaller number of countries.

These proposed developments of the structure of the UN are just one of the possible blueprints. But we shall not advance unless we dare to think in concrete terms like this. It is important to start focused and systematic efforts in this direction. In the Rio conference there was an excellent opportunity to start such a process, but no concrete specifications for the future UN were adopted there. However, active follow-up activities began. Let us hope that in 1995, on the fiftieth anniversary of the historic San Francisco Conference, we shall have a renewed UN system, adapted to the new global threats to security. That would be a worthy goal.

■ Greening Bretton Woods
Jacob D Werksman

Through the gun sights of an eco-activist few international institutions appear in greater need of greening than the World Bank. The World Bank and the affiliated international financial institutions known as the Bretton Woods group[*] have been accused of bankrolling ecological and economic disaster in the developing world, by promoting development projects that have denuded forests, depleted soils, and increased dependence on unsuitable energy sources. Gestures by the World Bank to introduce greener policies in response to these criticisms have been met with deep scepticisms and accusations of superficial "greenwashing" (Greenpeace, 1992).

The World Bank's most vocal critics, the non-governmental organizations (NGOs) with interests and constituencies in the area of environment and development, claim that the source of the World Bank's ecological disasters lie far deeper than the reach of recent reforms. For the World Bank to become truly responsive to environmental concerns it must be accountable for its policies and actions, not merely to its shareholders, but to the stakeholders in its projects — the countries, communities and individuals most affected by World Bank activities.

Mounting criticism of World Bank activities, despite its efforts at reform, has led some to conclude that it is incapable of reforming itself from within. Accountability will require not merely internal reform, but review of World Bank activities by an external authority.

In this context, many have looked to the United Nations (UN) to provide a framework for setting and monitoring compliance with internationally agreed environmental principles and standards. The 1992 UN Conference on Environment and Development (UNCED), demonstrated an ambitious global initiative in international policy-making aimed at integrating responses to environment and development concerns. Prominent on UNCED's agenda for the future is the use of international legal

---

[*] The term "World Bank" or "World Bank group" as used here loosely refers to the International Bank for Reconstruction and Development (IBRD), the International Development Association (IDA), the International Finance Corporation (IFC), and the Multilateral Investment Guarantee Agency (MIGA). The term "Bretton Woods" institutions, used here interchangeably with the "World Bank" often includes the General Agreement on Tariffs and Trade (GATT).

agreements on principles and standards for the achievement of environmentally sustainable development; and the strengthening of the UN's role in monitoring compliance with these agreements, including the compliance of the World Bank.

The first test for this new relationship will be the operation of the Global Environment Facility (GEF). The GEF was established by the World Bank, the United Nations Development Programme (UNDP) and the United Nations Environment Programme (UNEP) with the hope of playing a central role in the implementation of the international legal agreements or "conventions" entered into at UNCED. The UNCED negotiators, wary of ceding policy-making control to the World Bank, yet anxious for the World Bank's resources, approached the new relationship tentatively, and on the condition that the GEF be held accountable to the parties to the conventions and comply with UNCED principles. As the GEF is gradually restructured to conform to UNCED principles it promises to become the crucible for forging the first operational policies for sustainable development, linking the concepts of environment and development, and the institutions of the UN and Bretton Woods systems.

The debate over how these links should be made has prompted policy makers to reconsider the nature of the relationship between the World Bank group and the UN, to consider why World Bank environmental polices have failed in the past, and to explore whether the principles for sustainable development, agreed at UNCED, could be better achieved through a closer legal relationship between the UN and the Bretton Woods systems. While there are significant barriers to linking the two fundamentally different systems, UNCED has raised hopes that the set of principles and procedures for sustainable development, agreed at Rio, will produce a momentum towards institutional reform.

UNCED challenges international law to establish the process whereby the conflicting interests raised by environment and development concerns and the struggles between the UN and the Bretton Woods systems of governance, can be confronted and resolved. This process will involve an attempt to incorporate the cornerstones of sustainable development identified at Rio: the integration of environment and development on a transparent and equitable basis through the empowerment of all the stakeholders in the development process. In the context of the World Bank and the GEF, this process will encourage the empowerment of the people of developing countries, at both the governmental and non-governmental level, with the right to participate in and have access to information on the environmental and developmental design and assessment of World Bank projects.

Historical Overview: Incompatible and Conflicting Interests
International law and international governance, like any legal system, can be seen as a framework for resolving conflicting interests in pursuit of the common good. The spirit of international cooperation, prolific in the 1940s, engendered two fundamentally different international legal structures for sorting out the world's problems: the United Nations and the World Bank.

The United Nations and the World Bank: Creation and Constitution
The United Nations and its affiliated agencies have since provided a political forum for pursuing the common good by working to avoid and settle armed conflicts, alleviate

275

sickness and hunger, protect human rights and, with increasing intensity of effort, to protect the environment. The United Nations Charter was based loosely on the constitutions of the Western democracies that won the war. Each member state in the UN's principal political organ, the General Assembly, following the paradigm of representative democracy, holds the sovereign right to cast an equal vote. NGO representatives are routinely allowed to observe, to have access to information and to contribute their expertise and the concerns of their constituents. As the only intergovernmental organization with universal membership, the UN has been recognized as having a special authority to speak on issues, such as environment and development, that concern all the world's citizens (WCED, 1987).

The World Bank has focused its resources on alleviating poverty and promoting development in an effort to raise the standard of living in developing countries. The World Bank's Articles of Agreement are based on an equally venerable institution of Western democracy — the commercial bank. Within the World Bank's executive boardroom, respectful of the investors' right to protect their investment, directors' votes are weighted by the number of shares held in the World Bank, that is by the number of dollars each shareholder contributes to the World Bank's capital. Following the model of the traditional banker/client relationship, the World Bank closely guards much of the information it holds on its clients' projects. NGO participation in the design and implementation of World Bank policy and projects is minimal.

Although members of the same UN "family", the UN and the World Bank were intentionally separated at birth. They continue to be governed by a 1947 agreement, which expressly walls off the World Bank as an independent international institution, entitled to keep information confidential and to make loan decisions through the independent exercise of its own judgment (UN/IBRD, 1947). The UN was expected to be the world's central political organ, while the World Bank's Articles forbid it from making loans with "regard to political or other non-economic influences or considerations" (IBRD, 1989). For most of the history of these institutions, environmental concerns have been left to the UN's politicians and have been considered beyond the scope of the World Bank's "economic" considerations.

Since their creation, these two international legal "persons" have pursued their often overlapping development goals with limited success, in part due to their disjointed legal heritage. The United Nations struggles along like a legislature stripped of its power to tax and spend and unable, on its limited budget, to finance the ambitions of its resolutions and the wide scope of its mandate. The World Bank, self-regulating and largely unaccountable to the communities it aspires to help, manages its \$140 billion portfolio with a project failure rate staggering even by internal assessments (Wapenhans et al, 1992).

Cooperation or Discord?

To some extent the distinction between the UN and the World Bank is an artificial one in that membership in the two institutions closely overlap.[*] However, as has been frequently noted, structural differences at the international and the domestic level

---

[*] With the addition of Macedonia in March 1993, UN membership included 180 states; as of March 1993 the World Bank had 174 members.

prevent the two institutions from speaking with the same voice (Thacher, 1992).

The World Bank's decision-making system of "one dollar, one vote" precludes some of its members — i e, the developing countries in which the World Bank's projects are implemented — from participating in World Bank policy decisions to the full extent they can in the UN General Assembly. Furthermore, because the individuals in the ministries responsible for environmental matters in the UN system are often distinct from and subordinate to those dealing with financial matters through the World Bank's system of governance, member countries of both institutions appear to have difficulties in coordinating their environmental and development assistance policies on the international plane.

Thus, some countries that are shareholders in the World Bank may vote to adopt resolutions in the General Assembly and enter into treaties negotiated under the UN's auspices and find themselves without the voting power to carry through these policies at the World Bank. Similarly, other countries may undertake certain obligations under the political pressures of an open and more democratic UN, and then use their financial voting power to downplay the same obligations while closeted in the World Bank's boardroom. As a result, both the World Bank and its shareholder countries remain essentially unaccountable to UN policy-making.

As this discussion suggests, the power struggle between the two institutions masks a more fundamental conflict between the developed and the developing countries over the size and shape of the global development's agenda. The disjunction between the UN and the World Bank allows both groups to evade responsibility, by pointing to inadequacies in the institution over which they have less political control. The question is raised whether greater cooperation and accountability can be achieved by linking these two fundamentally incompatible systems, and, if so, what role an emerging international law of sustainable development can play in forging that link. Ideally such a link would ensure the integration of an internationally determined set of environmental principles and standards into the World Bank's development assistance at both the policy-making level and at the level of project implementation.

As discussed below, in the context of the GEF, accountability may best be achieved through international legal agreements based upon UNCED principles that establish procedures to oversee and assess whether the World Bank's governance, its management and its staff carry out policies as set by the international community. To operate effectively, such procedures would have to assure access to information about World Bank activities, and to input from communities affected by these activities.

A review of the World Bank's attempts to set and implement environmental policy will suggest that the UNCED's principles for the future are based, in part, upon lessons learned from the World Bank's relationship with the environment in the past.

The World Bank and the Environment

Past efforts to integrate environmental concerns into World Bank policy have fallen short of expectations. World Bank policies first began to address environmental concerns in the 1960s by lending on a relatively small-scale for particular environmental projects. The World Bank made considerable progress in designing projects to promote water sanitation, reduce urban pollution, prevent soil erosion and manage wildlife. But the World Bank's critics contended that the effect of this small-scale lending for environmental projects paled in comparison with the impact the World Bank's regular development lending was having on the environment. Real progress could only be made by integrating environmental concerns into all aspects of World Bank lending, not just those aimed specifically at improving the environment.

The effort to integrate the environment and development gained political momentum through various UN initiatives at developing international environmental law and policy, including the 1972 United Nations Conference on the Human Environment (UNCHE), the negotiation of the 1980 Declaration of Environmental Policies and Procedures Relating to Economic Development, and the work of the World Commission on Environment and Development (WCED). To some extent the World Bank has responded, by implementing both procedural and institutional reforms.

The World Bank's first attempt to integrate environmental concerns into the procedures of the World Bank project cycle was made with the introduction of environmental guidelines in 1970. These guidelines were monitored internally by the World Bank's Office of Environmental Affairs (OEA). Institutional inertia and a failure to commit resources at the appropriate stages of project selection and development have led many to conclude that these guidelines proved largely unsuccessful (Murgatroyd, 1990).

A more sophisticated attempt, intended to "apply state of the art practice on environmental assessment . . . to the subtleties of the World Bank's relationship with clients" and to "bring in the legitimate interest of various groups at the local level" was launched in 1989 by the World Bank's Operational Directive on Environmental Assessment (EA) (Piddington, 1992). Under this directive, the World Bank requires a preliminary screening of all projects for their environmental consequences as soon as a possible project is identified. Projects are then categorized by their potential environmental impact and subjected to varying degrees of environmental assessment, or to none at all (World Bank, 1992a).

The World Bank's EA directive conforms in principle with UNCED's recommendations for integrating environmental concerns into development policy; it fails, however, to incorporate opportunities for meaningful public participation. The concept of environmental assessment as a precondition for project approval derives from national laws, where it has worked to block government and private projects that threaten to damage the environment. The success of national application of this concept depends largely on the right to public participation in the EA process, and the right to challenge the EA's conclusions before an adjudicative authority. Thus, while the World Bank's EA process has, in theory, great potential for promoting environmentally sustainable development (Goodland and Daly, 1992), it has already come under sharp criticism. Internal World Bank and NGO evaluations of the EA directive in practice have revealed that the EAs are often superficial, underestimate and miscategorize the potential environmental impact of projects and fail to take into account the concerns of local peoples (Udall, 1993).

The World Bank's apparent inability to carry out its own policy directives has been consistently linked to the need for institutional reform to complement policy initiatives within the World Bank. The WCED, commissioned by the UN secretary-general to propose a "global agenda for change", identified the World Bank as especially influential in achieving sustainable development for providing "the largest single source of development lending and for its policy leadership which exerts a significant influence on both developing countries and donors". The WCED called for the establishment of a high level office within the World Bank with the authority to ensure the incorporation of sustainable development objectives and criteria into the World Bank's policies and programmes (WCED, 1987).

World Bank president Barber Conable, acknowledging that major institutional reform was necessary to integrate truly the environment into project development, established in 1987 the World Bank's Environment Department. The department, however, was relegated to the policy and research complex of the World Bank, and has not reached directly to the core of the World Bank's lending operations. Instead its role has been seen as being a "monitor and mentor" to regional operations (Piddington, 1992).

It is, perhaps, not surprising that in 1992, at the UN Conference on Environment and Development, the World Bank found itself, once again, the target of reformist criticism. In the months following Rio, the World Bank restructured its Environment Department. The department, still focused on policy and analysis, has now been given a tool with which to shape project selection. The various divisions of the department will design "best practice papers" to help policy-makers and project designers conform projects to what the World Bank considers the most environmentally friendly approaches.

Most recently, since January 1993, the restructured department has been placed under the authority of a newly created vice presidency for environmentally sustainable development. Within the World Bank's pyramidal structure, the Environment Department will be on the same level and under the direction of the same vice presidency as the Agriculture and Natural Resources Department and the Department on Transport and Urban Development (*Environment Bulletin*, 1993). It remains to be seen whether this reshuffling will produce a better integration of policy into practice.

Though the World Bank can be said to have made significant progress in establishing policies designed to promote sustainable development and environmental protection, and to have established institutional structures within itself for monitoring the implementation of these policies, the conclusions of UNCED suggest that the degree to which these policies are implemented and enforced will depend on deeper institutional reforms that open the World Bank's governance to accountability to those outside it. Without accountability, the World Bank's EAs and best practice papers may remain severed bits of policy, borrowed from domestic legal frameworks that depend on public participation and challenged for their legitimacy.

UNCED can be seen as an effort to provide this legitimacy by establishing a framework for external participation and accountability. The UN's past efforts toward this end have failed, primarily because of the largely symbolic nature of these initiatives that have produced only weak links between the World Bank and the UN.

The Narmarda Dam: A Case Study for Sustainable Development

The formidable nature of this challenge is illustrated by the controversy surrounding the World Bank's involvement in a hydroelectric and irrigation dam project on the Narmada River in north-western India. First proposed by the Indian government in 1946, this massive undertaking is intended to bring hydroelectricity, irrigation and drinking water to some 30 million people. The World Bank first became involved in the project in 1985 and committed $450 million in loans and credits, or about 15 percent of the total estimated cost of the project.

Although the World Bank's financial contribution represents a relatively small portion of the project's overall cost, it is generally recognized that bank involvement in any project is crucial to attracting financial resources from additional multilateral, bilateral and private sources of aid and loans.

As has been described, by the 1980s, the World Bank had begun to develop internal procedures for assessing the potential social and environmental impact of its projects. Accordingly, the World Bank negotiated with the Indian government what it claimed to be a comprehensive assessment of the environmental impact of the project and a plan for resettling local people who would be displaced by the dam's reservoir.

Soon after the project was under way, local communities, Indian NGOs and, later, the international NGO community, began to assess a social and environmental catastrophe well beyond what the World Bank's assessment procedures had revealed. Estimates now place the number likely to be displaced by the dam at over 100 000, a population described as impossible to relocate humanely (Rich, n d).

In response to growing local and international pressure, revelations of civil uprising, government crackdowns and human rights abuses among the villages in the dam's flood plain, the World Bank's president commissioned an unprecedented independent review of the World Bank's involvement in the project. The review, known as the Morse Commission Report and published in June 1992, found the World Bank management had abused and neglected stated World Bank policies on environment and resettlement, and that this attitude pervaded the World Bank's hierarchy of decision-making and project implementation. The review concluded that the primary cause was that "the World Bank is more concerned to accommodate the pressures emanating from its borrowers than to guarantee implementation of its policies" (Morse and Berger, 1992).

In March 1993, the World Bank, bowing under pressure, enforced its policies and drew up a newly negotiated series of "benchmark" conditions for continued World Bank involvement. The Indian government, unable to meet new requirements on environmental protection and resettlement, was forced to withdraw from the remaining $170 million of the loan package. There are, however, indications that the Indian government will continue with the project, without the World Bank's support, but free from international intervention (Anon, 1993).

The Narmada project reveals the outlines of the conflicts thrown up by the interface between environment and development, conflicts UNCED suggests the international law and policy of sustainable development will play a role in resolving. It provides a concrete example of the attitudes that contributed to the atmosphere and outcome of Rio, and to the articulation of the principles, standards and structures of UNCED.

UNCED and Agenda 21: Institutional Reform

The process that led to UNCED caused policy-makers within the UN agencies and the World Bank to consider, once again, the relationship between the environment and development, and the relationship between the two institutions. As chapter after chapter was added to Agenda 21, the estimated need for developing countries, in grant and concessional financing, to implement Agenda 21's policies rose to $125 billion a year between 1993 and 2000. It became clear that a new level of cooperation would have to be sought to ensure that unprecedented levels of resources could be directed towards environmental protection and that all resources dedicated to development were in harmony with the principles of sustainability

Agenda 21, which establishes a programme for action on sustainable development for the international community, is largely hortatory and recommendatory in nature and does not purport to blind directly UNCED participants to particular actions. It does, however, contain a remarkably detailed consensus of over 170 countries reflecting a general commitment to pursue the goals of sustainable development. Most significantly, it calls for the establishment of a high level Commission on Sustainable Development (CSD) to ensure the effective follow up of Agenda 21.

Agenda 21 contains extensive recommendations for the redirection and revitalization of the UN system, including the Bretton Woods institutions, towards the achievement of sustainable development. Central to these commitments is that the implementation of Agenda 21 shall be "based on an action- and result-oriented approach and consistent with the principles of universality, democracy, transparency, cost-effectiveness and accountability" (Section 38.2).

While virtually every aspect of Agenda 21's outline for sustainable development has implications for the World Bank's lending policies, the principles of Agenda 21, like the Stockholm principles of 20 years ago, will likely remain unimplemented without new and powerful structural and procedural mechanisms. To this end, the negotiators dedicated a subchapter to govern the "cooperation between United Nations bodies and international financial organizations", recognizing that: "the success of the follow-up to the conference is dependent upon an effective link between substantive action and financial support, and this requires close and effective cooperation between United Nations bodies and the multilateral financial organizations" (Section 38.40).

To ensure that the policies of Agenda 21 are followed, the conference recognized the need for institutional arrangements within the UN system to implement Agenda 21 and called upon the General Assembly, as the "supreme policy-making forum" of the UN system, to establish the CSD. In response to UNCED, the UN General Assembly adopted verbatim the conference's recommendations on the primary task of the CSD, which will be:

> *To monitor progress in the implementation of Agenda 21 and activities related to the integration of environmental and developmental goals throughout the United Nations system through analysis and evaluation of reports from all relevant organs, organizations, programmes and institutions of the United Nations system dealing with various issues of environment and development,* including those related to finance.
>
> (UNGA, n d)

Specifically, the General Assembly empowers the CSD to monitor the World Bank's activities and plans to implement Agenda 21, and invites the World Bank to submit regular reports to the CSD on the World Bank's progress (UNGA, n d). Agenda 21 envisages the NGO community playing a central role in this review process and recognizes that the United Nations system, including international finance and development agencies, should:

- design open and effective means to achieve the participation of non-governmental organizations, including those related to major groups, in the process established to review and evaluate the implementation of Agenda 21 at all levels and promote their contribution to it; and
- take into account the findings of non-governmental organizations' review systems and evaluation processes in relevant reports of the secretary-general to the General Assembly and all pertinent United Nations agencies and intergovernmental organizations and forums concerning implementation of Agenda 21 in accordance with its review process (Section 38.43).

Whether, and how effectively the CSD will monitor the World Bank's compliance with Agenda 21 remains to be seen. Hopefully the wide consensus reached at Rio signals a genuine commitment among the World Bank's controlling shareholder countries to open up the World Bank's operations to greater scrutiny, participation and oversight.

The first indications as to the sincerity of this commitment are likely to come from the specific relationship established at Rio between the parties to the UN Framework Convention on Climate Change and the World Bank's Global Environment Facility (GEF).

The Global Environmental Facility

The initial testing ground for the post-UNCED relationship between the UN and the World Bank has become the GEF, set up by the World Bank primarily in anticipation of new financial commitments arising out of UNCED. Since UNCED, the GEF has been designated the operator of the interim financial mechanism for the Climate Change Convention. The nature of this relationship has not yet been fully elaborated, but the legally binding nature of the convention, and the specific requirements it demands of the GEF, represent the first significant attempt to use international law to force the greening of a Bretton Woods offspring.

In 1987, the WCED's report had suggested that the World Bank develop a "special banking programme or facility linked to the World Bank [that] . . . could provide loans and facilitate joint financing arrangements for the development and protection of critical habitats and ecosystems, including those of international significance", and strongly recommended that additional financial resources be earmarked for the protection of the global commons (WCED, 1987).

Following the outlines of the WCED's suggestions and the encouragement of donor countries, the World Bank's board of executive directors established the GEF in 1991 (IBRD, 1991). The GEF was launched with a budget of approximately $1.3 billion to be allocated on a grant basis, over a three-year period. During these three years, known as the GEF's pilot phase, GEF funding was to be focused on four areas of global environmental concern that were becoming the focus of UN-driven policy making: climate change, biodiversity, pollution of international waters and ozone depletion.

Intended to be a model of cooperation between UN and Bretton Woods institutions, the GEF is described as a joint project between the UNDP, the UNEP and the World Bank. UNDP is to provide technical assistance, capacity building and project preparation, while UNEP is to provide strategic planning and to assure the scientific, technical and legal integrity of GEF projects. The World Bank describes its own role as managing the GEF's investment project cycle, acting as trustee, nominating the chairman to the GEF's governing body, and housing the GEF Secretariat (World Bank, 1992b).

GEF documentation nobly recites many of the same principles contained in Agenda 21. It promises that the GEF will be transparent and accountable to contributors and beneficiaries alike and that it will ensure universal membership and a broad and equitable representation of developing and developed countries in its decision-making procedures (World Bank, 1992b, para 2.05). Furthermore, the GEF promises to establish new structural mechanisms designed to guarantee follow through on these principles. Projects are to be overseen, directed and reviewed by a Participants' Assembly (PA) comprising all developed and developing countries participating in the GEF. To assist the PA and the GEF administration, an independent scientific and technical advisory panel (STAP) composed of experts from developed and developing countries, acting in their personal capacities, will provide advice on every stage of project selection and development (World Bank, 1992b). Finally, NGOs are to have a "major role to play in the identification, design and implementation of projects" (World Bank, 1992b).

Critics maintain that the GEF, in practice, has thus far fallen seriously short of its noble aspirations. Much of the criticism of the first stages of the GEF's operations surround the continued domination of the World Bank and its policies in the running of the GEF. During the GEF's pilot phase, membership in the GEF was limited to those countries wealthy enough to contribute a minimum of $4 million to the GEF's trust fund. As a result the GEF, just like the World Bank's board of executive directors, was dominated by developed countries during the period when much of the GEF's operational policy was being developed. Furthermore, the GEF's "democratic" governance procedures were under the direction of its powerful chairman, appointed by and an employee of the World Bank. Decisions were taken by consensus, as perceived and summarized by the chairman in his report.

Critics claim that the independent STAP, and the UNDP and UNEP, have had only a limited opportunity to influence project selection. As many as 80 per cent of the GEF's projects were prepared and approved by World Bank staff and are linked in some way to larger World Bank projects. STAP apparently has been denied access to relevant information about the World Bank projects to which GEF projects are linked (Udall, 1993). Furthermore, the GEF participants have thus far failed to reach a consensus on allowing NGOs to participate, even as observers. Instead, NGOs are limited to consultations held just prior to the GEF meetings, attended by the GEF administration but generally avoided by the participants. Some of the GEF's documentation of claims of having involved local NGOs in project development and implementation have proved difficult to verify (Greenpeace, 1992).

The GEF's fulfilment of the promise of universal membership has been gradual, and has been seen as an attempt to allow the donor countries to set the rules before the game begins. Even as larger numbers of developing countries are added to the roles of the GEF participants, traditional power struggles are emerging, blocking consensus on voting procedures and raising genuine fears that a newly democratized GEF will not yield UNCED's vision of an accountable and equitable cooperation, but political deadlock.

Hope that this deadlock could be broken, and that genuine reform will be introduced to the GEF, can be drawn from the legal force of the Climate Change Convention, which provides specific guidance on how the GEF, as the operator of the convention's financial mechanism, is to conform with UNCED principles. The political relationship between the main organ of the convention — the COP — and the GEF can be seen as roughly parallel to the political relationship between the UN and the World Bank. Just as in the UN General Assembly, developing countries will numerically and politically dominate the COP. Legally, however, the relationship is not parallel. Far from being an independent institution, the GEF is intended to serve the COP, which will determine the GEF's climate-related funding policies. Developed countries party to the convention, whether they are operating within the GEF's PA or through the World Bank's governance, must respect the text of the convention when discussing matters related to it. Thus, while the GEF as an institution is not a "party" to the convention, states party to the convention participating in the GEF are bound by international law to ensure that, in restructuring the GEF, they comply with the requirements and the principles of the convention.

Furthermore, the text of the convention codifies the developing countries' collective sovereign right to withdraw from the GEF. In an unprecedented move, the developing countries negotiating the convention accepted the GEF on the condition that it be reformed if it is to maintain a relationship with the convention. Thus, the convention provides that, within four years of entry into force, the COP may sever its relationship with the GEF and seek a different entity to operate its financial mechanism (UN, n d).

To prevent such a result and to shore up this new relationship, the specific terms of the convention can be read to require the parties to the convention to enter into an international legal agreement with the GEF to ensure its accountability to the parties and a long-term relationship between it and the convention. The closely negotiated text of the convention illustrates an attempt to use international law to translate UNCED principles into operational procedures.

Strong Links: An Agreement for Accountability

Article 11(1) of the convention requires that its financial mechanism be "accountable" to the COP. The convention anticipates this relationship will be established through an agreement between the COP and the GEF, as the entity entrusted with operating the financial mechanism.

Article 11 empowers the COP to decide on virtually every aspect of the financial mechanism's operational mandate, including its "policies, programme priorities and eligibility criteria" (UN, n d). This suggests that the COP will have to maintain a high degree of oversight and direction over the financial mechanism. Accordingly, the convention calls for the agreement between the COP and the GEF to establish modalities for the provision of regular reports to the COP (UN, n d). The agreement will also provide for the GEF to be made accountable to the COP through the assessment and review of particular funding decisions.

Thus, the general concept of accountability in Article 11(1), is supported by the broad procedural guarantees outlined in Article 11(3), which empower the COP to enter into an agreement with the GEF, to ensure that the convention's funding decisions conform to COP policies and that these decisions can be reconsidered in the light of COP policies (UN, n d).

It will be recalled that as the convention enters into force and the GEF's membership is made universal, parties to the convention may also become participants in the GEF (World Bank, 1992b). Legally, this relationship will provide an additional level of accountability, as the requirements of the convention will guide and bind the GEF's PA in convention-related decisions. In negotiating the agreement under Article 11(3), the COP is empowered to put in place procedures that bind the GEF at an institutional level, to ensure that the parties can exercise meaningful control over funding decisions to a degree that may not be provided through the PA. Such an agreement would provide a concrete legal link between a democratic body operating under the auspices of the UN and a Bretton Woods institution. Projects implemented by World Bank management would for the first time be subject to policy direction, review and revision by an open and democratic process.

A Restructured World Bank

In the hope of rallying the support of a sceptical NGO audience, the GEF's chairman, Mohammed T El-Ashry once described the GEF as a Trojan Horse, capable of seductively breaching the walls of the World Bank and unleashing progressive environmental policies on the World Bank's establishment. There is hope that Mr El-Ashry's metaphor will not prove hollow if the GEF is allowed the opportunity to demonstrate that greater success can be achieved through openness, democracy and accountability than through traditional World Bank operations.

A great deal of work will have to be done to devise the appropriate procedures and institutional arrangements to give shape to UNCED's vision of "accountability". The concept can encompass a wide range of meanings but certain elements have been recited often in the debate and have become a mantra for those restless for institutional reform. Universality, accountability, transparency, democracy and equity: close examination will have to be made of the implications of these words, as policy makers explore ways in which the catch words of UNCED can be translated into action, both at the level of the relationship between the GEF and the convention and between the World Bank and the UN.

References

Anon (1993) "India to Drop World Bank Dam Loans", *Financial Times*, 30 March
Environment Bulletin: A Newsletter of the World Bank Environment Community (1993) vol 5, no 1, Winter 1992/1993
Goodland, R and H Daly (1992) *Approaching Global Environmental Sustainability: A World Bank Environmental Working Paper*, World Bank, Washington, DC
Greenpeace (1992) *The World Bank's Greenwash: Touting Environmentalism while Trashing the Planet*, Greenpeace
IBRD (1989) Articles of Agreement III(4) vii
—— (1991) Resolution of the Board of Executive Directors, 14 March
Morse, B and T Berger (1992) *Sardar Sarorat: Report of the Independent Review*, Resource Futures International, Ottawa, Canada
Murgatroyd, C (1990) *The World Bank and Environmental Protection*, unpublished lay essay for LLM degree
Piddington, K (1992) "The Role of the World Bank", in A Hurrel and B Kingsbury, *The International Politics of the Environment*, Oxford University Press, Oxford
Rich, B (n d) *Memorandum: The Role of the World Bank After UNCED: The Need for Institutional Reform*

Thacher, P (1992) "The Role of the United nations", in A Hurrel and B Kingsbury, *The International Politics of the Environment*, Oxford University Press, Oxford

Udall, L (1993) Statement of Udall, Staff Attorney, Environmental Defence Fund, on Behalf of Environmental Defence Fund and Sierra Club before the Subcommittee on Foreign Operations, Export Financing and Related Matters, Committee on Appropriations, United States House of Representatives, 1 March

UN (n d) United Nations Framework Convention on Climate Change, Articles 11(4) and 11(3)(b).

UN/IBRD (1947) Agreement Articles I (2), I(3), Article IV(3), 15 November

UNGA (n d) United Nations General Assembly Resolution 47.191, para 3a

Wapenhans, W A et al (1992) *Report of the Portfolio Management Task Force*, World Bank, Washington, DC

WCED (1987) *Our Common Future: The Report of the World Commission on Environment and Development*, Oxford University Press, Oxford

World Bank (1992a) *The World Bank and the Environment: Fiscal 1992*, World Bank, Washington, DC

—— (1992b) *The Global Environment Facility: Beyond the Pilot Phase*, Working Paper No 1, 2–4

Sustainable Development: The Political and Institutional Challenge
David Pearce

The Political Challenge

The phrase "sustainable development" has staying power because most people want to believe in it. It survives because it appears to build bridges between the demands of environmentalists and developers. It sounds comforting — human wellbeing and economic security forever, not brought to heel by ecological collapse or social distress. It is an article of faith, and in that sense almost a religious idea, similar to justice, equality and freedom. Indeed, when it reaches a par with these grand goals, it will have arrived at the first stage in its long journey of transition.

The notion of a "sustainable" society is radical. Sustainable development confronts modern society at the heart of its purpose, because the human race is and always has been a colonizing species without an intellectual or institutional capacity for equilibrium (O'Riordan, 1993). Existing patterns of production, distribution and consumption thrive on creating environmental externalities in the form of pollution, habitat loss and ubiquitous waste disposal. Yet, it must be said that the present society is supported by a democracy that is led to believe that its best interests are served by minor adjustments to the status quo. This is buttressed by a general feeling of satisfaction among Western society's "contented majority" — the economically fortunate and politically dominant sections of society — with this state of affairs (Galbraith, 1992).

According to the Brundtland Report, the "modern" development process fails to meet human needs and often destroys or degrades the resource base. A pattern of human development that favours the rich and those of the current generation at the expense of the poor and those yet to be born is, by definition, unsustainable in the sense of the Brundtland Report, though potentially sustainable in the conventional sense of being able to last. However, it is still doubtful whether even the very basic needs of at least one billion of the world's poorest people can really be met without an enormous convulsion in the denial of expectations over future consumption of materials and energy among the very wealthy. Moreover, experience provides little support for the hope that it is technically possible to bring the existing global population up to the living standards of, say, France, without environmental disruption on an enormous scale. At the very least, there would need to be a serious and prolonged commitment to technology transfer, to scientific and managerial capacity building in the South and fundamental adjustments to the international systems of trade, debt and aid. All these points were raked over in the run-up to the Rio conference, and for the most part, appear as part of the "wish list" in Agenda 21.

From a political perspective, one of the most important of the fundamental principles of sustainable development is *fairness*. This does not just apply to the rights of future generations to be able, realistically, to adjust to what this generation bequeaths them. It also applies to rights of all present generations to enjoy fundamental democratic rights and access to sustained livelihoods. The social dimension states simply, but powerfully, that a sustained society is also a truly democratic society with rights of expression, dissent, participation, self reliance and equality of opportunity. Political and economic structures have to deliver social as well as environmental sustainability. This is the message that has still to be grasped by the politicians, and, indeed, most citizens.

The transition to sustainable development will be an intensely political process because it will create a new set of gainers and losers in society. This is hardly surprising since all patterns of development generate gainers and losers and a change to sustainable development will be no exception. Such a transition will also require active government intervention in markets through the provision of price and quantity incentives, especially through the introduction of environmental taxes and charges for using environmental assets.

The current political incentives are such that politicians have to be more concerned with generating policies that secure the short-term goal of re-election, rather than tackling the inevitably fraught transition towards more sustainable development. Ironically, it is probably democracy itself that is the greatest political barrier to a truly sustainable future. Without democracy, nothing can be achieved without losers, and losers can readily block some of the changes that are required for sustainable development. This potential conflict between what people want now and the interests of future generations is, of course, familiar in any democratic process. The conflict can be reduced only through persuasion of the majority that sustainable development is the right development path. Moreover, where there remains a conflict between the means of achieving sustainability and democratic wishes, the balance must lie with the perpetuation of democracy.

Any shift towards sustainability will inevitably be slow, taking generations, not years. Full sustainable development involves a cultural shift, not just economic and political tinkering. The goal is elusive, so we must learn to experiment and adjust towards sustainability, shedding failure and misunderstanding and capitalizing on success and support for well-intentioned trials. As Lee (1993) has put it, we need both a compass and a gyroscope: a "scientific" compass to chart our way, and a gyroscope to retain political and democratic stability as we move from one stage to the next. Table 8.3 outlines a possible compass and gyroscope.

Inevitably, the early stages of the transition are the most difficult: vision is very dim and resistance very strong. Much depends on building structures of support, understanding and learning capability rather than radical new policy measures that will be fought by an unprepared policy. There are three stages, the first two perhaps taking up to 20 years to complete, the third even longer. The stages can be characterized in four distinct dimensions: policy; economy; society and participatory structure. Arguably, the UK is not even fully at Stage 1. Even party political doctrine barely puts the parties on the road to Stage 2. Stage 3 does not appear to be in party strategists' minds.

The Institutional Challenge

Sustainable development is a process that must encompass every section of society and every role we play: citizens and parents, children and students, civil servants and teachers, business leaders and employees. Sustainability will not simply "happen"; neither can it be imposed "top down" by authoritarian governments. Nevertheless, the transition to sustainable development will still need to be managed, planned and administered. It also needs a sense of purpose — at least a hazy "vision" of where society is heading. Only governments can provide these things by taking the lead in the transition to sustainable development. Inevitably, this will require institutional change.

Table 8.3 A Possible Map of the Sustainable Transition

	Policy	Economy	Society	Discourse
Stage 1 Ultra weak sustainability	Lip service to policy integration	Minor tinkering with economic instruments	Dim awareness and little media coverage	Corporatist discussion groups; consultation exercises
Stage 2 Weak sustainability	Formal policy integration and deliverable targets	Substantial restructuring of micro-economic incentives	Wider public education for future visions	Round tables; stakeholder groups; parliamentary survelliance
Stage 3 Strong sustainability	Binding policy integration and strong international agreements	Full economic valuation; green accounts at business and national level; green taxes; offset	Curriculum integration; local initiatives as part of community growth	Community involvement; twinning of initiatives in the developed and developing world

References

Galbraith, J K (1992) *The Culture of Contentment*, Sinclair Stephenson, London

Lee, K N (1993) *Compass and Gyroscope, Integrity Science and Politics for the Environment*, Island Press, Washington, DC

O'Riordan, T (1993) "The Politics of Sustainability", in R K Turner (ed), *Sustainable Environmental Economics and Management*, Belhaven, London

Chapter 9 | EMPOWERMENT

Many people, particularly in the Third World, are severely limited by the weakness of their entitlements to adequate food, water and shelter, so they are unable to achieve sustainable livelihoods beyond the level of bare existence. Empowerment is the process though which entitlements are extended and strengthened. The first two readings examine the need of and the opportunity for women to gain control over their living conditions. Irene Dankelman and Joan Davidson consider women's wish to control the size of their family and constraints on their ability to control family size, and they discuss the benefits of family planning for women. Family planning is most effectively achieved as part of a broader programme of support to income, health, nutrition and education.

Caroline Moser discusses women's role in the long-term improvement of an informal settlement, showing what can be achieved by unaided women. Charlie Pye-Smith, Grazia Borrini Feyerabend and Richard Sandbrook extend the argument to examine ways in which communities can be helped to gain control over natural resources, allowing more effective and efficient management. Robin Sharp looks more broadly at the role of institutions in empowering people. He discusses participatory development, the development of opportunity, democracy, decentralization of power and the significance of central governments in fostering or hindering these aims.

Planning the Family:
A Woman's Choice
Irene Dankelman and Joan Davidson

In 1987, world population will pass five billion. It is growing at the rate of approximately a billion people every 12 years. Every minute it grows by 150; every day by 220 000; every year by over 80 million. Ninety per cent of this growth is in developing countries. . . . Is reaching 5000 million a triumph for humanity or a threat to its future?

(Salas, 1987)

If we lived in an ideal world, in which everyone — North and South, rich and poor — had access to the same amount and quality of resources and consumed as much (or as little) as anyone else; in which sustainable management of the natural world was fully integrated with development; in which the carrying capacity of land was recognized and honoured; in which appropriate technologies were available to all and practised widely, then the size of the world's population would be of great concern. Indeed, a 1983 FAO study concluded that with more irrigation and the wise application of other known technologies, the earth could produce enough food for everyone. And, if the rich consumed less, environmental degradation would be reduced.

But today's reality shows that society and the environment fall far short of this ideal. An enormous gap exists in consumption rates, in the resources available and in the ways in which those resources are managed between richer and poorer countries, and between the wealthy and the destitute within the same countries. In these circumstances, rapid population growth in the poorer countries exacerbates the problems of survival and accelerates the rate of resource degradation and in consequence, the burdens women must face.

When the present developed world passed through its demographic transition in the nineteenth century, "surplus" populations could be exported to relatively unpopulated countries. Today, no such solution exists for the people of the South, whose countries have an average growth rate of 2.5 per cent per year. With a projected world population in excess of 6000 million by the end of the century, and 90 per cent of growth taking place in developing countries, the struggle for survival of those who depend upon natural resources of food, fuel, water and building materials seems doomed to fail.

Overall, reducing population pressures on the environment is not simply a matter of limiting the numbers of those living in developing countries: major changes in development priorities are needed. Population control is one element of a complex web of radical decisions that are required to bring about sustainable development. But "present rates of population growth", argues the World Commission on Environment and Development (WCED, 1987), "cannot continue".

> *They already compromise many governments' abilities to provide education, health care, food security ... and ... raise living standards. This gap between numbers and resources is all the more compelling because so much of the population growth is concentrated in low-income countries, ecologically disadvantaged regions and poor households. ... Governments must work on several fronts — to limit population growth, to control the impact ... on resources, and with increasing knowledge, enlarge their range and improve their productivity; to realize human potential so that people can better husband and use resources; and to provide people with forms of social security other than large numbers of children. ... Giving people the means to choose the size of their families is not just a method of keeping population in balance with resources; it is a way of assuring — especially for women — the basic human right of self-determination.*

The Consequences for Women

"Women realize better than anybody else what an accelerated population growth rate means," says Makwavarara (1986), and certainly many Third World women do appreciate the problem. But they are victims of a harsh reality which militates against population control. Many Third World children do not survive to be adults; women are often left as sole providers for the household, with only their family to care for them in old age. Cultural and social values encourage large families. More children mean an extra work force and insurance for the future. As long as child mortality is high, the incentive to have more remains strong.

Increasingly, women in the South are acknowledging the heavy toll that continued childbirth and child-rearing exacts on their own and their children's health. Induced abortions which follow unwanted pregnancies — most taking place illegally and in unsanitary conditions — expose women to severe physical risks, and can permanently damage their mental health. It is estimated that at least 30 000 women in 1987 will not survive the experience, almost all of them in the Third World. Some demographers put the figure several times higher.

Pregnancy-related maternal and infant deaths are still unacceptably high in developing countries and could be reduced by family planning (IPPF, 1985a). One study, based on the Word Fertility Survey, which collected data from 29 developing countries between 1974 and 1981 and from interviews with some 150 000 women of reproductive years suggested that spacing all pregnancies at a minimum of two years would prevent 500 000 infant deaths each year in those countries.[*] Dr Fred Sai, population

---

[*] Information supplied by Frances Dennis, IPPF director of information, in 1987.

adviser to the World Bank, goes further. He estimates that family planning alone could save at least five million children and 200 000 maternal lives each year by helping couples to space their children and avoid high-risk pregnancies.

International Action

International assistance on population through the United National Fund for Population Activities (UNFPA) is a relatively recent development. Since its founding, the fund has been mainly involved in demographic trends and projections. Three important principles guide its work:

- the principle of national sovereignty in population matters;
- the provision of necessary information and services to individuals and couples to determine freely and responsibly the number and spacing of their children; and
- the notion that population goals and policies are integral parts of socio-economic development (Salas, 1986).

The International Conference on Population in Mexico in 1984 emphasized that it remains the free decision of couples themselves how many children they raise. Women, however, often have little say in the matter. The Mexico Conference recommended that "swift action must be taken to assist women in attaining full equality with men in the social, political and economic life of their countries. To achieve this goal, it is necessary for men and women to share, jointly, responsibilities in areas such as family life, child care and family planning" (Mexico City Declaration on Population and Development, August 1984).

The success of local projects that promote family planning along with health and child care shows that women do want to space their families better, and so reduce the number of children they have. This enhances their capacity to play a proper role in their local communities and to contribute to sustainable development.

But access to family-planning information and supplies — even for those who want them — is woefully inadequate. According to World Health Organization estimates, 300 million couples who want no more children still have no access to family-planning services. There are, moreover, powerful pro-natalist forces which seek to undermine assistance programmes for family planning. And women can suffer in other ways: there is continued evidence of iniquitous practices in the distribution of unsafe and inappropriate contraceptives, with Third World women being used as "guinea pigs" for new product testing.

An Integrated Approach

Women's development, education and emancipation are key factors in increasing the acceptance of family planning. The need for, and the viability of, an integrated approach that links family planning to other aspects of development — including improvements in income, health, nutrition and education — has been well demonstrated. Women have to identify their own priorities and must be enabled to participate at all stages of a project — planning, implementation and assessment (Huston, 1978 and see case study). The provision of information about family-planning methods and subsidized supplies is just one part of this effort.

One of the most experienced organizations offering family-planning information and services is the International Planned Parenthood Federation (IPPF) with its member family planning associations in more than 120 countries. In 1976, IPPF initiated the worldwide "Planned Parenthood and Women's Development" programme, focused on women in developing countries and with special reference to the poor in urban and rural areas who are often not reached by conventional development programmes. The objectives are:

- to enable women to work together;
- to teach them skills through training;
- to improve the status of women; and
- to improve the welfare of families through increasing family-planning knowledge and practice (IPPF, 1985b).

Many development activities have been included in the IPPF programme, ranging from income generation to the provision of community services, health care, skills and leadership training, the management of women's groups and responsible parenthood. Importantly, as the following case study shows, environmental action has been successfully incorporated into this integrated approach.

An Example from Nepal

More and more evidence is emerging of the usefulness of combining family planning with environmental action. The Family Planning Association of Nepal, for example, is coordinating a long-term project to help local people improve their self-sufficiency and reduce their birth rate. During 1987, some 150 000 fodder trees were planted by small farmers in the Sindhupalchowk district, northwest of Kathmamdu, and some 10 000 couples in the same area were protected against unwanted pregnancies. Some 60 per cent of people there live below the poverty line and, with over 11 people per cultivated hectare, the district has one of the highest population densities in the world. Poor diets are combined with a lack of sanitation, bad housing and polluted water. Only 15 per cent of the people are literate.

The project began in 1973 with the provision of basic health care and family planning, but expanded (with support from the US NGO World Neighbours and from Oxfam, UK) to promote increased agricultural productivity and family income by demonstrating improved fodder trees and soil conservation measures. Forests were disappearing through the collection of fodder in the dry season, and soil destruction followed. Now, a fast-growing Leuceana species, the "Ipil" tree, has been planted on the face of terraces, reducing soil erosion and allowing farmers to coppice the trees for fodder all year round. Stimulated by the project, local people have made other farming improvements and begun to accept family planning. This area now has one of the highest contraceptive use rates in Nepal and the birth rate is almost half the national average (Hamand, 1987). Not only the "hardware" of family planning, but a certain level of development, are necessary if couples are to be able to have fewer children.

References
Hamand, J (1987) "Fodder Trees and Family Planning in Nepal", in Earthwatch section, *People*, vol 14, no 3

Huston, P (1978) *Message from the Village*, The Epoch Foundation, New York

IPPF (1985a) *Annual Report*, IPPF, London

—— (1985b) *Experiences from Africa: Ghana, Kenya, Lesotho and Mauritius*, IPPF Africa Regional Office, Nairobi

Makwavarara, A (1986) "Women Realize Better than Anybody Else what an Accelerated Population Growth Rate Means . . .", *Ceres* (special issue on food, agriculture and women), FAO, Rome

Salas, R M (1986) *UNFPA and International Population Assistance*, UNFPA (1986) Reprint from *Harvard International Review*, March

—— (1987) *The State of World Population 1987*, UNFPA

WCED (1987) *Our Common Future*, Oxford University Press, Oxford

■ Women's Mobilization in Human Settlements: The Case of *Barrio* Indio Guayas
Caroline Moser

In Latin American cities low-income women work not only in their homes and in the factories but also in their neighbourhood communities. Along with men and children they are involved in residential-level mobilization and struggle over issues of collective consumption. The inadequate state provision of housing and local services over the past decades has increasingly resulted in open confrontation as ordinary people organize themselves to acquire land through invasion, or put direct pressure on the state to allocate resources for the basic infrastructure required for survival. This case study describes the critical role that women play in the formation, organization and success of local-level protest groups.

Acceptance of the sexual division of labour, and the home as their sphere of dominance, has meant that in many parts of Latin America women take primary responsibility for the provision of consumption needs within the family. This includes not only individual consumption needs within the household but also needs of a more collective nature at community level, with the point of residence thus extending spatially to include the surrounding neighbourhood. The extent to which it is seen as "natural" that women should assume such importance in residential-level struggle should be reflected both in the nature of their mobilization and the manner in which it is interpreted. If women's mobilization perceived as an extension of their realm of interest and power in the domestic arena, then it is most likely that it is in their roles as wives and mothers, rather than as people, that it is legitimized both by the women themselves and by their men.

The Development of Guayaquil and the Crisis of Collective Consumption
Within the Ecuadorian economy Guayaquil is the country's largest city, chief port and major centre of trade and industry. It is situated on lowlands 160 kilometres upstream from the Pacific Ocean. Historically, growth has been linked to the different phases of Ecuador's primary-export-oriented economy. As an industrial enclave, its population

growth has reflected the agricultural sector's declining capacity to retain its population as much as the city's potential to create industrial employment. It expanded rapidly during the 1970s at the time of the oil boom because of very high immigration rates, mainly from the surrounding rural areas. This helped to swell the population from 500 000 in 1960 to 1.2 million in 1982 and an estimated two million in 1988.

Guayaquil's commercial activity is focused around the 40 gridiron blocks of the original Spanish colonial city, which in the 1970s were encircled by the inner-city *turgurios* (rental tenements). To the north, separated on higher hilly ground, are the predominantly middle- and upper-income areas, while to the west and south are the tidal swamplands which provide the predominant area for low-income expansion. Settlement of this peripheral zone, known as the *suburbios* (suburbs), involved both the creation of solid land and the construction of incrementally built bamboo and timber houses linked by a complex system of catwalks. With most of the low-income population excluded, in effect, from the conventional housing market (public and private), "invasion" of the municipal-owned *suburbios* was, between 1940 and 1980, the predominant means by which access to both land and a form of shelter was obtained.

Indio Guayas is the name given by the local residents to an area of swampland, about ten blocks in size, located on the far edge of Cisne Dos. The settlement has no clear physical limits, but in 1978 it had some 3000 residents, the majority of whom belonged to the Indio Guayas neighbourhood or *barrio* committee. In 1978 Indio Guayas was a "pioneer settlement" of young upwardly mobile families, who had moved from inner-city rental accommodation. The community was representative of the lower-paid end of unskilled, non-unionized labour. The men were employed as mechanics, construction workers, tailoring outworkers, unskilled factory workers or labourers, while the women were employed as domestic servants, washerwomen, cooks sellers and dressmakers.

The motivation to "invade" this municipal floodland and acquire a 10 by 30 metre plot was primarily to own a home and thereby avoid prohibitive rents. The decision to acquire a plot was predominantly a family one. Both individuals and groups were involved in the initial process of cutting back the mangrove swamp and marking out the area. This work was carried out by men, as it was physically arduous and at times dangerous. It was only when the family occupied their plot that women became involved in the process of consolidating their home.

The majority of inhabitants (84 per cent) bought plots on which no house had been built. Consequently, this was a community heavily involved in house construction. A wide knowledge existed not only among professional construction workers but also among most family members. Women made daily repairs to their houses while living in them and children covered holes in the roof and papered the walls with newspaper to keep out the wind. The most important building materials were standardized with corrugated-iron roofs, split-cane walls, and wooden floors. Further upgrading was costly and therefore undertaken by few. It involved filling in the swamp under the house, replacing the wood floor with cement, and substituting bricks or breeze blocks for bamboo walls. Families worked on their own homes, with paid labour usually employed in the first, skilled stage of sinking and joining together the mangrove foundations on which the house rests. Although about a quarter of houses in the survey were built by paid labour, over 50 per cent were built mainly by the household, since the skills required were fairly rudimentary.

For most household construction of such a house was accomplished without major difficulties, other than sufficient cash for buying building materials. Far more problematical was the lack of basic infrastructure; it was this that caused communities to protest to the local municipality.

The Origins of Popular Participation

Community-level mobilization in the *suburbios* was neither automatic nor immediate. The development of self-help organization which occurred as areas of swampland were incrementally occupied by a heterogeneous population was the consequence of two interdependent experiences: the common experience within the community of struggling to survive in highly adverse conditions, and varying previous experience concerning the "institutionalized" procedure of petitioning political parties for services in return for votes.

Internal Factors
Plots were not always occupied immediately when acquired but were held as a future investment to be occupied when infrastructure had reached the area. The distance from the city centre, lack of electricity, running water, sewerage and above all roads, deterred families from living on their plots. Women were most reluctant to move because of the dangers to children of the perilous system of catwalks, the considerable additional burden of domestic labour under such primitive conditions and the very real fear of loneliness. It was the men, generally less concerned with issues such as these, who persuaded the family to move. But it was the women who bore the brunt, and the distress experienced by many in the early months and years should not be underestimated. Initially, walking on catwalks was so frightening that many crawled on hands and feet, venturing out as infrequently as possible. Acquiring water from the tanker or food from shops up to a mile away were costly, time-consuming and physically gruelling, with women recounting hazardous stories of wading miles through mud to acquire necessary provisions.

It was the struggle for survival in a situation where even water was a scarce and valuable commodity that forced women to develop and retain friendships with their neighbours, and gradually resulted in an increasing awareness among women of the need to try and improve the situation. Although women became aware of their common suffering, this experience itself did not always provide sufficient motivation for common action. Women did not question the fact that their responsibility for the domestic arena, which they saw as natural, made them the primary sufferers.

External Factors
The existence of a widely known procedure of petitioning for services in return for votes by self-help committees proved an important external catalyst for instigating popular participation among newly settled communities. The long history of *bario*-level committees in Guayaquil, beginning in the 1940s, was associated with a political system in which populist parties bought votes by providing infrastructure. Until the late 1960s, committees were short-lived, formed before elections and disbanded soon afterwards. It

was only in the late 1960s, with the post-Guevara tremors which shook liberal Latin America, that they took on a more "institutionalized" form. Along with the church, student, and middle-class women's organizations, which flooded the *suburbios* with dispensaries and clinics, came President Kennedy's Alliance for Progress programme, as a condition of a large United States Agency for International Development (USAID) grant for squatter upgrading, the Guayaquil Municipality was forced to create a Department of Community Development whose purpose was to assist poor communities to "fight for infrastructure". The 1972 Plan 240 to infill the mangrove swamps was organized around local *barrio* committees who formed by the hundred to ensure the arrival of infill. Although by 1976, when the project ceased for lack of funds (most committees had disbanded or existed only in name), the experience of local organization gained during this period had nevertheless been an important one for the *suburbio* inhabitants.

The Role of Women in the Formation of Barrio Committees

Barrio-level committees in the *suburbios* of Guayaquil contained both women and men members. The *barrio* committee performed a number of functions, particularly in the early stages of settlement consolidation, and it was the women members who took responsibility for much of the day-to-day work. The most important "external" function of the *barrio* committee was to petition for infrastructure, and when the infrastructure was provided, the committee had to ensure that the community's plan of work was implemented. In the committees the women were responsible for this work.

Although it was the women who urged their neighbours to form a committee, they did not automatically see themselves as leaders. Initially, women participated in protest out of desperation at their appalling living conditions. Then, out of a sense of duty, they moved into leadership positions over frustration at the corrupt management of the incumbent men presidents. Women had always formed the overwhelming majority of rank-and-file members. The committee saw itself as a group of predominantly women neighbours working together out of a common preoccupation with their living conditions. Over time, distinctions emerged between those few prepared to take on the difficult responsibility of presidentship and the majority who, for a variety of reasons, preferred to remain working at the rank-and-file level.

Since infrastructure was exchanged for votes, the number and commitment of ordinary members was critical to the success and long-term survival of the *barrio* committee. Although in most families both the men and women joined as members of the committee, it was the women who regularly participated. Where men did attend, their participation was neither regular nor reliable and was often undertaken after considerable pressure had been applied by both the committee and the women.

Political party leaders, administrative officials, and *barrio* men all saw it as natural that most of the participatory work should be undertaken by women: "because women have free time, while men are out at work". Although this may have been true for some, particularly during the daytime, it was also a convenient myth. Most women, throughout their adult lives, are involved not only in domestic and child rearing work but also in a diversity of income-earning activities, even though these are more likely to be undertaken from home. Time spent in mobilization was therefore detrimental both to domestic and to productive work, and women made considerable sacrifices, often risking their jobs as well as neglecting children, in order to participate. This attitude was reinforced by the women themselves. Just as it was natural for them to take full responsibility for domestic work in the home, women saw it as their responsibility to improve the living conditions of their family through participation in *barrio*-level mobilization. Equally they perceived themselves as benefiting most from, for instance, piped water, since the work of water collection and haulage was undertaken primarily by them.

Progress

Although the women of Indio Guayas perceived collective consumption needs in terms of infill, water, electricity, health care and education, these were not prioritized in any particular order. There was a strong sense of political pragmatism, of petitioning for the particular infrastructure they believed they would be most likely to get at any given time in exchange for votes. Since the late 1970s, when the study was undertaken, the *barrio* committee has achieved the following basic infrastructure:

- The area around and between the blocks has been infilled, though the internal area within each block has not;
- filling the swamp under the houses has been carried out by most families, individually;
- access roads surrounding the neighbouring land have replaced the catwalks;
- electricity has been installed; and
- a piped water system gets to the front of each house, though water pressure is too low to reach indoors.

To date there is still no sewerage system (households have individual septic tanks), drainage system or garbage collection.

Conclusion

Because of the escalating costs of housing programmes, site-and-service projects are not reaching low-income groups, and upgrading or other forms of self help have become more important. These rely substantially on community participation and, as the case study has shown, on the participation of women. It also shows that women participate with clearly defined objectives relating to practical gender needs such as better housing or infrastructure services — needs which are required by all the family but which women in their reproductive, productive, and community-managing roles see as their responsibility to provide.

■ What Next?
Charlie Pye-Smith and
Grazia Borrini Feyerabend

Decentralize Control over Natural Resources

For people to become active in environmental care a basic condition is that they have the authority and responsibility to do so. Much presumed "lack of care" arises because people do not feel in charge or, indeed, do not have the power to act. If a national or local government wants to involve people in the sound management of local resources, it can, first of all, review the legal basis for such an involvement. Private property of land is a well-known way of assuring local control over resources. (It does not, however, necessarily guard against abuse and waste). Communal property of land and/ or resources represents a significant alternative (Bromley and Cernea, 1989).

This is not the place to discuss the variety of legal arrangements for communal access to resources. What we wish to emphasize, however, is that private ownership is not a necessary condition for success and governments do not need to relinquish all their rights. On the contrary, a variety of co-management arrangements — such as long-term leases, limited resource-extraction permits, limited rights of use or of change of destination — are suited to combine formal ownership by the government with *people's security of access through time.* One example beyond those in the book serves to illustrate the point. In India, following the National Forest Policy of 1988, the forest departments of several states assigned to local communities the usufruct rights over their neighbouring forests. The rights included the extraction and use of all non-wood products and of a percentage share of the wood products — subject to successful forest protection and other conditions approved by the state. The local management plans were developed jointly by community organizations and state foresters, with the support of non-governmental organizations whenever necessary. The result? A clear reversal of forest degeneration and dramatic increases in productivity, all at minimal cost (Dhar et al, n d; Poffenberger, 1990).

This example — as well as several others collected in the book — suggests that governments have much to gain by decentralizing control and responsibility for local resources. The national regulatory framework can be left flexible enough to accommodate local peculiarities, but it is desirable that local regulations end up being specific and stringent (Conroy and Litvinoff, 1988; Drijver, 1990). Who is benefitting from local resources? Who is in charge, and responsible for their management? Who is directly accountable for the results? To whom? With what possible consequences? When questions such as these can be answered in a straightforward way, it is unlikely that the local environment is abandoned and degraded. As in many of our stories, local control over and responsibility for resources are the other face of local environmental care (Amalrik and Banuri, 1992).

Strengthen Local Institutions for Resource Management
Many readers will be familiar with wards, parishes, communes, *panchayats*, counties, districts and so on as their smallest units of local government. In an ideal world, government and communities merge at some point, and there is perfect coincidence of interests and intent. Sadly, this is extremely rare. In fact, it is rare even to find an explicit dialogue between many "authorities" and "communities", for instance to agree on common objectives and negotiate respective responsibilities. Many institutional arrangements for the management of resources, for instance, do not correspond to units of production and benefit. This makes little sense, since for a group of people to spend time and effort in environmental care they must perceive a clear link between the quality of management (including their work input) and the magnitude of benefits in return (Gow and VanSant, 1981; Borrini, 1991; Scoones and Matose, 1992). As pointed out by Marshall Murphree (1991) — effective care of resources may require that even single individuals providing differential inputs receive differential benefits.

An essential element of sound resource management is a local body that discusses, organizes, plans, takes action, responds on a human scale and, not least, provides for an equitable matching between inputs and benefits. Many such local bodies have existed as administrative units for centuries — examples are the community assemblies in Ecuador or the parishes in the UK. Others have only recently been recognized by state acts — such as the peasant associations in Mauritania or the development committees in Nepal. Some groups are mostly interested in the use of a particular resource, an example being the Mudialy cooperative, in Calcutta. Others, such as PACODET in Uganda, aim at a general improvement of living conditions. As elsewhere, the "local body" may not be directly in charge of resource management but has taken upon itself to convey the interests and concerns of people to appropriate authorities (Ghai, 1988; Renard, 1991; Uphof, 1991). In all cases, the important point is that local institutions exist, assume responsibility over local resources and are recognized by and accountable to both local people and national authorities. Amazingly, this essential aspect of organization — the effective link between national authorities and people — is so often ignored by the central governments and the development process.

Moreover, what in development jargon is referred to as "capacity building" rarely includes substantial attention and investments at the local level. But this is a mistake. Governments and development agencies can expect great returns if they strengthen local institutions for resource management and provide them with incentives to act. At least in part, cases are successful because local institutions have been recognized and nurtured. For instance, for years Zimtrust has been offering training, workshops and networking for the ward and community councils involved in CAMPFIRE. Similarly, leadership training by CERD played a key role in the development of effective local organizations in the Philippines. And Fundación Anai promoted local institutions in Costa Rica in many indirect ways. In their rotating fund programme, for instance, they asked communities to take collective responsibility for the individual repayment of loans, and only someone presented by a local "credit committee" was given access to loans. In this way, communities that wished their members to apply had to get organized.

Matchmake for Partnership and Support

Even when people and local institutions have a reasonable amount of control over local resources and possess the relevant skills, a community needs a catalytic impulse to get organized and act: the social equivalent of the grain of sand can be provided by leaders/organizers/facilitators who help the community pull its energies together, scout for external support and match various social actors for common goals. These leaders/facilitators can belong to the community or come from outside — moved by professional, political, religious motivations, or even by a not easily specified sense of solidarity and friendship.

In practice, what does the process entail? It can all begin by gathering community members around a project everyone easily approves and supports (such as a nursery in Costa Rica; recycling paper in Poland; or setting up a health care scheme, in Uganda). It may also begin by rallying people to solve a strongly felt problem (such as the depletion of fisheries in the Philippines, or the deterioration of trails in Nepal). Or it may begin by a systematic, interactive exploration of local needs and resources (as in participatory appraisal exercises such as the one we witnessed in Uganda). Specific action can then be agreed upon in community meetings and planning workshops. Action can also arise spontaneously because some individuals are highly motivated. The essential point is that one or more persons make it their business to catalyze the community's energy and ingenuity, and to look intelligently beyond its immediate boundary for the inputs and support that are not available locally. Such "matchmaking" usually links the community with governmental services and non-governmental support, be it from private individuals, business groups, international organizations, aid agencies, or any other body capable and willing to help.

Facilitators and matchmakers can be trained, and many development organizations are beginning to do just that. Even some aid agencies are currently examining how they can best "institutionalize" their support for PEC initiatives. Changes to a variety of elements in the work of organizations — from the attitude of professionals to disbursement procedures; from conditionality issues to programme formulation activities will have to be made (DGCS, 1991). A few governments are actively involved, for instance the government of Nepal, which is providing support to the lamas. Unfortunately this is rather uncommon (Poffenberger, n d; Peluso and Poffenberger, 1989; Gronow and Shrestha, 1990; Korten, 1980). More often than not, the grain of sand does not come from coherent governmental programmes but from the serendipitous initiative of community members, the personnel of non-governmental organizations or friends and concerned professionals from a variety of sectors.

A variety of forms of support can help a community engage in primary environmental care. Small grants, for instance, can make a world of difference. They have been used to enable community members to visit others and observe what they do, to prime local "rotating funds" or to import critical technology and tools. Similarly, credit schemes and matching funds can be used to increase a community's capital base and build upon existing knowledge and capabilities. Training in business management and technical skills allows people to begin new activities as do key material inputs such as seeds and tools. Often, legal assistance is required for communities to find out about and act upon their rights. Ongoing provision of simple and effective technical advice and technological innovations helps, as does support for communication and networking. Although the time frame of the experiences we examined varies from one year to several decades, it is the common perception of all the people we met that community initiatives fully develop over a long period, and thus require continuity of support (although not necessarily the same kind of support at various stages).

Last but not least, the success of the initiatives we encountered appears in no small measure tied to the approach and style of people involved — as both local players and external supporters. Human qualities like enthusiasm, perseverance, courage, patience, willingness to work hard, honesty, openness to new ideas and the capacity to communicate, although difficult to include in a "what next?" recipe, may be essential ingredients for replicating and spreading primary environmental care. At the root of everything well done, we always seemed to find generous people.

Make Markets Work for People

In many areas of the world, the *dominance* of market forces is a relatively recent phenomenon. Although exchange of products has been important in all human societies for thousands of years, it is only in the recent past that the fine tuning of subsistence in traditional communities has been shattered by the increasing local demand for cash. With that demand, surplus-generation and profits have become crucial in the decision-making of households and producers, with momentous consequences for local environments and communal life (Kitching, 1990). This phenomenon cannot be ignored. Moreover, it cannot be ignored that many community-based initiatives that appear sustainable and socially beneficial are related to business ventures and markets — including sophisticated and controversial international markets; and that many sound environmental-care practices require cash investments — which people are willing to make only when cash returns can be confidently expected. As a consequence, for governments and institutions interested in multiplying primary environmental care initiatives there is a clear indication that they should promote access to markets — and even create new markets wherever the local economic environment is sluggish and uncooperative. But *what kind of markets*?

Even in very remote places — as every traveller knows — there is little problem in finding soft drinks or avenues for exporting highly profitable raw materials. The markets we are talking about, however, are different. They are *regulated markets*, in which sustainable production is encouraged and an equitable flow of benefits is assured. In such markets, profits would reward those who produce with consideration for the environment and the health of workers, whose products contribute to meeting the needs of local people, and whose work creates more work in local communities. In this sense there is a great challenge ahead for policy-makers to develop and enforce appropriate regulations. To start, it is important to remove disincentives, such as low taxation for production processes that dump on society the cost of environmental damage and reduce local opportunities. Instead, products designed to respond to eco-logical *and* social criteria can be given incentives, with advantages for both producer and consumer communities and for the sustainable development of countries, much less the globe (McNeily, 1988). The same challenge applies to private and community-based business, which will hopefully respond with ingenious and socially responsible enterprise.

Among the ecological and social criteria that could identify positive initiatives are: the sustainability of production processes; the promotion of biological diversity and the protection of unique habitats and environmental functions; the strict compliance with public health regulations; the creation of jobs and the enhancement of local skills; the creation of widely spread rather than individual benefits; the reinvestment of profits in the producer community; and the promotion of community well-being and cultural identity. Beyond such general considerations, the meaning of a "regulated market" must be left unspecified — it is too dependent on the national economic situation and social background to be described in detail outside a specific context. Such markets, however, can be expected to reconcile the liberalization of trade (Repetto, 1993) with full protection and support to valuable ecological and socio-cultural environments.

It would be naïve to disregard the fact that a process by which communities acquire control over local resources, organize themselves in management institutions, strengthen their capabilities, enter into a variety of partnerships and gain full access to regulated markets, has fundamental political implications. Yet, this is not a political treatise. We gladly leave to others the task of articulating a coherent political message based on primary environmental care — if any can be. We only wanted to tell the stories — fascinating for us — of communities who have taken the future into their own hands. We offered our reflections on how their example can be replicated and expanded upon. They offered us many reasons to hope.

References

Amalrik, F and Banuri, T (1992) *Population, Environment and Responsibility*, IUCN, Pakistan, Islamabad

Borrini, G (ed) (1991) *Lessons Learned in Community-based Environmental Management*, ICHM, Rome

Bromley, D W and Cernea, M M (1989) *The Management of Common Property Natural Resources*, Discussion paper no 57, The World Bank, Washington, DC

Conroy, C and M Litvinoff (1988) *The Greening of Aid: Sustainable Livelihoods in Practice*, Earthscan, London

DGCS (1991) *Primary Environmental Care: Proposte Operative per la Cooperazione Italiana*, DGCS, Rome

Dhar, S K, Gupta, J R and Sarin, M (n d) "Participatory Forest Management in the Shivalik Hills: Experiences of the Haryana Forest Department", working paper no 5, Ford Foundation, New Delhi

Drijver, C (1990) "People's Participating in Environmental Projects in Developing Countries", *IIED Dryland Networks Programme Papers*, no 17, IIED, London

Ghai, D (1988) "Participatory Development: Some Perspectives from Grass-Roots Experiences", Discussion paper 5, UNRISD, Geneva

Gow, D D and J VanSant (1981) "Beyond the Rhetoric of Rural Development Participation: How Can It Be Done?", IRD Working Paper no 9, Development Alternatives, Washington, DC

Gronow, J and N K Shrestha (1990) *From Policing to Participation: Reorientation of Forest Department Field Staff in Nepal*, Nepalese Ministry of Agriculture and Winrock International, Kathmandu

Kitching, G (1990) *Development and Underdevelopment in Historical perspective: Population, Nationalism and Industrialization*, Routledge, London

Korten, D C (1980) "Community Organization and Rural Development: A Learning Process Approach", *Public Administration Review*, September–October, pp480–511

McNeily, J A, (1988) *Economic and Biological Diversity: Developing and Using Economic Incentives to Conserve Biological Resources*, IUCN, Gland, Switzerland

Murphree, M (1991) *Communities as Institutions for Resource Management*, Centre for Applied Social Sciences, University of Zimbabwe, Harare

Peluso, N and Poffenberger, M (1989) "Social Forestry in Java: Reorientating Management Systems", *Human Organization*, vol 48, no 4, pp333–44

Poffenberger, M (n d) "Joint Forest Management in West Bengal: The Process of Agency Change", *Sustainable Forest Management Working Paper*, no 9, Ford Foundation, New Delhi

—— (ed) (1990) *Forest Management Partnerships: Regenerating India's Forests*, Ford Foundation, New Delhi

Renard, Y. (1991) "Institutional Challenges for Community-Based Management in the Caribbean", *Nature and Resources*, vol 27, no 4, pp4–9

Repetto, R (1993) "Trade and Environment Policies: Achieving Complementarity and Avoiding Conflicts", *WRI Issues and Ideas*, July

Scoones, I and F Matose (1992) "Woodland Management in Zimbabwe: Tenure and Institutions for Sustainable Natural Resource Use", *Zimbabwe National Forest Policy Review*, Harare

Uphof, N (1991) "Local Institutions and Participation for Sustainable Development", *IIED Gatekeepers Series*, no 31, London

Organizing for Change: People Power and the Role of Institutions
Robin Sharp

The nature and scale of changes needed in all countries to achieve sustainable human development are increasingly well documented and understood. Many of these changes — political, technical and social — are spelled out in other chapters of this book. Critical to any chances of success in implementing them, however, is the complex chain of organizational mechanisms through which both the broad objectives and the specific planning targets must be articulated.

While they are in principle convergent, the pathways to sustainable development start from many points of the compass, often unconnected and mutually invisible. To be clear where they should take us, it is essential to understand the processes and the different levels of institutional machinery on which progress will depend.

This reading therefore seeks to identify some criteria for a system approach to sustainability. I ask what is meant by and what can be achieved through people's participation, how it grows out of democratic processes, how those processes in turn depend on a strong and appropriate structure of institutions, and how those institutions grow from and are supported by a root system of human resources.

The questions I shall discuss here are (1) how participatory decision-making and representative institutions can best be established in countries of the South with very diverse political and social traditions, and (2) whether the current approaches of international agencies and donors are moving in the right direction. Some of the issues raised are not equally applicable to all regions; particular weight has been given to the situation of sub-Saharan Africa, bearing in mind the current wave of political change in that region and the concentration there of foreign advice and interventions. Many of these issues, nevertheless, are of relevance to people and institutions in all countries.

Sustainable Development: The People's Role
The concept of sustainable development embodies a belief that people should be able to alter and improve their lives in accordance with criteria which take account of the

needs of others and which protect the planet and future generations. Thus people's rights and responsibilities form the crux of any discussion of sustainability.

People's movements in many countries have assumed the responsibility for challenging unsustainable systems or practices — the rape of tropical rainforests, industrial pollution, high-cost technologies for poor people or inequities in the distribution of wealth and resources. Where people have become aware of threats to their own or the world's future, these movements have accepted the responsibility of mobilizing to oppose them — sometimes even at the risk of their lives.

As for people's rights, the commitment of governments and development agencies to "popular participation" as a necessary ingredient of sustainable development has been enshrined in the Arusha Declaration on Popular Participation in Development (1990) and the Manila Declaration on People's Participation and Sustainable Development (1989). In one sense, this assertion of the right to participation does no more than reiterate a citizen's entitlement as set forth in the Universal Declaration of Human Rights, adopted by the UN General Assembly in 1948. However, its progressive elevation to a place of prominence on the development agenda reflects two more empirical factors.

The most recent impetus has been the upsurge of public demands for democracy in many countries and the consequent demise of repressive regimes. Second, and over a longer period, a wealth of evidence has been accumulated that development projects designed and implemented without the full involvement of the intended beneficiaries have had a high rate of failure — and conversely, that projects planned with them from the outset, on an appropriate scale and using their skills and resources, have had a relatively high rate of success.

Aid agencies have drawn the lessons from this experience and sought to incorporate participatory principles into their projects. While this is undoubtedly an advance, it is not yet sufficient evidence that aid interventions are enabling the people they mobilize to engage in a genuinely sustainable process of self-improvement. Sometimes a project is described as "sustainable" on the grounds simply of its survival beyond the phase of external support; but neither this, nor even its "success" measured by limited project goals, necessarily implies true sustainability.

Over and above these factors, there are two more fundamental arguments for people now to be demanding their voice in the future. Both have to do with the physical limits to expansionism, which has historically been at the core of the human experiment and which has provided an escape-valve when pressures have threatened to explode a society's stability.

One is that humanity's room for spatial expansion, hitherto taken for granted, has come to an end. Among other things, this means that the poorest of the world's people, who could previously as a last resort distance themselves from the powerful minorities seeking to exploit them or their resources, now have nowhere left to go. They must stand their ground or lose the struggle for survival, as the plight of indigenous peoples in many countries bleakly testifies.

The other argument concerns the limits of life support available from the biosphere. It challenges, on scientific grounds, the implicit assumption that development can mean a steady growth in material living standards for four-fifths of the world's people without curbing the consumption of the rest. While this analysis is not uncontested, its proponents insist that "sustainable development must be development without growth — but with population control and wealth redistribution — if it is to be a serious attack on poverty" (Daly, 1991).

Faced with these actual or anticipated limits, many of those concerned to achieve sustainable management of our "global village" have come to believe that democratic processes are essential for change, given that privileged minorities controlling power — nationally and internationally — will seldom if ever countenance the needed reforms.

The failure to institute such reforms up to now has left many governments in the South largely unaccountable for their actions, especially their massive accumulation of international debt, which is a principal reason for millions of people continuing to die of hunger and for the net flow of funds from South to North having reached US $50 billion a year. And if the borrowers are to blame, where is the accountability of the Northern and international lending agencies, who have been accessories — wittingly or otherwise — to massive misappropriation of their funds? More effective people's participation is necessary at both ends of the North–South axis if the costs of adjustment to a sustainable society are to be equitably shared and not simply loaded on to those least able to bear the burden.

For all the benefits they can induce, however, participatory systems are not a panacea. Consultations among NGOs in advance of the 1992 UNCED have led to their identifying a list of five criteria for sustainable development: Who initiates? Who decides? Who participates? Who benefits? And who controls? A report on the consultations added: "If the answer to all these questions is "the people", then *projects* can be assured of sustainability" (*Ecoforum*, 1991, emphasis added). This underlines an important distinction to be made between project-level participation — on a scale where direct democracy is often possible — and that in wider political fora, where the same cannot apply. Confusion frequently arises from use of the same term to mean different things (CWS and LWR, 1991). Participatory systems have up to now worked best at community or project level, where there are bonds of solidarity among the people and where, in the best cases, the five NGO criteria cited above can be met. But where they are introduced at a higher (for example, national) level to replace a rigid centralized authority, such systems — which are then necessarily representative, not direct — may unleash suppressed tensions and wreck the equilibrium previously maintained between rival social groups.

Whether at community or national level, for people to participate actively and without reward in public affairs costs them time and effort. In some cases it may well also entail financial or physical risk for those who find themselves in opposition to the majority. It is therefore not surprising if most people prefer to leave the business to others. Even in established democracies, the majority of citizens will only participate on a given issue when it directly effects their personal interests or seriously affronts their sense of justice. When we speak of participation, then what we should mean is the *opportunity* to participate.

This, in turn, raises the awkward question of what conditions constitute adequate opportunity. Many of these are culture or subject specific, but the most obvious include:

- full access to information on policy issues and development plans;

- freedom of association to permit the discussion of issues by all interested groups within the community; and
- regular meetings at which elected officials or the representatives of official agencies can receive and respond to the views of the community and be held accountable for the actions taken on its behalf (Gran, 1983).

These conditions, it goes without saying, will need to be realized in a wide variety of institutional forms, allowing for the forms themselves to change.

In looking to the future, there is a temptation to seek scenarios that describe a stable-state sustainable society, not least in respect of the institutions we believe would be necessary to maintain it. However, sustainable development cannot be a fixed destination; rather it is a process, as part of which our institutions and human resources can be moulded to meet the perceived priorities of the time. Those priorities will also change, depending partly on the extent to which they prove achievable and partly on the emergence of others that may seem more urgent.

In the end, the opportunity for people's participation in any society is determined by the quality of civil and political rights that they are accorded: in a word, political freedom. It is thus significant that the United Nations Development Programme's *Human Development Report*, in its initial work to construct an index of freedoms by country, detects a high correlation between human development and human freedom (UNDP, 1991).

Participation and Empowerment

When it is decided by the power brokers — usually governments or large donor agencies — that the people must be given a say in projects that affect them, their first step has often been to devise a process of consultation. The people are told what is to be done and their views are invited, but they are given no access to the decision-making process. When this is found inadequate, they are offered participation — a place, but often little real influence — in the policy-making or planning committees.

For the people to take charge of their own destiny, therefore, something more than participation is required. To encompass that "something more", the development community has adopted the term *empowerment*.

Empowerment literally means the granting of power to an individual or group for a specified purpose. But where is this power supposed to come from? The usual assumption is that it has to be transferred from a controlling authority, which implies a zero-sum transaction. And since those who hold power are seldom ready to relinquish it, some commentators suggest that "empowerment" may need to mean the struggle of the disadvantaged to achieve it (Hasan, 1991).

But there is also another kind of power that can be created where there was none before. This is empowerment through ideas, through education or, more specifically, through a process such as "education for consciousness", the method developed and spread in the 1970s by the Brazilian educator Paulo Freire (Freire, 1970, 1973). Here, empowerment is a positive-sum game, enabling people to understand not only why they are poor or disenfranchised but also what they can do about it — without waiting for concessions from authority.

This kind of empowerment is also frequently stimulated through participatory appraisal exercises at community level, giving villagers a clear sense of how they can improve their lives in practical ways. Much can be done to raise the consciousness of the poor and to help them understand the systems that restrict or oppress them, so that a confrontation with authority, if and when necessary, is more likely to yield benefits.

The Democratic Imperative

At the beginning of the 1990s, capitalist democracy appears to have emerged the victor from more than four decades of global confrontation with socialist central planning. Authoritarian regimes in many countries have suddenly found themselves facing a tidal wave of demands for civil liberties and a multi-party political system. A number have already gone under, and others seem certain to succumb. An era of rigid, autocratic governments in eastern Europe, much of Africa and other Third World countries appears to be coming to an end. Jubilant crowds in capitals from Bucharest to Bamako (Mali) have celebrated the demise of entrenched dictatorships.

Thus for many countries deprived of them hitherto, some measure of democracy and popular participation may now be on the way. But is it time yet to rejoice? As the nations of eastern Europe have quickly discovered, freedom from tyranny is no panacea for social and economic ills. The lesson will be much harder for emerging democracies in the South, especially those in Africa with scant resources to manage the transition. Therefore, if participatory systems are an essential underpinning for sustainable development, an assessment of the prospects for progress must begin with a review of what participation-in-development has meant and accomplished up to now.

Democracy as a system of government has had a chequered history. Following its codification by the city-states of ancient Greece, government by the people was subsequently forgotten in Europe for the best part of 2000 years, though it found expression in different forms in pre-colonial cultures as far apart as India and North America. From the sixteenth century and earlier, many Indian villages were self-sufficient and autonomous, governed by an unofficial council of elders and a number of village functionaries (Banuri, 1991).

When revived in a modified form in Europe and North America in the nineteenth and twentieth centuries, the democratic principles of the colonial powers were not generally extended to the governance of their territories in the southern hemisphere. So when these colonies in Asia and Africa gained their political independence after the Second World War — nearly a century and a half after most of South America — many gravitated towards the alternative model of the socialist bloc, which at the time seemed to offer many social and political benefits.

By the mid-1970s, halfway through the United Nations' Second Development Decade, many leading development thinkers had become aware that the conventional strategies propounded up to that time were not addressing the real problems. In 1975 an international team produced the outlines for what they called "another develop-ment" — needs-oriented, endogenous, self-reliant, ecologically sound and based on structural transformations. For this kind of development, it was stressed, "whether governments are enlightened or not, there is no substitute for the people's own, truly democratic organization" (Dag Hammarskjöld Foundation, 1975).

In fact, for the next 15 years, virtually until 1990, the international development community chose to turn a blind eye to the undemocratic nature of many governments in the South; indeed, the superpowers and some other Northern governments competed to support them for reasons of geopolitical or commercial interest. One result was that people's participation — and the development of indigenous institutions on which it depends — was in many countries conceivable only in the context of individual programmes or projects. Another was that independent groups embraced the idea of networking as a means of enabling people to participate in development planning and activities without being confined by the bureaucratic straitjacket of more formal institutions. National and international networks sprang up in many regions, providing an alternative institutional model for development promotion.

Over the past decade this commitment to participatory development has made significant progress, most notably in the practical work of non-governmental agencies and in methodologies devised by the more progressive research institutions. For many of the former it is now standard practice to try to involve the intended beneficiaries in the design, planning and management of projects, while the latter have developed a range of user-friendly techniques for participatory planning, such as farmer participatory research and rapid rural appraisal (RRA) (see McCracken, Pretty and Conway, 1988).

The hallmark of RRA is its reliance on simple techniques which can be understood and used by villagers themselves and which do not depend on literacy. They include the drawing of resource maps, seasonal calendars and diagrams to illustrate intra-village relationships, the ranking of people's priorities and preferences, and the use of folklore, songs and poetry, which can reveal much about the community's history, values and customs. Use of these techniques has spread with remarkable speed over the past five years, and nowhere more dramatically than in India (Pretty and Sandbrook, 1991).

These techniques represent an important advance. A difficult question, however, concerns the extent to which participatory development projects will be tolerated — or can retain their integrity — within a non-participatory political system. There are many countries where such projects have thrived at community level even though the national government has been anti-democratic; examples include countries as diverse as Kenya, Pakistan and Indonesia. Participatory projects have spread not only in the rural areas, where the governments in question could perhaps afford to ignore them, but also in urban areas, taking up problems such as housing and health care, water and sanitation.

Many centralist governments have not stood in the way of small-scale participatory initiatives, but there is a variable borderline beyond which such projects will find themselves in conflict with the government's assertion of its prerogative in policy-making. The viability of local-level participation in the absence of a positive enabling environment can only be measured on a case-by-case basis, but it will depend significantly on the spread of similar initiatives (strength in numbers) and the level up to which participation is permitted in the pyramid of social organizations.

In government-to-government aid programmes, with some honourable exceptions, the approach to people's participation has generally been to add on a token consultation process. The affected populations are then invited to give their views on a project already decided and about which they usually have little information. Some donor agencies are now moving this consultative process up to the preliminary planning phase, so the people's views may be taken into account; but consultation (an interview, a questionnaire) is not participation. The World Bank recently produced detailed guidelines for its staff on how to involve NGOs and community organizations in assessing the environmental impact of its projects (World Bank, 1991). The guidelines were presented as a recipe for the "participation" of these groups; but while they reflected much thought and sensitivity on appropriate methods of consultation they stopped well short of suggesting any direct involvement for such groups in project decision-making.

Who Defines Democracy?

In Africa, the "lost decade" of the 1980s has been described as synonymous with the failure of the state, which in its current form "has not managed to promote either development or popular participation" (ACORD, 1990). But the start of the 1990s has seen dramatic changes. Apart from the demise of nearly a dozen dictators, giving a new lease of life to the domino theory, potentially the most far-reaching change has been the decision of several major aid-giving nations to make their development assistance conditional on the recipient countries' progress towards democracy.

This new condition has been made possible by the ending of the Cold War, removing much of the rationale for shoring up unconstitutional client regimes. Whether or not such a political condition is considered to infringe a country's sovereignty, the pragmatic question is one of what kind of democracy it demands. Will the conditions imposed by the aid-givers really promote the empowerment of the people? The omens so far are not altogether encouraging.

To put first things first, there is now an authentic democratic groundswell of public opinion in many of the countries of the South themselves. For much of Africa, in particular, this opens up radical possibilities of renewal from within: the first chance, it could be argued, for the people of that region to redefine the parameters of their political organization since the pre-colonial era.

This process of renewal already has its own dynamic, independent of external pressures which may seek to reinforce it. These pressures may be helpful, where their purpose is to open up the range of available options. A measure of conditionality attached to human rights, for example, may be needed to deter governments from using political repression to protect themselves from the consequences of economic liberalization.

But pressure by Northern donors may equally prove counter-productive if they attempt to go beyond this to prescribe specific solutions, and this is what is happening at the present time. Furthermore, as commentators in the USA have noted, there is an assumption — central to the discussions of democratization among Northern policy-makers — that democracy and a free market are structurally linked (CWS and LWR, 1991). This again poses the question: are we all talking about the same thing?

For policy-makers brought up under a Western parliamentary form of government, the need for more than one political party to provide the checks and balances of a democratic system appears self-evident. Through the semblance is often greater that the reality, it seems to be the essential ingredient for public choice. As such, some Northern development agencies have adopted an almost evangelical fervour in urging multi-party democracy upon Southern countries looking for a new way forward. He is reminded of the words of Aldous Huxley (1927) more than 60 years ago when he observed: "For vast numbers of people the idea of democracy has become a religious idea, which it is a duty to try to carry into practice in all circumstances, regardless of the practical requirements of each particular case."

In the context of Africa today, one knowledgeable observer notes that "blanket demands for the rapid introduction of multi-party systems along Western lines do not always do justice to the complexity of the situation" (Hofmeier, 1991). That complexity includes several socio-political factors which differentiate the African from the Western reality. In particular, there is the risk of ethnic and/or religious antagonisms being manipulated and sharpened by the creation of competing political parties. Although various African leaders have found it convenient to invoke this as a justification of one-party rule, the danger of factional conflict is in many cases real — as, for example, in the case of Mali, where the overthrow of dictatorship has led to the creation of more than 40 political parties and aggravated hostility between the majority Bambara and the nomadic Tuareg of the north.

Quite apart from such inherent obstacles to political transformation, there is evidence that external pressures which stress form (for example multi-partyism) rather than substance make it fairly easy for autocratic rulers to construct a deceptive facade of democracy to satisfy them. Free elections present no problem; gerrymandering can ensure the desired result. Decentralization is easy; power is devolved to those who will do what they are told. And as Julius Nyerere has noted, corrupt governments can fearlessly assign their friends as puppeteers to run pseudo-independent political parties. In short, the forms of democratic practice are easily fudged. Even a genuine commitment to multi-party politics may only have the effect of segmenting the existing ruling class. Without a range of other measures, there is no guarantee that it will do anything to empower the people as a whole.

A further thorny question for those carrying the banner of sustainable development is whether governments introducing democratic systems will be more or less able to commit themselves to the kind of long-term development strategies their countries need. As in the West, short-term electoral opportunism can be expected to come to the fore, offsetting in varying degrees the gains of a more open and participatory system. With a time horizon of five years or less, elected governments face the inexorable logic that jam today will buy more votes than ovens for bread tomorrow. The nation's long-term economic health and the rights of future generations are not seen as the issues for a winning political manifesto.

The conclusion may be drawn that while sustainable development requires a participatory political process, the imposition of unfamiliar democratic forms without the necessary checks and balances in place is liable to prove socially divisive and counter-productive. What is needed, then, from the external supporters of political renewal in the South is less emphasis on form and more thoughtful attention to substance — that is, practical efforts to lay the groundwork for a pluralist society. As one distinguished African commentator has noted: "The needed transformation in the political process goes beyond multi-partyism or concessions granted by the government. It is necessary to strengthen civil society at all levels including peasants, workers and student movements, NGOs, professional associations, academic groups, etc" (Dambia, 1991).

A first appropriate step for external agencies in this process would be a constant and thorough monitoring of the observance of human rights. Related areas of attention should cover

> many different freedoms and institutions, such as the maintenance of the rule of law, the compulsory accountability of government bodies, the prevention of uncontrolled nepotism and other patronage, permission of a true pluralism of ideas, the unimpeded existence of different associations, interest groups and a free press, and finally as much separation as possible between parties (or the party) and the state or between the political and economic spheres.
>
> (Hofmeier, 1991)

To these could be added a campaign of public information and education, needed in many countries to raise people's awareness of the implications of an evolving democratic process and to give them the basic conceptual tools for participation.

The "Governance" Debate

Along with the new donor commitment to democracy in development has come a critical spotlight on the structure and efficiency of institutions in the developing world which are needed to support it. This debate on "good governance" was initiated by the World Bank in its long-term perspective study of sub-Saharan Africa (World Bank, 1989). While provoking controversy — and with good reason — it has done much to generate awareness that the best-laid plans for sustainable development will go nowhere without adequate institutional mechanisms to formulate policies and implement them.

At one level, the World Bank's concerns can be seen to focus primarily on the efficiency of economic management. In its long-term study emphasis is placed on the need for a "leaner, better disciplined, better trained and more motivated public service", public enterprises with managerial autonomy and monitorable performance indicators, and a greater role for local government. At another level, however, behind the assertion that "better governance requires political renewal", the World Bank's analysis is seen by some critics as highly ideological, suggesting that Western liberal democracy is the only path to development.

Put simply, an equation can be formulated to show that good governance = good decision-makers + good decisions + good implementation. And few would argue with the World Bank's general contention that the requirements include the rule of law, public accountability and the free flow of information. But beyond this, critics detect a tendency to write one blanket prescription for all countries — the same failure to disaggregate according to national and local conditions which they consider a principal flaw of the structural adjustment programmes of the 1980s.

So far the debate on governance has raised more questions than it has answered. For instance, harsh economic reforms demanded by the International Monetary Fund (IMF) and the World Bank in Africa have been more easily and effectively undertaken by authoritarian regimes, which have frequently imposed even more stringent controls to push the policies through. Furthermore, the budget cuts introduced with these reforms have often resulted in near-impossible working conditions in government, leading to a "brain drain" and yet lower performance by the very institutions on which the eventual outcome of the reforms depends. And Northern agencies have so far failed to come forward with offers of special help for governments prepared to initiate democratic reforms in difficult economic conditions.

Organizational Frameworks

On the basis of the foregoing analysis, we should now look at the organizational framework or structures which are needed if sustainable development policies are to work in practice. There are two fundamental questions to be asked about the direction of institutional change in the context of sustainability:

- What kind of democratic processes and machinery are necessary to unshackle the productive energies of the Third World populations and to convince them that new efforts will be for their own benefit?
- What are the conditions required to make such processes work?

What Processes?

People's participation is a multiform and dynamic process; it is not something that can be instituted simply by legislation, even though this will in most cases be a necessary condition. To have democratic rights on paper in no way guarantees the ability to exercise them. The process is multiform in the sense that it cannot be initiated from a single starting-point and achieved by a linear progression. An NGO in Borneo, Burundi or Brazil may want to operate in a participatory manner, but will be blocked at the start of its project — beneficiaries at community level are subject to cultural, political or economic domination by traditional chiefs, politicians or merchants — or if the central government denies the NGO access to information and refuses collaboration with its own extension services. Based on a case study from Peru, one analysis of citizen participation emphasizes that it must be understood within the context of political and governmental institutions that are complex and shifting, in which strange alliances abound and in which the motives to participate are conflicting (Peattie, 1990). Despite the complexities, democratic processes for sustainable development must *start from where the people are,* in terms of both place and socio-cultural environment. That this basic condition remains a dead letter in many parts of the world (and is broken by a good number of the model Western democracies) can be attributed essentially to two factors:

- over-concentration of political, commercial or social power in the hands of small minorities; and
- the resultant giantism of centralized institutions and top-heavy bureaucracies unable to respond either to needs or to opportunities.

However, cracks have recently been appearing in many of the monolithic national structures that control people's development in the South. Some interpret them as signs of a global trend towards decentralization and people power: perhaps even the "paradigm shift" for which some of the more progressive development thinkers have long been scanning the horizon.

Decentralization is said to be an idea whose time has come (Banuri, 1991). But how widespread is the empirical evidence for change in this direction? Without doubt, the strongest single impulse during the 1980s was provided by the structural adjustment programmes requiring many Southern governments to cut back social services and to divest themselves of unprofitable enterprises. Some cuts have left a vacuum; others led to a delegation of responsibilities to provincial and local levels of government but gave them little room to be more than executing agencies for the centre. Very few provided for a real transfer of power to the local agencies best placed to fill the gap, whether governmental or other.

Meanwhile, as illustrated by many examples in the present volume, a mass of evidence has been accumulated to show that decentralized development schemes are almost invariably those with the best track record. In most cases, though, these are schemes initiated at community or project level, and there is still little conclusive evidence that power relinquished by central governments will percolate to the grass roots.

Advocates of decentralization also have to overcome a number of objections from different quarters — for example, that it may encourage anarchy, that coordination between agencies and the enforcement of rules or laws will be more difficult, and that the rights of individuals or smaller groups will be hard to protect (Banuri, 1991). These are not concerns to be minimized, but assuming they can be satisfactorily resolved, action will be needed at various levels to promote a decentralized development model. More research is needed to define appropriate policies for international agencies and national governments. Better training is required for extension workers to develop strategies and programmes with the people, and for officials at national, intermediate and local levels to prepare and engage them in new ways of working and new inter-level relationships.

One important consequence of a shift in rights and responsibilities from central government to the local level should be an improvement in the management of resources — human, physical and financial. But for the system to work in this way, a local community must be able to obtain decision-making power over its own affairs. In other words, there must be an enabling environment — in particular, a framework of law and an organizational infrastructure though which representative bodies at community level can inform themselves on issues of the day and then transmit their views or decisions both to other communities and to the higher authorities. For this infrastructure to be effective, three essential requirements must be borne in mind:

- *transparency*, which means that the processes of decision-making must be open to public view and thus be seen to be free of interference from special interests;
- *accountability*, not only in the financial sense to guard against the poor management or misappropriation of funds, but also politically to ensure that agreed policies and programmes are carried through; and
- *freedom of information*, which requires independence for the press and other news media so that the people's right to participate in public affairs is backed up by the right to know.

What Conditions?

To make the necessary provision for these rights and responsibilities, governments must demonstrate their commitment to popular participation on a number of fronts:

- by establishing a proper legislative framework to give their commitment the force of law and by strengthening the integrity and powers of the judiciary in whatever ways are required to ensure compliance;
- by issuing instructions to public agencies and employees to ensure that legislation is respected, by providing any resources needed to reform existing institutions and practices, and by monitoring progress and publishing regular reports to highlight areas of success and/or difficulty; and
- by providing education and skills training at the community, district and provincial levels to produce an adequate cadre of trained and well-motivated people who will understand the values of, and be competent to manage, a participatory system.

The term "multi-partyism" is often used to imply that a political system that freely allows the establishment of political parties will, by definition, be democratic. This is a dangerous over-simplification. A multi-party system provides better protection for freedom of the individual, but it is not in itself enough. Just as important are the strength, orientation and credibility of the organizations that stand between the ordinary citizen and the state: the village committee, the rural workers' association, the schoolteachers' union, the handicrafts cooperative, the federation of women's groups, the national NGO consortium and many more.

It goes without saying that if these intermediate organizations are weak they will be poorly placed to represent the interests of those they speak for in any participatory system; indeed, for their constituents the system will not function. They must be strong in order to command credibility with their members/supporters and also with the higher organs of government with which they deal.

A good example is the NGO consortium of Zimbabwe, VOICE, which grew out of a pre-independence welfare organization and until recently experienced declining support among its members. Many felt that VOICE was unable to represent their interests effectively and that this restricted their scope for participation in development policy issues at national level. Under a recent restructuring and with a new name the National Association of NGOs (NANGO) — the consortium has adopted a new constitution and a centralized management structure, providing for more effective involvement of its members at all levels. A renewed sense of optimism and commitment is already evident.

Even with far greater human and technical resources, many social institutions considered to be the backbone of democracy in the North fail to meet the criteria of real participation. In countries of the South newly embarking on a democratic course, few of the preconditions exist for participation at the national level; there may nevertheless be room to build on traditional forms of collective decision-making at community level, which have the advantage of being established and well understood.

The Role of Institutions

People in the environment/development business are good at inventing the kind of magic passwords — such as "participatory appraisal", "good governance" and "sustainability" itself — that punctuate this chapter. Though reality lags behind, they give us a comforting sense of being on the right track. But what is needed to achieve the kind of harmonious balance implied by this occult vocabulary?

First and foremost, most analysts agree, is the need for effective machinery to carry and convert the sustainable development model from theory to practice. In simple terms, what is required is an interlocking network of institutions capable of acting as a power grid to harness and distribute a nation's human energy. Without such a matrix to articulate and give coherence to people's aspirations and efforts, no development can be built to last.

Scarcely more than a generation ago, India epitomized the misery of the Third World with widespread hunger and seemingly irreversible poverty. Today, more than 300 million Indians are still extremely poor, but the country has become the world's eighth largest industrial power, due in significant measure to its highly developed organizational infrastructure, which includes, from village level upwards, several thousand non-governmental groups active in every field of social and economic concern.

In other countries, however, and most notably in Africa, the development of formal institutions has until recently been confined to organs of central government and the ruling party. In the past, institution-building projects in the South by large aid agencies have also frequently been too short in duration and too narrow in their objectives.

A World Bank publication, acknowledging that institutional development is a slow process, says that its most successful attempts have been over long periods, "usually several decades". Institutional projects, which at first concentrated on only one or two issues, were found not to work very well; however, even when introduced into integrated rural or urban programmes they have still tended to produce poor results. Significantly, the most progress has been made in sectors of "high specificity" — such as finance, industry and advance technology, where standards and performance can be measured with precision — and the least in social or "people-oriented" activities such as rural development and health care (Israel, 1987).

This account of the World Bank's experience starts from a rather narrow definition of institutional development as being "the process of improving the ability of institutions to make effective use of the human and financial resources available". Arguably it should have the more fundamental purpose of evaluating the relevance of institutions — both individually and in relation to others — in addressing economic or social needs. Only with such terms of reference will institutions be identified that have outlived their purpose or, perhaps, had doubtful reasons to exist in the first place. The point is important because institutions are not a neutral factor in the development process; they represent values, which in turn represent the interests of some political or social group. As a consequence they can be highly exploitative. One school of thought maintains that in today's institutionalized society, health, learning, dignity, independence and creative endeavour are defined as little more than the performance of the institutions that claim to serve these ends (Illich, 1970).

In seeking to strengthen the institutional base for sustainable development, therefore, care must first be taken to ensure that the values are right and that both the scale and the orientation of any institution are appropriate. Only then is it time to address the technical questions about effective use of resources — and here again it must be remembered that the transfer of scientific, technical or managerial expertise to a given organization will not be enough to enhance its performance if constraints on its operation (upstream) or its outputs (downstream) remain unchanged.

321

So how should we visualize the kinds of institution that will support sustainable patterns of development?

The Micro Level

At community level, a viable institution will be one that represents people's ideas, interests and/or needs, which has their confidence and the power to communicate their views effectively in dealings with higher authorities. This presupposes a degree of decentralization of decision-making, and it assumes a capacity of both leaders and members of the community to take advantage of their rights. It requires that local institutions have access to information about national development and resource-use policies, plus the skills to interpret this information in order to formulate realistically their own expectations.

Local organizations must be the bedrock of any participatory development process. As well as giving people some say in the policy decisions that affect them, they can mobilize local resources, give better representation to women and adapt externally designed programmes to local conditions. Whether urban or rural, formal or informal, local organizations are among the most important and active in shaping their environment and can be crucial for sustainable resource use (Pretty and Sandbrook, 1991).

What, then, is needed to promote the development of institutions at the micro level and to facilitate their work? Before anything else, the right to organize. On this point one commentator has stressed that for the people to be empowered, the people must be "created" through institutions or collective organization. Others cite needs for cooperation with government agencies and technical assistance, while a study of housing and health in Third World cities lists four conditions for promoting community participation: representative governments at all levels; local government support; the adoption of a more community-based approach by government programmes; and the introduction of "community facilitators" to liaise with the government and other agencies.

The Meso Level

At the intermediate levels of social, economic and political organization — that wide stratum sandwiched between government and the grass roots — a more complex mix of technical, managerial and information-handling skills is needed to make the institutional machinery effective. In between the macro and the micro, this *meso* level of institutions includes provincial and district authorities, cooperatives, research and training institutions, the small-scale private sector, trade unions, religious groups and a range of independent, non-profit organizations. For this sector to function effectively in the national interest, it must cultivate the ability to face both ways: to interpret the grass roots to the centre and vice versa. This role is well established in certain countries of the South, but it is something new in those where the transmission of power has hitherto been unidirectional. It therefore calls for many new skills on the part of those who should provide a key interface between policy-makers and the mass of the people.

Three important elements in the meso-level infrastructure are federations of community groups and local government, both of which may straddle the micro-meso line, and NGOs. National and provincial federations of poor farmers or community organizations have developed in many countries. They range from the Federation des Groupements Naam, supporting as many as 200 000 peasant members in Burkina Faso, to the National Coordinating Body of Mexico's Urban Popular Movement (CONAMUP), an umbrella for dozens of urban groups throughout the country. Such federations can have a key role in mobilizing and sharing resources available within the movement, as well as providing an effective front for interaction and negotiation with government and external research or aid agencies (Bebbington, 1991).

A recurrent message of this book is that sustainable practices require a transfer of power and responsibility from central government to the local level. Given the importance that this attaches to the functions of local government, much will need to be done before most city, town and village administrations in the South are equipped for the task.

Decentralization has most often meant increased responsibilities for local government without any increase in its already inadequate financial resources or decision-making authority. In most urban centres, government already has no more than a minor role in housing construction, water supply, road building or other basic services — and in worse-case situations local government can have a negative influence, repressing community organizations and favouring investments that benefit a small elite.

Improving the quality and resources of local government should thus be a priority in any sustainable development strategy. Quality means that such authorities must be elected and accountable to the community, having well-defined powers commensurate with their responsibility for community affairs. To ensure an adequate degree of autonomy, local governments must also have access to independent sources of revenue — something that many national governments, and not only those in the South, do their best to resist.

Across most countries of Latin America, Asia and Africa, NGOs — either foreign or indigenous — have over the past two decades become principal actors in development at the meso level. At best they have proved more flexible, more innovative and more ready to introduce participatory approaches than official organizations. They have also successfully challenged many large-scale official development schemes that threatened the rights or resources of the poor.

For this reason NGOs are regarded with ambivalence if not suspicion by many governments. Given their control of substantial Northern funds, governments have been obliged to recognize them as partners in the development process. But for this partnership to have real meaning, NGOs and other organizations representing the people's interests must gain access to the policy-making process. In practice, they will only be accorded a meaningful role in policy formulation when they are able to demonstrate a thorough understanding of the technical and political constraints prevailing in any given sector. Even if nominally granted, access to the policy arena will be meaningless for people's organizations unless they are equipped to take advantage of it.

The policy role of Southern NGOs is actually or potentially one of their most important functions. This has been demonstrated in the past ten years by numerous groups in Asia and Latin America, which have formed networks and coalitions to campaign on issues of concern to their constituencies. In Africa, however, only a tiny handful of non-governmental groups have so far been able to develop anything like a policy platform. Some are now making new efforts in this direction, beginning with the skills required to underpin policy formulation.

Much more cross-fertilization and networking between meso-level institutions is needed to develop the consensus on strategies which must support participatory development goals. Among other things it demands a good degree of institutional flexibility.

The Macro Level

For a number of national governments, the last decade of the twentieth century has begun with a profound — and in some cases traumatic — reappraisal of the role of the state. The dismantling of the public sector in many Third world countries during the 1980s, under pressure from the IMF, was presented as an objective economic necessity. However, the institutional restructuring which this divestiture will entail for many countries of the South in the 1990s is being tied to an overtly political agenda. Some of this — the emphasis on democratic systems and people's participation — should help to cement the foundations for sustainable development. But there is a real danger that the demise of automatic regimes will be taken as evidence that the South now needs carbon copies of Western institutions to make democracy work. The already evident tendency of some donor countries to equate democracy with multi-party politics and free-market principles is a case in point.

The institutions of government in low-income countries vary so widely in both scope and quality that it is impossible to generalize about their needs. Some have efficient and well-staffed ministries working on clearly defined policies to promote sustainable development as far as their means allow. Others have little or no effective infrastructure and, in the case of the poorest countries of sub-Saharan Africa, few human resources or other means to start building it.

What can be said is that most countries should be seeking to strengthen their capacities in policy-making and in socio-economic and technical research, with three objectives in view:

- to enhance their economic independence by acquiring greater negotiating parity with Northern agencies on finance, aid and trade;
- to upgrade national research inputs to policy-making, thus reducing their dependence on external advice, which can seldom take full account of the critical indigenous factors of cultural and social relations; and
- to facilitate the process of institutional restructuring below government level by assisting in the identification of mechanisms and linkages required between the macro, meso and micro levels.

Institutions in the North

In countries of the North, meanwhile, a crescendo of voices urging environmental protection and "green" policies has brought a rapid growth of institutions committed to sustainable development over the past decade. Governments have set up new ministries of the environment and campaigns by non-governmental agencies have mobilized wide public support on many issues.

But popular support for sustainable development tends to stop short of policy areas where people perceive their own interests to be at stake. This means there is little or no public pressure for changes in international terms of trade or in resource-intensive consumerist lifestyles. To deal with these issues, Northern countries need more independent organizations able to analyse the costs and benefits of various policy options.

Internationally, much attention has been given in recent times to ways of reforming the institutions of global governance: the United Nations system, the World Bank and the IMF. In April 1991, a meeting of 30 world leaders convened in Stockholm by the Swedish prime minister, Ingvar Carlsson, concluded that "the United Nations is today not strong enough to deal with the tasks that face it. . . . [It] needs to be modernized and its organization updated" (Stockholm, 1991). In particular, their statement said that the UN needed to be able to handle the security dimension of economic and ecological issues at the Security Council level. Pointing out that the IMF and the World Bank had expanded their activities beyond those originally intended, the meeting called for a world summit on global governance to review these and related issues.

Human Resources

To achieve sustainable development, people must be able to participate in decisions that affect their lives. To provide for this participation requires a democratic political process with effective and accountable institutions at all levels. And institutions, to be effective, must be able to count on a supply of competent, well-motivated people to run them.

For countries of the South, therefore, the path of a sustainable future has to start with programmes of human resource development. Many in Asia and Latin America are already some way down this road; other countries — including most of Africa — have made little progress in recent years, and not a few are losing ground. The World Bank's long-term study of sub-Saharan Africa (World Bank, 1989) judged the quality of primary and secondary education in the region to be "low and declining", while higher education revealed an inappropriate mix of outputs, over-production of poor-quality graduates and high costs.

At one end of the educational spectrum, learning to read and write can empower the poor by enabling them to gain greater awareness of circumstances and changes that could improve their lives. At the other, Southern nations need highly trained specialists for policy-making, research, planning and management. In some countries, unbalanced spending on higher education has produced a surfeit of graduates in certain fields and a shortfall in others. Shortages of trained personnel have been exacerbated by the continuing "brain drain" of talent to the North, in some cases to jobs for the very aid agencies that affect to deplore it. There are estimated to be well over 100 000 trained Africans currently living in Europe and North America.

Setting out a strategic agenda for Africa in the 1990s, the World Bank suggested that, whatever the political vantage-points of different governments or organizations, there was "broad understanding, in particular, on the absolute priority to be given to human resource and institutional development" (World Bank, 1989). This is where any sustainable development must have its roots.

Conclusions

From this review of the structural elements of sustainability, two kinds of conclusion can be drawn: those of principle (what ought to be done, as change allows), and those of pragmatism (what can and cannot be done within existing constraints). But there is no fixed boundary between them. What is a distant ideal for one country may already be the accepted wisdom in another; what was unthinkable last year may be within reach today. Hence it would be invidious to attempt a demarcation between the two categories.

This extract has sought to show that organizing for change towards a sustainable global future hinges on the rights and responsibilities of people to participate in the decisions that affect their lives and those of future generations. It also demands the equitable sharing, North and South, of the costs of adjustment to a sustainable society.

To enable their people to exercise the right of participation, governments must guarantee civil and political rights including freedom of association, an independent judiciary and freedom of information. Participation can then lead to real empowerment through the provision of appropriate education, awareness raising and skills training to overcome the inequities perpetuated by the exclusion of the majority from the shaping of their own development.

Progress towards these goals presupposes the existence of or scope for democratic processes from the village to the global level. But these processes will be diverse; they cannot and must not be expected to conform to a particular model. International agencies and Northern governments need to exercise caution in attaching political conditions to aid programmes. There are severe limits on the extent to which a market-led economy can propel democracy in poor countries with few resources to manage the transition. Emphasis must be placed on the substance rather than the form of progress towards a pluralist society.

To manage change, it is suggested, requires in any country an interlocking network of institutions capable of acting as a power grid to harness and distribute a nation's energy. Much of the recent attention given to institutional development has focused on organizational efficiency. But institutions are not a neutral factor in development; often they are exploitative of the poor. More fundamental than their efficiency, some of the questions needing to be addressed concern the scale, orientation, relevance and values of institutions in relation to economic or social needs. At each level of organization (micro, meso and macro), enabling measures are required to help institutions fulfil their role. As a particular example, support for sustainable development calls for more coherent efforts — especially but not exclusively in the South — to strengthen the quality, representativeness and resources of local government.

Finally, as is now increasingly recognized, the precondition for any sustainable future lies in the mobilization of human resources to plan and manage it. A country's priorities for human resource development need to be assessed (or reassessed) not only according to the requirements of a given sector or institution but in light of the wider issues of sustainability.

Given the chance, we may conclude, people can make direct democracy work powerfully in favour of sustainable development. The more intractable problem is that of scaling up. Above the small-group or community level, systems of representative democracy have to reconcile many complex and conflicting pressures. They can only be expected to contribute to the goal of sustainability where social divisions are manageable and where there is a broad consensus on the ecological, economic and ethical criteria for a secure future. These three criteria — the ecological, the economic and the ethical — must be the measure of any organization for change in the twenty-first century.

References

ACORD (1990) *Democracy and Empowerment in Africa: The Challenge for NGOs*, ACORD, London

Banuri, T (1991) "Democratic Decentralization", mimeograph, IUCN, Islamabad

Bebbington, A (1991) *Farmer Organizations in Ecuador: Contributions to Farmer First Research and Development*, Sustainable Agriculture Programme Gatekeeper Series no 26, IIED, London

CWS and LWR (1991) "Democratization and Development: What Are We Talking About?" discussion paper for an NGO workshop, Washington, DC, May

Dag Hammarskjöld Foundation (1975) *What Now? Another Development*, Dag Hammarskjöld Foundation, Uppsala, Sweden

Daly, H (1991) "Sustainable Development is Possible Only If We Forgo Growth", *Development Forum*, vol 19, no 5, September–October

Dambia, P C (1991) "Governance and Economic Development", *Africa Forum*, no 1

Ecoforum (1991) vol 15, no 2, July

Freire, P (1970) *Pedagogy of the Oppressed*, Seaview Press, New York

—— (1973) *Education for Critical Consciousness*, Seaview Press, New York

Gran, G (1983) *Development by People: Citizen Construction of a Just World*, Praeger, New York

Hasan, M (1991) "Empowerment, Democracy, Participation and Development in Southeast Asia", *Development*, Journal of Society for International Development, no 1

Hofmeier, R (1991) "Political Conditions Attached to Development Aid for Africa", paper for a conference sponsored by Queen Elizabeth House, Oxford and the World Bank

Huxley, A (1927) *Proper Studies*, Chatto & Windus, London

Illich, I (1970) *Deschooling Society*, Harper & Row, New York

Israel, A (1987) *Institutional Development: Incentives to Performance*, World Bank, Washington, DC

McCracken, J A, J N Pretty and G R Conway (1988) *An Introduction to Rapid Rural Appraisal for Agricultural Development*, Sustainable Agriculture Programme, IIED, London

Peattie, L (1990) "Participation: A Case Study of How Invaders Organize, Negotiate and Interact with Government in Lima, Peru", *Environment and Urbanization*, vol 2, 1 April

Pretty, J N and R Sandbrook (1991) "Operationalizing Sustainable Development at the Community Level: Primary Environmental Care", paper for the Development Assistance Committee, OECD, Paris

Stockholm Initiative on Global Security and Governance (1991) *Common Responsibility in the 1990s*, Prime Minister's Office, Stockholm, April

UNDP (1991) *Human Development Report 1991*, Oxford University Press, Oxford

World Bank (1989) *Sub-Saharan Africa: From Crisis to Sustainable Growth. A Long-term Perspective Study*, World Bank, Washington, DC

—— (1991) "Community Involvement and the Role of Non-Governmental Organizations in Environmental Review", *Environmental Assessment Sourcebook*, vol 1, World Bank, Washington, DC

Chapter 10 | ENVIRONMENTAL ECONOMICS

The three selections on environmental economics represent two schools of economic thought on environment: the neoclassical and the alternative radical. Herman Daly is the leading exponent of alternative environmental economics. He argues that the inestimable laws of thermodynamics and a range of fundamental ethical considerations determine that present rates of economic growth cannot continue. A steady state economy must be achieved. Many will find his suggestions for limits on personal freedoms to be unacceptable, but his analysis points out the difficulty of achieving an equitable, democratic, political response to the physical and metaphysical limits to growth.

Rather than accept the need for a radical redesign of the world, governments, intergovernmental institutions and businessmen favour the use of market mechanisms as incentives to modify people's behaviour towards more environmentally acceptable actions. Lester Brown, Christopher Flavin and Sandra Postel discuss the scope for the use of environmental (green) taxes, which they see as complementary to regulation through legislation. Anil Markandya examines the use of tradable pollution permits as an alternative to green taxes in achieving reductions in carbon dioxide levels. Tradable pollution permits are already used in the Los Angeles Basin as a method of reducing air pollution by gases and smoke.

The Steady-State Economy: Alternatives to Growthmania
Herman Daly

The economy grows in physical scale, but the ecosystem does not. Therefore, as the economy grows it becomes larger in relation to the ecosystem. Standard economics does not ask how large the economy should be relative to the ecosystem. But that is the main question posed by steady-state economics. Standard economics seeks the optimal allocation of resources among alternative uses and is, at best, indifferent to the scale of aggregate resource use. In fact it promotes an ever-expanding scale of resource use by appealing to growth as the cure for all economic and social ills. While not denying the importance of optimal allocation, steady-state economics stresses the importance of another optimum — the optimum scale of total resource use relative to the ecosystem. These contrasting visions are represented in Figure 10.1.

What is Steady-State Economy?

A steady-state economy (SSE) is an economy with constant stocks of artefacts and people. These two populations (artefacts and people) are constant, but not static. People die and artefacts depreciate. Births must replace deaths and production must replace depreciation. The "input" and "output" rates are to be equal at low levels so that life expectancy of people and durability of artefacts will be high. Since the input flow of matter-energy equals the output flow then both populations are constant, the two flows may be merged into the concept of "throughput". The throughput flow begins with depletion, followed by production, depreciation and finally pollution as the wastes are returned to the environment. The economy maintains itself by this throughput in the same way as an organism lives by sucking low-entropy matter-energy (raw materials) from the environment and expelling high-entropy matter-energy (waste) back to the environment (Georgescu-Roegen, 1971). In SSE this throughput must be limited in scale so as to be within the regenerative and assimilative capacities of the ecosystem, insofar as possible.

It is important to be clear about what is not constant in the SSE. Knowledge and technology are not held constant. Neither is the distribution of income nor the

STANDARD ECONOMICS   STEADY-STATE ECONOMICS

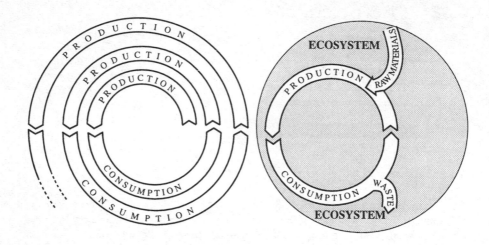

Note: Standard economics considers ever-growing cycles of production and consumption but does not consider the role of the supporting ecosystem. Such a view can encourage an economy that can ultimately strain the surrounding environment. Steady-state economics considers cycles of production and consumption that take the surrounding ecosystem into account and try to achieve a state of equilibrium with it.

Source: "Towards a New Economic Model", *Bulletin of the Atomic Scientists*, April 1986.

Figure 10.1 Contrasting Visions

allocation of resources. The SSE can develop qualitatively but does not grow in quantitative scale, just as planet Earth, of which the economy is a subsystem, develops without growing. Neoclassical growth models notwithstanding, the surface of the Earth does not grow at a rate equal to the rate of interest! Neither can the physical stocks and flows that make up the economy continue for long to grow at compound interest. As Nobel laureate chemist and underground economist Frederick Soddy noted long ago (Daly, 1980a): "You cannot permanently pit an absurd human convention, such as the spontaneous increment of debt (compound interest), against the natural law of the spontaneous decrement of wealth (entropy)."

The concept of the SSE can be clarified by analogy to a steady-state library, an idea that has attracted the attention of some librarians who realize that their stock of books cannot continue to grow exponentially. A steady-state library would have a constant stock of books. Whenever a new book is added, an old one must be got rid of. The rule would be to add a book only if it were qualitatively better than some other book whose place it would take. The steady-state library would continue to improve qualitatively, but its quantitative physical scale would remain constant. Likewise for a steady-state economy. The end of physical accretion is not the end of progress. It is more a pre-condition for future progress, in the sense of qualitative improvement.

One might object to this argument on the grounds that conventional economic growth is not defined in physical units but in terms of GNP, which is in units of value, not tons of steel or barrels of oil. It is quite true that GNP is in value units, because this is necessary to aggregate diverse physical units by means of a common denominator that bears some relation to the degree to which diverse things are wanted. Nevertheless, a dollar's worth of GNP, just like a dollar's worth of gasoline or wheat, is an index of physical quantities. In calculating growth in real GNP, economists correct for price changes in order to capture only changes in quantity. It is also true that GNP includes services, which are not physical things. But a service is always rendered by something physical, either a skilled person or a capital good, over some time period. Growth in the service sector does not at all escape physical constraints. In any case the SSE is defined in physical terms, not as zero growth in GNP.

What is Growthmania?
The above definition of a steady-state economy stands in great contrast to the regime of economic growthmania characteristic of the modern world. Economic growth is currently the major goal of both capitalist and socialist countries and, of course, of Third World countries. Population growth is no longer a major goal for most countries, and in fact a slowing of demographic growth is frequently urged in spite of considerable retrogression on this issue by the Reagan administration. But the usual reason for urging slower demographic growth is to make room for faster economic growth. Economic growth is held to be the cure for poverty, unemployment, debt repayment, inflation, balance of payment deficits, pollution, depletion, the population explosion, crime, divorce and drug addition. In short, economic growth is both the panacea and the *summum bonum*. This is growthmania. When we add to GNP the costs of defending ourselves against the unwanted consequences of growth and happily count that as further growth, we have hyper-growthmania. When we deplete geological capital and ecological life-support systems and count that depletion as net current income, then we arrive at our present state of terminal hyper-growthmania.

World leaders seek growth above all else. Therefore to oppose growth, to advocate a SSE, is not something to be done carelessly. One must present good reasons for believing that the growth economy will fail and also offer good reasons for believing that an SSE will work. That is the aim of the remainder of this article.

Origins of the Growth Dogma
How did we come to believe so strongly in the dogma of economic growth? What vision of the world underlies this commitment to continuous expansion, and where does it go wrong? Open any standard introductory text in economics, and in the first chapter you will find a circular flow diagram. In this diagram, exchange value embodied in goods and services flows from firms to households and is called the national product, while an equal flow of exchange embodied in factors of production returns from households to firms and is called national income. The picture is that of an isolated system. There are no inflows or outflows connecting the circular flow to its "other", the environment.

If we think only in terms of abstract exchange value, the picture is reasonable. If we think in terms of money, the physical token of exchange value, the picture is not unreasonable, but is no longer strictly correct because, though money flows in a circle, on each circuit it wears out a bit. New money must be minted or printed to make up for worn-out money. Thus there is a physical throughput associated with the circulation of currency. Yet we argue that with money the circular flow is dominant and the through-put is identical. But when we shift to real goods and services making up national income, the real physical processes of production and consumption, then the through-put is dominant and the circular flow is identical. Yet we find leading textbooks proclaiming that "the flow of output is circular, self-renewing, and self-feeding" and that "the outputs of the system are returned as fresh inputs" (Heilbroner and Thurow, 1981). One wonders what "fresh" could possibly mean in this context of an isolated circular flow? The authors were trying to explain how the circular flow is replenished so it can go on for another round. But in an isolated system, replenishment must be internal. A self-replenishing isolated is a perpetual motion machine! Replenishment requires a throughput. Abstract exchange value may circulate in an isolated system because it has no physical dimension. Money may be thought of as flowing in a circle even though some throughput is required. But real production and consumption are in no way circular. They are based on linear throughput beginning with depletion and ending in pollution. An economy is an open system, not an isolated system. Connections to the larger environment cannot be abstracted from without losing the most essential fact. In the circular flow vision, matter is arranged in production, disarranged in consumption, rearranged again in production, and so forth. Nothing gets used up. The first law of thermodynamics can be appealed to in support of this vision: matter can be neither created nor destroyed, only rearranged. Economic growth is just a question of speeding up the circular flow, and if nothing is used up there are no limits to growth, there is no problem of replenishment from the outside.

Of course this picture flatly contradicts the second law of thermodynamics, which says, in effect, that the capacity to rearrange indestructible building blocks is not itself indestructible. It gets used up irrevocably. As we have seen, the standard vision sees the economy as a perpetual motion machine. The gravity of such a contradiction for any theory is indicated by Sir Arthur Eddington (1953):

> *The law that entropy increases — the Second Law of Thermodynamics — holds, I think, the supreme position among the laws of nature. If someone points out to you that your pet theory of the universe is in disagreement with Maxwell's equations — then so much the worse for Maxwell's equations. If it is found to be contradicted by observation — well, these experimentalists do bungle things sometimes. But if your theory is found to be against the Second Law of Thermodynamics, I can give you no hope; there is nothing for it but to collapse in deepest humiliation.*

Economists, however are not without some excuses for their predicament. They do not really deny that raw materials come from the environment, or that waste returns to the environment. But economic theory developed at a time when the environment was considered an infinite source and sink because it was so large relative to the economy. Since the throughput flow went from an infinite source to an infinite sink it involved no scarcity and could, presumably, be abstracted from for purposes of economic theory. But economic growth means that the scale of the economy gets bigger, and it is now no longer reasonable to treat it as infinitesimal relative to the ecosystem. It is time for the concept of throughput to displace the circular flow from the centre stage of economic theory (Daly, 1985).

If such a restructuring of economic theory is to be avoided, then the assumption of infinite sources and sinks must be in some way maintained, or else a substitute premise that has similar logical consequences must be found. The latter strategy has been more common and consists in discovery of an "ultimate resource", which is both infinite in amount and infinitely substitutable for other resources, and therefore has the same limits-abolishing effect as the original premise of infinite sources and sinks for physical resources. This "unlimited resource" is variously referred to as technology, information, knowledge, or the human mind. Anyone who asserts the existence of limits is soon presented with a whole litany of things someone once said could never be done but subsequently were done. Certainly it is a dangerous business to specify limits to knowledge. But it is equally dangerous to presuppose that the content of new knowledge will abolish old limits faster than it discovers new ones. The discovery of uranium was new knowledge that increased our resource base. The subsequent discovery of the dangers of radioactivity did not further expand the resource base, but contracted it. Before getting carried away with the idea that the human mind is an "ultimate resource" that can generate endless growth, let us remember that, while certainly not reducible to physical or mechanical terms, the mind is not independent of the physical body. "No phosphorus, no thought", as Frederick Soddy put it. Or as Loren Eisley reminds us, "The human mind, so frail, so perishable, so full of inexhaustible dreams and hunger, burns by the power of a leaf." Minds capable of such insight ought to be capable of showing more restraint toward leaves and phosphorus than is usually exhibited by our growth-bound economy. Mere knowledge means little to the economic system unless it is embodied in physical structures. As Boulding reminds us, capital imprinted on the physical world in the form of improbable arrangements. But knowledge cannot be imprinted on any kind of matter by any kind of energy. The constricted entry point of knowledge into the physical economy is through the availability of low-entropy resources. No low-entropy resources, no capital — regardless of knowledge, unless the second law of thermodynamics is abolished.

It has been said that the best measure of a scientist's influence is how long he can hold up progress in his own discipline. By this measure, the editors of the major economics journals are probably the most influential scientists of all time! Continuing to study economies only in terms of the circular flow model is like studying organisms only in terms of the circulatory systems, without ever mentioning the digestive tract. Yet that is what the mainline professional journals, in their dogmatic commitment to growth, insist on.

Money Fetishism

Money fetishism is a particular case of what Alfred North Whitehead called the "fallacy of misplaced concreteness", which consists in reasoning at one level of abstraction, but applying the conclusions of that reasoning to a different level of abstraction. It is to argue that since abstract exchange value flows in a circle, so does real GNP. Or since money can grow forever at compound interest, so can real wealth. What is true for the abstract symbol or token of wealth is held to be true for concrete wealth itself. This is money fetishism.

Arx, and Aristotle before him, pointed out that the danger of money fetishism arises when society shifts its focus from use value to exchange value. Simple commodity production, the sequence of C–M–C' (commodity–money–other commodity) begins and ends with a concrete use value embodied in a commodity. Money is merely an intermediary facilitating exchange, the object of which is to acquire an increased use value. C' is a greater value than C, but both are limited by their specific purposes. One has, say, greater need for a hammer than a knife, but has no need for two hammers, much less of 50. As simple commodity production gave way to capitalist circulation the sequence shifted to M–C–M' (money–commodity–more money). The sequence begins and ends with money capital, and the commodity or use value is an intermediatory step in bringing about the expansion or exchange value. M' is greater than M, representing growth in abstract exchange value, which does not impose its own concrete limits. One dollar of exchange value is not as good as two, and 50 dollars is better still, and a million is much better, and so on. Unlike concrete use values, which spoil or deteriorate when hoarded (due to entropy), abstract exchange value can accumulate indefinitely without spoilage or storage cost. In fact exchange value grows by itself; it earns interest. But as Soddy told us, we cannot permanently pit an absurd human convention against a law of nature. The physical limit to growth at the micro level imposed by the absurdity or accumulating use values has been bypassed by accumulating exchange value (money and interest-bearing debt). But unless the aggregate of real concrete wealth can grow as fast as the accumulations of abstract exchange value, there will be a devaluation of exchange value (inflation) or some other form of debt repudiation or confiscation in order to bring accumulations of exchange value back into equality with accumulations of real wealth.

Money fetishism and growthmania are alive and well in a world in which banks in wealthy countries make loans to poorer countries, and when the debtor countries cannot make the repayment the banks simply make new loans to enable the repayment of interest on old loans, and thereby avoid taking a loss on a bad debt. The exponential snowballing of the debt that results when new loans are needed to pay interest on old loans cannot continue. The result is that somehow real growth in the debtor countries will also snowball. The international debt crisis is a clear symptom of the basic disease of growthmania. Too many accumulations of money are seeking ways to grow exponentially in a world in which the physical scale of the economy is already so large relative to the ecosystem that there is not much room left for exponential growth of anything having a physical dimension.

The paper economy offers more scope for "growth" than the real economy. Mergers, takeovers, "greenmail", tax-avoidance schemes, and other forms of rent seeking seem more profitable than production of commodities. Accountants, investment bankers and tax lawyers make more money than engineers because manipulating abstract symbols is easier than rearranging concrete materials into more useful structures. M–M' replaces M–C–M'. Commodity use values disappear altogether and with them all the natural limits to the expansion of exchange value. The "paper economy" is the result.

Limits to Growth: Biophysical and Ethicosocial

Biophysical conditions limit the possibility of economic growth even in cases where growth may still be desirable. Ethicosocial conditions limit the desirability of growth even in cases where growth is still possible.

Three interrelated conditions — finitude, entropy, and complex ecological inter-dependence — combine to provide the biophysical limits to growth. The growth of the economic subsystem is limited by the finite size of the total ecosystem, by its dependence on the total system as a source for low-entropy inputs and a sink for high-entropy waste outputs, and by the intricate ecological connections that are more pervasively disrupted as the physical scale of the economic subsystem grows relative to the enveloping ecosystem. Moreover, these three limits interact. Finitude would not be so limiting if everything could be recycled, but entropy prevents complete recycling of matter and forbids any recycling of energy. The entropy law would not be so limiting if environmental sources of low entropy and sinks for high entropy were infinite, but both are finite. The fact that both sources and sinks are finite, plus the entropy law, means that the ordered structures of the economic subsystem are maintained at the expense of creating a more than offsetting amount of disorder in the rest of the system. If the part of the system that pays the entropy bill is the sun (as in traditional peasant economies), then we need not worry. But if the disorder is imposed mainly on parts of the terrestrial ecosystem (as in modern industrial economies), then we need to count the cost of that disorder.

The disordering of the ecosystem (depletion and pollution) interferes with the life-support services rendered to the economy by other species and by natural biogeo-chemical cycles. The loss of these services should surely be counted as a cost of growth, to be weighed against benefits at the margin. But, as we have already seen, our national accounts do not do this. Indeed we now count the extra economic activity made neces-sary by the loss of free natural services as further growth. If the source of our drinking water becomes polluted, then we need more purification plants, and up goes GNP.

Even when growth is still biophysically possible, other factors may limit its desirability. Four ethicosocial propositions limiting the desirability of growth are considered below.

1. The desirability of growth financed by drawdown of geological and ecological capital is limited by the opportunity cost imposed on future generations. Since future people cannot bid in present markets, we cannot reasonably expect current resource prices to reflect opportunity costs beyond ten or fifteen years in the future.

2. The desirability of growth financed by takeover of the habitats of other species is limited by the extinction or reduction in the number of sentient subhuman species whose habitat disappears. The loss of natural services rendered by these species (their instrumental value to us) was considered under the heading of biophysical limits. The issue here is the intrinsic value of these species as centres of sentience and creatures of God. It is not suggested that subhuman species "utility" should count equally with that of humans, even if it were possible for these creatures to bid in the marketplace. But surely their feelings of pleasure and pain deserve a weight greater than zero in our cost-benefit analyses. Even Jeremy Bentham, from whom economists took their utilitarian philosophy, was of this opinion.

3. The desirability of aggregate growth is limited by its self-cancelling effects on individual welfare. Growth in rich countries is, at the current margin, dedicated to the satisfaction of relative rather than absolute wants. Welfare increments are more a function of changes in relative position than of absolute level of consumption. After some level of absolute income is reached, we must agree with J S Mill that, "Men do not desire to be rich, but to be richer than other men". Aggregate growth cannot possibly make all people richer than other people! Relative improvement is a zero sum game in the aggregate.

4. The desirability of growth is limited by the corrosive effects on moral capital of the very attitudes that foster growth, such as glorification of both self-interest and the technocratic-reductionistic world view. On the demand side of the market, growth is stimulated by greed and acquisitiveness. On the supply side, technocratic scientism proclaims limitless expansion and preaches a reductionistic, mechanistic philosophy that, despite its success as a research programme, has serious shortcomings as a world view. As a research programme, it furthers power and control, but as a world view it leaves no room for purpose, much less any distinction between good and bad purposes. "Anything goes" is a convenient moral stance for a growth economy because it implies that anything also sells. Expanding power and shrinking purpose lead to uncontrolled growth for its own sake. To the extent that growth has a well-defined purpose, it is limited by the satisfaction of that purpose. For example, if growth were really for the sake of the poor, we would limit it to producing things needed by the poor, and would stop when the poor were no longer poor. But if growth must never stop, then we must never define our purposes too clearly, lest they should be attained and we lose our reason to grow!

The Issue of Optimal Scale

If growth must never stop, then neither should we measure the costs of growth in our national accounts, lest we discover that they become equal to the benefits at the margin and thus define an optimal scale beyond which it would be anti-economic to grow! By discovering the existence of such an optimal scale, we would threaten ourselves with a question to which we do not know the answer: namely, how can we shift from a growth economy to a steady-state economy without risking economic collapse? It is nonsensical to advocate growing beyond the optimum, but politically risky to advocate nongrowth. What to do?

The answer given by some neoclassical economists is, "don't worry, the market will automatically keep us from growing beyond optimal scale even if such were likely, which it is not because technical progress pushes aside all apparent limits to growth".

For all its virtues, technological advance cannot escape the entropy law, nor can the market register the cost of increasing its own scale relative to the ecosystem. The market measures the relative scarcity of individual resources; it cannot measure the absolute scarcity of resources in general, of environmental low entropy. The best we can hope for from a perfect market is a Pareto optimal allocation of resources (i e a situation in which no one can be made better off without making someone else worse off). Such an allocation theoretically could be attained at any scale, just as it is theoretically attainable for any distribution of income.

Most of the consequences of increasing scale are experienced as pervasive external costs. Services and amenities that were free at a smaller scale become scarce at the larger scale. Once the growing scale has turned formerly free goods into scarce goods, then it is certainly better to give them positive prices than to continue to behave as if their price were zero. But there remains a prior question. How do we know that we were not still better off at the smaller scale, before the free good became an economic good? Perhaps we are just always making the best of an increasingly bad situation. The optimal allocation of resources (Pareto optimum) is one thing. The optimal scale of the economy relative to the ecosystem is something else entirely. As growth in scale forces us to turn previously free goods into economic goods, it swells GNP but may reduce welfare, even if the newly scarce goods are optimally priced.

There is an instructive parallel between the relation of scale to the price system and the more familiar relation of distribution to the price system. It is well known in economic theory that the price system in pure competition would attain an efficient allocation of resources in the sense of a Pareto optimum. It is further known that Pareto optimality is independent of the distribution of ownership of physical resources — i e there is a Pareto-efficient allocation for any distribution, including unjust distributions. Therefore the social goal of distributive justice must be pursued independently of (but not necessarily in conflict with) the price mechanism. Likewise, I suggest, for the question of scale of throughput. At any stage of growth, at any stage of throughput, the price system can optimally allocate the given volume of throughput among alternative uses. But just as there is nothing in the price system that can identify the best distribution of ownership according to criteria of justice, neither is there anything that allows the price system to determine the best scale of throughput according to ecological criteria of sustainability. Just as Pareto optimal allocation may coexist with a socially unjust distribution, so may it coexist with an ecologically unsustainable scale. Indeed, there is a sense in which the unsustainable scale is simply an unjust distribution with respect to future generations.

Perhaps an analogy will clarify this important point. Consider a boat. Suppose we want to maximize the load that the boat carries. If we place all the weight in one corner of the boat it will quickly sink or capsize. Therefore we spread the weight out evenly. To do this we may invent a pricing system. The heavier the load in one part of the boat the higher the price of adding another pound in that place. We allocate the weight so as to equalize the cost per additional capacity used in all parts of the boat. This is the internal equimarginal rule for allocating space (resources) among heavy objects (alternative uses) so as the maximize the load carried. This pricing rule is an allocative mechanism only, a useful but dumb computer algorithm that sees no reason not to keep on adding weight and allocating it optimally until the optimally loaded boat sinks, optimally of course, to the bottom of the sea. What is lacking is an absolute limit on scale, a recognition that the boat can displace only so much water, a rule that says, "stop when total weight is one ton, or when the waterline reaches the Plimsoll mark". Price is only a tool for finding the optimal allocation. The optimal scale is something else. The market by itself has no criterion by which to limit its scale relative to the environment. Its basic thrust of exchange value accumulation at the micro level, amplified by Keynesian policies at the macro level, is towards continuous growth in GNP, which under present conventions of national accounting, implies a growing scale of throughput.

Transition from Growth to the Steady-State

A realistic discussion of a transition cannot assume a blank slate, but must start with the historically given initial conditions currently prevailing. These given initial conditions I take to be the institutions of private property and the price system. The basic institutions must be bent and stretched, but not abolished, because we lack the wisdom, the leadership, and the time to replace them with something novel. This consideration lends a fundamental conservatism to a line of thought that will nevertheless appear quite radical to many.

A complementary design principle for guiding our speculations on the transition is to seek to combine micro freedom and variability with macro stability and control. This means, in practice, relying on market allocation of an aggregate resource throughput whose total is not set by the market, but rather fixed collectively on the basis of ecological criteria of sustainability and ethical criteria of stewardship. This approach aims to avoid both the Scylla of centralized planning and the Charybdis of the tragedy of the commons.

From the definition of a steady-state economy in the introduction to this reading, it is clear that it requires two kinds of limits: limits on the population of human bodies; and limits on the population of artefacts. A third limit, not derivable from the definition, but important in the interest of justice, is to impose limits on the degree of inequality in the distribution of artefacts among people — i e limited inequality in the distribution of income. How could these three limits be institutionalized so as to achieve necessary macro level control with the minimum sacrifice of freedom at the micro level?

The population of artefacts could be limited by controlling its "food supply", the throughput. By limiting the aggregate throughput at the point of origin (depletion) we indirectly limit the scale of physical stocks, and indirectly limit pollution outflow as well, at least in a gross quantitative sense. There remains the important problem of controlling the qualitative nature of wastes (degrees of toxicity and biodegradability) that would have to be dealt with separately by pollution taxes or standards. Several institutions could be used to limit depletion. Elsewhere I have suggested a depletion quota auction, and Talbot Page has suggested a national *ad valorem* severance tax, (Daly, 1980b).

In the depletion quota auction, the resource market would become two-tiered. In the first tier the total amount to be extracted of each resource category would be set by a government agency and auctioned off in divisible units as rights to purchase or extract the resource up to the specified amount. Purchase of the depletion quota allows entry into the second tier of the market, which would be a private competitive market. In addition to paying the market price to the extracting company, the purchaser must present the previously purchased depletion quota rights that the firm will present to auditors at tax time. The scheme sets total quantity centrally, but leaves the decentralized price system to determine allocation of the fixed total among alternative uses.

The severance tax alternative is similar. By taxing depletion, we lower the throughput to some socially determined level judged to be within ecosystem tolerance limits. Once again aggregate throughput is controlled, yet the allocation at the micro level is left to the market. The advantage of the severance tax is that it is administratively simpler. Indeed, Page argues that it amounts to nothing more than reversing the algebraic sign of the existing depletion allowances. Instead of subsidizing depletion we would tax it. The disadvantage of the tax is that the aggregate throughput is controlled only indirectly and less tightly than with a depletion quota. Quantity as well as price is free to vary, whereas in the quota system all adjustment is in price. The ecosystem is sensitive to quantities, not prices, so the quota system is safer ecologically. Yet the severance tax is simpler administratively and more likely to gain support as a first step.

Either of these institutions will have the following effects: (1) reduce the levels of depletion and pollution, and limit the scale of the aggregate stock of artefacts; (2) raise relative prices of resources, which will force greater efficiency in resource use; (3) result in a large revenue or rent to the government in the form either of tax or auction receipts. This third consequence ties in with limits on inequality.

Higher resource prices would by themselves likely have a regressive effect on income distribution, much like a sales tax. However, this effect can be more than offset by distributing the receipts progressively. Inequality might be limited simply by setting minimum and maximum income limits. The minimum might work along the lines of a negative income tax and be financed by the resource rents collected by the government. In this way we would serve the goal of efficiency by high resource prices, and serve the goal of equity by redistributing the resource rents resulting from the higher prices that in turn result from limits on the scale of throughput.

The minimum income and negative income tax ideas have some political support, but the maximum income does not. Many fear that a maximum would dull incentives and reduce growth. But if growth is no longer the *summum bonum*, then incentives at the top become less important. A range of inequality would continue to exist to reward real life differences in effort, risk and conditions of work. Incentive differentials are important, and fairness in a larger sense is certainly not served by trying to equalize all incomes. But probably a factor of ten difference would be a sufficient range of functional inequality. The incentives argument for unlimited inequality is much exaggerated, especially in the USA. Japanese auto executives reportedly make about six to eight times what assembly-line workers earn. American auto executives make about 15 times the wage of the unionized assembly-line worker. Furthermore US workers are laid off when sales drop, while managers keep their jobs, usually with no cut in salary, whereas in Japan everyone shares the burden of bad times. It is very clear that this larger inequality had not resulted in the US auto industry being more efficient than the Japanese! In fact it may be that the richer the managers become the less incentive they have to work hard, and the greater the resentment and uncooperativeness of workers who know that they will be laid off at the first sign of recession.

The proper range of inequality is a subject for further research, reflection, and debate, once the principle of a limited range of inequality is accepted.

Regarding limits to population, there are the many possibilities, ranging from the coercive Chinese system to complete *laissez faire*. My own favourite institution is that first suggested by Kenneth Boulding: exchangeable birth quotas issued in an aggregate amount corresponding to replacement fertility, distributed equally among individuals, but reallocated voluntarily by sale or gift. This plan combines macro control with micro freedom to a very high degree. However, the idea of reproduction rights being exchanged on a market is for many people unacceptable, and some cannot even distinguish between selling a legal right to reproduce and selling a baby. How some people can get so upset with this proposal while accepting the current "rent-a-womb" practices and the Nobel Laureate sperm bank for single mothers is beyond me. In any case debate on this controversial issue detracts attention from the other institutions that do not depend on it. Therefore, for present purposes I will invite the reader to substitute his or her own population policy. I mention this one for logical completeness only.

The proposed institutions have the advantage of being capable of gradual application during a transition period. Initially the depletion quotas could be set high, near current levels (or severance taxes low), and applied first only to energy, the most general of resources. The distributive limits could be initially set far apart. Birth quotas could be used in amounts not much different from actual fertility. Once the institutions were in place the limits could be tightened, like the jaws of a vice, as gradually as desired. Of course in a democratic society they could also be loosened to the point of being totally ineffective, if the political will be lacking.

There may, of course, be better ways of stretching and bending the institutions of private property and the market system than the ones I have suggested. But I think one is obliged to call out an initial price to start the bidding. He does not believe that his price will actually be the sale price, but without a specific starting point the trial and error feedback of bidding will never get started. Nor will the feedback process of critical discussion begin as long as economists think that the concept of the SSE is not worth "bidding on" — as long as they remain committed to the illusion of growthmania.

There are many further problems and issues in the transition to an SSE, such as international trade adjustments between growing and steady-state economies, and legitimate Third World needs for further growth up to a sufficient level. These are important issues that merit discussion. But in a sense it is premature to discuss further these problems of transition as long as we have not yet firmly established that: (1) the growth economy is unworkable; and (2) the SSE is, in broad outline, a feasible and desirable alternative.

The first order of business is to make that case as clearly and cogently as possible. However, that is unlikely to be sufficient. The Keynesian revolution did not occur because Keynes's arguments were so compellingly lucid and unanswerable. It was the Great Depression that convinced people that something was wrong with an economic theory that denied the very possibility of involuntary unemployment. Likewise it will probably take a great ecological spasm to convince people that something is wrong with an economic theory that denies the very possibility of an economy exceeding its optimal scale. But even in that unhappy event, it is still necessary to have an alternative vision ready to present when crisis conditions provide a receptive public.

References
Daly, H E (1980a) "The Economic Thought of Frederick Soddy", *History of Political Economy*, vol 12, no 4
—— (ed) (1980b) *Economics, Ecology, Ethics*, W H Freeman Company, San Francisco
—— (1985) "The Circular Flow of Exchange Value and the Linear Throughput of Matter-Energy: A Case of Misplaced Concreteness", *Review of Social Economy*, 43 (3) pp279–97
Eddington, A (1953) *The Nature of the Physical World*, Cambridge University Press, New York
Georgescu-Roegen, N (1971) *The Entropy Law and Economic Process*, Harvard University Press, Cambridge, MA
Heilbroner, R and L Thurow (1981) *The Economic Problem*, Prentice-Hall, New York

■ Green Taxes
Lester Brown, Christopher Flavin and Sandra Postel

Many serious threats to humanity's future — from climate change and ozone depletion to air pollution and toxic contamination — arise largely from the economy's failure to value and account for environmental damage. Because those causing the harm do not pay the full costs, unsuspecting portions of society end up bearing them — often in unanticipated ways. People in the USA, for example, annually incur tens of billions of dollars in damages from unhealthy levels of air pollution, but car drivers pay nothing at the gas pump for their part in this assault. Similarly, if farmers pay nothing for using nearby waterways to carry off pesticide residues, they will use more of these chemicals than society would want, and rural people will pay the price in contaminated drinking water (Cannon, 1990).

Taxation is an efficient way to correct this shortcoming, and a powerful instrument for steering economies toward better environmental health. By taxing products and activities that pollute, deplete, or otherwise degrade natural systems, governments can ensure that environmental costs are taken into account in private decisions — whether to commute by car or bicycle, for example, or to generate electricity from coal or sunlight. If income or other taxes are reduced to compensate, leaving the total tax burden the same, both the economy and the environment can benefit.

Opinion polls show that a good share of the public thinks more should be spent on protecting the environment, but most people abhor the idea of higher taxes. By shifting the tax base away from income and toward environmentally damaging activities, governments can reflect new priorities without increasing taxes overall (Harris, 1991).

So far, most governments trying to correct the market's failures have turned to regulations, dictating specifically what measures must be taken to meet environmental goals. This approach has improved the environment in many cases and is especially important where there is little room for error, such as disposing of high-level radioactive waste or safeguarding an endangered species. Taxes would be a complement to regulations, not a substitute. Environmental taxes are appealing because they can help meet many goals efficiently. Each individual producer or consumer decides how to adjust to the higher costs. A tax on air emissions, for instance, would lead some factories to add pollution controls, others to change their production processes, and still others to redesign products so as to generate less waste. In contrast to regulations, environmental taxes preserve the strengths of the market. Indeed, they are what economists call corrective taxes: they actually improve the functioning of the market by adjusting prices to better reflect an activity's true cost (Kneese, 1980; Pearce et al, 1989; Goulder, 1990).

In a minor form, environmental or so-called green taxes already exist in many countries. A survey by the Organization for Economic Cooperation and Development turned up more than 50 environmental charges among 14 of its members, including levies on air and water pollution, waste and noise, as well as various product charges, such as fees on fertilisers and batteries. In most cases, however, these tariffs have been set too low to motivate major changes in behaviour, and have been used instead to raise a modest amount of revenue for an environmental programme or other specific purpose. Norway's charge on fertilizers and pesticides, for instance, raises funds for programmes in sustainable agriculture — certainly a worthy cause — but is too low to reduce greatly the amount of chemicals farmers use in the short term (OECD, 1989).

There are, however, some notable exceptions. In the United Kingdom, a higher tax on leaded petrol increased the market share of unleaded petrol from 4 per cent in April 1989 to 30 per cent in March 1990. And in late 1989, the US Congress passed a tax on the sale of ozone-depleting chlorofluorocarbons (CFCs) in order to hasten their phaseout, which the nation has agreed to do by the end of the decade, and to capture the expected windfall profits as the chemicals' prices rise. The most widely used CFCs are initially being taxed at $3.02 per kilogram ($1.37 per pound), roughly twice the current price; the tax will rise to $6.83 per kilogram by 1995 and to $10.80 per kilogram by 1999. During the first five years, this is expected to generate $4.3 billion, which will be added to the government's general revenues, (EC, 1990; US House of Representatives, 1989; Weisskopf, 1989).

A comprehensive set of environmental taxes, designed as part of a broader restructuring of fiscal policy, could do much more to move economies quickly onto a sustainable path. Most governments raise the bulk of their revenues by taxing income, profits and the value added to goods and services. These are convenient ways of collecting money, and ones that often serve an important redistributive function, but such taxes distort the economy by discouraging work, savings and investment. Substituting taxes on pollution, waste and resource depletion could improve both the environment and the economy, and be done in a way that keeps the total tax structure equitable.

A comprehensive green tax code would alter economic activity in many areas. It would place fees on carbon emissions from the burning of coal, oil and natural gas, and thereby slow global warming. It would penalize the use of virgin materials, and thus encourage recycling and reuse. It might, among other things, charge for the generation of toxic waste, and so foster waste reduction and the development of safer products, and for emissions of air pollutants, thus curbing acid rain and respiratory illnesses. And it might impose levies on the overpumping of groundwater, which would encourage more efficient water use.

An analysis of eight possible green taxes for the USA suggests that they can raise substantial revenues while working to protect the environment. (See Table 10.1). Determining tax levels that reduce harm to human health and the environment without damaging the economy is complicated; the ones shown here are simply for illustration. Because some taxes have multiple effects (a carbon tax for example, would lower both carbon and sulphur dioxide emissions by discouraging fossil fuel consumption) and because the taxed activities will decline even before taxes are fully in place, revenues shown in the table cannot be neatly totalled. But it seems likely that the eight levies listed here could raise something of the order of $130 billion per year, allowing personal income taxes to be reduced by about 30 per cent.

Table 10.1 USA: Potential Green Taxes

Tax Description	Quantity of Taxed Activity	Assumed Charge[1]	Resulting Annual Revenue[2] (bn $)
Carbon content of fossil fuels	1.3 bn tons	$100 per ton	130.0
Hazardous wastes generated	266 m tons	$100 per ton	26.6
Paper and paperboard produced from virgin pulp	61.5 m tons	$64 per ton	3.9
Pesticide sales	$7.38 bn	half of total sales	3.7
Sulphur dioxide emissions[3]	21 m tons	$150 per ton	3.2
Nitrogen oxides emissions[3]	20 m tons	$100 per ton	12.0
Chlorofluorocarbon sales[4]	225 m kilos	$5.83 per kilo	1.3
Groundwater depletion	20.4 m acre-feet	$50 per acre-foot	1.0

Notes: (1) Charges shown here are for illustration only, and are based simply on what seems reasonable given existing costs and prices. In some cases several taxes would exist in a given category to reflect differing degrees of harm; the hazardous waste tax shown, for instance, would be the average charge. (2) Since revenue would diminish as the tax shifted production and consumption patterns, and since some taxes have multiple effects, the revenue column cannot be added to get a total revenue estimate. (3) The Clean Air Act passed in October 1990 requires utility sulfur dioxide emissions to drop by 9m tons and nitrogen oxide emissions by 1.8m tons by the end of the decade. (4) This tax already exists. Revenues shown here were expected for 1994.
Source: Worldwatch Institute. The original cites eight sources for the data on the table.

A team of researchers at the Umwelt und Prognose Institut (Environmental Assessment Institute) in Heidelberg proposed a varied set of taxes for the former West Germany that would have collectively raised more that 210 billion deutsche marks ($136 billion). The researchers analysed more than 30 possible "ecotaxes", and determined tax levels that would markedly shift consumption patterns for each item. In some cases, a doubling or tripling of prices was needed to cut consumption substantially. Halving pesticide use, for example, would require a tax of the order of 200 per cent of current pesticide prices (Teufel, 1988).

Phasing in each environmental tax over, say five or ten years would ease the economic effects and allow for a gradual adjustment. The tax on carbon emissions from fossil fuels is the one likely to raise the most revenue in most industrial countries. Levied on the carbon content of coal, oil and natural gas, an effective charge must be high enough to reduce emissions of carbon dioxide, now the official goal of more than a dozen industrial nations. Carbon taxes went into effect in Finland and the Netherlands in early 1990; Sweden began collecting carbon taxes in January 1991. Unfortunately, none of these levies seems high enough to spur major changes in energy use. In the case of Sweden, however, a hefty sulphur dioxide tax, which also went into effect in January 1991, combined with the small carbon tax, may encourage measurable reductions in fossil fuel burning, (the original cited 17 sources).

In September 1990, the 12 environment ministers from the European Community (EC) gathered in Rome to discuss the possibility of Community-wide green taxes. Though they failed to reach agreement, the meeting placed environmental taxes squarely on Europe's political agenda. The EC environment commissioner, Carlo Ripa di Meana, himself supports a common EC tax on carbon emissions, as do Belgium, Denmark, France, and Germany. The less wealthy EC members fear, however, that a harmonized tax would be too high, jeopardizing their growth, while the Netherlands worries that it might be too low. Even if Community-wide taxes are not set, it seems likely that other countries will introduce them individually over the next few years, (MacKenzie, 1990; Gardner, 1991).

In the USA, energy tax proposals have languished in the Congress. With little support for energy efficiency and renewable sources coming from the Bush administration, all that Congress approved in 1990 was a 5 cents-a-gallon increase in the federal petrol tax. Such a meagre additional charge will do little to discourage motorcar use or reduce carbon emissions (US House of Representatives, 1989).

Of all the energy taxes possible, that on carbon — levied on coal at the mine, on oil at the wellfield or dock and on natural gas at the wellhead — would most efficiently and effectively reduce carbon dioxide (CO_2) emissions. An August 1990 study by the US Congressional Budget Office (CBO) examined the effect of phasing in a carbon tax over the next decade, beginning with $11 per ton of carbon in 1991 and rising to $110 per ton in 2000 (in 1988 dollars). When fully implemented, the tax would generate an estimated $120 billion in revenues, (Maize, 1990; CBO, 1990).

The CBO estimates that the fee of $110 per ton of carbon would raise oil and natural gas prices by about half over the levels currently projected for 2000, and the expected price of coal — the most carbon-rich of the fossil fuels — by 256 per cent. This would encourage industries and consumers to invest in efficiency measures and to switch to non-carbon energy sources (CBO, 1990).

The model used by CBO that best reflects business and consumer responses to changed energy prices shows that CO_2 emissions would be 37 per cent lower than now projected in the year 2000, while the nation's energy efficiency would improve 23 per cent. The nation would also meet the much discussed international target of cutting CO_2 emissions 20 per cent from the 1988 level by the year 2005. The model projects a drop of $45 billion in the gross national product in 2000, a modest 0.6 per cent, which could likely be avoided by pairing the carbon tax with reductions in income or other taxes (CBO, 1990).

Completely shifting the tax base away from income and towards environmental concerns would not be desirable. Income taxes are usually designed to make the wealthy pay proportionally more; green taxes, on balance, would not serve this equity goal. Hefty carbon charges, for instance, would cause heating oil prices to rise, imposing a heavy burden on low-income households, who spend a greater share of their income on this essential item. To offset this undesirable impact, income tax rates would need to be lowered even more for poorer people. Government payments could compensate the very poor, the elderly and others who may not pay any income taxes at all now but who might experience higher living costs under an environmental tax code.

Another reason to blend income and environmental taxes is that green-tax revenues would diminish as production and consumption patterns shift away from taxed activities. Environmental levies would therefore be a less constant source of revenue over time than income taxes. Once businesses and consumers have adjusted to the new tax scheme, revenues from green taxes and income taxes would strike a more stable balance. Besides their help in reshaping national economies, green taxes can also raise funds for global initiative that require transfers from rich countries to poorer ones, including slowing global warming, preserving tropical forests and biological diversity, and protecting the ozone shield. Such transfers would serve as partial payment for the ecological debt industrial countries have incurred by causing most of the damage to the global environment thus far. An extra tax of $10 per ton of carbon emitted in industrial countries (excluding eastern Europe and the Soviet Union) would initially generate $25 billion per year for a global fund (Starke, 1990).

Reshaping fiscal policy to be an instrument of environmental restoration may be difficult at a time when policymakers are concerned with the economic slow-down in much of the world and with revitalizing the flagging economies of the former Soviet bloc. Yet nothing lasting will be gained by the continued pursuit of growth at the environment's expense.

References

Cannon, S (1990) *The Health Costs of Air Pollution: A Survey of Studies Published 1984–1989*, American Lung Association, New York

CBO (1990) *Carbon Charges as a Response to Global Warming*; income tax receipts from US Department of Commerce, Bureau of the Census, *Statistical Abstract of the United States, 1990*, Washington, DC

EC (1990) *Report of the Working Group of Experts from the Member States on the Use of Economic and Fiscal Instruments in EC Environmental Policy*, European Community Commission, Brussels

Gardner, D (1991) "Green Hopes Rise in a Grey Area", *Financial Times*, 13 May

Goulder, L H (1990) *Using Carbon Charges to Combat Global Climate Change*, Standford University, Standford, California

Harris, L et al (1989) *The Rising Tide: Public Opinion, Policy and Politics*, Americans for the Environment, Washington, DC

Kneese, A V (1980) *The United States in the 1980s*, The Hoover Institution, Standford, California

MacKenzie, D (1990) ". . ..as Europe's Ministers Fail to Agree on Framework for Green Taxes", *New Scientist*, 29 September

Maize, K (1990) "Budget Summit Looking at Carbon Tax", *The Energy Daily*, 1 June

OECD (1989) *Economic Instruments for Environmental Protection*, OECD, Paris

Pearce, D et al (1989) *Blueprint for a Green Economy*. Earthscan, London

Starke, L (1990) *Signs of Hope: Working Towards Our Common Future*, Oxford University Press, Oxford

Teufel, D et al (1988) *Okosteuern als marktwirtschaftliches Instrument im Umweltschutz: Vorschlage fur eine okologische Steuerreform*, Umwelt und Prognose Institut, Heidelberg, West Germany

US House of Representatives (1989) "Omnibus Budget Reconciliation Act of 1989, Conference Report to Accompany HR 3299", Washington, DC

Weisskopf, M (1989) "A Clever Solution for Pollution: Taxes", *Washington Post*, 12 December

Global Warming: The Economics of Tradable Permits
David Pearce, Scott Barratt,
Anil Markandya, Edward Barbier,
Kerry Turner and Timothy Swanson

National and international taxes may be used as a means of controlling atmospheric trace gases (ATGs), the principal one of which is carbon dioxide. One can think of such a tax as a "price" for the right to emit ATGs into a global environmental sink. Once the price is fixed, emissions are adjusted and the task before the regulatory authority is to set the right tax, or price, so that the desired level of emissions is obtained. However, the problem can be approached in another way. The regulators could specify the emissions reductions and then allow the market mechanism to determine the price. It would work through the issuance of ATG permits, which would be traded, perhaps on some kind of exchange, and from which a price would emerge. This price would be the equivalent of a tax.

In a simple model, with the demand for permits — or equivalently the costs of reducing ATGs — known with certainty, the two approaches should result in the same outcome.

This can be seen with the aid of a diagram (Figure 10.2). On the vertical axis are the additional (or marginal) costs of reducing emissions in two different countries: a rich developed country and a poor developing country. The rich country has a higher level of emission to start with but a lower marginal cost of reducing emissions than the developing country. If we combine the two marginal reduction costs, we obtain the overall marginal cost curve for reductions in emissions. Note that total emissions (OB) are the sum of the individual emissions (OF for the poor country plus OC for the rich country). If we want to reduce emissions from OB to OE, a tax of T* should be imposed. With this tax the poor country would cut back emissions from OF to OG, and the rich country would cut back from OC to OD. The reason for each country cutting back by precisely that amount is that it equates the tax to marginal cost of reduction. Any further cutbacks would imply a cost of reduction greater than the tax payment saved, a cutback less than that would imply a unit tax payment greater than the cost of a unit reduction. The sum of FG and CD is equal to BE. Note also that with a tax of T* the revenue collected from the poor country would be OG × T* and from the rich country OD × T*. The two together amount to OE × T*.

With a permit system, the regulatory authority would issue a total number of permits equal to OE. Each country's demand for permits is now given by its marginal costs of abatement function. At a price for the permits of T* the poor country would demand OG permits and the rich country would demand OD permits. Between them, the total demand for permits is then exactly equal to the supply and the market for permits is exactly cleared at a price of T*. Note that the total payments for the permits are exactly the same as the payments of taxes: OG × T* by the poor country and OD × T* by the rich country.

If the two methods of control have the same solution, why then do some economists argue in favour of one rather than the other? The reasons lie in the impact of uncertainty on the solution and in the details under which the two systems operate.

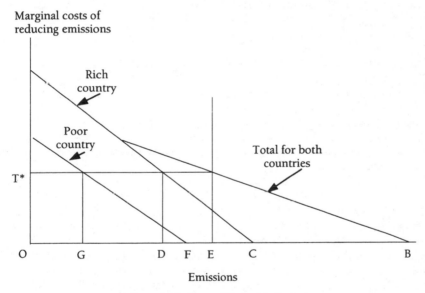

Figure 10.2 *Costs of Reducing Emissions*

Taxes and Permits: The Impact of Uncertainty

The central assumption made so far, which is clearly violated, is that these reduction cost curves are known with certainty. They are not, and there is considerable argument about that the costs of reducing ATGs are. In the presence of uncertainty, a tax may result in a level of reduction that is different from the desired reduction; on the other hand, a permit system could result in a cost of reduction on the participants that is different from the anticipated cost. Both types of error have adverse implications. If a change results in too low a reduction in emissions, the effect in terms of global climate change could be serious. On the other hand, an issue of permits that is too small could result in very high costs of reduction in terms of forgone growth of output and a decline in living standards.

As a matter of common sense, economists argue that one should go for price-based controls when the potential losses from incorrectly estimating costs are relatively large, and for quantity-based controls when the potential losses from achieving the emission reduction targets are relatively large. In the case of global climate change, it is hard to say which of the two costs are greater. However, in the case of permits, there is scope for mitigating any unforeseen high cost of reduction by adjusting the allocation of permits, or recycling the revenues collected by the sale of permits in an appropriate manner. With the tax solution, one cannot adjust the emission reduction effects in the same way, although one could adjust taxes in future periods if the observed rates of emission reduction were too low or too high. As long as taxes are flexible, this would be an acceptable solution, but the setting and changing of international taxes may prove too difficult to implement and therefore not amenable to the kinds of adjustments that are required. Also, it should be noted that where taxes have been employed as environmental control instruments in other contexts, the level of changes has consistently tended to be too low (Opschoor and Voss, 1989).

Setting the Target

With a permit system, one of the key task is to define the target level of reductions. For ATGs the targets being discussed are almost entirely in terms of carbon dioxide emissions. For example, the Toronto target, set in 1989 by a group of concerned citizens, called for a 20 per cent reduction in CO_2 emissions from 1988 levels by 2005. More recently, discussion has focused on a target of stabilizing global CO_2 emissions at 1990 levels by 2005. This latter target (which is consistent with the Nordwijk Declaration of 1990 made by the environment ministers of several countries) is based on an "ecological sensitivity value", whereby an ecologically tolerable rate of global warming is thought to be about 0.1 degrees Celsius per decade. To limit warming to this level, one would need to phase out CFCs and to reduce CO_2 emissions by around 20 per cent compared to the projected 2005 levels.

The choice of a target based on such an "ecological sensitivity" criterion turns out to be considerably stricter than one that would appear to emerge from a comparison of costs and benefits of global warming. A detailed worldwide analysis of the damages arising from global warming has not been carried out, but it is interesting to note that on the basis of the evidence from a preliminary US-based study, extrapolated to all countries, a lower emissions target would be indicated (Nordhaus, 1990; Ayres and Walter, 1990).

The other aspect of the targets for reductions is the fact that only CO_2 emissions are considered; these account for only half of all ATGs. This is mainly because CO_2 emissions are more readily monitored than other ATGs (apart from CFCs). The latter are being dealt with through the Montreal Protocol, and the feeling is that politically it is easier to negotiate agreements in gas by gas bans. From an efficiency point of view, however, such a procedure could involve considerably higher costs. It might be cheaper to allow some countries to reduce other ATGs, or to exploit their carbon sink capacities, rather than cut back on carbon emissions. This possibility is not allowed for.

Allocating the Permits

How would a permit system work in practice? A central authority could act as an auctioneer and, using a bidding process (open or closed), would allocate CO_2 permits for fixed periods of time. Bids would be made by governments on the basis of what they felt the demand for emissions in their respective countries would be. However, we have no experience with such an auction applying in this context, and for what would be large sums of money. Just to get an idea of what would be involved: emissions of CO_2 worldwide in 1987 were around 19 million metric tons, or around 5 billion tons of carbon. If a permit price of £20 to £30 per ton of carbon were to emerge — a plausible range, according to some estimates (Grubb, 1990) — the revenue raised would be in the range of $100–150 billion! Any authority controlling such sums would be very powerful, probably too powerful for governments to be willing to give it a mandate.

The alternative solution is to allocate permits to countries on the basis of existing emissions, or on some other criterion. Trading would then take place between countries, with those whose costs of reducing emissions are lower than the average selling permits, and those with relatively high emission reduction costs buying permits. An exchange or clearing house would be useful, but not essential, and the financial transfers involved would be smaller than in open auction. The key issue here, of course, is how the initial allocation is made. In other applications of permit systems (McGartland and Oates, 1985; Tietenburg, 1990) the commonest method is to allocate permits in proportion to current use. This criterion, known as grandfathering, would result in the largest number of permits being given to the developed countries (46 per cent) and eastern Europe (29 per cent); and the minority going to developing countries (26 per cent). Given the higher aspirations for economic growth in the developing world, such an allocation would be considered extremely inequitable. More importantly, developing countries would never accept a system based on such an allocation. Much the same applies to an allocation based on GDP — i e each country receives permits in proportion to its share of the world's GDP.

A seemingly just way to allocate tradeable permits would be on the basis of population. After all, if the global environment is a truly public good, each of us has an equal share in it. On that basis, however, the giant nations of India and China would get the lion's share and the rich countries would have to purchase back a lot of permits at a significant cost. Some have argued that such a transfer from the rich to the poor is warranted anyway, and it would be a good way of enforcing the transfer of resources from the North to the South. However, such a view fails to realize that an agreement on global warming has to be based on a broad consensus, with each country finding the terms acceptable. A population-based allocation of permits would not command such a consensus, any more than a GDP — or grandfathering — based one.

Considerable thought has been given to alternative rules for allocating permits that are both "fair" and acceptable. For the GDP-based allocation system, it has been argued that account should be taken of the fact that exchange rates do not reflect purchasing power, and that a country's allocation should be based on its "true" as opposed to its dollar-value GDP. Another adjustment that has been proposed is to allocate permits on the basis of adult populations, rather than total populations. The argument here is that a total-population rule may encourage population growth, or at least reduce the incentives for population control, in the interests of getting more permits. Incidentally, since the fast-growing populations of developing countries tend also to have a larger non-adult share, this rule redresses some of the advantage given to those countries by the population rule.

The essential problem remains, however, that whatever rule is to be used has to command universal acceptability. Developing countries, with projected economic growth rates of 5 per cent per annum and more, are simply unwilling to agree to any measures that would involve more than a marginal reduction in that rate of growth. Hence, the allocation of permits has to be sufficient for them to be able to pursue their growth targets. If that is to be the case, the developed countries will have to cut back their emissions by even more. Conflict could also arise from the way in which permits are allocated on the grounds of inequity of previous cutbacks. For example, a country such a France has very low emissions of CO_2 because it has pursued a programme of nuclear power generation. If the rule for allocating permits did not recognize that, it would face a much higher cost of meeting the global target than a country that had not pursued such a programme. Finally, there are other considerations of "need". What about countries, such as Canada and Finland, where energy needs are high because of the climate? Or countries such as Australia, where much of the indigenous fuel (coal) has a high carbon content?

For all these reasons, it is unlikely that a global sharing of permits can ever be agreed. What is possible, however, is for groups of countries in similar positions to agree targets. If such targets are undershot, or likely to be overshot, these countries may also agree to some informal arrangement for trading their respective surpluses or deficits. In fact this was the way permit trading in the environmental sphere arose in the first place, and much the same could happen with regard to CO_2 emissions.

Experience With Permit Trading

Experience with permit trading in general is mixed. Under the bubble concept in the USA, firms that had over-achieved their Clean Air Act targets could transfer their surplus reductions to other firms. In fact much of the trading that took place under this arrangement was intra-corporation, and the overall market for genuine trade was quite thin (thought to number only a few hundred). However, there may be special reasons why permit trading was a failure in this context. Hahn (1989) argues that it was partly the result of the administrators being unwilling to encourage such trade because of the criticisms of environmentalists. The latter have been against such trading on the grounds that it conferred the "right to pollute". In the context of permits for CO_2, such objections might be less severe.

On economic grounds, the evidence in favour of trading is quite strong. Tietenberg (1990) has shown that such schemes could cost anything between five and ten times less than schemes involving direct regulations. If this were to hold for CO_2, the savings worldwide would be enormous. For example, if emissions were to be reduced by 20 per cent over current levels, the reduction would be around one billion tons of carbon. Assuming an efficient cost of £20 to £30 per ton (see above), the total cost would be in the region of £20 to £30 billion. An inefficient system costing five times as much would cost £100 to £150 billion! Hence if these cost savings could be achieved, there would be a strong case for a permit trading system.

Another difficulty that has emerged from the trading experience with permits is the tendency of the more powerful traders to hoard them. Given uncertainties regarding the future availability of permits, and the desire to gain monopoly power, traders have responded in a number of cases by hoarding. The same could happen with permits for greenhouse gases, if rich countries buy up permits to keep poor countries from producing goods that would compete with their own in the international markets.

Finally, Tietenberg has argued that permit systems in the USA have encouraged technological progress in pollution control. This is particularly true in the case of the substitution of water-based solvents for solvents using volatile organic compounds (VOCs). The reason is simply that with permit trading there is a continuous incentive for purchasers to find ways of reducing their demands for permits.

Conclusions for the Use of Permits to Control Greenhouse Gas Emissions

What are the implications of the experience in permit trading for the control of greenhouse gas emissions? The arguments in favour are the clear economic benefits that could be derived, and the encouragement that the system offers for continued technological developments that limit emissions through increased energy efficiency. On the negative side are the difficulties with actual trading arrangements, and the possibility of countries hoarding permits and using monopoly power to eliminate competition. What must also be borne in mind is the fact that any agreed trading system would work only if the countries party to such an agreement were to continue to be satisfied that the system worked. This acts as a positive force in so far as it discourages hoarding and other destabilizing behaviour, but it also acts as a negative force because it would need only a few bad experiences with the system for it to collapse and the whole arrangement to fail.

Given all these objections — and in view of the difficulties with allocating permits in the first place — it is very unlikely that a full permit system can be instituted for greenhouse gases in the foreseeable future. What could happen, however, is that limited trades take place, based on targets for reductions in emissions that are partly regional and partly based on the level of development. Such trading is not to be sniffed at; it can generate considerable benefits and may, in time, be the precursor to a global trading arrangement. As an alternative to a global carbon tax, it certainly deserves serious consideration.

References

Ayres, R and J Walter (1990) "Global Warming: Abatement Policies and Costs", International Institute of Applied Systems Analysis, Laxenberg, Austria, mimeograph

Grubb, M (1990) *The Greenhouse Effect: Negotiating Targets*, Royal Institute of International Affairs, London

Hahn, R (1989) "Economic Prescriptions for Environmental Problems: How the Patient Followed the Doctors" Orders", *Journal of Economic Perspectives*, vol 3, no 2, pp95–114

McGartland, A and W Oates (1985) "Marketable Permits for the Prevention of Environmental Deterioration", *Journal of Environmental Economics and Management*, vol 12, pp207–28

Norhaus, W (1990) "To Slow or Not to Slow: The Economics of the Greenhouse Effect", Department of Economics, Yale University, mimeograph

Opschoor, J B and Voss, H B (1989) Application of Economic Instruments for Environmental Protection in OECD Countries, OECD, Paris

Tietenberg, T (1990) "Economic Instruments for Environmental Regulation", *Oxford Review of Economic Policy*, vol 6, no 1, pp17–33

■ Acronyms and Abbreviations

ACORD	Agency for Cooperation and Research in Development
ADI	integral development association
AGGG	Advisory Group on Greenhouse Gases
AIDS	acquired immune deficiency syndrome
ANDA	Associacão Nacional de Defensivas, Brazil
ATG	atmospheric trace gas
BULOG	Government of Indonesia Procurement Programme
CAMPFIRE	Communal Area Management Programme for Indigenous Resource Exploitation
CBA	cost-benefit analysis
CBO	Congressional Budget Office
CDAC	Carbon Dioxide Assessment Committee
CEDARENA	Centre for Environmental Law and Natural Resources (Costa Rica)
CFC	chlorofluorocarbon
CHCN	Committee of the Health Council of the Netherlands
CITES	Convention on International Trade in Endangered Species
COMECON	Council for Mutual Economic Assistance
CONAMUP	National Coordinating Body of Mexico's Urban Popular Movement
COP	Conference of the Parties
CSCE	Conference on Security and Cooperation in Europe
CSD	Commission on Sustainable Development
CWS	Church World Service
DGF	the General Forestry Directorate
DNA	deoxyribonucleic acid
DNPWM	Department of National Parks and Wildlife Management
EA	Environmental Assessment
EC	European Community
ECLAC	Economic Commission for Latin America and the Caribbean (UN)
ECO SOC	Economic and Social Committee
EEB	European Environmental Bureau

EEC	European Economic Community
EEZ	exclusive economic zone
EFTA	European Free Trade Association
EIA	environmental impact analysis
EPA	Environmental Protection Agency
FPN	National Parks Foundation of Costa Rica
EUROPICA	European Programme in Chemistry of the Atmosphere
FAO	Food and Agriculture Organization (UN)
FRG	Federal Republic of Germany
GATT	General Agreement on Tariffs and Trade
GEF	Global Environment Facility
GHG	greenhouse gases
GNP	gross national product
GOI	government of Indonesia
G77	'Group of 7' (negotiating group of over 100 developing countries)
HEI	high-external input
HYVs	higher yielding variety
IADP	Intensive Agricultural Development Programme
IBM	International Business Machines
IBPGR	International Board for Plant Genetic Resources
IBRD	International Bank for Reconstruction and Development
ICC	International Chamber of Commerce
ICI	Imperial Chemical Industries
ICJ	International Court of Justice
ICMR	Indian Council of Medical Research
ICRW	International Convention for the Regulation of Whaling
ICSU	International Council of Scientific Unions
IDA	Institute for Agrarian Development
IDA	International Development Association
IFC	International Finance Corporation
IGBP	International Geosphere–Biosphere Programme
IIASA	International Institute for Applied Systems Analysis
IMF	International Monetary Fund
IPCC	Intergovernmental Panel on Climate Change
IPCS	International Programme on Chemical Safety
IPM	integrated pest management
IPPF	International Planned Parenthood Federation
IPSEP	International Project for Sustainable Energy Paths
IR	infrared
IRENA	Institute of Natural Resources and Environment (Nicaragua)
IRRI	International Rice Research Institute
IUCD	intra-uterine contraceptive device
IUCN	International Union for Conservation of Nature and Natural Resources
IWC	International Whaling Commission

KWDP	Kenyan Woodfuel Development Programme
LDC	less-developed country
LEI	low-external input
LDC	London Dumping Convention
LWR	Lutheran World Relief
MAG	Ministry of Agriculture and Livestock
MCL	Monteverde Conservation League
MIC	methyl isocyanate
MIGA	Multilateral Investment Guarantee Agency
MIRENEM	Ministry of Natural Resources, Energy and Mines
MNC	multinational corporation
MV	modern variety
NAMMCO	North Atlantic Marine Mammals Conservation Organization
NANGO	National Association of NGOs
NATS	sodium thiosulphate injections
NC	Nature Conservancy
NCS	National Conservation Strategy
NEIC	newly emerging industrial country
NGO	non-governmental organization
NGO	nongovernmental organization
NIA	National Irrigation Authority
NIC	newly industrializing country
NIMBY	Not-In-My-Back-Yard
NMP	new management procedures
NOAA	National Oceanic and Atmospheric Administration
NPR	nominal protection rate
NRC	National Research Council
OEA	Office of Environmental Affairs
OECD	Organization for Economic Cooperation and Development
OPEC	Organization of Petroleum Exporting Countries
OTA	Office of Technology Assessment
PA	Participants' Assembly
PCB	polychlorinated biphenyl
PCIJ	Permanent Court of International Justice
PEC	Primary Environmental Care
PIC	Prior Informed Consent
R & D	research and development
RA	Rainforest Alliance
RIAA	Reports of International Arbitral Awards
RMP	revised management procedures
RRA	rapid rural appraisal
SADCC	Southern Africa Development Coordination Conference
SARA	Superfund Amendment and Reauthorization Act
SCEP	Study of Critical Environmental Problems
SIRDO	Integrated Systems for Waste Recycling (Mexico)
SMIC	Study of Man's Impact on Climate

357

SOLAR	Stratification of Livestock in Arid Regions
SPC	South Pacific Commission
SPN	National Parks Service
SSE	steady-state economy
STAP	scientific and technical advisory panel
T & V	training and visit
UCC	Union Carbide Corporation
UN	United Nations
UNCED	United Nations Conference on Environment and Development
UNCHS	United Nations Centre for Human Settlements
UNCLOS	United Nations Convention on the Law of the Sea
UNDP	United Nations Development Programme
UNEP	United Nations Environment Programme
UNESCO	United Nations Education, Scientific and Cultural Organization
UNFPA	United National Fund for Population Activities
UNICEF	United Nations (International) Children's (Emergency) Fund
UNWEO	United Nations World Environment Organization
UOI	Union of India
USAID	United States Agency for International Development
UV	ultraviolet
VOC	volatile organic compound
WCED	World Commission on Environment and Development
WCS	World Conservation Strategy
WHO	World Health Organization
WMO	World Meteorological Organization
WWF	World Wide Fund for Nature

■ Sources of Information

Chapter 1: Biodiversity

Ayres, Ed, "Many Marine Mammal Populations Declining", in Lester Brown et al, *Vital Signs 1993–4*, Earthscan Publications, London, 1994

Munson, Abby, "The UN Convention on Biological Diversity", in Michael Grubb et al, *The Earth Summit Agreements*, Earthscan Publications, London, 1993

Murray, Martyn, "The Value of Biodiversity", in Gwyn Prins (ed) *Threats Without Enemies*, Earthscan Publications, London, 1993

Prescott-Allen, Robert, "Conservation of Wild Genetic Resources", in Christine and Robert Prescott-Allen, *Genes from the Wild*, Earthscan Publications, London, 1988

Rose, Greg and Saundra Crane, "The Evolution of International Whaling Law", in Philippe Sands (ed) *Greening International Law*, Earthscan Publications, London, 1993

Utting, Peter, "Costa Rica", in Peter Utting, *Trees People and Power*, Earthscan Publications, London, 1993

Chapter 2: Climate Change and Energy

Hill, Robert, Phil O'Keefe and Colin Snape, "Energy Planning", in Robert Hill et al, *The Future of Energy Use*, Earthscan Publications, London, 1994

Krause, Florentin, Wilfred Bach and John Kooney, "A Target-Based, Least Cost Approach to Climate Stabilization", in Florentin Krause at al, *Energy Policy in the Greenhouse*, Earthscan Publications, London, 1991

Chapter 3: Population

Ecologist, The, "'Carrying Capacity', 'Over Population' and Environmental Degradation", in The Ecologist, *Whose Common Future?*, Earthscan Publications, London, 1993

Lappé, Frances Moore and Rachel Shurman, "The Population Debate", in Frances Moore Lappé and Rachel Shurman, *Taking Population Seriously*, Earthscan Publications, London, 1989

Rowley, John and Johan Holmberg, "Stabilizing Population: The Biggest Challenge", in Johan Holmberg (ed) *Policies for a Small Planet*, Earthscan Publications, London, 1992

Shiva, Mira, "The Politics of Population Policies", in Vandana Shiva (ed) *Close to Home*, Earthscan Publications, London, 1993

Chapter 4: Agriculture

Conway, Gordon and Edward Barbier, "Pricing Policy and Sustainability in Indonesia", in Gordon Conway and Edward Barbier, *After the Green Revolution*, Earthscan Publications, London, 1990

Patnaik, Utsa, "Economic and Political Consequences of the Green Revolution in India", in Ben Crow et al, *The Food Question*, Earthscan Publications, London, 1990

Pretty, Jules et al, "Regenerating Agriculture: The Agroecology of Low External Input and Community-Based Development", in Johan Holmberg (ed) *Policies for a Small Planet*, Earthscan Publications, London, 1992

Chapter 5: Industrialization and Pollution

Hardoy, Jorge and David Satterthwaite, "Environmental Problems", in Jorge Hardoy and David Satterthwaite, *Squatter Citizen*, Earthscan Publications, London, 1989

Jaising, Indira and C Sathyamala, "Legal Rights . . . and Wrongs: Internationalizing Bhopal", in Vandana Shiva (ed) *Close to Home*, Earthscan Publications, London, 1993

Koch, Matthias and Michael Grubb, "Agenda 21", in *The Earth Summit Agreements*, Earthscan Publications, London, 1993

Robins, Nick and Alex Tresoglio, "Restructuring Industry for Sustainable Development", in Johan Holmberg (ed) *Policies for a Small Planet*, Earthscan Publications, London, 1992

Weir, David, "Run into the Wind", in David Weir, *The Bhopal Syndrome*, Earthscan Publications, London, 1988

Chapter 6: Urbanization and Health

Cairncross, Sandy, Jorge Hardoy and David Satterthwaite, "The Scale of the Problem", in Jorge Hardoy et al (eds) *The Poor Die Young*, Earthscan Publications, London, 1990

Dankelman, Irene and Joan Davidson, "Human Settlements: Women's Environment of Poverty", in Irene Dankelman and Joan Davidson, *Women and Environment in the Third World*, Earthscan Publications, London, 1988

Hardoy, Jorge and David Satterthwaite, "The Search for Shelter", in Jorge Hardoy and David Satterthwaite, *Squatter Citizen*, Earthscan Publications, London, 1989

Hardoy, Jorge and David Satterthwaite, "Urban Growth as a Problem", in Jorge Hardoy and David Satterthwaite, *Squatter Citizen*, Earthscan Publications, London, 1989

Chapter 7: The Commons

Ecologist, The, "The Commons: Where the Community has Authority", in The Ecologist, *Whose Common Future?*, Earthscan Publications, London, 1993

Grainger, Alan, "Improving Livestock Raising", in Alan Grainger, *The Threatening Desert*, Earthscan Publications, London, 1990

Gray, Kevin, "The Ambivalence of Property", in Gwyn Prins (ed) *Threats Without Enemies*, Earthscan Publications, London, 1993

Stone, Christopher D, "Defending the Global Commons", in Philippe Sands (ed) *Greening International Law*, Earthscan Publications, London, 1993

Toulmin, Camilla, Ian Scorer and Joshua Bishop, "The Future of Africa's Drylands", in Johan Holmberg (ed) *Policies for a Small Planet*, Earthscan Publications, London, 1992

Chapter 8: Environmental Security and Environmental Institutions

Pearce, David, "Sustainable Development: The Political and Institutional Challenge", in David Pearce, *Blueprint 3: Measuring Sustainable Development*, Earthscan Publications, London, 1993

Sands, Philippe, "Enforcing Environmental Security", in Philippe Sands (ed) *Greening International Law*, Earthscan Publications, London, 1993

Vavrousek, Josef, "Institutions for Environmental Security", in Gwyn Prins (ed) *Threats Without Enemies*, Earthscan Publications, London, 1993

Werksman, Jacob D, "Greening Bretton Woods", in Philippe Sands (ed) *Greening International Law*, Earthscan Publications, London, 1993

Chapter 9: Empowerment

Dankelman, Irene and Joan Davidson, "Planning the Family: A Woman's Choice?", in Irene Dankelman and Joan Davidson, *Women and Environment in the Third World*, Earthscan Publications, London, 1988

Moser, Caroline, "Women's Mobilization in Human Settlements: The Case of Barrio Indio Guayas", in Sally Sontheimer (ed) *Women and the Environment: A Reader*, Earthscan Publications, London, 1991

Pye-Smith, Charlie and Grazia Borrini Feyerabend, "What Next", in Charlie Pye-Smith, and Grazia Borrini Feyerabend with Richard Sandbrook, *The Wealth of Communities*, Earthscan Publications, London, 1994

Sharp, Robin, "Organizing for Change: People Power and the Role of Institutions", in Johan Holmberg (ed) *Policies for a Small Planet*, Earthscan Publications, London, 1992

Chapter 10: Environmental Economics

Daly, Herman, "The Steady-State Economy: Alternative to Growthmania", in Herman Daly, *Steady State Economics*, Earthscan Publications, London, 1992

Brown, Lester, Christopher Flavin and Sandra Postel, "Green Taxes', in Lester Brown et al, *Saving the Planet*, Earthscan Publications, London, 1992

Pearce, David, Scott Barratt, Anil Markandya, Edward Barbier, Kerry Turner and Timothy Swanson, "Global Warming: The Economics of Tradable Permits", in David Pearce et al, *Blueprint 2: Greening the World Economy*, Earthscan Publications, London, 1991

■ Index